The Reel Cowboy:
Essays on the Myth
in Movies and Literature

The Reel Cowboy

Essays on the Myth in Movies and Literature

by

BUCK RAINEY

McFarland & Company, Inc., Publishers
Jefferson, North Carolina, and London

Other Books by Buck Rainey

The Saga of Buck Jones
The Fabulous Holts
The Cowboy: Six Shooters, Songs, and Sex
Shoot-Em-Ups
Saddle Aces of the Cinema
Heroes of the Range
The Life and Films of Buck Jones: The Silent Era
The Life and Films of Buck Jones: The Sound Era
Those Fabulous Serial Heroines
The Shoot-Em-Ups Ride Again
Sweethearts of the Sage

Frontispiece: Randolph Scott in *A Lawless Street* (1955)

British Library Cataloguing-in-Publication data are available

Library of Congress Cataloguing-in-Publication Data

Rainey, Buck.
    The reel cowboy: essays on the myth in movies and literature /
by Buck Rainey.
        p.   cm.
    Includes filmographies, bibliographical references and index.
    ISBN 0-7864-0106-0 (library binding : 50# alk. paper)   ∞
    1. Western films — United States — History and criticism.
2. Cowboys and literature.   3. Wild West shows — United States.
I. Title.
PN1995.9.W4R33   1996
791.43'6278 — dc20   96-3191
                                                                                CIP

Manufactured in the United States of America

McFarland & Company, Inc., Publishers
  Box 611, Jefferson, North Carolina 28640

Dedicated to
William (Bill) McDowell,
a long-time friend and
a film researcher with few peers

Acknowledgments

Many sources were used in the preparation of this book; however, I wish especially to recognize the following:

American Film Index
American Film Institute Catalog, Feature Films, 1911–1920
American Film Institute Catalog, Feature Films, 1921–1930
Contemporary Authors (various volumes)
Variety (various issues)
Shoot-Em-Ups
William (Bill) McDowell

Contents

Introduction

That the cowboy is one of the most romantic figures in American history is uncontested. Few other characters have received more attention in the pages of books and magazines, or have had more film footage devoted to them than has this almost legendary vestige of the West. Yet the true cowboy has seldom been uncovered by either authors or directors. The image that the world has of the cowboy is one of three types — depending mainly on one's age: the one of the silent, strong, bashful, and virginal deliverer of damsels popular with the generations before 1935; the gaudy, guitar-strumming, crooning mutations of the late 1930s and 1940s; or the virile, violent types that appeared in the 1960s.

The movies have perpetuated, perfected, and extended the cowboy myth to such a degree that the average person cannot easily differentiate reality from myth when thinking about the cowboy. More likely than not, "cowboy" conjures up memories of Saturdays at the neighborhood theater and Buck Jones, Tom Mix, Gene Autry, and other movie cowboys dashing across the prairie to save the heroine from a "fate worse than death." Old memories, and the movies and personalities that gave life to them, constitute a piece of nostalgic history that is pleasant to remember, to savor, to cherish, and to perpetuate. And so Chapter 1 will recall the "reel" cowboys of yesteryear and how their make-believe West was different from the real West and the authentic cowboy.

Part II presents the movies based on the writings of America's favorite western writers. Topping them all in popularity was Zane Grey, whose writing, according to critics, was atrocious and whose characters were as wooden as a cigar-store Indian, but who somehow had a gift for storytelling. It was Grey who made "western" a generic term, and whose success prompted other writers to follow in his footsteps. The output of western literature has never faltered — William MacLeod Raine, Max Brand, Luke Short, Ernest Haycox, on down to Louis L'Amour, who has outsold then all, including Zane Grey. Much of their work has been used as the story line for movies, sometimes with astronomical profits.

Just as Zane Grey once dominated the West, James Oliver Curwood held reign over the Northwest. Much of his work, even more so than that of Zane Grey, was adapted for motion pictures. No writer has ever equaled him in popularity as a writer about "God's Country"—his term for the great Northwest. He dealt with a type of life exactly suited to his time, with the vague imaginings of the rank-and-file citizen, and he instinctively availed himself of the conventional literary devices that made for popularity. Even in France he reached a lofty pinnacle hitherto reserved for Upton Sinclair and Jack London. But there were others, too, who wrote of the great white trails of the North and Northwest and whose writings easily translated to the screen. Foremost among these writers were Jack London and Rex Beach.

Part III will focus specifically on Curwood, London, and Beach. Millions of people have experienced vicarious thrills in the ruggedness of America's Northern frontier through these authors' stories and movies based on their work.

The cinema cowboys' experience on the sawdust trail is an interesting bit of cowboy history that needs, first, discovery; and second, preservation. Both the circus and the wild west show provided a kaleidoscopic panorama of glittering pageantry in which a number of cinema cowboys found a niche—on the road to success, during their moviemaking days, or on the downhill slide to oblivion. Part IV tells their story. It is not a potpourri of reminiscences of wild west shows and the cowboys and cowgirls who participated in them. Rather, it is a chronicle of a special few movie cowboys who, at one time or another, traveled the sawdust trail.

PART I

The Reel Cowboy

Chapter 1

The Reel Cowboy's
Drift from Realism

No discussion of the cowboy would be complete without some attention to the reel cowboy, for it is he, the cinema cowboy of yesteryear along with the cowboy of literary fiction, that has provided the basis for the popular misconception of the wild west of the 1800s and early 1900s. To the chagrin, perhaps, of historians whose scholarly reposits of factual information barely reap enough in sales to pay publication costs, the world has turned to writers such as Zane Grey, Louis L'Amour, Luke Short, Peter Field, Peter Kyne, and Jackson Gregory to formulate its impression of the West, receiving for the billions of dollars spent on western fiction a sensationalized, glorified, romanticized, distorted, imaginative, and downright inaccurate impression of the American cowboy that has given body and form to the legend that now exists about the cowboy and his era. But, worse still, millions have in part formulated their image of the West and of the cowboy from reading pulp magazines authored by nameless numbers of writers depending mainly on their own imagination to paint in words a commercially marketable cowboy.

The pulps had many predecessors in the low-priced heroics field of the dime novel and story-paper serials. Ned Buntline, the pen name of a long-time writer named Edward Z.C. Judson, made a fortune in fictionalizing the exploits of an obscure William F. Cody. The first of these stories, "Buffalo Bill, the King of the Border Men," began running in Street and Smith's *New York Weekly* in 1869.[1] Other wild west heroes followed, the most notable being Deadwood Dick and Kit Carson. Completely fictional heroes such as the Rio Kid, Jim Hatfield, and Zorro were also created.

In 1919 *Western Story Magazine* made its appearance, and within one year had a circulation of 300,000 per issue.[2] Other pulps followed — magazines

Revised from the Cowboy: Six-Shooters, Songs, and Sex, *edited by Charles W. Harris and Buck Rainey. New edition, copyright © 1976 by the University of Oklahoma Press.*

such as *Triple-X Western, Dime Western, Ace Western, New Western, West, Western Adventures, Golden West, North-West, Six-Gun, Spicy Western, Crack Shot, Double Action, Ranch Romances, Wild West Weekly, Thrilling Ranch Stories, Texas Rangers, The Rio Kid, Popular Western, Far West,* and *Ace High.* Thus were added more mythical interpretations of the West and the cowboy by hundreds of gregarious writers — most of whom knew little about the West — seeking to make their fortunes catering to the insatiable appetites of Americans for cheap, vicarious thrills. And, to put it kindly, the average American, reading four or five pulps a week, preferred western realism in heavily diluted doses.

Many famous western writers got their start in the pulps before graduating to the better magazines and the hardcover books — Zane Grey, William MacLeod Raine, Walt Coburn, James Hyndrix, W.C. Tuttle, Max Brand, Clarence Mulford, and Ernest Haycox, to name a few. It was Max Brand (Frederick Faust) who stated the guiding formula for most pulp stories *and* B-western movies when he said: "Action, action, action is the thing. So long as you keep your hero jumping through fiery hoops on every page you're all right. The basic formula I use is simple: good man turns bad, bad man turns good. Naturally, there is considerable variation on the theme.... There has to be a woman, but not much of a one. A good horse is much more important."[3]

Ramon Adams in his excellent work on the cowboy commented as follows:

> No class of men were ever so unfaithfully represented and in consequence so misunderstood and unfairly judged by people generally, as the old-time cowboy has been. He suffered severely from the bad publicity of ill-informed writers who had no real conception of his life and work. They pictured the rough, crude, brutal aspects of the cattle country; the reckless, happy-go-lucky visits to town, the careless use of the six-shooter, the drinkin', the fightin', practical jokes that were rough, the gamblin', and the profanity. All them things were subjects for the writer who painted, in the most lurid colors, slanderous accounts for eager Eastern readers ... but still, in spite of all that's been wrote 'bout 'im, them who knowed 'im best and lived with 'im found 'im to be good-natured and a rollickin' whole-souled feller, quick to do a kindness, and as quick to resent an insult.[4]

It is perhaps easier merely to shrug one's shoulders and verbalize a cliché, "Beauty is in the eye of the beholder," than it is to seriously try to define the cowboy. For at the mention of the word cowboy at least 100 different images are fashioned in the minds of as many people. Some will think of the heroes of wild west stories, or rodeo performers, or movie actors; others the guitar-picking yodelers of radio, television, and stage, or the dude ranch wrangler, or the wild west show performer; still others, more realistically, the vaquero of Texas, the wild roughrider of the plains, or the present-day rancher of the

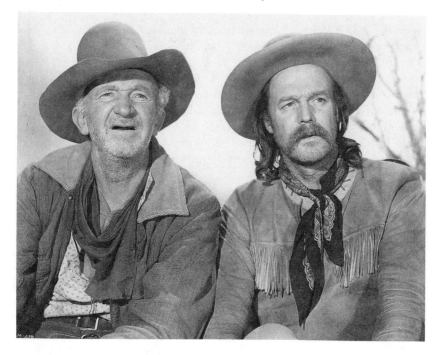

Walter Brennan and Hal Taliaferro (Wally Wales) in *Red River* (United Artists, 1948).

great Southwest. For the cowboy has become part of a make-believe world in which each of us has fashioned him in the image that suits our own requirements.[5]

The cowboy captured the imagination of the world, and few groups have been commercialized as intensively as the poor cow tender. Thousands of books have been written about him, thousands of films made about him, and millions of dollars lavished on cowboy toys, regalia, and paraphernalia. Yet the public, with an insatiable appetite, has continued to devour every morsel of cowboydom put on the market.

The cowboy may have been merely a unique occupational type who was concerned with cow work on the range: raising, rounding up, branding, trailing, haying, and mending. But the American propensity to venerate folklore has enshrined him as a creature beyond and above the law: a cavalier, or caballero, who rode with the gods and who rode like a devil; a man who carried his own rules loaded in his holster; and a man who enforced those rules according to his interpretation — a mounted prosecuting attorney, judge, jury, and executioner who dispatched all cases on the spot.[6]

As one of America's truly unique contributions to culture, the cowboy seems destined to live on forever in that favored corner of our hearts reserved for vicarious thoughts about experiences that — because of a combination of circumstance, era, and cowardice — we shall never personally have.

Seeing an occasional film such as *Stagecoach* (1939), *The Covered Wagon* (1923), *Shane* (1953), *The Iron Horse* (1924), *The Searchers* (1956), *Red River* (1948), *Butch Cassidy and the Sundance Kid* (1969), or *Dances with Wolves* (1990) could hardly have the lasting effect that the film output of Buck Jones, Tom Mix, Bob Steele, Tex Ritter, and confrères had from week to week, month to month, and year to year. Millions of boys and girls grew to adulthood during fifty years of B westerns from 1903 to 1954, thoroughly enmeshed in the continuing heroics of these bigger-than-life performers who were always cowboys, not something different each time they were seen.

When I was growing up in the twentieth-century version of the age of innocence, — the 1920s and 1930s — my best and closest friends were "reel" cowboys. I knew and loved them all: Ken Maynard, Hoot Gibson, George O'Brien, Gene Autry, Bill Cody, and Tim McCoy, all of whom were intimate acquaintances. I shared their adventures, and it was when Buck Jones smooched with Loretta Sayers in *The Fighting Sheriff* (Columbia, 1931) that I knew the first terrible pangs of unrequited love. It mattered not that the B westerns of yesteryear were devoid of much substance, we (we being literally millions of people) loved them then and remember them now as the most entertaining movies ever made and the finest aggregation of stars ever to inhabit Hollywood.

It has been estimated that for the decade following 1935 the western was so entrenched as a movie staple that the genre comprised about 25 percent of all films made in the United States, and that almost all westerns made after 1930 up until after World War II were B westerns.[7]

For those movie patrons not attuned to the B genre, the allegiance of so many people for the low-budget, "hay burner" western — while demonstrating little enthusiasm for major westerns — is hardly understandable. Few "A" westerns have been taken seriously by those who are identified as "oater," "horse-opera," "sagebrusher," "shoot-'em-up," "formula western," or "programmer western" fans. While a western fan might travel a long distance to catch an old Charles Starrett or Reb Russell oater, just as likely they would not step across the street to see a western starring the likes of Clint Eastwood or Tom Selleck; not unless one of the "accepted" cowboys had a supporting role in it. John Ford films have drawn respect from western enthusiasts, but primarily because Ford worked mostly with stars of the caliber of Hoot Gibson, Harry Carey, Buck Jones, Tom Mix, John Wayne, and George O'Brien. This being the case, Ford could be forgiven for an occasional transgression, when he made a western without any true cowboy stars in it.

The present generation has not experienced the thrill of attending a weekend matinee at a local theater to see a new western, along with a two-reeler comedy and the latest episode of an exciting cliffhanger. Perhaps in this age of sophistication, antiheroes, and declining moral standards, a young person cannot be expected to understand the thrill of ecstasy reverberating through one's body at the sight of Tim McCoy icily staring down an opponent; Buck Jones in white hat, astride his white horse Silver, riding in pursuit of that ace villain Charlie King with his black hat and riding a black horse; Yakima Canutt dashing across the prairie on his steed at top speed, standing erect with the reins in his teeth and pumping lead with both hands; or Tom Tyler knocking the bad boys in all directions in a saloon free-for-all. One must have lived through these to fully appreciate them. Today's goose pimples, acquired at viewing one of the old shoot-'em-ups, were earned 30 to 50 years ago by youngsters clutching their dimes and fighting for a place in line at the popcorn counter.

Arthur McClure and Ken Jones, in one of the many books on the western films, write as follows:

> The popularity of the "B" western was an extension of the cowboy myth in American life. Historian Carl Becker noted that Americans are prone to cling to what he called "useful myths." The western film hero received an adoration and continuing loyalty of amazing proportions. Villains were hissed with equal fervor. Westerns moved audiences emotionally as no other type of film. The emotional conditioning provided by these films, and the durability of that conditioning should never be underestimated by historians of American life. Some historians have dismissed the "B" western as simply a novelty or tasteless fad with no real substance or significance. However, it is entirely possible that in the midst of the confusion and uncertainty created by the Depression and World War II audiences sustained many of their "faiths" by identifying with such admirable and powerful symbols of straight-forward righteousness as seen in the "B" westerns.[8]

They go on to say that the B westerns were "fascinating historical examples of the romantic flavor of a haunting nostalgia for a more individualistic and flamboyant past," and that "the B western was very much a part of the evasion of reality in a mundane world."[9]

By 1900 Edison's kinetoscope — moving pictures — was well established and motion pictures were being accepted by the public. Films were short — less than one reel — and were merely incidents caught at random or staged by enterprising photographers representing the emerging companies that would give birth to a full-fledged industry. Films were — if it can possibly be imagined — worse efforts than the most offensive home movies made by doting parents at their children's birthday parties. There were no stories, no plots, no acting as such, and no direction: nothing. Nothing, that is, but exposed film of moving trains, the seashore, prize fights, and circus acts. No theaters existed for the exclusive showing of film; rather, the innumerable one-reelers were shown as intermission entertainment in vaudeville houses, kinetoscope parlors, penny arcades, and museums across the country.

Changes occurred rapidly after the turn of the century, though. In spite of the crudeness of the moving pictures of that day, they were catching on. One must remember that these were not being watched by the cynical, sophisticated audiences of 80 years later, but by people caught up with the novelty of seeing pictures actually move. Nickelodeon theaters grew in number, and moving picture companies were formed to exploit the medium. Anything that moved would draw an audience in the beginning, but the novelty began to wear thin; so producers were, of necessity, becoming more innovative. The public liked movies that told a story, albeit simple and short.

Edwin Porter, employed by the Edison Company, was quick to catch the mood of the public and hastened to put together a film concerning a western railroad robbery (although filmed in New Jersey), *The Great Train Robbery*, in 1903. The rest is motion picture history. This 740-feet, 9-minute film was the first serious attempt at a story. In addition, it had a western plot and introduced many principles of motion picture production followed by later filmmakers — the close-up, the chase, changing locales, cutting from one scene to another, a climax, specially designed props, the escape, cliffhanger action, stop motion, and even a musical interlude (long before Ken Maynard or Gene Autry). And it introduced the first western star, G.M. "Broncho Billy" Anderson, playing three parts. Scheduled for a fourth part, that of a posse member, he fell off his horse and thus was not seen in this capacity. Hardly an auspicious beginning for the screen's first cowboy star!

The western genre's start predated *The Great Train Robbery* (1903) by about five years, although it was a very inauspicious and shaky one. The Edison Company had committed to film a number of one- and two-minute vignettes of cowboys, Indians, buffalo, Indians scalping cowboys, cattle roundups, and such, and even William F. (Buffalo Bill) Cody had been filmed during his wild west act. And so it was that the company in 1898 filmed a short tableau entitled *Cripple Creek Bar-Room*, devoid of a moving story and only a few minutes in length. Nevertheless, it did contain a cast who were coached in what they were to do, and it did attempt to realistically depict life in a Cripple Creek saloon. The seed had been planted.

Subsequent to *The Great Train Robbery*, other films such as Porter's *Rescued from an Eagle's Nest* (1907); D.W. Griffith's *The Massacre* (1912), *Fighting Blood* (1911), and *The Last Drop of Water* (1911); Selig's *Boots and Saddles* (1909); and Thomas Ince's *War of the Plains* (1911) contributed bits and pieces to what would become the tried-and-true, bread-and-butter formula for countless sagebrush heroes over a period of nearly 80 years.

These early western opuses appealed to the multitudes, and filmmakers hastened to quench the public's seemingly insatiable thirst for this new type of action entertainment. The western story remained very popular with movie audiences, particularly when coupled with a new screen innovation: romance.

G.M. Anderson remained in the film business, first going to work for

Vitagraph, then, in partnership with George Spoor, organizing Essanay Film Manufacturing Company. It prospered, and Anderson eventually established a West coast studio in Niles, California. It was here that he was to produce, direct, and star in the highly successful Broncho Billy westerns that would cause an industry to be formed within an industry: the cowboy movie. Because he was unable to find an actor to play in the westerns he wanted to make, Anderson became a cowboy and made close to 200 one- and two-reelers before his career ground to a halt about 1920. His first one-reeler, *Bronco Billy and the Baby*, was made in 1908 and established the basic good bad-man character of Broncho Billy.

The public lapped up Anderson's heroic characterization of a good bad-man who aids a stricken child and is reformed by love, and so both the name and the characterization (with many variations) stuck. The Billy character had genuine charm, was basically realistic, and could supply sentimentality and action in equal doses.[10] However, Anderson, is not usually thought of as a realist.

Realism is a somewhat nebulous quality, one hard to pin down and describe appropriately. Most B westerns had within them elements of both reality and myth, for if the cowboy had been depicted solely as he actually was — a mostly drab, hardworking, hard drinking, illiterate, shabbily dressed, oversexed, and unambitious drifter — there would have been little audience for such movies. No, there had to be a bigger-than-life hero. Consequently, ingredients of most westerns from the mid–1920s on, which were accepted without thought, particularly by youngsters, included the following:

1. *Clean, unlingering, unsuffering deaths.* Did you ever stop to wonder why everyone died so conveniently, so quickly, sparing our hero the frustration and responsibility associated with caring for a villain he has shot out on the range somewhere?

2. *Cowless cowboys.* Where did all the cows go? And why did we call them cowboys when, in fact, most of the time they were marshals or Texas Rangers or just drifters? Only in a minority of westerns was the cowboy star ever depicted as a working cowboy.

3. *Well-lodged hats.* Yes, gravity, force, or "all hell turned loose" never seemed to be able to separate a cowboy's fancy Stetson from his head. It was an interesting phenomenon when you think about it.

4. *Unerring accuracy.* In spite of the poor weapons of the late nineteenth century, our nonchalant heroes always seemed able to shoot the gun out of a man's hand at 50 yards, without aiming and without hitting the antagonist's hand. And what about those shots from the hip that cut the hangman's rope from across and halfway down the street?

5. *Perpetual summers.* I wonder why there was never winter in the West? Like the bears, the cowboy seemed to hibernate in the winter, and our only glimpse of him or of the West was invariably in a summer setting.

6. *Corpses galore!* As Duncan Renaldo (of Cisco Kid fame) once said, "There have been more people killed in westerns than ever populated the West!" Killing seemed to be taken nonchalantly in many westerns, as if it were an everyday occurrence. And there was hardly ever an inquest or legal red tape for our hero, who might have finished off six or seven men in as many minutes; nor did such killings ever seem to rest heavily on his mind.

7. *Biological freaks.* Most of the heroines in westerns had but a single parent, nearly always a father. Less than 1 percent of them ever had a living mother in the film.

8. *Perpetual-firing six-shooters.* The six-shooters that fired 15 times without reloading would certainly be collector's items today if we could get our hands on them. I wonder where the Durango Kid got that pistol anyway?

9. *Sarsaparilla drinking, girl-shy heroes.* It was always strange that the cowboys thought asexual thoughts only — must have been all that sarsaparilla! History reveals that the typical cowboy definitely had an eye for the ladies, and they weren't too particular either. A cowboy took his woman where and when he could. The youthfulness and virility of the men, devoid of normal comforts, and the scarcity of women drove them to seek outlets in the seedy surroundings provided by dancehalls, saloons, and cribs, all anxious for their patronage.[11]

10. *"Fists only" heroes.* A guy, cowboy hero or not, had to be a little stupid not to pick up a chair, break a whiskey bottle, run, or pull a gun in the face of a dozen hoodlums out to kill him. As Joe Franz and Ernest Choate point out in their excellent work, *The American Cowboy, The Myth and the Reality* (1981), the real cowboy seldom fought with his fists — either in a crowded barroom or teetering on the edge of a sheer canyon — not if there were a gun or a knife handy. The cowboy had courage with a six-gun, or in the face of one, and the law of the West permitted a gun in protecting one's life, but fighting with fists on foot was demeaning and not for white men.

11. *Full musical orchestrations.* I never could figure out where all the music was coming from out there on the desert when Gene Autry or Roy Rogers was riding along singing to his horse. I could have sworn that either the whole Lawrence Welk Orchestra or Bob Wills and His Texas Playboys were hidden behind a boulder somewhere.

12. *Superior social graces.* Where did the cowboy heroes obtain the culture they displayed — speech, etiquette, education? Certainly not out in the barn, or behind it in the haystack with the neighborhood girl, or closely trailing the south end of a herd of cattle headed north along the Chisum Trail.

13. *Ambiguous film titles.* A title such as "Outlaws of Cherokee Pass" for some reason seemed odd at times when there was neither a town nor a pass by that name in the movie. And downright misleading were such titles as *Conquest of Cheyenne* when the heroine, it turns out, is named Cheyenne and is the subject of the conquest rather than a booming, lawless frontier town.

14. *Instantaneous recovery.* After a bruising battle with several bad men weighing no less than 200 pounds each, the hero would come up with all his teeth intact, bloodless, his clothes immaculately clean, and with a smile on his face. In thousands of B westerns the hero never had any teeth knocked out or his nose broken!

15. *Ridiculous wearing apparel.* Can you believe a cowboy in the 1870s or 1880s wearing a costume like that of Gene Autry, Tom Mix, Roy Rogers, or William Boyd? Not if he wanted to live a long time!

16. *Happy endings only.* You could always count on the fact that the hero would be vindicated, win the girl or ride off into the horizon, as he so wished, and bring about the downfall of the lawless element. The hero's luck in this respect seldom wavered. And when was the last time you saw any B western star meet his death at the end of a film? In spite of thousands of rounds of ammunition fired in B westerns over a period of 50 or 60 years the cowboy stalwarts always seemed to dodge that fatal bullet.

17. *Physical Adonises.* Why was the hero nearly always six feet tall, muscular, clean shaven, handsome? And was it necessary for him, at the conclusion of a knockdown and drag-out encounter with two dozen villains in a western drinking hell, to appear in his close-ups as though he had just left the beauty shop?

18. *Unencumbered heroes.* Very seldom was the hero of a B western laden with the responsibilities that beset the ordinary man. He seldom, if ever, was married, seldom presented as a widower with children, and almost never had a mother or father or maiden aunt to look after.

19. *Simple plot structures.* The scene was pretty commonplace: a dusty one-street town; one young, beautiful woman; one outlaw gang headed by the town's leading citizen, one saloon serving as the social gathering place; and one hero. Few were the times when there was a deviation from this basic structure — yet western towns came in all sizes; some of them had several beautiful women worth fighting for or rescuing; some had more than one gang; and, upon occasion, a town might even have several heroes capable of thwarting the nefarious plans of the villain and of vying for the affections of the girl(s).

20. *Artificial chivalric code.* Why did the hero have to wait for the villain to make the first move? Widespread dismay among audiences would have resulted had cowboy favorites drawn their guns and fired first at an adversary; yet, in the real West, heroes such as Wild Bill Hickock or Wyatt Earp never had any twinge of conscience about taking the initiative in life-threatening situations. In the old west the good guy in a fracas might also pick up a chair and smash it to smithereens over the head of his opponent, yet cinema cowboys were restrained from doing so.

21. *Nonsmoking, nondrinking cowpokes.* It is a rather safe assumption that in the West of the late 1800s and early 1900s that a good percentage of the

male population either smoked, chewed, or drank or engaged in all three. Yet cinema cowboy heroes invariably had no such vices.

22. *Gloved gunmen.* One only needs to attempt to draw and fire a six-shooter with gloved hand to realize how ridiculous it is to be wearing gloves when one's life depends on a fast draw and accurate shot. Yet heroes from Tom Mix (who started the practice) to Gene Autry have worn them. Why? Possibly because pulling and tugging at them while attempting dialogue in a stationary position gave the star something to do with his hands and resulted in less self-consciousness.

23. *Moronic sidekicks.* What sheriff, marshal, or ranger in the real old west would have tolerated a sidekick as bumbling and idiotic as the characters created by Al St. John, Dub Taylor, Smiley Burnette, Fuzzy Knight, and other second bananas? In reality, one's life was on the line and partners were needed who knew what to do and did it — quickly and effectively.

24. *Bullet-proof horses.* It seems that the hero's horse was just as lucky as the hero. In spite of all the lead flying around as the posse or outlaw gang pursued the hero, never did a slug connect with that relatively large target: the horse. The horse, like the hero, was invincible. One knew that from the beginning of a picture. It was never assumed, even by the youngest child in the audience, that either the hero or his horse were every in any real danger of being killed.

25. *Indians/savages; Mexicans/greasers' syndrome.* In at least 90 percent of B westerns Indians and Mexicans were depicted as subhuman or inferior beings. From the movies' infancy Indians were stereotyped as dumb, painted, animalistic savages and Mexicans as dirty, treacherous, knife-wielding misfits. Killing either was nothing to worry about, for both Indian and Mexicans were entirely dispensable. The negative cultural stereotypes of Indians and Mexicans dominated most westerns, while the pure Anglo hero functioned as a preserver of civilization. All in all, the treatment was unrealistic, unfair, misleading, and downright degrading.

26. *Nonblack west.* As history has recorded, Negroes helped to open and hold the West. They worked as cowboys, law officers, became outlaws, fought Indians, trapped wild horses, and performed in rodeos. In fact, a significant percentage of cowboys were black. Yet the Negro was a missing element in the B western.

We could go on, but we hope that the point has been made that few western movies were ever completely realistic. However, for our purposes, we can define realism as believability with regard to plots, characterizations, action, dress, authenticity of story, sets, and locales, dialogue, and quality of acting.

But back to Broncho Billy. For a man who knew nothing about the West, Anderson produced horse operas with a surprising ring of authenticity to them. The customs were sometimes a little strange, and the dialogue subtitles were often overdone, in the manner of western pulp fiction. But the stories were strong, and the films themselves were nicely directed, photographed, and edited.[12] They were often surprisingly strong and vigorous in their action content, with elaborately constructed and absolutely convincing western town sets. A trifle dour in the later Hart tradition, Anderson presented a reasonably realistic and not too glamorized portrait of the frontier's manhood.[13] Truly, Anderson made the first "series" westerns and was the first cowboy star of the movies. His films established westerns as a genre, one in which erstwhile cowboys such as Mix, Jones, Maynard, Gibson, and Boyd would excel in the basic formula laid down by the man from New Jersey.

Much of the credit for western realism in the early years of silent film production goes to Thomas Ince and D.W. Griffith, both of whom produced superb little westerns having characteristics similar to both the A and B westerns of later years. Griffith's *The Battle of Elderbush Gulch* and *The Massacre* both vividly depict the rawness of the West, sparing none of its savagery, while Ince's *The Massacre* was one of the first films ever to present the Indian in a sympathetic light.

Griffith and Ince each made a number of one- and two-reel (a reel could vary from 10–14 minutes; hence, a two-reeler usually ran about 25 minutes) westerns in the pre–1920s, all of them fairly realistic with regard to stories, scenery, costume, and action. Griffith's output included remarkably realistic little gems such as *The Stage Rustler, The Redman and the Child, The Goddess of Sagebrush Gulch, The Last Drop of Water, The Gold Seekers, The Twisted Trail, The Wanderer, The Sheriff's Baby, A Pueblo Legend,* and *Two Men of the Desert.* Being a master technician who possessed considerable finesse both as a director and film editor, Griffith developed to a fine art the use of panoramic shots and running inserts, both techniques adding a sense of reality to his films. Not interested in complicated plots per se, he leaned toward presenting situations and then directing his actors and actresses to the hilt, sapping every bit of talent they might muster. Significantly, he did not create a cowboy star, as did Anderson, nor did he produce series westerns. What he did accomplish was to partially create the mold out of which came the realistic westerns of series cowboys Carey, Hart, Holt, Scott, Wayne, and confrères.

Thomas Ince, remembered today as the man who brought William S. Hart to the screen, turned out a great many westerns and had a preference for strong plots and action scenes, as well as for telling the story of the Indian. *Across the Plains, The Heart of an Indian, The Raiders, The Lieutenant's Last Fight,* and *Custer's Last Fight* were illustrative of his films, which became guidelines for later practitioners of the art of serious western film production.

Many pre–1920 western films stressed realism. There were no cowboy heroes in white hats and gaudy clothes twirling pearl-handled six-shooters as they casually, almost contemptuously, faced half a dozen degenerates "collected by the broom which swept hell." During the period 1908 to 1913 Broncho Billy Anderson made the films that most closely resembled the B westerns of the 1920s, 1930s, and 1940s; but even his work, as already noted, attempted to project western realism as Anderson envisioned it to be from reading the pulp western magazines and dime novels of the day.

Realism, or at least semi-realism, reigned supreme until the early 1920s, when Tom Mix and cohorts caused a shift in popularity to the nonrealistic, streamlined westerns that were to predominate until the end of the genre in 1954. Dustin Farnum's *The Squaw Man* (1913), William Farnum's *The Spoilers* (1914), and *Last of the Duanes* (1918), William Duncan's *The Range Law* (1913), J. Warren Kerrigan's *The Covered Wagon* (1923), George O'Brien's *The Iron Horse* (1924), and others too numerous to mention kept stark realism in the forefront, with solid acting, good locations, strong stories, appropriate costuming, great camera work, and logical action. The cowboy was not glorified — his weaknesses were emphasized many times. He could drink, smoke, desire a woman, be a sloppy dresser, and slow on the draw, ride a cayuse (a native range horse) that was rejected by everyone else, and he could even wind up quite dead in the final reel — something that never happened to Gene Autry, Rex Bell, or Tim McCoy in all their years as cowboy heroes.

The pre–1920 years were indeed formative years. The western movie, as a distinct form of motion picture entertainment, was born before hardly anyone knew the industry was pregnant. And like other infants, the western genre struggled to survive its own blunders and oppression from outside forces. But the "hoss opera" mastered life, grew rapidly, and prospered; by 1920 it was an industry within an industry, with its own horde of stars and technicians especially trained for bringing the wild west to life on the screen each week. As the nation entered upon the peaceful decade of the 1920s westerns — good, bad, and mediocre — were rushing in to fill the need for film of the rapidly growing number of small-town theaters, much as a thundering herd of buffalo in the real wild west of yesteryear might converge upon a valley of lush, green grass and plentiful water.

But it is the series western stars who are so fondly remembered by thousands of people today, the ones who created the image of the cowboy held by those same thousands, and it is on their careers and influence that we will concentrate now. The star system developed gradually, and during the period 1915–54 a herd of reel cowboys rode the silver screen into the hearts of the world.

When realism in the western B movie is discussed, the two names invariably mentioned are Harry Carey and William S. Hart. Carey actually predated Hart by about five years, since he entered movies about 1908. However, it is not until around 1915 that he became almost exclusively a western star. Hart's western career began when he joined Triangle Studios in 1914, then later moved to Artclass, and he remained a western star until his retirement in 1925 as a result of his refusal to streamline his films. Both Hart and Carey were Easterners; yet, ironically, they made more authentic cowboy movies than did their contemporaries with true Western backgrounds.

Hart brought authenticity and a kind of poetry to the western. He had a driving, bull-headed passion to make realistic westerns rather than fake ones demonstrating flashy showmanship antics. And, although he arrived on the film scene after Anderson and Mix and retired while Mix was still in his prime, his contributions to westerns were original, and their influence was of greater importance than those of Anderson and Mix. As a youth, Hart had spent some time in the Dakota Territory, but his adult years had been spent as a stage actor in the East. Brought to California by his friend Thomas Ince in 1914, Hart was cast as the villain in a couple of two-reel westerns starring Tom Chatterton, and then was starred in *The Bargain* and *On the Night Stage.* To the surprise of everyone, including Hart, these two features proved highly popular, and he was placed under contract as star and director of his own films. The Hart era was underway. Hart is credited with being the epitome of western film realism, and he developed to a fine art the good bad-man motif. His costume was an unforgettable trademark — a flat-brimmed Stetson with four dents, boots rising above the knee, and a flowing neckerchief — and most of all a strong, silent expression that indicated a man of granite will.[14]

Hart loved the West and was determined to put the truth, the poetry, and the history of the West on film. His films were raw, unglamorous, and gutsy, the costumes and livery trappings accurate, the ramshackle western towns and their inhabitants like untouched Matthew Brady photographs, the sense of dry heat ever present, and the clouds of dust everywhere.[15]

Hart was the embodiment of the strong, silent hero of the saddle, respectful of all women, kind to children, and he loved his horse. He brought sentimentality into his films while avoiding the romanticism common to most other westerns. Yet the drab and stark existence he demonstrated soon became a negative image of the very stereotype he had sought to destroy. Its validity was as questionable as that which it replaced.[16]

Hell's Hinges (1916) is a classic Hart western, one of his very best. The story concerns the seduction of a minister by a local prostitute, a good bad-man (Hart) who falls in love with the minister's sister after being hired to run him out of town, and the destruction of the town by burning, as of Sodom of old. It was a masterpiece of realism, and as different from the formula westerns of Roy Rogers or Reb Russell as night from day. But by 1925 the public had tired of Hart's stern-faced, uncompromising westerns, which had become formalized in their own unique way. Rather than change his style and cater more to the public's interest in slick, fresh, escapist westerns, Hart chose retirement after the release of his finest western of all — *Tumbleweeds* (United Artists, 1925).

In commenting on Hart's contributions to realism and his stressing of the morality inherent in the West's history, George Fenin and William Everson note as follows: "Life in the old West was certainly a lawless one in many communities, but the generalized concept of the shooting down of endless villains and ranchers without so much as a second glance at the corpses is very much at odds with fact. A killing was as serious a matter in the West as it was in the East, although admittedly the justice meted out was a less standardized one.... The Westerns of William S. Hart recognized this principle; there was no casual extermination of badmen in the Hart-Ince Pictures."[17]

Hart's films made one feel as if he were actually living a part of the West's history, not merely being entertained, and his films accomplished this without resorting to quasi-documentary presentation.

Harry Carey was second only to Hart as an exponent of realism, his brand being more palatable to the masses than Hart's. Like many of the early favorites who epitomized the western hero on the screen, he was born in the East and knew nothing about cowboying when he made his first western, *Bill Sharkey's Last Game*, on Staten Island in 1908 for D.W. Griffith. He became a Griffith regular and moved with the director to California in 1913, when Griffith decided he would seek his fame and fortune in the film colony springing up there. Harry alternated between westerns and straight drama.

A Griffith one-reeler produced about 1911 for busy nickelodeon trade was *The Sheriff's Dilemma*, a film in which Harry plays what would be called today an antihero. He is an on-again, off-again sheriff who also happens to be a bit of a tippler. One of his earliest western successes was *The Wanderer* (1912); as a drifter, Harry saves two settlers and goes on his way, leaving them to a happy future with no knowledge of his having saved them. He was to play the part of a lovable drifter often, just as Hart many times duplicated his good badman theme.[18]

Fenin and Everson, in their excellent history of the western movies, state with regard to the westerns of the 1920s:

> Only two Western stars remained in any way in the Hart tradition: Harry Carey and Buck Jones. In actual fact, Carey's taciturn characterization predates Hart's in that he was active in the early Biograph Westerns for Griffith. Perhaps partly because his leathery and non-youthful appearance so dictated, Carey avoided the "streamlined" Westerns that Maynard, Gibson, and Fred Thomson made so popular. His were always Westerns of the old school, sometimes a little slow on action, but always strong on plot, with a definite sign of Hart's influence. Carey's *Satan Town* (1926), for example, was a very creditable lesser *Hell's Hinges* (1916). Respect for womanhood was a staple ingredient with Carey, and in *The Prairie Pirate* (1925), a good Carey film for Hunt Stromberg, this extended to another typical Hart plot motivation — the death of the hero's sister (she commits suicide when threatened with rape by the villain) and the tracking down of the man responsible.[19]

The authors are correct in their comparison of the films of Carey and Hart. Both stressed strong, often sentimental stories, always insisting upon

Harry Carey in _The Vanishing Legion_ (1931).

realism. The moral rectitude of Carey's films was no less than that shown in those of Hart, yet he continued as a popular star, making films in the Hart mold long after the public had tired of Hart's screen characterizations. The difference seemed to lie in the two stars' personalities. Often likened to Will Rogers, Carey could empathize with his audience more successfully than Hart. His personal charm somehow struck a responsive chord in his audience, and people warmed to him. That wrinkled face, those kindly eyes, and the boyishly innocent smile captured his audience. In addition, his characters were always a little more human, more flexible, than those of Hart. And by no means least, Harry Carey was a better actor than Hart. He grew on you and became a part of you, without your conscious realization of the fact. Other heroes came and went — Hart, Hoxie, Stewart, Acord, Maloney, Duncan, and Thomson — but Carey was always there. Like mother and dad and the old home town with its familiar haunts, Carey was there to return to when the glamorous heroes had shot their wad and ridden into the sunset for the last time.

Jon Tuska, noted film historian and former publisher of *Views and Reviews*, a quarterly magazine of the reproduced arts, said, "Harry Carey as a screen cowboy was quite dissimilar to William S. Hart. His personality was engaging with a comfortable self-sufficiency. He was incapable of Hart's moral intensity and lacked utterly Hart's penchant for sustained melodrama. Carey's natural humor and charm resulted in a characterization that, in some way, anticipated Will Rogers."[20]

Carey left Biograph in 1915 to join Universal, where he teamed with director John Ford in a long series of Cheyenne Harry movies, first two-reelers and then feature westerns. Carey was Ford's first big star, and the famed director said, "He was a great actor, and we didn't doll him up — made him sort of a bum, a saddle tramp, in a dirty blue shirt, and old vest and patched overalls."[21]

Glenn Shirley, commenting on *Straight Shooting* (1917), the first Carey-Ford full-length feature (which also featured Hoot Gibson, another Ford favorite), stated,

> The William S. Hart influence is apparent, both in austerity of production and the intermingling of good and bad in both the good guys and bad guys.
> In these early pictures, Hart's "good badman" style even overlapped Carey's role as "Cheyenne Harry." Generally there was showmanship and polish, a more epic and grander view of man and the land, and a deliberate striving for realism and detail typical of Ford in later years.[22]

By 1919 Carey was one of Universal's hottest properties, and his salary jumped to $1,250 a week. He and Ford continued as a team for another three years, with the plots continuing strong and unusual, always uncomplicated. *Marked Men* (1919) was an early version of Peter B. Kynes's "The Three Godfathers" and a Ford favorite. Carey, after 1922, worked for R-C Pictures, Steller, PDC, and Pathé, continuing to grind out exceptionally well-scripted realistic filmfare such as *The Man from Red Gulch* (1925), *Silent Sanderson* (1925), and *The Seventh Bandit* (1926). And although his fame never matched that of Hart or the streamlined cowboys discussed below, his films probably presented West and the cowboy in a truer light than did even those of Hart.

The third major cowboy star to maintain some roots in western realism was Charles (Buck) Jones, generally conceded to be the most popular and most beloved of all motion picture cowboys. He was the only major western star other than Harry Carey and Randolph Scott (and maybe Bill Elliott in his later years of semi–A westerns) to retain much of Hart's approach to the making of westerns. Featuring a laconic personality, with a true love of the West and its lore, Buck's westerns were in the middle between the extreme and gaudy showmanship of Tom Mix, Fred Thomson, Yakima Canutt, and Ken Maynard and the austere, heavy plots of Hart and Carey. His westerns — nearly all of which were superior in production values to the majority of programmer westerns of the time — were a happy blend of action, humor, good stories, and restrained realism.

Jones was among the first to break away from the grim, poker-faced heroes continuously portrayed by Hart, and the fact that he once received more fan mail than matinee idol Clark Gable is a good example of the wide popularity he enjoyed.[23] Jones could not bring himself to dress in tawdry uniforms or perform in a flamboyant manner, and the action scenes in his films were usually justified by the story development far more than those of Mix, in whose films such scenes were quite often included merely to give Tom a chance to show off his fancy riding ability. But Buck could ride and fight with the best of them (a real Oklahoma cowboy, he had worked for the 101 Ranch Wild West Show and later was with the Ringling Brothers' Circus as a rider), and he rarely used a double. He could also act: a feat beyond the reach of many celluloid cowboys. Consequently, he was often provided with first-rate actresses as female leads and stories that had adult appeal as well as the necessary ingredients to appease the action appetite of youngsters.

Jones made about 60 westerns for Fox Studios during the 1920s, after starting his career in 1917 as a Universal stuntman and graduating to small parts in Franklyn Farnum, William Farnum, and Tom Mix westerns in 1918 and 1919. His first starring film was *The Last Straw* in early 1920, and he worked for Fox until 1928, finally overtaking Tom Mix in popularity in the latter part of the decade. Although there was lightheartedness in the Jones films, and plenty of excitement as Buck and Silver swung into action, there was also romance and solid stories that were believable.

Buck seemed to be the epitome of masculinity, magnanimity, virtuosity, and courage and he rode into the hearts of millions on his equally popular white horse Silver, carving himself a permanent niche not only in the hearts of those who loved him but in the pages of movie history as well. The Buck Jones Rangers, a youth fan organization, alone numbered from 3–5 million boys at one time, and it is probably safe to say that Jones, through his exemplary life, clean films, and unusual dedication to the welfare of impressionable youth, probably did more to shape the moral fiber of adolescents than did 100 ministers combined. It was an age of heroes, and Buck Jones came along to fulfill his destiny as truly a heroes' hero. He made adult westerns before there was such a differentiation in films, yet they were also kiddie westerns. No other cowboy star was as successful as Buck in attracting a general audience.[24]

Tuska writes as follows:

> The image that Buck projected on the screen for most of his career was that of the athletic, rugged, sincere, and capable all–American male. There was horse-play and honesty in his characterizations. While no drinker, he occasionally smoked. He was not restricted by the conventions of glamour which, to an extent, prompted Ken Maynard and Tom Mix to be almost incredibly clean-cut. Buck was a friendly, a warm, genuine personality, the kind of person one would immediately choose for a pal. This image was carefully constructed and went over well with audiences.[25]

For 20 years children throughout the United States clip-clopped along neighborhood streets, slapping their thighs while playing at being Buck astride Silver. In the sweltering heat of summer and the icy gusts of winter, loyal young fans (and older ones too) would brave the elements trudging to theaters showing the new Buck Jones movie, never for one moment considering letting an ice storm or a heatwave deter them, even when — as was usually the case in the 1920s and 1930s — there was no automobile transportation. And the fondest memories of childhood for tens of thousands of Depression-era kids include backyard shootouts in which Buck and confrères such as Ken Maynard and Tim McCoy overcame the dastardly villains who dared to usurp the forces of righteousness. To say that Buck Jones was a strong moral force is an understatement of his charisma and influence.[26]

Stone of Silver Creek (Universal, 1935) is illustrative of the difference between a Jones film and a routine B western of the time. There was little shooting, riding, or fisticuffs until the final reel, and it was very much like Carey's *Satan Town* or Hart's *Hell's Hinges* in its austerity and evangelistic fervor. In the story Jones is T. William Stone, a saloon owner, who gets a one-half interest in a mine when he turns in two gamblers who cheated one of his saloon customers in a card game. Stone's new partner has a daughter who induces Stone to go to church. He swells the congregation by offering free drinks for church attendance. The new minister is — to quote the *Film Daily Review*— a regular guy, and he and Stone are rivals for the girl. The gamblers come back to Buck's saloon for revenge, and in the following fight the minister is wounded. The preacher gets the girl; Buck gets religion and one of his old girlfriends who has come back to the saloon to work for him. Buck sure was no prude!

Jones became king of the cowboys in the early 1930s and remained the most popular movie cowboy until finally overtaken by the cowboy mutation, Gene Autry. At Buck's death in 1942 he had just completed a series of Rough Riders films with Tim McCoy and Raymond Hatton for Monogram, a series that was both popular and semi-realistic.

Among the other cowboys of the time, there were a few whose films stressed realism to a great extent. Jack Holt, who starred in a Zane Grey series for Paramount in the 1920s, was one of the greatest western heroes of the period, playing a no-nonsense type of hero in well-budgeted films that paid close attention to western realism. Holt's Paramount films far exceeded the attempts of other studios to film the old West as Grey dreamed and wrote it. The emphasis in these films was on story and production values. Curiously enough, virile, steely jawed Holt was the only cowboy hero who got by with having a mustache. This was a period when the mustache was symbolic of evil. Holt's career continued throughout the 1930s and 1940s; however, his last important western was Columbia's *The End of the Trail* (1936), adapted from a Zane Grey story entitled "Outlaws of Palouse." Beautiful in its pathos and simplicity, and excellently directed, acted, and photographed, the film presents Holt at his dramatic best. No true western buff could forget Jack as Dale Brittenham, ex–Rough Rider, walking to the gallows leaving behind both the girl he loves and his best friend, who was forced to bring him to justice.[27]

Holt was one of the first to make adult westerns. Oddly, he has been practically ignored by western film historians, even though he was almost exclusively a western star for a decade. In his day, however, he romped through wild western adventures and achieved greater fame and fortune than his son Tim was ever able to accomplish, even though Tim is justly hailed as one of the better actors who made westerns.

Minor stars Roy Stewart and Art Acord made fairly realistic westerns. Acord achieved considerable popularity as a Universal star in the period 1915–20 and throughout the 1920s. A real, rugged Oklahoma cowboy, he preferred just the simple essentials in cowhands' duds and usually projected a rather realistic view of the cowpoke.

Roy Stewart had taken Hart's place at Triangle in 1917 and for a decade was a cowboy star for various studios. His best and most realistic series was for Sunset Productions in the mid–1920s, in a group of historical westerns: *Buffalo Bill on the U.P. Trail*, *With General Custer at the Little Big Horn*, and *With Kit Carson Over the Great Divide*. His *Daniel Boone Through the Wilderness* remained quite faithful to the popular concept of the backwoods' hero. Only George O'Brien in his 1936 *Daniel Boone* brought more realism to the portrayal of Boone.[28]

During the 1930s, Fox and RKO Radio each produced a fine series with O'Brien, extrovert without equal, who was for a decade one of the top luminaries in the western film world. He brought to the genre a quality of acting and action seldom seen. At Fox in the 1920s, he had been John Ford's favorite star and had the male lead in the academy award–winning *Sunrise* (a non–Ford film). His Fox westerns, in particular — based mostly on Zane Grey stories — were well made and certainly believable, even though O'Brien sometimes came on like Tom Mix or Ken Maynard in the action sequences. In keeping with his popularity, his westerns were budgeted at from $200,000–300,000 each, as compared with $15,000–60,000 normally expended on B westerns.[29] *Robber's Roost, The Last Trail, Thunder Mountain, Riders of the Purple Sage,* and *Last of the Duanes* certainly stand up well with the best of Hart and Carey in overall realism. But his RKO series in the late 1930s consisted of the super-streamlined westerns of the type turned out by Maynard, Steele, McCoy, Boyd, and Brown, although O'Brien's films were more polished and realistic in the sense that they were well scripted, filmed on location, well cast, and competently edited.[30]

Buster Crabbe and Randolph Scott each made some fine westerns at Paramount in the 1930s that established them as western stars of some importance and, in addition, were very realistic, adult westerns, not dissimilar to those of Hart and Carey. Again, many of them were based on Zane Grey stories. Both men became major western stars in the 1940s and Scott continued making realistic westerns right up to the 1960s. Scott was very similar to Hart, not only in looks but in mannerisms as well. His westerns, John Wayne notwithstanding, were the most realistic ones produced during the 1950s, and he had a tremendous adult following. But his films were too adult, too realistic for the young fans, and he was not looked upon and remembered as a Saturday matinee hero in the same way as youngsters fondly remembered the screen adventures of Wild Bill Elliott, Charles Starrett, or Allan (Rocky) Lane.

Tom Keene in the early 1930s was a popular RKO western star in a slick series of polished little B gems. But in 1936–37 he made several historical westerns for Crescent that reeked with realism and were made on a larger scale than regular western programmers. However, they failed to win over the juvenile audiences, who preferred the hell-for-leather, thrill-a-second action that was provided by Maynard, Steele, Bell, Perrin, Lease, and numerous others who made escapist westerns.[31]

In the late 1940s and early 1950s William Elliott, formerly known as Wild Bill, made first-class westerns in the Hart tradition. David Carroll Everson states as follows:

> Unquestionably the most interesting aspect of this series was the realistic quality of the hero's personal conduct. While Elliott remained essentially a man of integrity, at the same time he upset many of the Boy Scout behavior codes by which most of the cowboy heroes had abided since Tom Mix's day. Foremost among these of course was a taboo on alcoholic drinking.... Elliott drank the hard stuff whenever it seemed logical for him to do so—and in fairness to him he frequented restaurants too, something that other cowboy heroes rarely seemed to find necessary. When he played an outlaw, or a reformed outlaw, he was just that—not a lawman posing as a bad guy ... he could also be ruthless, selfish, and even unsportsmanlike, sufficiently sensible not to mind holding a gun on an unarmed opponent and beating the truth out of him if the circumstances warranted.[32]

Significant, however, is the fact that in attaining his adult audience Elliott lost his juvenile one. Few cowboy stars could hold both—Jones did, and for a while so did Autry, Mix, and O'Brien. But it was the rare star who could play to the general audience and keep them coming back for more.

If we can conveniently categorize movie cowboys into three groups—realists, semi-realists, and mythics—by far the largest number would have to be classified as semi-realists. This group became dominant about 1920 and remained so until the demise of the genre in 1954, although in the last decade the mythics numbered almost as many. As the term implies, semi-realist westerns had both elements of realism and escapism in them, with the fantasy elements dominant.

Without question, the greatest of all semi-realists—and many believe the greatest of all western stars ever—was Tom Mix, the embodiment of the world's yearning for a bigger-than-life hero. Tom was for real, in spite of exaggerated studio ballyhoo as to his exploits. He was a real cowpoke and lawman in Oklahoma in the early 1900s (although he was born in Pennsylvania), a bartender in Oklahoma City, a rider for the Miller Brothers' 101 Wild West Show, the Wildman Wild West Show, and the Will A. Dickey's Circle D Wild West Show.

Tom's first big break came in 1909, when, hired by the Selig Company as a cowboy extra, he was featured in a bronco-busting sequence in *Ranch Life in the Great Southwest*. The one-reeler was advertised as "The greatest western picture ever put before the public." It was probably one of the first filmed sequences of rodeo events, and was filmed near Dewey, Oklahoma.[30] Tom became a popular star at Selig, performing feats that not even stuntmen like Dave Sharpe or Yakima Canutt would perform today without considerable thought and planning. Sometimes things happened that were not in the scripts, such as the time in 1910, while filming a jungle thriller titled *Back to the Primitive*, that Tom barehandedly wrestled a leopard that had attacked the heroine, Kathlyn Williams.

By 1916 Mix had become Selig's top western star, and his brand of westerns was catching on, although he was still several years away from overtaking Hart in popularity. Tom was still making only one- and two-reelers. Author Paul Mix writes as follows:

> Tom's screen personality was well established by this time and he definitely wanted his pictures to be accepted as a form of proper family entertainment. He was proud that any mother could take her child to see a Tom Mix movie. He boasted that he never drank or smoked while on the screen. Tom was always the good guy—never the neurotic anti-hero torn between good and evil. Tom usually helped a girl in distress and won her heart in the end. Tom didn't really prefer to kiss the horse instead of the girl! Occasionally, the movie ended with Tom kissing the girl, but more often, they merely held hands and smiled affectionately at each other. Tom was rough on villains, although he seldom

killed one in a movie. He roped plenty of them and defeated many in a good old-fashioned fist fight. He would of course use his gun to blast the villain's gun out of his hands.[31]

Mix established a formula for the sexless western that lasted into the 1950s when the new realism returned romance somewhat in films like *High Noon* and *Shane*. Cowboys from Hoot Gibson and Ken Maynard to Roy Rogers and Gene Autry were all heir to the Mix flirt-and-run legacy, and these Mixian heroes — to the glee of youngsters who bought comic books and cap guns embossed with their names — were more infatuated with horses and pearl-handled revolvers than with their leading ladies.[32]

In 1917 Tom was induced by William Fox to come and work for him, and it was at Fox that Tom made his greatest westerns. By 1920 he had overtaken Hart in popularity, and he remained the most popular screen cowboy until the advent of sound.

Tom was not a western purist. He did on the screen what he knew best how to do. He rode hard, performing daredevil stunts calculated to keep the audience on the edge of their seats.[33]

Gradually, a deliberate type of circus format was created for the Mix films. They were full of fights and chases, essentially realistic in such details as costuming and locations, but emphatically escapist in dramatic terms. No serious issues were ever raised by the Mix plots, and nobody was expected to take them too seriously. As their popularity increased, the story lines tended to become even less realistic.[34]

Mix was everything Hart was not. He wore a frilly cowboy suit and a flamboyant ten-gallon hat that made Hart's simple leather trousers seem ragged in comparison. Hart would cinematically shoot to kill, as it was really done in the West, but Mix only grazed the bad guys, nicked the tops of their heads so they fainted long enough to bring them in for a fair trial.[35] Being a tough-as-nails westerner himself, Mix's performances naturally carried authority, but otherwise his films were breezy, cheerful, streamlined, aimed at a wide audience, careful not to contain elements that might disturb children, and free of serious romantic entanglements.[36] In short, he polished the mythic image of the cowboy until it gleamed and almost singlehandedly ushered in the age of the nonrealistic, romanticized western.[37]

Above all, Tom Mix and Tony represented the finest in vicarious thrills and escapist entertainment. The cowboy, in his broad-brimmed white Stetson, and the well-groomed, white-stockinged chestnut horse rode together to fame and fortune. The fancy duds and hand-carved boots were never intended to represent the working clothes of the average cowboy — neither were the intricate stunts intended to represent the everyday happenings in the life of a cowboy. The costume and stunts exaggerated the adventure and romance of the old west and the audience loved every minute of it.[38]

After Hart and Ford, Tom Mix unquestionably was the greatest single influence on the western in its formative years. "Where Hart had instilled realism in the western and John Ford was to provide its poetry, Mix's greatest contribution to the genre was showmanship. He turned the western into an entertainment industry, created many of the traditions of the action western, and achieved a popularity and box-office value equaled by no other star."[39] Most important of all, he gave the western to the children and the young at heart.

Ken Maynard, too, was one of the greatest movie cowboys ever to sit in a saddle. And, like his friend Tom, Ken was something of a ladies' man, heavy drinker, and hell-raiser off the screen. He had traveled with a number of wild west shows and with Ringling Brothers before entering movies in the mid–1920s. He was also, at one time, the world's champion trick rider. He tended to go overboard on trick riding and elaborate stunting, and rooftop chases were his specialty. Millions thrilled at the exploits of Ken and his horse Tarzan in both silent and sound features, and he earned and squandered several million dollars during his 20-year career as a horse opera star.

Red Raiders (First National, 1927) is a particularly illuminating example of the really slick and well-made westerns of the 1920s. Aside from a consideration of the stars involved, it is as big a picture as *Stagecoach* and other epics. The action is staged on a massive scale, and the entire picture seems dedicated to the proposition that action matters far more than plot.[40] Another film, *Senior Daredevil* (First National, 1926), had for its climax a spectacular sequence of Maynard racing a convoy of wagons loaded with food to a town starved and besieged by villains. Several critics compared this sequence with the chariot race in *Ben Hur* for the excitement it generated.[41]

In *Fiddlin' Buckaroo* and *Strawberry Roan* (both Universal, 1933) Maynard introduced musical instruments and complex musical numbers. This, the musical western, was perhaps an inevitable development following the introduction of sound and dialogue. It helped renew the popularity of the western, and, in Maynard's pictures at least, was never allowed to interfere with the action.[42] However, the day came when Ken made the mistake of allowing a young man by the name of Gene Autry to sing a couple of numbers in the movie *In Old Santa Fe* (Mascot, 1934). The western was never the same again.

Maynard had charm and a screen personality that endeared him to millions of people of all ages and classes. His horse Tarzan was a sensitive, highly intelligent creature whose own personality complemented that of Ken. Together, Ken and Tarzan "allowed theatre-goers to pretend, to take part in a fantasy far-removed from the bleak realities of the depression and the frightful rejection of the faith of the frontier which the circumstances of the modern world imposed upon them."[43]

A name synonymous with cowboy movies is that of Hoot Gibson, clown prince of horse operas for 25 years. Hoot dared to be human, and discovered a great secret: audiences like human beings. They could be thrilled when Bill Hart blew into a saloon full of bad men and shot out all the lights. Just the same, they knew that when the lights went on again, steel-eyed Hart would be standing there with his pistols smoking and the floor would need a dozen janitors to sweep out the corpses. With Hoot you never could tell. He might well be the one on the floor, and audiences worried about him. His horse could throw him 20 feet. His gun would jam. His pack mule paid him "no never mine," and even the heroine blackened his eye.[44]

Hoot had won the all-around cowboy championship at age 17 in Pendleton, Oregon, and was appearing in Universal two-reelers in 1917 after having spent several years in minor parts at Vitagraph, Kalem, and Selig. By 1920 he was ready for stardom and was given the lead in *Action*, directed by his buddy John Ford. The public liked him. The action in his films was usually at a frenzied pace and the comedy refreshing. Strangely, Hoot's films appealed as much to parents as to children, probably even more. By 1925 Hoot was earning $14,000 a week, just $3,000 less than the salary commanded by Mix. Hoot remained a top star throughout the 1920s, playing usually a clowning, fumbling, all-thumbs hero, but during the 1930s his popularity declined considerably, and he was relegated to minor star status.

Fred Thomson's popularity transcended a following by western fans alone. Next to Mix he was the most successful cowboy star of the 1920s, earning nearly $2.5 million in a career that lasted only six years. His films were very much in the mold of Mix and Maynard as far as flamboyant action, and he probably was a better athlete than either.[45]

Thomson's movies were streamlined and showy, they specialized in action for its own sake, and presented a customary superficial and glamorized picture of the West. His clothing had a dude-like appearance too, much as that of Mix. But Thomson himself was far from a phony; he had a pleasant personality and was a fine athlete. Most of the trick stunts in his films he performed without a double, and his effortless acrobatics were often introduced in the interests of comedy.[46] Thomson had been a minister; therefore, he stressed strong moral values, avoided sex and undue violence, intended his films to be a good influence on youth as well as entertaining them, and often included subplots that he felt would be meaningful to youngsters.[47] In 1928 it seemed that he and his handsome white horse Silver King might ride on forever, conquering everything in their paths, but he was taken ill and died on Christmas Day.

Bob Steele has to be rated as one of the top cowboy stars of all time, including both the silent and sound era. Few western stars have had careers as long as that of the "little giant of westerns," whose activities have encompassed silents, sound, and television. It would take several pages just to list the titles of Steele's many films and television appearances during his lengthy career. His first starring western was *The Mojave Kid* (FBO, 1927), but he had already been in movies for five years. Although rather short in height for a cowboy star, he proved that he could handle all the action the role called for, whether it was stunt riding or the fist fights for which he became so well known.[48] Bob's westerns were mostly straightforward, assembly-line affairs, but they were always entertaining, and Steele was a fine, believable actor. As did most of the other stars, Bob sometimes made surprisingly realistic films; for example, *Driftin' Sands* (1928), *Near the Trail's End* (1930), *The Land of Missing Men* (1930), *The Man from Hell's Edges* (1932), *Smoky Smith* (1934), and *Wildfire* (1945). Bob shared "most handsome" honors with Rex Bell, Tim Holt, and Charles Starrett, and romance was usually included in his films. However, it was never allowed to mire the action.

Tim McCoy was one of the most authentic cowboys ever to appear in shoot-'em-ups. As a boy he worked on cattle ranches in Wyoming and became an authority on Indian sign language. After serving in World War I, he became an aide to General Scott, Indian fighter of the late nineteenth century and later army chief of staff. McCoy was ranked by General Scott as one of ten best Indian sign talkers in the U.S. Army.[49]

McCoy presented a strong, handsome figure, with virile qualities that made him an appealing star. His first series, at MGM in 1927–28, was a realistic, high-budgeted group of historical westerns featuring authentic Indians and locales, and Tim dressed in what he felt was the proper attire of the period. The films played the MGM circuit of plush theaters, but, because the action content was sometimes slow-paced, the juvenile audience did not take to him as they did to Mix, Jones, and Maynard.

There was really no other cowboy star like McCoy in personality and manner. Throughout his long, illustrious career he maintained a military aloofness that set him apart from his contemporaries. Traces of the same personality were to be found in William Boyd and Allan Lane, yet they did not command the awed respect that McCoy invariably did. Only Jack Holt came close to demonstrating the same qualities that set McCoy apart, and an icy stare from either man was apt to melt even the most courageous soul.[50]

McCoy, whether or not a popcorn-munching kid realized it, was different. The audience really did not expect to see him crawl up on a bucking bronc à la Gibson or Mix to engage in fantastic riding stunts such as those performed by Kermit Maynard, Ken Maynard or Yakima Canutt, or to give and take in a face-to-face slugfest with half a dozen villains in every picture. Somehow it wasn't expected of this straight-backed, coldly reserved, glove-wearing hero with the distinguishing black suit and wide-brimmed white Stetson. Rather, it was expected that he would draw his pearl-handled pistol with the speed of greased lightning (Tim was acknowledged as the fastest draw of the movie cowboys), foil the attempts of all who would despoil and bring dishonor to the range, win the hand of the heroine if he so pleased, and bring a quality of acting and charm to the screen not usually seen in westerns of the B category. And this he did with gusto in a career that lasted sixteen years.[51]

Johnny Mack Brown, ex-football great from Alabama, began his screen career in 1928 at MGM and played opposite such lovelies as Greta Garbo, Norma Shearer, and Joan Crawford before being costarred along with Wallace Beery in *Billy the Kid* (1930). After many dramatic roles, Johnny eventually drifted into westerns in the early 1930s and remained in the genre for 20 years. He was a most believable western ace, possessing all the attributes necessary for success as a cowboy (riding ability, physique, good looks, and athletic prowess) and with the added asset of being an exceptionally good actor. He was a fixture at Universal and Monogram from 1939 to 1953 and consistently made fine, compact little-formula westerns that never failed to entertain. "Always the good guy or an undercover agent from start to finish, there was little chance of casting this Southern gentleman as anything else. Johnny just exuded those wholesome qualities that make a family hero, which worked to his advantage by attracting not only the kids as fans, but many of their parents as well."[52]

Charles Starrett and John Wayne, too, came to the screen via their football heroics. Starrett, from 1935 to 1952, had the longest reign for any cowboy star at a single studio. Although he is best remembered today for the 65 Durango Kid films he starred in, his best films were the ones made from 1937 to 1945. Starrett was extremely handsome, well built, a good actor, and highly personable.[53] Wayne starred in a 1932 series of B westerns for Warner Brothers, after spending several years as a supporting actor. In 1933 he went to work for Lonestar/Monogram, later working for Mascot/Republic, where he eventually became a member of the highly popular Three Mesquiteer trio, along with Ray Corrigan and Max Terhune. Wayne was a believable cowboy and handled action very well. In fact, he and Yakima Canutt developed the science of screen fighting while working together in early sound features.

Wayne laid claim to overthrowing the boy scout image of the screen cowboy—a claim not unjustified. For a long time he loped along on the white horse wearing the white hat before *Stagecoach* (1939) changed things for him. "When I came in the western man never lost his white hat and always rode the white horse and waited for the man to get up again in the fight. Following my dad's advice, if a guy hit me with a vase I'd hit him with a chair. That's the way we played it. I changed the saintly Boy Scout of the original cowboy hero into a more normal kind of fella."[54] After *Stagecoach* and the completion of his Three Mesquiteer contract, Wayne graduated to A films and continued to turn out first-class westerns far more realistic in story and presentation than the normal B western.

Many outstanding athletes, whether or not they knew one end of a cow from the other, have parlayed athletic prowess into cowboy stardom in the movies. For example, in 1934 a handsome young athlete could be seen charging onto the screen as a rip-snorting, hell-bent-for-leather cowboy in the tradition laid down by Tom Mix. The picture was *The Man from Hell* and the star was Reb Russell, an All-American from Kansas that Knute Rockne called "the greatest fullback I ever saw." Reb was a great athlete and looked like a million dollars on his white gelding Rebel in action sequences. But in dialogue or romantic interludes, he sounded and looked like almost nothing. As Reb laughingly said, "I needed two expressions as a cowboy hero—constipation and relief." But his films, like other independent westerns of that era, made money. Whereas Paramount might take more of the proceeds of a Mae West film as rental, a theater manager could book Reb Russell westerns for a weekend, pay a flat rental of $25, pack his theater, and pocket nearly all the proceeds.[55]

About the time Russell was making his series, another athlete, Kermit Maynard (brother of Ken), was signed by Ambassador Pictures to star in a series of outdoor action films. Kermit had won world championships for both trick and fancy riding and had starred earlier in a silent series (1927) after coming to Hollywood as a football hero.[56]

One of the greatest athletes to grace a saddle was Buster Crabbe, the swimming ace from Hawaii, who, before the end of 1933, had won a gold medal for the 400-meter freestyle event in the 1932 Olympics and set a dozen world records in swimming. Forty years later he was still setting world records in the senior citizen competitions. During the 1930s he starred in some very realistic Zane Grey westerns, but he is primarily remembered for his cheapie westerns (in many of them playing a whitewashed Billy the Kid turned hero) with Al St. John from 1941 through 1946 at PRC Studios and as the king of the sound serials (such as *Flash Gordon*, *Tarzan the Fearless*, *Buck Rogers*, *Red Barry*, *Flash Gordon Conquers the Universe*, and *King of the Congo*). As the last of the great serial stars and one of the few remaining B western stars of the golden age of the movies, he was a popular figure at western and serial film festivals until his death in 1983.[57]

Yakima Canutt, a star in the 1920s and later a character actor, stuntman, and second unit director, was probably the greatest athlete of all. Before entering movies he was a champion of many events in the rodeo world, and some of his wild westerns (for example, *The Devil Horse*, 1926) even put Tom Mix to shame. Art Acord and Jack Hoxie, two of Universal's top cowboys in the silent period, were also rodeo champions. Acord was an authentic Oklahoma cowboy and rodeo performer who entered movies about 1909 and became extremely popular as a western lead. His drinking caused Universal to fire him a number of times; popularity caused the studio to rehire him, but he could never kick the drinking habit. Hoxie was a big fellow and has been called an amiable oaf whose large frame made him seem clumsy and whose expression suggested that his mind was a complete blank except when the director told him to pantomime a specific emotion. However, his critics conceded that on a horse he was something else again, an expert rider and stuntman.[58] In the silent era he achieved tremendous popularity but faded with the coming of sound, though he did make a series of six sound features for a small independent outfit called Majestic. And, in his defense, these films are not bad in comparison with the other independents of the day.

In 1928 Tom Tyler, another athlete and movie star, established a new world weightlifting record in the senior heavyweight class by lifting a total of 760 pounds. This record would remain unbroken for nearly 14 years.

George O'Brien was light-heavyweight boxing champion of the Pacific Fleet during World War I. Bob Steele, William Russell, and William Duncan were also noted as boxers. Many of the early western stars were authentic rodeo and wild west show performers; for example, Buck Jones, Ken and Kermit Maynard, Fred Burns, Bud Osborne, Neal Hart, Bill Cody, Buffalo Bill, Jr., Pee Wee Holmes, Fred Humes, Don Coleman, Bob Custer, Ted Wells, Sunset Carson, Bill Patton, and Buddy Roosevelt. Their natural ruggedness, aided by scriptwriters, directors, and cameramen, created in the minds of millions the mythic cowboy who was virtuous to a fault, physically perfect, handsome, and a super athlete. Although not necessarily rodeo or wild west performers, other real cowboys became screen cowboys too — Wally Wales, Pete Morrison, Edmund Cobb, William Fairbanks, and Al Hoxie.

Other semi-realist cinematic cowboys in the 1920s and early 1930s, although not real-life cowboys or professional athletes, were Jack Perrin, Leo Maloney, William Desmond, Rex Bell, Rex Lease, Lane Chandler, Franklyn Farnum, Wallace MacDonald, and Guinn (Big Boy) Williams, each of whom attained respectable following of fans. In the late 1930s came Tim Holt, whose western series at RKO maintained high standards until the very end of B western production in 1954. Tim projected the nice, clean-cut, handsome young cowboy that most of us like to think did exist. He was the epitome of what western movie fans wanted their heroes to be, and he never disappointed his fans on screen or off.[59]

Donald (Red) Barry was another popular cowboy who combined dramatic roles with westerns and whose career extended into the television era. Coming to the screen as Red Ryder in Republic's 1940 serial *The Adventures of Red Ryder*, Barry's westerns were mostly tautly wrought little gems that often stressed the dramatic rather than physical conflicts in the stories.[60] His husky voice set him apart from other western stars, as did his stature; but what he lacked in size was more than compensated by his intestinal fortitude. Like Bob Steele, Barry was one of the best scrappers to appear in B westerns.[61]

One cowboy star who simply cannot be passed over without comment is William Boyd, the nonathletic, dramatic actor who was a Cecil B. DeMille protégé for years before being launched into the Hopalong Cassidy westerns in 1935. A distinguished figure, usually dressed in black and riding a snow-

Charles Starrett and the Sons of the Pioneers.

white horse called Topper, Boyd was projected as soft-spoken and retiring, presenting more the father figure than the hard-hitting, rough-fighting stereotype western hero; on some occasions he even came across as a genuine gentleman.[62] You might say he was the Ben Cartwright of the pretelevision era. His portrayal won instant approval from audiences and launched Boyd on a series that was to span 13 years and produce 66 films. Boyd's distinct screen persona was one of the most pleasing ever presented to viewers, and a single flash of his smile and a quick burst of his hearty laughter alone were worth the price of admission to one of his films — unless, of course, one insisted in a reasonable amount of realism in his or her screen fare. In that case, the "Hoppys" were in trouble. The movies were usually filmed on location in more picturesque areas than the minor studios used, primarily because a good deal more money and time were spent on their production; they had well-written scripts and relatively long running times.[63]

Robert Livingston, Rod Cameron, Dave O'Brien, Russell Hayden, Bill Elliott, Ray Corrigan, and Allan (Rocky) Lane all made westerns that were predictable, and the heroes they played were above reproach. You could always count on their keeping the cowboy's reputation untarnished, as clean as the driven snow. And speaking of snow, although there was no basis for it in the real West, the color white played an important part in the westerns of the 1930s and early 1940s. The trend to white hats was led by such stars as Starrett, Wayne, Livingston, Maynard, Jones, McCoy, Allen (Bob), Ritter, and Baker. White horses were introduced by Jones (Silver), Maynard (Tarzan), Boyd (Topper), Ballew (Sheik), Starrett (Raider), Russell (Rebel), Perrin (Starlight), Scott (White Dust), Ritter (White Flash), and Thomson (Silver King). Pearl-handled guns were used by a number of stars. The traditional symbol of purity in the western film had completed the flow from Stetson and revolver handle to "old faithful." Not until milkiness had been overdone could an off-white charger again achieve status.[64]

The 1930s, especially, were a veritable heaven for those millions who loved the escapist adventures of innumerable sagebrush cavaliers who galloped inexorably through film after film filled with exploding six-shooters, bone-crunching fist fights, and unbelievable stuntwork, but which were inefficaciously realistic.

Mythicism, of course, made its way into the western film from the very beginning. Hart, Carey, Anderson, Holt, and a few others fought it hard, while Jones, O'Brien, and Stewart, among others, tolerated it in reasonable doses only. Mix, Maynard, McCoy, Gibson, and other streamlined cowboys took larger doses, while keeping their feet in the stirrups of semi-realism.

But sound brought music to the western genre, and with the introduction of the singing cowboy the essence of reality (and any pretense of such) disappeared from the screen.[65]

Gene Autry was a singer of country music on a Chicago radio station in 1933 when Nat Levine of Mascot Pictures met him. Although Autry was not much to look at physically, Levine detected an elusive quality about him that he thought might be worth an investment. Ken Maynard was creating problems, westerns were in a slump, and Nat was looking for something fresh. Thus, Gene Autry entered the Hollywood scene. It took a year of tutoring in acting and horsemanship (Reb Russell helped him learn to ride and found a gentle horse for him in the form of Champion) before the studio dared turn him loose on the screen in a cliffhanger entitled *Phantom Empire*, a bizarre science-fiction western. The rest is screen history.[66]

The remarkable thing about the Autry westerns is how quickly they, and Autry, improved and acquired a definite style of their own. Autry never aspired to the acting standards of a Buck Jones, but, on the other hand, his scripts seldom required it. Warmth and geniality were enough. His films were given modern trappings (cars, airplanes, and radio stations) and plots quite often touched on contemporary politics, big business, and social problems.[67] The sandy-haired, blue-eyed, gum-chewing vocalist soon became the top box-office star of his field. Personal appearances in rodeos and on stage and a string of hit records broadened his national following. With his ever-increasing income, he built a vast financial empire that ranged from oil wells to radio stations to a major league baseball team. By 1950 his holdings were estimated at $4.7 million, and by 1970 his worth was figured at over $100 million.[68]

While it is true that Autry left much to be desired as an actor, was only a marginal action-adventure performer, and only a fair musician, he managed to combine these qualities in a unique package that spelled cash and plenty of it wherever he appeared.[69] He adopted what he called his cowboy's code. In 93 movies — from 1934 to 1954 — he never shot first, hit first, hit a smaller man, took a drink, or smoked. He never took unfair advantage of anyone, never broke his word, or rarely kissed a leading lady.[70] And most of the other cowboys followed his code too.

Although Autry's films were entertaining and immensely popular, the mythic content completely obliterated realism. For example, *Strawberry Roan* (Columbia, 1948) opens with the Autry singers and stooges performing the theme song, with full orchestral accompaniment, while stringing a fence. And in *Mexicali Rose* (Republic, 1939), when villain Noah Beery's recording of the title song is broken, Autry takes over and continues the song, a full orchestra accompanying him right out there on the prairie with the banditos forming a male chorus![71]

Autry's success brought forth many imitators, and the musical range was soon grazed to capacity. No one matched Gene's success, although Roy Rogers came close and, like Gene, became a millionaire many times over. Rogers had a likable personality and his charisma about equaled that of Autry. Roy did not star in his first western, *Under Western Stars*, until 1938, four years after Autry's initial starring vehicle, *Tumbling Tumbleweeds*, shook the western film world. The ultra-streamlined westerns of Autry and Rogers brought together, in weird fashion, the standard ingredients of the old-time westerns (chases, cattle stampedes, gunslinging, and saloon fights) with contemporary elements (night clubs, radio, television, chorus girls, high-powered guns, jet-rockets, and uranium deposits).[72]

The first Autry imitators were Dick Foran, Tex Ritter, and Smith Ballew. Ritter was the most successful singing cowboy after Autry and Rogers and was an authentic Texan, although without any cowboy background. Ballew had the best voice of them all and was also a Texan. His background was in music, and during the late 1920s and early 1930s he was a very popular bandleader and vocalist. Foran was probably the most competent actor-singer and went on to become a successful dramatic actor after his stint as a singing cowboy. Fred Scott, George Houston, James Newill, Jimmy Wakely, Ray Whitley, Eddie Dean, John King, Bill (Cowboy Rambler) Boyd, Art Davis, Art Jarrett, Monte Hale, Tex Williams, Kirby Grant, and Ken Curtis all found a measure of fame and fortune in musical westerns. Only two singing cowboys were anything near to being real cowboys before strapping on a guitar and riding Hollywood's cinematic trails: Bob Baker and Rex Allen. Both hailed from Arizona, and Baker had been a working cowboy and rodeo performer. Allen had grown up on a ranch and so knew something about cowboy life. Baker's career was short, although he was handsome, had a better voice than Rogers or Autry, was rugged, and turned out a series of well-made westerns. Bad handling by his studio, Universal, was the primary cause of only a brief career in movies. Allen, who got into films only five years before the termination of series westerns, is still semi-active today as an entertainer on television, on the rodeo and state-fair circuit, as a recording artist, and in Walt Disney nature films.

Any concern for realism was thrown out of the window with the coming of the crooners and pluckers, but the musical western was not the only bastardization of the West. In the late 1940s production standards slipped, as costs rose and the market for B westerns shrank. Charles Starrett, a good actor who deserved better, was foisted on audiences as the Durango Kid, a masked fighter for justice, in a series of cheaply made pictures. But the youngsters ate it up, and the series continued profitably for nearly ten years. Even earlier, in 1938, the Lone Ranger had made his appearance. The Cisco Kid dated back to the 1920s, and in the 1940s was portrayed by Cesar Romero, Duncan Renaldo, and Gilbert Roland. Renaldo — a former member of the Three Mesquiteers — was the most successful in the role, especially on television. Zorro, too, had a long screen history. The Avenger, the Eagle, and other masked hero mutations appeared, and the heroines even got in the act as super women behind masks. Then came the whip crackers: Whip Wilson and Lash LaRue. It was more then the genre could stand. And so the B western died in 1954, after putting up a heroic struggle against the onslaught of television and the closing of small theaters across the country.

In its final years, 1946–54, the quality of the average B western reflected the illness that had beset the industry. The genre died a peaceful death with the conclusion of a short-lived series starring Wayne Morris (previously unassociated with westerns), for Allied Artists, and the completion of the last serial ever made, Columbia's *Perils of the Wilderness* (1956), starring Dennis Moore, long a member of the B western fraternity of featured players. Of course, B westerns have continued to be made on a nonseries basis, but the old-fashioned shoot-'em-ups that provided yesteryear's thrills and generated a mythical concept of the cowboy shared by millions throughout the world are gone, evidently forever.

In the 1950s and 1960s old stereotypes of roles and role limitations for both men and women started falling away. The period brought the psychological western, a cinematic attempt to talk out our historical neuroses and psychoses. What westerns had in common was a jaundiced view of various elements of the western myth and the traditional western of bygone days.[73]

The psychological western, though excellent in its way, led to a definite emasculation of the genre as a whole. The double-action Freud ousted the double-action Colt and, speaking generally, the transition was a deplorable one. It led to numerous films in which the hero was a nonhero—a coward.[74]

The traditional western formula, pitting white hats against black hats, was discarded in favor of films loaded with every conceivable sick and quirkish plot element. The dramatic punch of straightforward western action with heroes, heroines, sidekicks, horses, heavies, and Indians doing what they do best was debased by the weight of neuroses and social ills dumped on the western range.

Since the 1960s western heroes have often been presented as obsessed, neurotic characters whose motives are questionable and whose means are despicable—men who live by their own rules rather than society's—white-hatted heroes and virginal heroines were displaced by sagas emphasizing characterization and psychoanalysis at the expense of hell-bent-for-leather western high jinks. Western myths and archetypes were singularly treated with glibness or contempt. In fact, a number of films have purposely strived for demythologization of the West and to parody the western by poking fun at myriad familiar genre clichés.[75]

I wonder how many today sit with pipe and newspaper in a lounge chair before a television set watching mediocre fare and longing to see once again the cinematic cowboy heroes of yesterday's Saturdays dashing across the prairie on their favorite steeds in pursuit of arch-villains such as Roy Barcroft, George Chesebro, or Charles King? I suspect that large numbers would prefer this opportunity, even though they can catch a different type of mythic western drama on television. The reel cowboys of B films left a great legacy to millions upon millions of young boys (and a few girls too). They left us a dream—a dream that we could conveniently tuck away in our minds and enjoy whenever we wished. And in the dead of winter, as I sit comfortably gazing into the burning logs of the fireplace, with the howling wind outside providing an eerie, chilling tune as snow is driven relentlessly against the windows, I dream my dreams—for a few minutes freed from the frustrations and concerns of a job, of children, or of the world.

I help my hero to escape death at the hands of assorted villains, dash furiously down mountain trails with him in many thrill-packed adventures, and empathize with him as he romances his way through never to be forgotten features. I envy him in those oft-recalled love scenes with heroines who captured my heart 50 years ago, and I inwardly chuckle at the antics of my hero and his horse when they decide to clown around.

After tamping fresh tobacco into my pipe, I reach for the coffee pot to refill a now empty cup, light the pipe, and gaze at the dying flame of the match against a backdrop of pine logs sputtering and flickering in the fireplace. Then I drift again into dreams of long-past Saturdays from the age of innocence.

And so the dreams continue, year after year. The logs burn low, the flames flicker into an abyss of darkness, the chill creeps in, and, suddenly, reality in all its harshness is thrust upon me — and I start to worry again. But the dreams will return — dreams of things that can never be again — and how wonderful it is to have a brief respite from the real world and to have had a boyhood filled with heroes such as Buck Jones, Bob Steele, and Hoot Gibson. They have done themselves proud providing the best entertainment ever given a youngster and teaching simple moral lessons that would sustain a world. So what if the image projected was somewhat different from that of the typical real-life cowboy? Deep down we knew it was fantasy, even as children.

PART II

Western Literature as Hollywood Filmed It

Chapter 2

Zane Grey

Topping all western writers in popularity at the time of his death in 1939 was Zane Grey, whose writing was considered atrocious by his critics and whose characters, they believed, were as wooden as a cigar-store Indian, but who somehow had a knack for storytelling. It was Grey who made western a generic term, and the output of western literature has never faltered — William MacLeod Raine, Max Brand, B. M. Bower, Luke Short, Ernest Haycox, Larry McMurtry, on down to Louis L'Amour, who has outsold them all, including Grey. Their work converts to movies directly, with sometimes astronomical profit.

Grey reigned as the most popular western fiction writer for the last 20 years of his life. And, five decades after his death, he is still one of the two most revered writers of the genre, sharing honors with Louis L'Amour. This, in spite of literary critics rating him more impressive as a phenomenon than as a writer and labeling all of his novels adolescent fantasies set in a never-never land of romance and adventure. But whatever their literary merits, Zane Grey novels were and still are eagerly devoured by readers worldwide and have been made and remade into profitable movies. No other popular writer mirrored the age in which he lived so powerfully and yet so eloquently.

Grey had so many unpublished book manuscripts (some had appeared in serial form in magazines) at the time of his death that his publisher, Harper and Row, decided to publish one each year until the supply was exhausted. The last one, *Boulder Dam*, appeared in 1963.[1]

Even Grey critics — and they are numerous and vociferous — concede his popularity with the masses. After all, they can do little else, since his approximately 85 books have sold in excess of 40 million copies.

And speaking of the critics, their opinion of Grey as a sensational, hack writer is short of unanimous, even while they concede that his works retain a vast popularity with working people that is unique, incredible, and inexplicable. Zane Grey is not merely the most famous western writer of all time; he is the one American author of whom it can be said that he has evolved,

38

quite literally, into an American tradition, as much as fireworks on the fourth of July, the neighborhood tavern, or apple pie and cheese.[2]

Like his contemporary, Edgar Rice Burroughs, Grey's popularity has mainly depended on the common man, the literally unsophisticated; the cultural sophisticates have tended to ignore or condemn his works. But no other writer has ever had such an influence on western literature as did Grey; and even today, over a century after his birth, his books are selling over 1 million copies a year in various trade editions, thanks in large measure to the vast new audience acquired in recent years through the paperback market. Apparently, there are still those who need a code of ethics; an inspiration to higher morals; a challenge for their ventures and ambitions; and someone to bring chivalry back into their lives. They have found these things in the writings of Zane Grey, an institution in his time.

Writer Burton Rascoe, writing in the *Saturday Review of Literature* in 1939, summed up the appeal of Zane Grey thus: "Grey brought about the vicarious wish-fulfillment of millions of sedentary workers in the office warrens of cities and industrial towns — of imprisoned men to whom a new Zane Grey novel was a splendid escape into a wild, free dreamland of limitless horizons, where the problems of life are reduced to the simplest elements and where justice triumphs over evil, the wages of courage and uprightness are true love and genuine happiness, and where man may breathe in freedom."

Grey was indeed a romantic, and he wrote romantic novels of the American West. To him romanticism was tantamount to love. The West encouraged love affairs with nature, especially the wild beauty of open spaces, and with rugged individualism. He wrote about the westerner in the way that non-westerners wanted him to, developing a western mythology that helped turn that area into the most romanticized area of the United States. The West, to Grey, was just as much an idea in the United States as it was a geographical region. Perhaps the West did not offer the charm with which Grey endowed it, but that was not the most important point. The significant thing was that Americans thought the West had all these qualities.[3]

For the same reason, Burrough's highly imaginative tales of Pullicidar, Tarzan of the Apes, and John Carter of Mars touched the reading hearts of the masses. He wrote about places, things, and people we all hoped existed and liked to fantasize about. It was escapism run amok in Burroughs' case, but the world loved it.

However, Grey, unlike Burroughs, had actually been a part of the West. Whereas Burroughs had never been in Africa, or the center of the earth, or on Mars or Venus, Grey had trudged the deserts and mountains of the West. But he has never received due credit for the comparatively high degree of realism in his books. His cowboys, for example, actually raise cattle, get tired, dirty, drunk, and curse (albeit mildly) when angry. And Grey was philosophically a child of his times. In an age that extolled moral incorruptibility, the manly virtues and the strenuous life, Grey's novels revealed a world in which those values reigned supreme.[4]

Grey was sincere; he thought his view of the West was essentially true, even if slightly romanticized. Critics, however, were always quick to chop away at the foundation of Grey's west. "Nothing shows more clearly how far away Mr. Grey's world is from actuality," says T. K. Whipple, referring to Grey's treatment of sex. "His Texas is not in the Union, but in fairyland." Whipple cites instances of Grey's heroes and heroines living and traveling together in the wilderness in perfect innocence.[5]

But, as Topping points out in his essay on Zane Grey, one must note a more realistic side to Grey's novels as well. For one thing, they abound in rapes, both attempted and successful. *The U.P. Trail* features a whorehouse madam as a major character and describes her establishment in great detail. Also, in both that novel and *Riders of the Purple Sage*, female breasts are bared (although only for medical reasons in both cases). All this is remarkable and realistic for pre–1920 fiction.[6]

The First Zane Grey Films

It was inevitable that Grey's romanticized West would find its way to the screen. Beginning with *The Border Legion*, released by Goldwyn in January 1919, the name Zane Grey on a movie marquee became a distinct asset.

Grey's early experiences with moving picture companies and agents were neither financially rewarding nor happy ones. For several years prior to World War I he attempted to get his stories onto the screen, his first efforts centering around *Desert Gold*, *The Light of Western Stars*, *Riders of the Purple Sage*, and *The Heritage of the Desert*. The year was 1914. However, the first actual sale of movie rights to a Grey book was to William Fox for a flat fee of $1,500 for *Riders of the Purple Sage*. Under the contract, Grey received no royalties from the movie. It was not released until mid–1918, one month after the release by Goldwyn of *The Border Legion*.

It was not long before Grey's asking price had zoomed to $25,000 a picture — and he received it, thanks to the business acumen of Mrs. Grey. For it was she who handled most of the business matters while Zane concentrated on his writing and fishing. One thing Grey did insist on, however, was a clause in his contracts with motion picture studios that forced them to shoot part of each picture in the actual locales of the stories. Thus, Arizona was often frequented by Paramount and Fox for location shooting, as it was a favorite locale of Grey stories.

William Farnum was the first actor to be closely associated with Zane Grey westerns and was the personal choice of Grey to depict Jim Lassiter in *Riders of the Purple Sage*. Subsequently, he starred in *The Rainbow Trail*, *The*

Last of the Duanes, and *Lone Star Ranger*, all for Fox. Ironically, when he had fallen from stardom and became a character actor, he appeared in the 1941 remake of *Riders of the Purple Sage* that starred George Montgomery, an actor Farnum had been cofeatured with in Republic's classic serial of 1938, *The Lone Ranger*. At the time Montgomery was billed as George Letz, his real name.

In 1919 Grey entered into partnership with Benjamin H. Hampton to form Zane Grey Productions for the purpose of producing movies based on Grey's works. *Riders of the Dawn*, based on *The Desert of Wheat*, was the first film by the company and starred Roy Stewart, the cowboy star who replaced William Hart at Triangle. Stewart's encore film was *The U.P. Trail*. What is eminently characteristic about this production, in addition to its atmospheric touch, is the last shot of a spectacular shooting scene. In this the smokescreen emanating from the revolvers becomes so thick that the human figures erect or falling are like mere silhouettes against the background. It is a unique bit of photography and one that reflects the efficiency of the cameraman. Kathlyn Williams is effective in the part of Beauty, coloring the role with an essential hardness in mimicry that offers a great contrast to the soft, sweet features of Marguerite De La Motte as the naive, unsophisticated girl from the parochial school.

Both *Riders of the Dawn* and *The U.P. Trail* showed a profit, were of reasonable production quality, adhered more closely to the books than would most of the later films adapted from Grey novels, and enhanced the career, albeit temporarily, of Stewart. Zane Grey Productions, however, was shortlived. *Desert Gold*, with Elmo Lincoln (of Tarzan fame), *The Man of the Forest*, with Claire Adams, Robert McKim, and Jean Hersholt, and *The Mysterious Rider*, again with Robert McKim and Claire Adams, rounded out the total output of the company.

Grey found the many problems associated with producing films not to his liking and he resented the amount of time it took from his writing, even though in actuality Hampton did the filmmaking and wrestled with the day-to-day operational problems. In late 1919 Grey bought out Hampton and sold the company to Famous Players Lasky. The sale included the old Brunton studios which housed Zane Grey Productions. The studio then became Paramount, and it still occupies the same location today. Thereafter, Grey contented himself with contracting with others for the filming of his books.

The Last Trail was brought to the screen by Fox in 1921 with Maurice B. Flynn, Eva Novak, and Wallace Beery heading up the cast. Flynn portrays a stranger whom Eva Novak shelters from the sheriff, who thinks him to be a bandit. Wallace Beery, Eva's fiancée, is jealous and has Flynn arrested. Later, he attempts to blow up a dam and steal the company payroll but is captured by Flynn, who has secretly been sent by the company to investigate Beery. Although the film's source was *The Last Trail*, a story of early days in the Ohio

Valley, it would be hard to find any similarity in the stories. Such was the case with most of the Grey tales.

For example, *The Last Trail* was made by Fox in 1927 with Tom Mix as the star. In this version Mix saves the person played by Lee Shumway and his wife from an Indian attack, and as a result the couple name their first son after Tom. Later, Shumway — as sheriff of Carson City — is killed, placing his son in Tom's care before he succumbs. Later, a stagecoach race is conducted under the supervision of a U.S. express agent to determine who gets a government contract. Tom supports an old contractor whose daughter, played by Carmelita Geraghty, he has fallen in love with. He is opposed by a bandit leader, played by William Davidson, who lines up his men as contestants in the race. But justice triumphs and Tom wins the race and the girl, as well as capturing all the crooks who attempted to escape with stolen loot.

Neither the 1921 or the 1927 version bears any resemblance to the Grey novel about the Ohio Valley and Wetzel, frontiersman, but the author's name above the title was worth a cool $25,000 royalty to Grey.

The Zane Grey–produced *Mysterious Rider* of 1921 adhered better to the story line of the novel and retained the character names. Robert McKim, usually a villain, plays Hell Bent Wade, the stranger who ultimately proves to be the father of Columbine (Claire Adams), the girl he befriends.

But in the Jack Holt version made by Paramount in 1927 Hell Bent Wade (Jack) is a rancher who struggles to uncover the ruthlessness of a crooked Spanish land grant holder and prove that he and his fellow ranchers have legally paid for their ranches. In the end he finds happiness with the heroine, who is now a girl called Dorothy King (played by Betty Jewel) rather than his daughter, Columbine.

Zane Grey, Jack Holt, and Paramount: A Winning Combination

The one man most associated with Zane Grey films during the 1920s was iron-jawed, virile Jack Holt. His Paramount westerns based on Grey stories were among the finest produced in the decade.

Holt had started in movies as a stuntman in *Salomy Jane* in 1914. By 1916 he was starring in Universal's *Liberty, a Daughter of the U.S.A.*, the first western serial ever made. Roles in *A Desert Wooing* and *The Squaw Man* (both 1918) followed, but a three-year hiatus in nonwesterns befell him before he was cast by Cecil B. DeMille in *The Call of the North* in 1921. *While Satan Sleeps* and *North of the Rio Grande* further convinced the Paramount brass of Holt's competency as a western hero and the decision to star him in the company's series of super westerns was a unanimous one in the front office.

In the opinion of many, Paramount made the best Zane Grey westerns ever produced, although the Fox westerns, to be discussed later, certainly provided stiff competition. But as a whole, the Paramount westerns exceeded in quality the attempts of others to bring to life the West as Grey lived and fantasized it. Emphasis was on story and production values, and stars such as Holt, Gary Cooper, Randolph Scott, and Buster Crabbe gave them the polish they deserved.

Wanderer of the Wasteland (1924) was the first of the Grey novels to be brought to the screen as a Holt vehicle, with most of the scenes shot in two-strip technicolor. Although this production was the best colored screen effort put forth up to that time, it might have been just as interesting if it had been made as a black and white, enhanced by tinting and toning. In fact, the most dramatic scenes in the film are not the colored ones, but those in the desert that are tinted a most effective sepia.

Obviously, Holt put his whole soul into the portrayal of the hero and his characterization of Adam Larey was possibly the best acting job he had done to that point. One of the most compelling situations in the film was when Holt is shown suffering from gnawing hunger in the sun-scorched desert. He is almost insane and even the sight of a rattlesnake prompts him to attack the reptile as if he wanted to eat it. You see the rattlers at the end of the reptile's tail and then the sudden stab it makes at its victim, who is found unconscious.

Director Irvin Willat and actor Holt, with fine support from Noah Beery and Billie Dove, sustain the suspense in a thoroughly gripping story. Paramount remade it in 1935 with Dean Jagger and Edward Ellis in the roles played earlier by Holt and Beery. The RKO version (1945) starring James Warren had nothing to do with the Zane Grey story, other than use of the title.[7]

Holt next made *The Thundering Herd* (1925), a film that deviated considerably from the Grey story. Lois Wilson and Noah Beery were featured. An interesting sidelight to this film is the granting of star status to Tim McCoy (he was listed sixth in the cast) by film historians Fenin and Everson.[8] Holt plays a buffalo hunter out to stop Noah Beery from starting an Indian war. Complicating matters is Holt's love for Beery's daughter. The scenery is beautiful, the acting good, and William Howard's direction one of his better efforts.

Gary Cooper was an extra in *The Thundering Herd*. Paramount remade the story in 1933 with Randolph Scott and Judith Allen in the roles played originally by Holt and Wilson. Noah Beery repeated his role in the sound version, which used considerable cannibalized footage from the Holt films. Paramount followed this practice of cutting up the Holt films for insertion into remakes to the point where no complete copies exist of most of the Holt westerns. They were so good, it seems, that it cost them their lives.[9]

Paramount would dress the casts of the sound film in clothing identical to that worn in the original outdoor scenes and put the actors through their paces on the back lot or in Griffith Park. Then they spliced in, from the negative of the original, all the mid-distant and distant action scenes plus the outdoor panorama to create the illusion of a lavishly produced film. They even had Randolph Scott and Buster Crabbe wear mustaches in several of the films, and in one film, *The Mysterious Rider* (1933), used Kent Taylor, who bore a superficial resemblance to Holt. Thus, in *Forlorn River* (1937) you see Buster Crabbe in the closeup shot, but the fellow riding into Bryce Canyon, with the magnificent scenery in the background, is actually Jack Holt. Pictures cannibalized in addition to *The Mysterious Rider* and *Forlorn River* were *The Thundering Herd*, *The Vanishing Pioneer*, and *Wild Horse Mesa*.

Holt plays a drunken gunfighter in *The Light of Western Stars* (1925). He summons up enough decency to help a lady in trouble, Billie Dove, and falls in love with her; then subsequently fights to recover her cattle from rustlers headed by Noah Beery. In the sound remake in 1930, Richard Arlen assumes the Holt role, while Victor Jory had the lead in the Harry Sherman production released by Paramount in 1940.

Ingenue Billie Dove is again an inspiration for hero Holt in *Wild Horse Mesa*, Grey's beautiful story of wild horses caught by running them into a barbed wire corral. Holt, as Chance Weymer, a trail rider, fights to save the herd and wins the love of the delectable Dove to boot. The film is about the most faithful of all Grey adaptations. Although leisurely in its pacing, it makes up for it with a good solid story and action sequences that are well done. Composed of virtually all exteriors, *Wild Horse Mesa* is also beautifully photographed. True, it is not overly paced with action, and it takes its time getting under way. Neither hero nor villain appear until two reels into the film. But if nothing else, this is indicative of an unusual fidelity to the original Grey story. Very few adaptations have done more than pay lip service to his originals; very often the same story has been remade several times, each time with a totally different plot. Sometimes, the Grey originals on which they were based just do not exist at all, Grey being paid merely for the use of his name, or perhaps a plot outline scribbled on the back of an envelope!

Paramount twice filmed *Born to the West*. In the 1926 film, Jack Holt plays Colorado Dare Rudd, who seemingly lives a charmed life. Set in those halcyon days when beer was served in huge glasses and men wore flowered waistcoats, the acting is quite good. Holt wins the heroine, Margaret Morris, and the villain dies a violent death.

In 1937 the studio remade the story with Johnny Mack Brown and John Wayne in the roles played earlier by Holt and Bruce Gordon and, upon rerelease, retitled it *Hell Town*. The story was also published serially as *Open Range* (with only slight alteration in story and with character name changes) and filmed by Paramount under that title with Lane Chandler and Betty

Compson starring. And, to add to the confusion, Harper and Brothers later published the book under the title *Valley of Wild Horses*.

Jack Holt completed *Forlorn River* and *Man of the Forest* in 1926, each film a lavishly mounted western and extremely successful at the box office. Both negatives were cut up later and included in the Crabbe and Scott remakes. In *Forlorn River* Jack is Nevada, familiar to Grey enthusiasts as the hero of two Grey novels. Raymond Hatton, Tom Santschi, and Arlette Marchal help Holt vividly bring the story to the screen.

Exteriors were shot in Zion National Park and Bryce Canyon in Utah. Holt, a reformed outlaw, strives to suppress his love for the fiancée of Edmund Burns (Ben Ide), who saved his life; but, in the end, true love flourishes as he saves the girl's live and she declares her love for him.

Likewise, in *Man of the Forest* Jack, as Milt Dale, keeps his batting average with the ladies intact as he saves Georgia Hale from a fate worse than death at the hands of Warner Oland (Charlie Chan to a later generation of moviegoers), after having been jailed for kidnapping her himself earlier in an attempt to protect her from scoundrels who planned to force her to deed a ranch to them.

The Vanishing Pioneer (1928) was an original story for the movies and was, as far as is known, the only original screenplay Zane Grey did. Although it has been confused with *The Vanishing American*, it is not the same story, for it revolves about a western settlement of pioneer descendants who are threatened with the loss of their water supply through the encroachments of nearby townspeople. Jack Holt is a hard-fisted rancher leading the fight for water rights. The film also serves as Tim Holt's screen debut, playing John Ballard as a 7-year-old, while his father plays the adult Ballard.

The Vanishing Pioneer was remade during 1935 with Randolph Scott starring. And, as with so many of the Jack Holt originals, the scenic shots were cannibalized from the silent version. The billing of the picture was "Adolph Zukor presents Zane Grey's *Rocky Mountain Mystery* with Randolph Scott — from Zane Grey's story, *The Vanishing Pioneer*."

The Water Hole (1928) is a curious mixture of unbelievable comedy and melodrama, based on the Zane Grey story of the same title. Holt does exceedingly well with the part of an Arizonian angry with Nancy Carroll and her father. Jack, with the acquiescence of the father, decides to teach her a lesson by pretending to kidnap her and making her care for him in some deserted cliff dwellings. John Boles is the fiancee who puts in an appearance to rescue his sweetheart. There are some beautiful desert scenes in technicolor. The story is prefaced by a farcical sequence depicting Eve tempting Adam, and there is a silly series of scenes in which Nancy flirts with Jack.

Holt's role in Grey's *Avalanche* (1928) was particularly suited to his talents. His portrayal of Honest Jack Dunton, a gambler in a frontier western town, who turns crooked in order to send his ward to college, was an exceptionally good one. The theme of the story centers around the affection of two men for each other and the romantic problem that threatens to estrange them. The story was adapted for the screen by Paramount's ace writers J. Walter Ruben and Sam Mintz. The human qualities of the story, the masterly portrayals by the cast, and the intimate picture of life in an early Western town account for the popularity that *Avalanche* enjoyed.

Sunset Pass (1930) rounded out Holt's work at Paramount. The film was shot on location near Flagstaff, Arizona, with Holt cast as a marshal out to catch cattle rustlers. In the process he falls in love with the rustler's sister, played by Nora Lane. John Loder is Nora's crooked brother killed by Jack when he refuses to reform. In 1933 Paramount remade the story with Tom Keene, Kathleen Burke, and Randolph Scott in the principal roles. The RKO version (1946) with James Warren used little more than the title.

Besides those with Jack Holt, Paramount also filmed other Grey stories during the 1920s. Those with Richard Dix as star were perhaps the most important. *To the Last Man*, with Lois Wilson and Noah Beery featured, was released in September 1923; *The Call of the Canyon*, likewise with Wilson and Beery, in December 1923. Both were directed by Victor Fleming.

In the former film Richard and Lois are members of two feuding families. The conflict leaves only the two as survivors in the end. In the latter film Richard plays Glenn Kilbourne, an Easterner who goes to Arizona to regain his Eastern fiancée; the fiancée wins back his love from an Arizona girl; and the Arizona girl winds up marrying B western favorite Tom London, going under his real name of Leonard Clapham at that point in his career.

The best of the Dix westerns, however, is *The Vanishing American* (1925), in which he plays the Indian Nophaie, hopelessly in love with Lois Wilson, a white schoolteacher, and frustrated and abused by a crooked Indian agent — Noah Beery. Jesse Lasky devoted ten reels to unfolding this great Grey classic, which was filmed in Monument Valley, Utah. It was an important film from the standpoint of presenting sensitively the plight of the American Indian. However, the studio made many changes in the story — so many, in fact, that it was hardly recognizable as that authored by Grey.

In addition to the Holt and Dix westerns and those films already mentioned, Paramount brought to the screen during the 1920s *The Heritage of the Desert*, *The Border Legion*, *Code of the West*, *Desert Gold*, *Drums of the Desert*, *Nevada*, *Open Range*, *Under the Tonto Rim*, and *Stairs of Sand*. *Nevada* was one of Gary Cooper's first hits; *Under the Tonto Rim* helped to establish Richard Arlen as a western actor; and *Stairs of Sand* starred Wallace Beery in the title role. Each of these films, as with the Holt and Dix ones, were made on budgets of $125,000–150,000 each.

The Zane Grey–Fox Westerns of the 1920s and 1930s

After using William Farnum and Maurice Flynn as leads in their first few Grey westerns, Fox decided to cast Tom Mix, fast overtaking William Hart as the most popular screen cowboy, as Grey's hero Buck Duane in *The Lone Star Ranger* (1923). It was followed by *The Last of the Duanes* (1924), *Riders of the Purple Sage* (1925), *The Rainbow Trail* (1925), and *The Last Trail* (1927), making a total of five Zane Grey westerns for the extrovert Mix.

Tom was miscast in these, and *Riders of the Purple Sage* was probably his poorest film. The character Mix played was too subdued for the personality he had developed over the years. But, in spite of the miscasting, Mix's name, combined with that of Grey, was enough to assure box-office success.[10]

Zane Grey's fame grew until his name on a movie poster automatically meant huge box-office returns. His name frequently was in larger letters than that of the stars. Few writers have ever attained this status.

During the Depression days of the 1930s, Grey still received $25,000 for each book, while most westerns were being written by staff writers for as little as $25 per week. Ernest Haycox was the second highest paid author at that time, but his top price was the $5,000 he received for the short story "Stage to Lordsburg," which became the film *Stagecoach*.[11]

In 1930 Fox remade *The Lone Star Ranger* with George O'Brien, who was much more adept at bringing Grey's heroes to the screen than Mix. Equally adept as an athlete and as a flamboyant extrovert, O'Brien also had considerable acting ability, his repertoire of emotions being far greater than the two possessed by Mix, constipation and relief.

Fox proceeded to make a series of high-class westerns with O'Brien, most of them based on Grey novels. Not to be confused with the low-budget quickie programmers of the 1940s and 1950s, the O'Brien westerns were budgeted at up to $200,000 (back when inflation had not yet eroded the value of the dollar) and four to six weeks were allocated for the production of each, utilizing such locations as Monument Valley, various locations in California, and distant locations in Utah, Arizona, Colorado, Montana, and Nevada.[12]

The O'Brien-Fox westerns were on a par with the best of Buck Jones, Ken Maynard, Tim McCoy, and William Boyd films made during the 1930s; in fact, surpassing all of them in production values. And when Fox decided to end the long-running O'Brien series (non–Grey stories alternated with Grey yarns), George signed with RKO for a similar series of quality westerns.

Fox released only two additional Grey westerns during the remainder of the 1930s. *King of the Royal Mounted* (1936) was based on the comic strip of the same name, which had been created by Grey, and featured Robert Kent and Rosalind Keith. *Roll Along Cowboy* (1937) was based on a future published novel, *The Dude Ranger*. The film starred singing cowboy Smith Ballew and featured Cecilia Parker and Gordon Elliott (later to achieve B-western immortality as Wild Bill Elliott). Operating on a budget of around $125,000, Sol Lesser, the producer, shot much of the picture at scenic Lone Pine, California.

Paramount in the 1930s and 1940s

During the early 1930s the Paramount Studio was in a tight financial position. The change over to sound production had been expensive and with the Depression theater attendance was low; thus, receipts were down. To stimulate business most of the first-run movie houses had changed to double features; however these theaters wanted both movies to be quality productions. However, with the advent of sound, most of the major studios believed that westerns were out and so had stopped making these movies and had released most of their western contract players.

With improved sound techniques they soon discovered that there was indeed a demand for westerns. During the 1920s Paramount had produced the series of Zane Grey westerns starring Jack Holt. All of these were quality features made with generous budgets and shot on location with Holt during all of his riding and fight scenes. Someone in the Paramount production department came up with an idea that enabled Paramount to produce a series of quality westerns on a tight budget. The use of stock scenic shots or single action scenes — for example, a stagecoach wreck or spectacular fall — was not unique, but in this instance most of the films were made by outfitting all of the players in the later version with costumes identical to those worn by the actors in the silent version, as previously mentioned. Because Jack Holt was no longer with Paramount, the actors who took over his roles in the sound versions wore mustaches. Then all of the scenic shots, all of the distant action shots, most of the mid-distant action shots, and even some fleeting close action shots were cut out of the silent movies and spliced into the new sound films. Some of these remakes were shot entirely in the studio and on the Paramount back lot, and a couple of them did go on location for a few scenes. By extremely clever work on the part of the directors, the cameramen, the editors, and cutters the two versions were put together and the end result was a quality product made on a low budget.

During the 1930s O'Brien's chief competition in Zane Grey westerns came from Randolph Scott, whom Paramount put into medium-budget, realistic Grey westerns backed up by the old Jack Holt silent footage that would have cost a fortune to reshoot. This footage was so effectively inserted into the new films that none but the really discriminating, astute film buffs realized it had been done. Scott became the epitome of the Grey hero with a series of ten high-caliber Zane Grey westerns: *Wild Horse Mesa, Heritage of the Desert, The Thundering Herd, Man of the Forest, Sunset Pass, To the Last Man, The Last Roundup, Wagon Wheels, Home on the Range,* and *Rocky Mountain Mystery.*

Luckily, Henry Hathaway was given the directorial assignment on a number of the Scott movies, and they turned out to be among the finest westerns of the era. Film historian Tuska has written as follows:

> I cannot help thinking that perhaps Hathaway came closest to the romantic spirit of the Grey novels. To the rugged beauty and endurance of the land was added the idyllic experience of first love. Whether the heroine was Sally Blane, Esther Ralston or Verna Hillie, Hathaway chose them for their innocence, their pluck, their gameness. They were sensuous without ever being overtly carnal, vibrant without being vulgar. His $90,000 budgets did not permit Hathaway to encompass grandeur, other than use of stock footage; but intense working with his players allowed him to sustain a poetic lyricism that glowed quietly on the silver screen.[13]

In 1931 Paramount made *Fighting Caravans*, starring Gary Cooper, Ernest Torrence, Fred Kohler, and Lily Damita. Although a big production, it bore little resemblance to the novel and was somewhat sluggish. However, it was popular and turned a good profit.

Wagon Wheels (1934), starring Randolph Scott, used much footage left over from *Fighting Caravans* and was also supposedly based on Grey's novel. It took a vivid imagination or keen mind to see the connection between film and novel.

Another important Grey star at Paramount was Buster Crabbe, who had a principal supporting role in *To the Last Man, Man of the Forest, The Thundering Herd* and *Wanderer of the Wasteland* before being given star billing in the studio's adaptation of Grey's *Nevada* (1935), a good little western that earned a good return on investment.

Nevada was followed by *Drift Fence* in 1936, also a film version of the Grey novel. Buster plays Slinger Dunn, a tough rancher who comes to the aid of a Texas Ranger, Tom Keene, and a young tenderfoot rancher, Benny Baker. Reputedly, more than 5,000 steers were used for the spectacular stampede scene where the drift fence is torn down.[14]

Next in line for Crabbe was *Desert Gold* (1936), in which he starred as the Indian Moya. Tom Keene again played second lead and Robert Cummings, Marsha Hunt, Monte Blue, Raymond Hatton, and Walter Miller provided excellent support in this memorable study in human nature set against a desert backdrop.[15]

In 1936 Crabbe starred in Paramount's *The Arizona Raiders*, an adaptation of Grey's *Raiders of Spanish Peaks*, and *Arizona Mahoney*, based on *Stairs of Sand*. Both were excellent minor films, far above the standards of most programmer westerns but ranking below the higher-budgeted Scott westerns. Crabbe made his last Grey film, *Forlorn River*, in 1937, playing the cowboy Nevada and turning in a good performance. June Martel was the girl Nevada loved. Interestingly, the screen's first Lone Ranger, Lee Powell, was ninth-billed in the cast.

Paramount continued to capitalize on the Grey fame in 1938, 1939, and 1940 by releasing *Thunder Trail* (based on *Arizona Ames*), starring Gilbert Roland and Charles Bickford, and *Born to the West* (aka *Hell Town*), starring John Wayne and Johnny Mack Brown, as well as a series of four better than average westerns produced by Harry Sherman. The films were *The Mysterious Rider, Heritage of the Desert, Knights of the Range,* and *The Light of Western Stars.* Featured were such players as Victor Jory, Jean Arthur, Donald Woods, Russell Hayden, and Douglas Dumbrille. Paramount ceased production of Grey westerns with the completion of *The Light of Western Stars* in 1940.

Mention should be made of *The Woman Accused* (1933), which appears to have been the brainchild of Rupert Hughes, a friend of Zane Grey. Hughes wrote the first chapter of the book and sent it to Vicki Baum, who in turn wrote a chapter and sent it to Zane Grey. He did his turn with the pen (chapter 3) and sent it to another, and so on until ten authors had written a ten-chapter book. It is amazing that Paramount could get a movie out of it. The story is not a western but is all about a woman who killed her ex-lover and goes on the run. Cary Grant and Nancy Carroll starred in the movie.

Reenter Jack Holt and Randolph Scott

In the latter part of 1936 Jack Holt was at Columbia making one of his best-remembered films, *End of the Trail*, adapted from the Zane Grey story "Outlaws of Palouse." The story was originally published as a magazine feature. Later retitled "The Horse Thieves," it was included in the Walter Black edition in the volume *Blue Feather and Other Stories.* Actually, about all that remains of the Grey story in the film is the names of three of the characters: Dale Brittenham, Bill Mason, and Bob Hildreth. The plot is a direct remake of *The Last Parade* (1931) in a different time frame.

Harry Cohn, Columbia president, was paranoid about title changes. Practically every Columbia film was shot under a working title and in some instances released under a title, withdrawn, and then reissued with a new title before the film had even had a complete national showing. *End of the Trail* started out as "Outlaws of Palouse" with Holt and Jean Arthur. Frank Capra preempted Arthur for one of his movies and the film was started again with Louise Henry under the title, *The Man Without Fear.* At the last minute the title was changed to *End of the Trail*, even though Columbia had done a western with Tim McCoy a couple of years earlier with the same title. Filmographers, who aren't too careful, understandably get the two films confused.

The film was a popular one, enhanced by the Grey and Holt names and a good story that finds Holt and Big Boy Williams as Spanish-American War veterans in love with the same girl, Louise Henry. The film was Jack's last great solo-starring western, a well-scripted, well-acted motion picture achieving high production value on a small budget and tugging relentlessly at the heart strings of the viewer.[16]

After several years away from Grey westerns, Randolph Scott came back in 1941 as star of the technicolor 20th Century–Fox film *Western Union*. However, Fenin and Everson state the story was written by a Fox contract writer and that no such book ever existed prior to the movie. They contend that following release of the film interest in the nonexistent book by Grey's fans was so strong that a book based on the film was actually written, published, and credited to Zane Grey, who had died in 1939, two years earlier.[17]

It would be interesting to know how these authors came up with this story. *Western Union* was definitely written by Grey. It was printed (according to plate codes) during September 1939 and was released for sale October 20, 1939. On the same date Harper (the publisher) sent Grey a publicity telegram of congratulations. On October 21 Grey spent the day in a bookstore in Pasadena autographing copies of the book. On the morning of October 23 he died of a heart attack. Because of the close proximity of Grey's death to the time of publication, a rumor started that claimed the story was a posthumous work.

True, the book differs in style from Grey's earlier works, but Romer Grey (Zane's son) explains it thus: his father was recovering from a stroke and, as therapy, Romer suggested the plot to his father. Grey, who always did his own copy, wasn't able to do so and he dictated the work. Since he wasn't used to dictation, his thought processes were somewhat altered. According to biographer Frank Gruber, *Western Union* was written in 1933 but not published until 1939. Gruber had access to Grey's diary while writing the Grey biography.[18] As to a contention that the movie was not based on the novel but used the title only, that also is false. What is true is that there were evident changes. Seldom does a movie follow the book in close detail; however, a reading of the book and a viewing of the film will reveal many of the same characters. And the plot — well, how many plots can you get from stretching a telegraph wire?[19]

Scott's best Grey western came in 1947, at Columbia, where he made *The Gunfighters*, based on the novel *Twin Sombreros*. This film, too, was in color but lacked the impact of *Western Union*.

Fox Tries Again

In 1941, after a five-year hiatus, Fox made *Riders of the Purple Sage* and *The Last of the Duanes*, both featuring their new western star George Montgomery. Unfortunately, Montgomery was sidetracked into dramatic films and no more westerns were made with him in the cast. He was replaced by football star John Kimbrough in *Lone Star Ranger*, after which the studio dropped the series when Kimbrough flopped as an actor.

RKO, Republic, and Others

Evidently, few of the smaller, independent companies could afford Grey's asking price for the motion picture rights to his works. Or it could be that the cost of bringing to life a Grey western was the stumbling block. Whichever was the case, only W. W. Hodkinson, Benjamin B. Hampton, and Tiffany — other than the short-lived Zane Grey Productions — tried prior to 1940. Tiffany's seven-reel *Lightning* (based on Grey's essay of the same title) was an interesting and valiant attempt by a small (and for a while, successful) company to capitalize on the Grey appeal.

Robert Frazer and Guinn (Big Boy) Williams play horsewrangler brothers out to capture the wild stallion Lightning in the mountains of Utah. They fail. Later, during a fling in Chicago, they meet and flirt with Margaret Livingston and Jobyna Ralston, two entertainers. The girls take their money and skip town. Back in Utah, Lightning, attracted to Frazer's pet mare, Bess, invades their camp and takes her away. Frazer and Williams give chase into the desert, where they come upon the girls after their plane has been forced down while flying over the territory. The boys "kidnap" them and put them to work, but the girls escape and are almost killed in a sandstorm. However, the brothers rescue them and also subdue Lightning. All ends well, with the girls evidently repentant and in love with the cowboys. And Lightning seems glad to be civilized, if it means being with Bess.

As it was to be expected, perhaps, Republic entered the Zane Grey film story via the serial route, the studio being a specialist in cliffhanger productions. Grey's popular comic strip "King of the Royal Mounted" was produced as a 12-chapter serial in 1940 under the same title and was followed in 1942 by a sequel, *King of the Mounties*. Both serials starred Allan Lane, who later became a popular B-western star. Zane Grey wrote only a brief outline of the story for the King comic strip. His son Romer Grey wrote the story and the Big Little Books. Later "King of the Royal Mounted" appeared as a series of comic books bearing Zane Grey's name.

Republic likewise made a version of *The Border Legion*, a formula western starring Roy Rogers. *The Vanishing American* was released in 1955 and featured Scott Brady and Forrest Tucker in a rather weak adaptation of the Grey classic. And Republic has the credit for producing the last Zane Grey feature film to date, *The Maverick Queen*, released in 1956 and starring Barbara Stanwyck as Virginia Banion, a Virginia-born beauty who goes to Wyoming following the loss of her family in the Civil War and becomes known as the Maverick Queen, because she takes every unbranded steer and puts her brand on it. In Rich Springs Barbara also operates the Maverick Queen Hotel, which becomes a rendezvous for the notorious Wild Bunch outlaw gang, with whom she works hand-in-glove. Love and trouble enter her life in the person of Barry Sullivan, a Pinkerton detective posing as Jeff Younger, nephew of the infamous Younger brothers. In the end, Barbara is regenerated through her love for Barry but is killed in helping to save his life.

Two Zane Grey films were produced in Australia. One, *Rangle River*, starred Victor Jory, whose talent shone out against the rest of a mostly amateurish Australian cast. Margaret Dare, the young Australian leading woman, had considerable visual charm, but her voice reminded the audience of the troubles that Jack Hoxie and Ken Maynard had with dialogue — and they did not have an Australian accent to further complicate matters.

The story of *Rangle River* revolves around two cattle ranches in Australia. The owner of one gets a contract to supply the local freezing works and his hated rival immediately dams the local river, leaving his enemy's cows to expire of thirst. The sudden drying-up of the river arouses suspicion, but it is not until a plane is chartered by a visiting Englishman that the dam is discovered. Knowing that the game is up, the villain dynamites the dam, intending that the flood would sweep away his rival's herds. But the heroic stockrider, Jory, is everywhere at once — at the ranch, getting the cattle moved to the higher levels, and a few seconds later at the villain's abode belting him with a stock whip.[20]

The film has its peccadilloes; but at least it is intelligible and has some dramatic shape about it, providing 90 minutes of lively entertainment. Granted, it does not possess the spectacular values of a *Cimarron*, *Trail of the Lonesome Pine*, or *Dances with Wolves*, but in a quiet way it is interesting. Certainly, the scenery alone was worth the price of admission.

Grey is reported to have written the film scenario for *White Death* (1936) on the back of an order for marlin bait, sold it to a local Australian producer for several thousands of dollars, and then consented to star in the film for a further fee. At any rate, he did write the story, it was made in Australia by Barrier Reef Productions, and Grey did star in it.

The story of *White Death* pivots around a 20-foot shark that has terrorized whites and blacks alike, a plot not unlike that of *Jaws*, made nearly four decades later. Grey comes to the island determined to catch the monster. The film had only one woman in the cast, Nola Warren, age 17, a young Sidney girl who plays the part of the daughter of a financial missionary whose wife and other daughter have been killed by the shark. Filming was at Haymar Island, at the northern end of the Whitsunday Passage and was in production six to eight weeks.

RKO Pictures took over production of Grey westerns in 1944, mainly using only the titles and Grey's name, with the stories completely unrelated to the novels. Robert Mitchum starred in a pair, *Nevada* and *West of the Pecos*; James Warren in three, *Wanderer of the Wasteland*, *Sunset Pass*, and *Code of the West*; and Tim Holt in three, *Under the Tonto Rim*, *Wild Horse Mesa*, and *Thunder Mountain*. *West of the Pecos* had also been filmed by the company in 1934 on a larger budget and with Richard Dix and Fred Kohler heading the cast.

Universal, surprisingly, tried only one Grey western, *Red Canyon* (1949), based on *Wildfire*. George Sherman directed and Howard Duff and George Brent starred. No one seemed inspired, least of all the stars. Character actors Edgar Buchanan, Chill Wills, Denver Pyle, and John McIntire tried their best to lift the film out of the doldrums, but with little success.

In 1955 United Artists released *Robber's Roost* with George Montgomery, Richard Boone, and Sylvia Findley in the lead roles. The film partially adhered to the original story and was fairly entertaining, though it did not make a lot of money for the producers.

Conclusion

It has now been 40 years since the last Grey western film, *The Maverick Queen*, was released in theaters. There can be little doubt as to Zane Grey's influence on the western movie, just as his books influenced the western story. While his books sometimes seem complex, the plots are simple. With but few variations, his formula remained the same. It is easily recognized in western stories today, and so it was with the movies. In recent years there has been an effort to make the western more mature, but even in these there is often the Zane Grey influence. During the days of the B westerns, however, his influence rode strong through all of them.[21]

It seems a shame that Grey and the western film in general have fallen from favor with movie audiences. For there are so many good Grey stories yet to be brought to the screen; for example, *Betty Zane*, *The Spirit of the Border*, *Boulder Dam*, *The Wilderness Trek*, *30,000 on the Hoof*, *Majesty's Rancho*, *The Arizona Clan*, *Black Mesa*, *The Shepherd of Guadeloupe*, and *Stranger from the Tonto*. In addition, there are many stories filmed previously that deserve refilming for today's audiences.

Hopefully, cinema tastes will change and the western will once again come into vogue, and with it the works of Grey. Imagine, if you will, Grey's beautiful story of a basically gentle but strong man and his faithful beast of burden on the fringes of Death Valley. *Tappan's Burro*, in technicolor and with Tom Selleck as the star, could be a real movie experience.

Grey was a prolific writer of short stories as well as of full-length novels, and these works could sustain a weekly television show for several seasons if they were to be utilized as scripts. To date, the Grey warehouse of stories has only been superficially tapped, with more stories not cinematized than those that have been filmed. The television series "The Zane Grey Theater" was merely an exploitation of the famous author's name, for the segments were not based on his work.[22]

Zane Grey Novels in Chronological Order

Betty Zane, 1903; *The Spirit of the Border*, 1906; *The Last of the Plainsmen*, 1908; *The Last Trail*, 1909; *The Short-Stop*, 1909; *The Heritage of the Desert*, 1910; *The Young Forester*, 1910; *The Young Pitcher*, 1911; *The Young Lion Hunter*, 1911; *Riders of the Purple Sage*, 1912; *Ken Ward in the Jungle*, 1912; *Desert Gold*, 1913; *The Light of Western Stars*, 1914; *The Lone Star Ranger*, 1915; *The Rainbow Trail*, 1915; *The Border Legion*, 1916; *Wildfire*, 1917; *The U.P. Trail*, 1918; *The Desert of Wheat*, 1919; *Tales of Fishes*, 1919; *The Man of the Forest*, 1920; *The Redheaded Outfield and Other Baseball Stories*, 1920; *The Mysterious Rider*, 1921; *To the Last Man*, 1922; *Tales of Lonely Trails*, 1922; *The Day of the Beast*, 1922; *Wanderer of the Wasteland*, 1923; *Tappan's Burro and Other Stories*, 1923; *Roping Lions in the Grand Canyon*, 1924; *The Call of the Canyon*, 1924; *Tales of Southern Rivers*, 1924; *The Thundering Herd*, 1925; *Tales of Fishing Virgin Seas*, 1925; *The Vanishing American*, 1925; *Tales of an Angler's Eldorado, New Zealand*, 1926; *Under the Tonto Rim*, 1926; *Tales of Swordfish and Tuna*, 1927; *Forlorn River*, 1927; *Nevada*, 1928; *Wild Horse Mesa*, 1928; *Don, the Story of a Lion Dog*, 1928; *Tales of Fresh-Water Fishing*, 1928; *Fight-ing Caravans*, 1929; *The Wolf Tracker*, 1930; *The Shepherd of Guadeloupe*, 1930; *Sunset Pass*, 1931; *Zane Grey's Book of Camps and Trails*, 1931; *Tales of Tahitian Waters*, 1931; *Arizona Ames*, 1932; *Robber's Roost*, 1932; *The Drift Fence*, 1933; *The Hash Knife Outfit*, 1933; *The Code of the West*, 1934; *Thunder Mountain*, 1935; *The Trail Driver*, 1936; *The Lost Wagon Train*, 1936; *An American Angler in Australia*, 1937; *West of the Pecos*, 1937; *Majesty's Rancho*, 1938; *Raiders of Spanish Peaks*, 1938; *Knights of the Range*, 1939; *Western Union*, 1939; *30,000 on the Hoof*, 1940; *Twin Sombreros*, 1941; *Stairs of Sand*, 1943; *The Zane Grey Omnibus*, 1943; *Wilderness Trek*, 1944; *Shadow on the Trail*, 1946; *Valley of Wild Horses*, 1947; *Rogue River Feud*, 1948; *The Deer Stalker*, 1949; *The Maverick Queen*, 1950; *The Dude Ranger*, 1951; *Captives of the Desert*, 1952; *Zane Grey's Adventures in Fishing*, 1952; *Wyoming*, 1953; *Lost Pueblo*, 1954; *Black Mesa*, 1955; *Stranger from the Tonto*, 1956; *The Fugitive Trail*, 1957; *The Arizona Clan*, 1958; *Horse Heaven Hill*, 1959; *The Ranger and Other Stories*, 1960; *Blue Feather and Other Stories*, 1961; *Boulder Dam*, 1963; *The Reef Girl*, 1977; *Savage Kingdom*, 1979.

Zane Grey Filmography

Riders of the Purple Sage (Fox, June 1918) 6 reels; William Farnum, Mary Mersch, William Scott, Murdock Mac-Quarrie, M. B. Robbins, Katherine Adams, Nancy Caswell, J. Holmes, Charles Clary, Jack Nelson, Buck Jones (unbilled); D/SP: Frank L. Lloyd.

The Rainbow Trail (Fox, September 1918) 6 reels; William Farnum, Ann Forrest, Mary Mersch, William Burress, G. Raymond Nye, Genevieve Blimm, Milton Ross, Nancy Caswell, Buck Jones (unbilled); D: Frank L. Lloyd; SP: Charles Kenyon, Frank L. Lloyd.

The Light of Western Stars (Sherman United, September 1918) 6 reels; Dustin Farnum, Winifred Kingston, Joseph Swickard, Virginia Eames, Burt Apling; D: Charles Swickard; SP: Roy Clements.

The Border Legion (T. Hayes Hunter Productions/Goldwyn, January 1919) 6 reels; Hobart Bosworth, Blanche Bates, Eugene Strong, Horace Morgan, Russell Simpson, Arthur Morrison, Bull Montana; D: T. Hayes Hunter; SP: Victor de Villers, Laurence Marston; P: T. Hayes Hunter.

Riders of the Dawn (Zane Grey Productions, May 1919) 6 reels; Roy Stewart, Claire Adams, Norman Kerry, Robert McKim, Frederick Starr, Violet Schram, Frank Brownlee, Marie Messenger, Arthur Morrison, Nelson McDowell, Charles Murphy; D: Jack Conway; SP: William H. Clifford, L. V. Jefferson. Note. Based on *The Desert of Wheat*.

The Lone Star Ranger (Fox, June 1919) 6 reels; William Farnum, Louise Lovely, G. Raymond Nye, Charles Clary, Lamar Johnstone, Frederick Herzog, Irene Rich, Leonard Clapham (Tom London); D: J. Gordon Edwards; SP: Charles Kenyon.

The Last of the Duanes (Fox, September 1919) 6 reels; William Farnum, Louise Lovely, Frankie Raymond, Harry De Vere, Charles Clary, G. Raymond Nye, Clarence Burton, Lamar Johnstone, Henry J. Hebert, Edward Hatton, Genevieve Blinn, Frederick Herzog, Orra Gardner, Leonard Clapham (Tom London), John Murphy; D: J. Gordon Edwards; SP: Charles Kenyon.

Desert Gold (Zane Grey Productions, November 1919) 6 reels; Elmo Lincoln, Eileen Percy, Margery Wilson, Walter Long, Edward Coxen, Lawson Butt, Russell Simpson, Arthur Morrison, William Bainbridge, Robert Kortman, Frank Lanning, Frank Brownlee, Mary Jane Irving, Louise Winston, Joe Halquin; D: T. Hayes Hunter; SP: Fred Myton.

The U.P. Trail (Zane Grey Productions/W. W. Hodkinson, November 1920) 7 reels; Roy Stewart, Kathlyn Williams, Joseph J. Dowling, Robert McKim, Marguerite De La Motte, Frederick Starr, Charles B. Murphy, Virginia Caldwell, Walter Perry, George Berrell; D: Jack Conway; SP: William H. Clifford.

The Man of the Forest (Zane Grey Productions/W. W. Hodkinson, June 1921) 7 reels; Carl Gantvoort, Claire Adams, Robert McKim, Jean Hersholt, Harry Lorraine, Eugenia Gilbert, Frank Hayes, Charlotte Pierce, Charles B. Murphy, Frederick Starr, Tote Du Crow; D: Benjamin B. Hampton; SP: Howard Hickman, Richard Schayer, W. H. Clifford.

The Mysterious Rider (Zane Grey Productions/W. W. Hodkinson, October 23, 1921) 6 reels; Carl Gantvoort, Claire Adams, Robert McKim, James Mason, Walt Whitman, Frederick Starr, Maude Wayne, Frank Hayes, Aggie Herring; D: Benjamin B. Hampton.

The Last Trail (Fox, November

Jack Holt and unidentified actress in *The Mysterious Rider* (Paramount, 1926).

1921) 7 reels; Maurice B. Flynn, Eva Novak, Wallace Beery, Rosemary Theby, Charles K. French, Harry Springler, Harry Dunkinson; D: Emmett J. Flynn; SP: Jules Furthman, Paul Schofield.

When Romance Rides (Goldwyn, April 1922) 5 reels; Claire Adams, Carl Gantvoort, Jean Hersholt, Harry Van Metter, Charles Arling, Tod Sloan, Frank Hayes, Mary Jane Irving, Audrey Chapman, Helen Howard, Stanley Bingham, Walter Perkins, Babe London, John Beck; D: Elliot Howe, Charles O. Rush, Jean Hersholt; P/SP: Benjamin B. Hampton. Note. Based on *Wildfire*.

Golden Dreams (Goldwyn, June 1922) 5 reels; Rose Dione, Claire Adams, Norris McKay, Carl Gantvoort, Audrey Chapman, Ida Ward, Bertram Grassby, Frank Leigh, Gordon Mullen, Pomeroy Cannon, Frank Hayes, Babe London, Mary Jane Irving, Walter Perkins, Harry Lorraine, C. B. Murphy, William Orlamond, D. J. Mitsoras; D/SP: Benjamin B. Hampton. Note. Story idea was suggested by Grey.

The Lone Star Ranger (Fox, September 9, 1923) 6 reels; Tom Mix, Billie Dove, L. C. Shumway, Stanton Heck, Edward Peil, Frank Clark, Minna Redman, Francis Carpenter, William Conklin, Tom Lingham, Tony (a horse); D/SP: Lambert Hillyer.

To the Last Man (Famous Players–Lasky/Paramount, September 23, 1923) 7 reels; Richard Dix, Lois Wilson, Noah Beery, Robert Edeson, Frank Campeau, Fred Huntley, Edward Brady, Eugene Pallette, Leonard Clapham (Tom London), Guy Oliver, Winifred Greenwood; D: Victor Fleming; SP: Doris Schroeder.

The Call of the Canyon (Famous Players–Lasky/Paramount, December

16, 1923) 7 reels; Richard Dix, Lois Wilson, Marjorie Daw, Noah Beery, Ricardo Cortez, Fred Huntley, Lillian Leighton, Helen Dunbar, Leonard Clapham (Tom London), Edward Clayton, Dorothy Seastrom, Laura Anson, Charles Richards, Ralph Yearsley, Arthur Rankin, Mervyn Leroy; D: Victor Fleming; SP: Doris Schroeder, Edfrid Bingham.

The Heritage of the Desert (Famous Players–Lasky/Paramount, January 1924) 6 reels; Bebe Daniels, Ernest Torrence, Noah Beery, Lloyd Hughes, Ann Schaeffer, James Mason, Richard R. Neill, Leonard Clapham (Tom London); D: Irvin Willat; SP: Albert Shelby Le Vino.

Wanderer of the Wasteland (Famous Players–Lasky/Paramount, June 1924) 6 reels; Jack Holt, Noah Beery, George Irving, Kathlyn Williams, Billie Dove, James Mason, Richard R. Neill, James Gordon, William Corroll, Willard Cooley; D: Irvin Willat; SP: George C. Hull, Victor Irvin; Supv: Lucien Hubbard. Note. Filmed in technicolor.

The Last of the Duanes (Fox, August 24, 1924) 7 reels; Tom Mix, Marian Nixon, Brinsley Shaw, Frank Nelson, Lucy Beaumont, Harry Lonsdale; D: Lynn Reynolds; SP: Edward J. Montagne.

The Border Legion (Famous Players–Lasky/Paramount, October 1924) 7 reels; Antonio Moreno, Helen Chadwick, Rockliffe Fellowes, Gibson Gowland, Charles Ogle, James Corey, Edward Gribbon, Luke Cosgrave; D: William K. Howard; SP: George Hull.

The Thundering Herd (Famous Players–Lasky/Paramount, March 7, 1925) 7 reels; Jack Holt, Lois Wilson, Noah Beery, Raymond Hatton, Charles Ogle, Tim McCoy, Lillian Leighton, Eulalie Jensen, Stephen Carr, Maxine Elliott Hicks, Edward J. Brady, Pat Hartigan, Fred Kohler, Robert Perry; D:

William K. Howard; SP: Lucien Hubbard.

Riders of the Purple Sage (Fox, March 15, 1925) 6 reels; Tom Mix, Beatrice Burnham, Arthur Morrison, Seesel Ann Johnson, Warner Oland, Fred Kohler, Charles Newton, Joe Rickson, Mabel Ballin, Charles Le Moyne, Harold Goodwin, Marion Nixon, Dawn O'Day, Wilfred Lucas; D: Lynn Reynolds; SP: Edfrid Bingham.

Code of the West (Famous Players–Lasky/Paramount, April 6, 1925) 7 reels; Owen Moore, Constance Bennett, Mabel Ballin, Charles Ogle, David Butler, George Bancroft, Gertrude Short, Lillian Leighton, Edward Gribbon, Pat Hartigan, Frankie Lee; D: William K. Howard; SP: Lucien Hubbard.

The Rainbow Trail (Fox, May 24, 1925) 6 reels; Tom Mix, Anne Cornwall, George Bancroft, Lucien Littlefield, Mark Hamilton, Vivian Oakland, Thomas Delmar, Fred De Silva, Steve Clements, Doc Roberts, Carol Halloway, Diana Miller; D/SP: Lynn Reynolds.

The Light of Western Stars (Famous Players–Lasky/Paramount, June 22, 1925) 7 reels; Jack Holt, Billie Dove, Noah Beery, Alma Bennett, William Scott, George Nichols, Mark Hamilton, Robert Perry, Eugene Pallette; D: William K. Howard; SP: George C. Hull, Lucien Hubbard.

Wild Horse Mesa (Famous Players–Lasky/Paramount, September 14, 1925) 80 mins.; Jack Holt, Noah Beery, Billie Dove, Douglas Fairbanks, Jr., George Magrill, George Loving, Edith Yorke, Bernard Siegel, Margaret Morris, Eugene Pallette; D: George B. Seitz; SP: Lucien Hubbard.

The Vanishing American (Famous Players–Lasky/Paramount, October 15, 1925) 10 reels; Richard Dix, Lois Wilson, Noah Beery, Malcolm McGregor, Shannon Day, Kocki, Charles Crockett, Bert Woodruff, Guy Oliver, Joe Ryan,

Bernard Siegel, Bruce Gordon, Charles Stevens, Richard Howard, John Webb Dillon; D: George B. Seitz; SP: Ethel Doherty, Lucien Hubbard.

Desert Gold (Famous Players–Lasky/Paramount, April 19, 1926) 7 reels; Neil Hamilton, Shirley Mason, Robert Frazer, William Powell, Josef Swickard, George Irving, Edward Gribbon, Frank Lackteen, Richard Howard, Bernard Siegel, George Rigas, Ralph Yearsley, Aline Goodwin; D: George B. Seitz; SP: Lucien Hubbard; Supv: Hestor Turnbull.

Born to the West (Famous Players–Lasky/Paramount, June 14, 1926) 6 reels; Jack Holt, Margaret Morris, Raymond Hatton, Arlette Marchal, George Siegmann, Bruce Gordon, William A. Carroll, Tom Kennedy, Richard Neill, Edith Yorke, E. Alyn Warren, Billy Aber, Jean Johnson, Joe Butterworth; D: John Waters; SP: Lucien Hubbard.

Forlorn River (Famous Players–Lasky/Paramount, September 27, 1926) 6 reels; Jack Holt, Raymond Hatton, Arlette marchal, Edmund Burns, Tom Santschi, Joseph Girard, Christian J. Frank, Albert Hart, Nola Luxford, Chief Yowlachie, Jack Moore; D: John Waters; SP: George C. Hull.

Man of the Forest (Famous Players–Lasky/Paramount, December 27, 1926) 6 reels; Jack Holt, Georgia Hale, El Brendel, Warner Oland, Tom Kennedy, George Fawcett, Ivan Christie, Bruce Gordon, Vester Pegg, Willard Cooley, Guy Oliver, Walter Ackerman, Duke R. Lee; D: John Waters; SP: Fred Myton; Adapt: Max Marcin; AP: B. P. Schulberg.

The Mysterious Rider (Famous Players–Lasky/Paramount, March 5, 1927) 6 reels; Jack Holt, Betty Jewel, Charles Sellon, David Torrence, Tom Kennedy, Guy Oliver, Albert Hart, Ivan Christie, Arthur Hoyt; D: John Waters; SP: Fred Myton, Paul Gangelin; AP: B. P. Shulberg.

The Last Trail (Fox, January 23, 1927) 6 reels; Tom Mix, Carmelita Geraghty, William Davidson, Frank Hagner, Lee Shumway, Robert Brower, Oliver Eckhardt, Tony (a horse); D: Lewis Seiler; SP: John Stone.

Drums of the Desert (Famous Players–Lasky/Paramount, June 4, 1927) 6 reels; Warner Baxter, Marietta Millner, Ford Sterling, Wallace MacDonald, Heinie Conklin, George Irving, Bernard Siegel, Guy Oliver; D: John Waters; SP: John Stone. Note. Film based on "Desert Bound," but publication undetermined.

Lightning (Tiffany, July 15, 1927) 7 reels; Jobyna Ralston, Margaret Livingston, Robert Frazer, Guinn (Big Boy) Williams, Pat Harmon, Lightning (a horse), Lady Bess (a horse); D: James C. McKay; SP: John Francis Natteford. Note. Film based on the essay of the same title in *Hosses* magazine.

Nevada (Famous Players–Lasky/Paramount, August 8, 1927) 7 reels; Gary Cooper, Thelma Todd, William Powell, Philip Strange, Ernie S. Adams, Christian J. Frank, Evan Christy, Guy Oliver; D: John Waters; SP: John Stone, L. G. Rigby.

Open Range (Famous Players–Lasky/Paramount, November 5, 1927) 6 reels; Betty Bronson, Lane Chandler, Fred Kohler, Bernard Siegel, Guy Oliver, Jim Corey, George Connors, Flash (a dog); D: Clifford S. Smith; SP: John Stone, J. Walter Ruben. Note. Based on the serialized magazine story.

Under the Tonto Rim (Paramount Famous–Lasky, February 4, 1928) 6 reels; Richard Arlen, Alfred Allen, Mary Brian, Jack Luden, Harry T. Morey, William Franey, Harry Todd, Bruce Gordon, Jack Byron; D: Herman C. Raymaker; SP: J. Walter Ruben; AP: B. P. Schulberg.

The Vanishing Pioneer (Paramount Famous–Lasky, June 23, 1928) 6 reels; Jack Holt, Sally Blane, William Powell, Fred Kohler, Guy Oliver, Roscoe Karns,

Tim Holt, Marcia Manon; D: John Waters; SP: J. Walter Ruben, John Goodrich, Ray Harris. Note. Film based on an original screenplay by Grey.

The Water Hole (Paramount Famous–Lasky, August 25, 1928) 7 reels; Jack Holt, Nancy Carroll, John Boles, Montague Shaw, Ann Christy, Lydia Yeamans Titus, Jack Perrin, Jack Mower, Paul Ralli, Tex Young, Bob Miles, Greg Whitespear; D: F. Richard Jones. Note. Film based on the story of the same name in *Collier's* magazine.

Avalanche (Paramount Famous–Lasky, November 10, 1928) 6 reels; Jack Holt, Doris Hill, Baclanova, John Darrow, Guy Oliver, Dick Winslow; D: Otto Brower; SP: Sam Mintz, Herman Mankiewicz, J. Walter Ruben. Note. Publication undetermined.

Sunset Pass (Paramount–Lasky, February 9, 1929) 6 reels; Jack Holt, Nora Lane, John Loder, Christian J. Frank, Pee Wee Holmes, Chester Conklin, Pat Harmon, Alfred Allen, Guy Oliver; D: Otto Brower; SP: J. Walter Ruben, Ray Harris.

Stairs of Sand (Paramount Famous–Lasky, June 8, 1929) 6 reels; Wallace Beery, Jean Arthur, Phillips R. Holmes, Fred Kohler, Chester Conklin, Guy Oliver, Lillian Worth, Frank Rice, Clarence L. Sherwood; D: Otto Brower; SP: Agnes Brand Leahy, Sam Mintz, J. Walter Ruben.

The Long Star Ranger (Fox, January 5, 1930) 7 reels; George O'Brien, Sue Carol, Walter McGrail, Warren Hymer, Russell Simpson, Roy Stewart, Lee Shumway, Colin Chase, Richard Alexander, Joel Franz, Joe Rickson, Oliver Eckhardt, Caroline Rankin, Elizabeth Patterson, Billy Butts, Delmar Watson, William Steele, Bob Fleming, Ralph Le Fevre, Ward Bond, Jack Perrin, Hank Bell, Delmar Watson, Jane Keckley; D: A. F. Erickson; SP: Seton I. Miller, John Hunter Booth; AP: James Kevin McGuinness.

The Light of Western Stars (Paramount, April 19, 1930) 8 reels; Richard Arlen, Mary Brian, Harry Green, Regis Toomey, Fred Kohler, William LeMaire, George Chandler, Syd Saylor, Guy Oliver, Gus Seville; D: Otto Brower, Edwin H. Knopf; SP: Grover Jones, William Slavens McNutt.

The Border Legion (Paramount, June 28, 1930) 8 reels; Richard Arlen, Jack Holt, Fay Wray, Eugene Pallette, Stanley Fields, E. H. Calvert, Ethan Allen, Syd Saylor; D: Otto Brower, Edwin H. Knopf; SP: Perry Heath, Edward E. Paramore, Jr.

The Last of the Duanes (Fox, August 31, 1930) 6 reels; George O'Brien, Lucille Browne, Myrna Loy, Walter McGrail, James Bradbury, Jr., Nat Pendleton, Blanche Frederici, Frank Campeau, James Mason, Lloyd Ingraham, Willard Robertson, Roy Stewart, Dick Alexander; D: Alfred L. Werker; SP: Ernest Pascal; AP: Edward Butcher, Harold B. Lipsitz.

El Ultimo De Los Vargas (Fox, 1930) 6 reels; (Spanish version of *The Last of the Duanes*) George J. Lewis, Luana Alcaniz, Juan de Landa, Vincente Pedula, Martin Garralaga, Carmen Rodriquez, Julian de Landa; D: David Howard; SP: Ernest Pascal; Spanish dialogue: F. Mores de la Torre.

Fighting Caravans (Paramount, February 14, 1931) 91 mins.; Gary Cooper, Ernest Torrence, Lily Damita, Fred Kohler, Tully Marshall, Eugene Pallette, Roy Stewart, May Boley, James Farley, James Marcus, Eve Southern, Donald MacKenzie, Syd Saylor, E. Alyn Warren, Frank Campeau, Charles Winninger, Frank Hagney, Jane Darwell, Irving Bacon, Iron Eyes Cody, Merrill McCormick, Harry Semels, Chief Big Tree; D: David Burton, Otto Brower; SP: Edward E. Paramore, Keene Thompson, Agnes Brand Leahy. Note. Rereleased as *Blazing Arrows.*

Riders of the Purple Sage (Fox,

October 28, 1931) 59 mins.; George O'Brien, Marguerite Churchill, Noah Beery, James Todd, Yvonne Pelletier, Stanley Fields, Lester Dorr, Shirley Nail; D: Hamilton MacFadden.

The Rainbow Trail (Fox, January 3, 1932) 60 mins.; George O'Brien, Cecilia Parker, Roscoe Ates, Minna Gombell, James Kirkwood, Ruth Donnelly, Landers Stevens, Robert Frazer, Niles Welch, William L. Thorne; D: David Howard; SP: Barry Connors, Philip Klein.

Heritage of the Desert (Paramount, September 30, 1932) 63 mins.; Randolph Scott, Sally Blane, Vince Barnett, Guinn (Big Boy) Williams, J. Farrell MacDonald, David Landau, Gordon Westcott, Susan Fleming, Charles Stevens, Fred Burns, Hal Price, Jim Corey, Jack Pennick; D: Henry Hathaway; SP: Harold Shumate, Frank Partos.

Wild Horse Mesa (Paramount, November 25, 1932) 65 mins.; Randolph Scott, Sally Blane, Fred Kohler, James Bush, George F. Hayes, Charley Grapewin, Buddy Roosevelt, Lucille LaVerne, Jim Thorpe, E. H. Calvert; D: Henry Hathaway; SP: Frank Clark, Harold Shumate.

The Golden West (Fox, December 3, 1932) 74 mins.; George O'Brien, Janet Chandler, Marion Burns, Onslow Stevens, Julia Swayne Gordon, Everett Corrigan, Edmund Breese, Sam West, Arthur Pierson, Bert Hanlon, Hattie McDaniel, Charles Stevens, Stanley Blystone, George Regas, Dorothy Ward, Sam Adams, Ed Dillon, Chief Big Tree, John War Eagle; D: David Howard; SP: Gordon Rigby. Note. Film based on *The Last Trail*.

Robbers' Roost (Fox, January 1, 1933) 64 mins.; George O'Brien, Maureen O'Sullivan, Maude Eburne, William Pawley, Ted Oliver, Walter McGrail, Doris Lloyd, Reginald Owens, Frank Rice, Bill Nestell, Clifford Santley, Gilbert Holmes, Vinegar Roan; D: David Howard; SP: Dudley Nichols.

The Mysterious Rider (Paramount, January 20, 1933) 62 mins.; Kent Taylor, Lona Andre, Gail Patrick, Warren Hymer, Berton Churchill, Irving Pichel, Cora Sue Collins, E. H. Calvert, Sherwood Bailey, Niles Welch, Clarence Wilson; D: Fred Allen; SP: Harvey Gates, Robert Niles.

The Woman Accused (Paramount, February 17, 1933) 73 mins.; Cary Grant, Nancy Carroll, John Haliday, Irving Pichel, Louis Clahern, Norma Mitchell, Jack LaRue, John Lodge, Lona Andre, Harry Holman; D: Paul Sloane. Note. Film based on a 10-chapter magazine serial of which Grey wrote chapter 3; other writers were Rupert Hughes, Vicki Baum, Vina Dalmar, Irvin S. Cobb, Gertrude Atherton, J. P. McEvoy, Ursula Parrott, Polan Banks, and Sophie Kerr.

Smoke Lightning (Fox, February 17, 1933) 63 mins.; George O'Brien, Virginia Sale, Douglas Dumbrille, Betsy King Ross, Nell O'Day, Frank Atkinson, Morgan Wallace, Clarence Wilson, George Burton, Fred Wilson; D: David Howard; SP: Gordon Rigby, Sidney Mitchell. Note. Film based on "Canyon Walls."

The Thundering Herd (Paramount, November 24, 1933) 59 mins.; Randolph Scott, Judith Allen, Barton MacLane, Harry Carey, Buster Crabbe, Noah Beery, Sr., Raymond Hatton, Frank Rice, Dick Rush; D: Henry Hathaway; SP: Jack Cunningham, Mary Flannery.

Under the Tonto Rim (Paramount, April 7, 1933) 63 mins.; Stuart Erwin, Verna Hillie, Raymond Hatton, Fuzzy Knight, Kent Taylor, Fred Kohler, John Lodge, Pat Farley, Alan Garcia, George Narvie, Marion Bardell, Ed Brady; D: Henry Hathaway; SP: Jack Cunningham, Gerald Geraghty.

Sunset Pass (Paramount, May 26, 1933) 61 mins.; Randolph Scott, Tom Keene, Kathleen Burke, Harry Carey, Fuzzy Knight, Noah Beery, Vince Barnett, Kent Taylor, Tom London, Pat

Farley, Charles Middleton, Bob Kortman, James Mason, Frank Beal, Al Bridge, Leila Bennett, Nelson McDowell, George Barbier, Patricia Farley, Christian J. Frank; D: Henry Hathaway; SP: Jack Cunningham, Gerald Geraghty.

Life in the Raw (Fox, July 7, 1933) 62 mins.; George O'Brien, Claire Trevor, Warner Richmond, Francis Ford, Greta Nilsen, Gaylord Pendleton, Alan Edwards, Nigel De Brulier; D: Louis King; SP: Stuart Anthony. Note. Exact Zane Grey story not authenticated.

The Last Trail (Fox, August 25, 1933) 59 mins.; George O'Brien, Claire Trevor, El Brendel, Lucile LaVerne, Matt McHugh, Edward J. LeSaint, J. Carrol Naish, Ruth Warren, George Reed, Luis Albertson; D: James Tinling; SP: Stuart Anthony.

Man of the Forest (Paramount, August 25, 1933) 62 mins.; Randolph Scott, Harry Carey, Verna Hillie, Noah Beery, Larry (Buster) Crabbe, Barton McLane, Guinn (Big Boy) Williams, Vince Barnett, Blanche Frederici, Tempe Piggot, Tom Kennedy, Frank McGlynn, Jr., Duke Lee, Lew Kelly, Merrill McCormack, Hank Bell, Fred Burns, Jim Corey, Jack Hendricks; D: Henry Hathaway; SP: Jack Cunningham, Harold Shumate. Note. Rereleased by Favorite Films as *Challenge of the Frontier.*

To the Last Man (Paramount, September 15, 1933) 70 mins.; Randolph Scott, Esther Ralston, Noah Beery, Jack LaRue, Larry (Buster) Crabbe, Fuzzy Knight, Barton MacLane, Gail Patrick, Muriel Kirkland, Egon Brecher, James Eagles, Eugénie Besserer, Harlan Knight, Shirley Temple, Bobs Watson, James Burke, Buck Connors, Harry Cording, Ethan Laidlaw, James Mason, Blackjack Ward; D: Henry Hathaway; SP: Jack Cunningham.

The Last Roundup (Paramount, May 1, 1934) 65 mins.; Randolph Scott, Barbara Fritchie, Barton MacLane, Fuzzy Knight, Monte Blue, Charles Middleton, Richard Carle, Dick Rush, Ben Corbett, Fred Kohler, James Mason, Bud Osborne, Bob Miles, Buck Connors, Frank Rice, Jim Corey, Sam Allen, Jack M. Holmes; D: Henry Hathaway; SP: Jack Cunningham. Note: Based on *The Border Legion.*

Wagon Wheels (Paramount, September 15, 1934) 56 mins.; Randolph Scott, Gail Patrick, Billie Lee, Leila Bennett, Jan Duggan, Monte Blue, Raymond Hatton, Olin Howland, J. P. McGowan, James Marcus, Helen Hunt, James Kenton, Alfred Delcambre, John Marston, Sam McDaniels, Eldred Tidbury, E. Alyn Warren, Pauline Moore, Ann Sheridan, Lew Meehan, Harold Goodwin, Fern Emmett; D: Charles Barton; SP: Jack Cunningham, Charles Logan, Carl A. Buss.

The Dude Ranger (Principal/Fox, September 29, 1934) 65 mins.; George O'Brien, Irene Hervey, Syd Saylor, LeRoy Mason, Henry Hall, James Mason, Sid Jordan, Alma Chester, Lloyd Ingraham, Earl Dwire, Si Jenks, Lafe McKee, Jack Kirk, Hank Bell; D: Edward F. Cline; SP: Barry Barringer; P: Sol Lesser, John Zanft.

West of the Pecos (RKO-Radio, December 1, 1934) 68 mins.; Richard Dix, Martha Sleeper, Samuel S. Hinds, Fred Kohler, Sleep 'n' Eat (Willie Best), Louise Beavers, Maria Alba, Pedro Regas, G. Pat Collins, Russell Simpson, Maurice Black, George Cooper, Irving Bacon; D: Phil Rosen; SP: Milton Krims, John Twist.

Home on the Range (Paramount, February 1, 1935) 65 mins.; Randolph Scott, Ann Sheridan, Dean Jagger, Jackie Coogan, Fuzzy Knight, Ralph Remley, Philip Morris, Frances Sayles, Addison Richards, Clarence Sherwood, Evelyn Brent, Allen Wood, Howard Wilson, Albert Hart, Richard Carle,

Jack Clark, Joe Morrison, Alfred Delcambre; D: Arthur Jacobson; SP: Harold Shumate; P: Harold Hurley. Note. Based on *The Code of the West*.

Rocky Mountain Mystery (Paramount, March 1, 1935) 63 mins.; Randolph Scott, Charles (Chic) Sale, Mrs. Leslie Carter, Kathleen Burke, George Marion, Sr., Ann Sheridan, James C. Eagles, Howard Wilson, Willie Fung, Florence Roberts; D: Charles Barton; SP: Edward E. Paramore, Jr., Ethel Doherty; P: Harold Hurley. Note. A remake of *The Vanishing Pioneer*.

Wanderer of the Wasteland (Paramount, September 9, 1935) 7 reels; Dean Jagger, Larry (Buster) Crabbe, Gail Patrick, Raymond Hatton, Fuzzy Knight, Edward Ellis, Benny Baker, Al St. John, Trixie Frigans, Monte Blue, Charles Walton, Anna Q. Nillson, Tammany Young, Stanley Andrews, Alfred Delcambre, Pat O'Malley, Glenn (Leif) Erickson, Marina Shubert, Kenneth Harlan, Jim Thorpe, Bud Osborne, Robert Burns; D: Otto Lovering; SP: Stuart Anthony; P: Harold Hurley.

Thunder Mountain (Atherton/Fox, September 27, 1935) 7 reels; George O'Brien, Barbara Fritchie, Frances Grant, Morgan Wallace, George F. Hayes, Edward J. LeSaint, Dean Benton, William N. Bailey; D: David Howard; SP: Dan Jarrett, Don Swift; P: Sol Lesser.

Nevada (Paramount, November 29, 1935) 7 reels; Larry (Buster) Crabbe, Kathleen Burke, Monte Blue, Raymond Hatton, Glenn (Leif) Erickson, Syd Saylor, William Duncan, Richard Carle, Stanley Andrews, Frank Sheridan, Jack Kennedy, Henry Rocquemore, William L. Thorne, Harry Dunkinson, Barney Furey, William Desmond, Frank Rice; D: Charles Barton; SP: Barnett Weston, Stuart Anthony.

Drift Fence (Paramount, February 14, 1936) 56 mins.; Larry (Buster) Crabbe, Katherine DeMille, Tom Keene, Benny Baker, Glenn (Leif) Erickson, Stanley Andrews, Effie Ellser, Richard Carle, Jan Duggan, Irving Bacon, Walter Long, Chester Gan, Dick Alexander, Bud Fine, Jack Pennick; D: Otto Lovering; SP: Stuart Anthony, Robert Yost; P: Harold Hurley. Note. Rereleased as *Texas Desperadoes*.

Desert Gold (Paramount, March 27, 1936) 58 mins.; Larry (Buster) Crabbe, Robert Cummings, Marsha Hunt, Tom Keene, Glenn (Leif) Erickson, Monte Blue, Raymond Hatton, Walter Miller, Frank Mayo, Philip Morris; D: James Hogan; SP: Stuart Anthony, Robert Yost; P: Harold Hurley.

The Arizona Raiders (Paramount, June 28, 1936) 54 mins.; Larry (Buster) Crabbe, Raymond Hatton, Marsha Hunt, Jane Rhodes, Johnny Downs, Grant Withers, Don Rowan, Arthur Aylesworth, Richard Carle, Herbert Hayward, Petra Silva; D: James Hogan; SP: Robert Yost, John Drafft; P: A. M. Botsford. Note. Based on *Raiders of Spanish Peaks*, even though not published until 1938; rereleased as *Bad Men of Arizona*.

King of the Royal Mounted (20th Century–Fox, September 11, 1936) 61 mins.; Robert Kent, Rosalind Keith, Jack Luden, Alan Dinehart, Frank McGlynn, Grady Sutton, Arthur Loft; D: Howard Bretherton, SP: Earle Snell; P: Sol Lesser.

White Death (Barrier Reef Productions/B.E.F. Films, 1936) 78 mins.; Zane Grey, Alfred Frith, Nola Warren, John Weston, Jim Coleman, Harold Colonna; D: Edwin G. Bowen. Note. Filmed in Australia.

Rangle River (Columbia/National Studios, 1936) 90 mins.; Victor Jory, Margaret Dare, Robert Coote, Rita Paunceford, Georgie Sterling, Cecil Perry; D: Clarence Badger. Note. Released in United States by J. H. Hoffberg; TV title: "Men with Whips."

End of the Trail (Columbia, October 31, 1936) 70 mins.; Jack Holt, Louise Henry, Douglas Dumbrille, Guinn (Big Boy) Williams, George McKay, Gene Morgan, John McGuire, Edward J. LeSaint, Frank Shannon, Erle C. Kenton, Hank Bell, Art Mix, Blackie Whiteford, Blackjack Ward, Edgar Dearing; D: Erle C. Kenton; SP: Harold Shumate. Note. Based on "Outlaws of Palouse."

Arizona Mahoney (Paramount, December 4, 1936) 58 mins.; Larry (Buster) Crabbe, June Martel, Robert Cummings, Joe Cook, Marjorie Gateson, John Miljan, Dave Chasen, Irving Bacon, Richard Carle, Billie Lee, Fred Kohler, Fuzzy Knight, Si Jenks; D: James Hogan; SP: Robert Yost, Stuart Anthony. Note. Based on *Stairs of Sand*.

Forlorn River (Paramount, July 2, 1937) 56 mins.; Larry (Buster) Crabbe, June Martel, John Patterson, Harvey Stephen, Chester Conklin, Lew Kelly, Syd Saylor, William Duncan, Rafael Bennett, Ruth Warren, Lee Powell, Oscar Hendrian, Robert Homans, Purnell Pratt, Larry Lawrence, Tom Long, Merrill McCormack, Vester Pegg, Buffalo Bill, Jr., (Jay Wilsey), Hank Bell; D: Charles Barton; SP: Stuart Anthony, Robert Yost. Note. Rereleased by Favorite Films as *River of Destiny*.

Roll Along Cowboy (Principal/20th Century–Fox, October 18, 1937) 55 mins.; Smith Ballew, Cecilia Parker, Stanley Fields, Gordon (Bill) Elliott, Wally Albright, Jr., Ruth Robinson, Frank Milan, Monte Montague, Bud Osborne, Harry Bernard, Budd Buster, Buster Fite, and his Six Saddle Tramps, Herman Hack, Sheik (a horse); D: Gus Meins; SP: Dan Jarrett; P: Sol Lesser.

Thunder Trail (Paramount, October 22, 1937) 58 mins.; Gilbert Roland, Charles Bickford, Marsha Hunt, J. Carrol Naish, James Craig, Monte Blue, Barlowe Bourland, Bill Lee, Gene Reynolds, William Duncan, Lee Shumway, Ray Hanford, Gertrude Simpson,

Ed Coxen, Vester Pegg, Lucien Littlefield, Hank Bell, Bob Clark, Frank Cordell, Carol Holloway, Slim Hightower, Partner Jones, Cecil Kellogg, Jack Moore, Guy Schultz, Ed Warren, Tommy Coats, Alan Burk, Danny Morgan, Jack Daley; D: Charles Barton; SP: Robert Yost, Stuart Anthony. Note. Based on *Arizona Ames*.

Born to the West (Paramount, December 10, 1937) 59 mins.; John Wayne, Marsha Hunt, Johnny Mack Brown, John Patterson, Monte Blue, Syd Saylor, Lucien Littlefield, Nick Lukats, James Craig, Jack Kennedy, Vester Pegg, Earl Dwire, Jim Thorpe, Jennie Boyle, Alan Ladd, Lee Prather, Jack Daley; D: Charles Barton; SP: Stuart Anthony, Robert Yost. Note. Rereleased as *Hell Town*.

The Mysterious Rider (Paramount, September 21, 1938) 73 mins.; Douglas Dumbrille, Sidney Toler, Russell Hayden, Stanley Andrews, Weldon Heyburn, Charlotte Fields, Monte Blue, Earl Dwire, Glenn Strange, Jack Rockwell, Leo McMahon, Arch Hall, Ben Corbett, Price Mitchell, Ed Brady, Dick Alexander, Bob Kortman; D: Lesley Selander; SP: Maurice Geraghty; P: Harry Sherman.

Heritage of the Desert (Paramount, March 17, 1939) 74 mins.; Donald Woods, Evelyn Venable, Russell Hayden, Robert Barrat, Sidney Toler, C. Henry Gordon, Paul Guilfoyle, Paul Fix, Willard Robertson, Reginald Barlow, John (Skins) Miller, Frankie Marvin; D: Lesley Selander; SP: Norman Houston, Harrison Jacobs; P: Harry Sherman.

Knights of the Range (Paramount, February 23, 1940) 68 mins.; Victor Jory, Russell Hayden, Jean Parker, Britt Wood, J. Farrell MacDonald, Morris Ankrum, Ethel Wales, Rad Robinson, Raphael (Ray) Bennett, Edward Cassidy, Eddie Dean, The King's Men; D: Lesley Selander; SP: Norman Houston; P: Harry Sherman.

Jack Holt, Richard Arlen, and Stanley Fields in Zane Grey's *Border Legion* (Paramount, 1930).

The Light of Western Stars (Paramount, April 10, 1940) 67 mins.; Victor Jory, Russell Hayden, Jo Ann Sayers, Noah Beery, Jr., J. Farrell MacDonald, Ruth Rogers, Tom Tyler, Rad Robinson, Eddie Dean, Esther Estrella, Alan Ladd, Georgia Hawkins, Morris Ankrum, Earl Askam, Lucio Villegas, Bob Burns, Merrill McCormick; D: Lesley Selander; SP: Norman Houston; P: Harry Sherman.

King of the Royal Mounted (Republic, September 20, 1940) 12 chapters; Allan Lane, Robert Strange, Robert Kellard, Lita Conway, Herbert Rawlinson, Harry Cording, Bryant Washburn, Budd Buster, Stanley Andrews, John Davidson, John Dilson, Paul McVey, Lucien Prival, Norman Willis, Tony Paton, Ken Terrell, Charles Thomas, Bill Wilkus, Ted Mapes, Major Sam

Harris, George Plues, Frank Wayne, Richard Simmons, Loren Riebe, Wallace Reid, Jr., William Justice, William Stahl, John Bagni, Earl Bunn, Curley Dresden, George DeNormand, Bud Geary, Dave Marks, Robert Wayne, William Kellogg, Tommy Coats, Alan Gregg, Danny Sullivan, Walter Low, George Ford, Bob Jamison, Dale Van Sickel, Al Taylor, Cy Slocum, Douglas Evans, Duke Taylor, Jimmy Fawcett, Duke Green, David Sharpe; D: William Witney, John English; SP: Franklyn Adreon, Norman S. Hall, Joseph Poland, Barney A. Sarecky, Sol Shor; AP: Hiram S. Brown, Jr. Note. Based loosely on the comic strip created by Grey.

The Border Legion (Republic, December 5, 1940) 58 mins.; Roy Rogers, George F. Hayes, Carol Hughes, Joseph Sawyer, Maude Eburne, Jay

Novello, Hal Taliaferro (Wally Wales), Dick Wessell, Paul Porcasi, Robert Emmett Keane, Ted Mapes, Fred Burns, Post Parks, Art Dillard, Chick Hannon, Charles Baldra, Jack Montgomery, Jack Kirk, Eddie Acuff, Monte Montague, Pascale Perry, Bob Card, Ed Piel, Ed Brady, Lew Kelly, Curley Dresden, Art Mix, Bob Woodward; D/AP: Joseph Kane; SP: Olive Cooper, Louis Stevens.

Western Union (20th Century–Fox, February 21, 1941) 94 mins.; Robert Young, Randolph Scott, Dean Jagger, Virginia Gilmore, John Carradine, Slim Summerville, Chill Wills, Barton MacLane, Russell Hicks, Victor Kilian, Minor Watson, George Chandler, Chief Big Tree, Chief Thunder Cloud, Dick Rich, Harry Strange, Charles Middleton, Addison Richards, Irving Bacon, Tom London, Reed Howes; D: Fritz Lang; SP: Robert Carson; AP: Harry Joe Brown.

The Last of the Duanes (20th Century–Fox, September 26, 1941) 57 mins.; George Montgomery, Lynne Roberts, Eve Arden, Francis Ford, George E. Stone, William Farnum, Joseph Sawyer, Truman Bradley, Russell Simpson, Don Costello, Harry Woods, Andrew Tombes, Lew Kelly, Arthur Aylesworth, Ann Carter, Russ Clark, Paul E. Burns, Harry Hayden, Tom London, LeRoy Mason, Lane Chandler, Syd Saylor, Ethan Laidlaw, Tim Ryan, Paul Sutton, Walter McGrail; D: James Tinling; SP: Irving Cummings, Jr., William Conselman, Jr.

Riders of the Purple Sage (20th Century–Fox, October 10, 1941) 56 mins.; George Montgomery, Mary Howard, Robert Barrat, Lynne Roberts, Kane Richmond, Patsy Patterson, Richard Lane, Oscar O'Shea, James Gillette, Frank McGrath, LeRoy Mason; D: James Tinling; SP: William Buckner, Robert Metzler; P: Sol M. Wurtzel.

Lone Star Ranger (20th Century–Fox, March 20, 1942) 58 mins.; John Kimbrough, Sheila Ryan, Jonathan Hale, William Farnum, Truman Bradley, George E. Stone, Russell Simpson, Dorothy Burgess, Tom Fadden, Fred Kohler, Jr., Eddy Waller, Harry Holden, George Melford, Tom London; D: James Tinling; SP: William Conselman, Jr., George Kane, Irving Cummings, Jr.

King of the Mounties (Republic, October 10, 1942) 12 chapters; Allan Lane, Gilbert Emery, Russell Hicks, Peggy Drake, George Irving, Abner Biberman, William Vaughn, Nestor Paiva, Bradley Page, Douglas Dumbrille, William Bakewell, Duncan Renaldo, Francis Ford, Jay Novello, Anthony Warde, Ken Terrell, Harry Cording, Carleton Young, Tom Steele, Stanley Price, Tommy Coats, Duke Taylor, Duke Green, Bob Jamison, Jack Kenney, Forrest Taylor, David Sharpe, Frank Wayne, Pete Katchenaro, Kam Tong, Earl Bunn, Hal Taliaferro, Sam Serrano, Joe Chambers, Tor Johnson; D: William Witney; SP: Taylor Caven, Ronald Davidson, William Lively, Joseph O'Donnell, Joseph Poland; AP: W. J. O'Sullivan. Note. Based loosely on the comic strip created by Grey.

Nevada (RKO-Radio, December 1, 1944) 62 mins.; Robert Mitchum, Anne Jeffreys, Nancy Gates, Craig Reynolds, Guinn (Big Boy) Williams, Richard Martin, Harry Woods, Edmund Glover, Alan Ward, Harry McKim, Wheaton Chambers, Philip Morris, Emmett Lynn, Bryant Washburn, Larry Wheat, Jack Overman, George DeNormand, Virginia Belmont, Russell Hopton, Sammy Blum, Mary Halsey, Patti Brill, Bert Moorhouse, Margie Stesart; D: Edward Killy; SP: Norman Houston; P: Sid Rogell, Herman Schlom.

West of the Pecos (RKO-Radio, June 18, 1945) 68 mins.; Robert Mitchum, Barbara Hale, Richard Martin, Thurston Hall, Rita Corday, Russell Hopton, Bill Williams, Bruce Edwards,

Harry Woods, Perc Launders, Bryant Washburn, Philip Morris, Martin Garralaga, Ethan Laidlaw, Larry Wheat; D: Edward Killy; SP: Norman Houston; P: Herman Schlom.

Wanderer of the Wasteland (RKO-Radio, October 18, 1945) 67 mins.; James Warren, Richard Martin, Audrey Long, Robert Barrat, Robert Clarke, Harry Woods, Minerva Urecal, Harry D. Brown, Tommy Cook, Harry McKim, Jason Robards, Sr.; D: Edward Killy, Wallace Grissell; SP: Norman Houston; P: Herman Schlom.

Sunset Pass (RKO-Radio, October 1, 1946) 59 mins.; James Warren, Nan Leslie, Jane Greer, Steve Brodie, John Laurenz, Robert Clarke, Harry Woods, Harry Harvey, Robert Barrat, Frank O'Connor, Carl Faulkner, Slim Balch, Roy Bucko, Buck Bucko, Artie Ortego, Charles Stevens, George Plues, Clem Fuller, Bob Dyer, Boyd Stockman, Slim Hightower, Robert Bray, Florence Pepper; D: William Berke; SP: Norman Houston; P: Herman Schlom.

Code of the West (RKO-Radio, February 2, 1947) 57 mins.; James Warren, Debra Alden, John Laurenz, Robert Clarke, Steve Brodie, Rita Lynn, Carol Forman, Harry Woods, Raymond Burr, Harry Harvey, Phil Warren, Emmett Lynn; D: William Berke; SP: Norman Houston; P: Herman Schlom.

Thunder Mountain (RKO-Radio, June 15, 1947) 60 mins.; Tim Holt, Martha Hyer, Richard Martin, Steve Brodie, Richard Powers (Tom Keene), Virginia Owen, Harry Woods, Jason Robards, Sr., Robert Clarke, Harry Harvey; D: Lew Landers; SP: Norman Houston; P: Herman Schlom.

The Gunfighters (Columbia, July 1, 1947) 87 mins.; Randolph Scott, Barbara Britton, Dorothy Hart, Bruce Cabot, Charley Grapewin, Steven Geray, Forrest Tucker, Charles Kemper, Grant Withers, John Miles, Griff Barnett, Charles Middleton; D: George Wagner; SP: Alan LeMay; P: Harry Joe Brown. Note. Based on *Twin Sombreros*.

Under the Tonto Rim (RKO-Radio, August 1, 1947) 61 mins.; Tim Holt, Nan Leslie, Richard Martin, Richard Powers (Tom Keene), Carol Forman, Tony Barrett, Harry Harvey, Jason Robards, Sr., Lex Barker, Robert Clarke, Jay Norris, Steve Savage, Herman Hack; D: Lew Landers; SP: Norman Houston; P: Herman Schlom.

Wild Horse Mesa (RKO-Radio, November 21, 1947) 60 mins.; Tim Holt, Nan Leslie, Richard Martin, Richard Powers (Tom Keene), Jason Robards, Sr., Tony Barrett, Harry Woods, William Gould, Robert Bray, Richard Foote, Frank Yaconelli; D: Wallace Grissell; SP: Norman Houston; P: Herman Schlom.

Red Canyon (Universal-International, April 1949) 82 mins.; Howard Duff, Ann Blyth, George Brent, Edgar Buchanan, John McIntire, Chill Wills, Jane Darwell, Lloyd Bridges, James Seay, Edmund MacDonald, David Clarke, Denver Pyle, Willard Willingham, Hank Patterson, Ray Bennett, Hank Worden, Edmund Cobb, John Carpenter; D: George Sherman; SP: Maurice Geraghty; P: Leonard Goldstein. Note. Based on *Wildfire*.

Robber's Roost (United Artists, May 30, 1955) 82 mins.; George Montgomery, Richard Boone, Sylvia Findley, Bruce Bennett, Peter Graves, Warren Stevens, Tony Romano, William Hopper, Leo Gordon, Stanley Clements, Joe Bassett, Leonard Geer, Al Wyatt, Boyd Morgan; D: Sidney Salkow; SP: John O'Dea, Sidney Salkow, Maurice Geraghty; P: Robert Goldstein, Leonard Goldstein.

The Vanishing American (Republic, November 17, 1955) 90 mins.; Scott Brady, Audrey Totter, Forrest Tucker, Gene Lockhart, Jim Davis, John Dierkes, Gloria Castillo, Julian Rivero, Lee Van Cleef, George Keymas, Charles

Stevens, Jay Silverheels, James Millican, Glenn Strange; D: Joseph Kane; SP: Alan LeMay; P: Herbert J. Yates.

The Maverick Queen (Republic, May 3, 1956) 92 mins.; Barbara Stanwyck, Barry Sullivan, Scott Brady, Mary Murphy, Wallace Ford, Howard Petrie, Jim Davis, Emile Meyer, Walter Sande, George Keymas, John Doucette, Taylor Holmes, Pierre Watkin; D: Joseph Kane; SP: Kenneth Gamet, DeVallon Scott; AP: Joseph Kane.

Chapter 3

Other Writers of the West

Though Zane Grey deserves most of the credit for establishing western as a generic term, he was faced with plenty of competition in this arena. This chapter pays tribute to the other western authors who gained fame and popularity through their writings and whose works were often translated to the screen. It should be remembered that filmmakers often took considerable license when adapting stories to the screen. Sometimes little more than the character names or title remained in the film version. But there were films that often followed closely the books and short stories they were based on.

Marvin H. Albert

Marvin Albert has had six of his stories adapted to the screen. *Duel at Diablo* was based on *Apache Rising*; *Rough Night in Jericho* was from *The Man in Black*; and *The Ugly Ones* was an adaptation of *The Bounty Killer*. *The Law and Jake Wade, Bullet for a Badman* (based on his novel *Renegade Posse*), and *The Don Is Dead* credited Albert with both story and screenplay.

Albert, born in 1924 in Philadelphia, is an author and editor. He has been employed in varying situations, including positions as copyperson for the *Philadelphia Record*, magazine editor, researcher for *Look* magazine, and television and motion picture scriptwriter. In World War II he served as chief radio officer on liberty ships.

A prolific writer, Albert has also written under the pseudonyms Ian MacAlister, Al Conroy, Albert Conroy, and Nick Quarry. Detective stories have been his specialty.

While Marvin H. Albert spent much of his early writing career creating traditional hard-boiled detective stories, both in novel and screenplay form, his recent novels are "marked by a multiple point of view, a complex plot, [and] a global arena of conflict," asserts Shelly Lowenkopf in *Twentieth-Century Crime and Mystery Writers*. Lowenkopf notes that while Albert is a "journeyman" who makes intermittent mistakes of plot or characterization, she admits that he "can see drama, conflict, and tension in any gathering of two or more characters, and, at his best, moves forth with fluid ease." 1983's *Operation Lila* is typical of the author's latest work, as *New York Times Book Review* contributor Peter Andrews remarks: "Balanced against such occasional lapses [of plot] is some first-class adventure story writing. The plot rips along in good style and makes all of the mandatory stops." The critic concludes that *Operation Lila* is "a sturdy piece of work that provides spirited entertainment."[1]

The following is a summary of his principal writings as Marvin H. Albert: *Lie Down with Lions*, 1955; *The Law and Jake Wade*, 1956; *Apache Rising*, 1957 (published in England as *Duel at Diablo*, 1966); *Broadsides and Borders*, 1957; *The Long White Road: Sir Ernest Shackleton's Adventures*, 1957; *The Bounty Killer*, 1958; *Renegade Posse*, 1958; *That Jane from Maine*, 1959; *Pillow Talk* (screenplay novelization), 1959; *Rider from Wind River*, 1959; *The Reformed Gun*, 1959; *All the Young Men* (screenplay novelization), 1960; *Come September*, 1961; *Lover Come Back* (screenplay novelization), 1962; *Move Over, Darling* (screenplay novelization), 1963; *Palm Springs Weekend*, 1963; *Under the Yum-Yum Tree* (screenplay novelization), 1963; *The VIPs*, 1963; *The Outrage* (screenplay novelization), 1964; *Honeymoon Hotel*, 1964; *Posse at High Pass*, 1964; *What's New, Pussycat?* (screenplay novelization, 1965; *Strange Bedfellows* (screenplay novelization), 1965; *The Divorce: A Re-Examination of the Great Tudor Controversy*, 1965; *Do Not Disturb*, 1965; *The Great Race*, 1965; *A Very Special Favor* (screenplay novelization), 1965; *The Gargoyle Conspiracy*, 1975; *Becoming a Mother* (coauthor), 1978; *The Dark Goddess*, 1978; *The Corsican*, 1980; *The Medusa Complex*, 1981; *Hidden Lives*, 1981; *Operation Lila*, 1983; *The Golden Circle*, 1985; *Back in the Real World*, 1986; *The Stone Angel*, 1986; *Get Off at Babylon*, 1987; and *Long Teeth*, 1987.

This is the summary of his writings as Anthony Rome, Ian MacAlister, or Mike Barone: *Miami Mayhem*, 1967; *My Kind of Game*, 1962; *The Lady in Cement*, 1962; *Driscoll's Diamonds*, 1973; *Skylark Mission*, 1973; *Strike Force 7*, 1974; *Crazy Joe*, 1974; and *Valley of the Assassins*, 1975.

Another pseudonym, Al Conroy, includes the following work: *Clayburn*, 1961; *Last Train to Bannock*, 1963; *Three Ride North*, 1964; *The Man in Black*, 1965; *Death Grip*, 1972; *Soldatol*, 1972; *Blood Run*, 1973; *Murder Mission*, 1973; and *Strangle Hold!* 1973.

Albert Conroy, yet another pseudonym, is credited with the following: *The Road's End*, 1952; *The Chislers*, 1953; *Nice Guys Finish Dead*, 1957; *Murder in Room 13*, 1958; *The Mob Says Murder*, 1958; *Mr. Lucky* (novelization of TV series), 1960; *Devil in Dungarees*, 1960; and *The Looters*, 1961.

Finally his writing as Nick Quarry included these: *Trail of a Tramp*, 1958; *The Hoods Come Calling*, 1958; *The Girl with No Place to Hide*, 1959; *No Chance in Hell*, 1960; *Till It Hurts*, 1960; *Some Die Hard*, 1961; *The Don Is Dead*, 1972; and *The Vendetta*, 1972.

Films Based on Marvin H. Albert's Writings

The Law and Jake Wade (MGM, 1958) 86 mins.; Robert Taylor, Richard Widmark, Patricia Owens, Robert Middleton, Henry Silva, DeForest Kelley, Burt Douglas, Eddie Firestone; D: John Sturges; SP: William Bowers; P: William Hawks.

Bullet for a Badman (Universal, 1964) 80 mins.; Audie Murphy, Darren McGavin, Ruta Lee, Beverly Owen, Skip Homeier, George Tobias, Alan Hale, Jr., Berkeley Harris, Edward C. Platt, Kevin Tate, CeCe Whitney, Mort Mills, Buff Brady, Bob Steele; D: R. G. Springsteen; SP: Mary and Willard Willingham; P: Gordon Kay.

Duel at Diablo (United Artists, 1966) 103 mins.; James Garner, Sidney Poitier, Bibi Andersson, Dennis Weaver, Bill Travers, William Redfield, John Hoyt, John Crawford, John Hubbard, Kevin Coughlin, Jay Ripley, Jeff Cooper, Ralph Bahnsen, Bobby Crawford; D: Ralph Nelson, SP: Marvin H. Albert, Michel M. Grilikhes; S: *Apache Rising*; P: Ralph Nelson, Fred Engel.

Rough Night in Jericho (Universal, 1967) 104 mins.; Dean Martin, Jean Simmons, George Peppard, John McIntire, Slim Pickens, Don Galloway, Brad Weston, Richard O'Brien, Carol Anderson, Steve Sandor, Warren Vanders, John Napier; D: Arnold Laven; SP: Sidney Boehm, Marvin H. Albert; S: *The Man in Black*; P: Martin Rackin.

The Ugly Ones (United Artists, 1968) 96 mins.; Richard Wyler, Tomas Milian, Ella Karin, Mario Brega, Hugo Blanco, Glenn Foster, Ricardo Canales, Lola Gaos, Saturno Cerra, Manuel Zarzo, Tito Garcia, Antonio Iranzo, Ferdinand Sanchez Polack, Enrique Navarro; D: Eugenio Martin; SP: Don Prindle, Eugenio Martin, Jose G. Maesso; S: *The Bounty Killer*; P: Giuliano Simonetti.

The Don Is Dead (Universal, 1973) 115 mins.; Anthony Quinn, Frederic Forrest, Robert Forster, Al Lettieri, Angel Tompkins, Charles Cioffi, Jo Anne Meredith, J. Duke Russo, Louis Zorich, Ina Balin, George Skaff, Robert Carricart, Anthony Charnota, Abe Vigoda, Frank de Kove, Joseph Santos; D: Richard Fleischer; SP/S: Marvin H. Albert; P: Hal B. Wallis.

Tom W. Blackman

Tom Blackman has written some good westerns, with his own film adaptations being equally good. *Colt .45* is a prime example. However, he is mostly a scenarist, adapting the stories of other writers to the screen.

Films Based on Tom Blackburn's Writings

Colt .45 (Paramount, 1950) 104 mins.; Randolph Scott, Zachary Scott, Ruth Roman, Lloyd Bridges, Alan Hale, Ian MacDonald, Chief Thunder Cloud, Walter Coy, Luther Crockett, Charles Evans, Buddy Roosevelt, Hal Taliaferro (Wally Wales), Art Miles, Barry Reagan, Howard Negley, Aurora Navarro, Paul Newland, Franklyn Farnum, Ed Piel, Sr., Jack Watt, Carl Andre, Royden Clark, Kansas Moehring, Warren Fisk, Forrest R. Colee, Artie Ortego, Stanley Andrews, Zon Murray, Bud Osborne, Clyde Hudkins, Jr., Ben Corbett, Leroy

Johnson, Richard Brehm, Dick Hudkins, Leo McMahon, Bob Burrows, William Steele; D: Edward L. Marin; SP/S: Tom W. Blackburn; P: Saul Elkins.

Short Grass (Allied Artists, 1950) 82 mins.; Rod Cameron, Cathy Downs, Johnny Mack Brown, Raymond Walburn, Alan Hale, Jr., Morris Ankrum, Jonathan Hale, Harry Woods, Marlo Dwyer, Riley Hill, Jeff York, Stanley Andrews, Jack Ingram, Myron Healey, Tris Coffin, Rory Mallison, Felipe Turich, George J. Lewis, Lee Tung Foo, Kermit Maynard; D: Lesley Selander; SP/S: Tom W. Blackburn; P: Scott R. Dunlap.

Sierra Passage (Monogram, 1951) 81 mins.; Wayne Morris, Lola Albright, Lloyd Corrigan, Alan Hale, Jr., Roland Winters, Jim Bannon, Billy Gray, Paul McGuire, Richard Karlan, George Eldridge, Zon Murray, John Doucette, Paul Bryar; D: Frank McDonald; SP: Tom W. Blackburn, Warren D. Wandberg, Sam Rosca; P: Lindsley Parsons.

Raton Pass (Warner Brothers, 1951) 84 min.; Dennis Morgan, Patricia Neal, Steve Cochran, Scott Forbes, Dorothy Hart, Basil Ruysdael, Louis J. Heydt, Roland Winters, James Burke, Elvira Curci, Carlos Conde, John Crawford, Rudolpho Hoyos, Jr.; D: Edwin L. Marin; SP: Tom W. Blackburn, James R. Webb; S: Tom W. Blackburn.

Cavalry Scout (Monogram, 1951) 78 mins.; Rod Cameron, Audrey Long, Jim Davis, James Millican, James Arness, John Doucette, William Phillips, Stephen Chase, Rory Mallison, Eddy Waller, Paul Bryar; D: Lesley Selander; SP: Dan Ullman, Tom B. Blackburn; P: Walter Mirisch.

Cattle Town (Warner Brothers, 1952) 71 mins.; Dennis Morgan, Philip Carey, Rita Moreno, Paul Picerni, Amanda Blake, George O'Hanlon, Ray Teal, Jay Novello, Bob Wilke, Sheb Wooley, Charles Meredith, Merv Griffin, A. Guy Teague, Boyd Morgan, Jack Kenney; D: Noel Smith; SP: Tom W. Blackburn; P: Bryan Foy.

Riding Shotgun (Warner Brothers, 1954) 75 mins.; Randolph Scott, Wayne Morris, Joan Weldon, Joe Sawyer, James Millican, Charles Buchinsky (Bronson), James Bell, Fritz Field, Richard Garrick, Victor Perrin, John Baer, William Johnstone, Kem Dibbs, Alvin Freeman, Edward Coch, Jr., Eva Lewis, Lonnie Pierce, Mary Lou Holloway, Boyd Morgan, Richard Benjamin, Jay Lawrence, George Ross, Ray Bennett, Jack Kenney, Jack Woody, Allegra Varron, Frosty Royse, Jimmy Mohley, Ruth Whitney, Bud Osborne, Budd Buster, Buddy Roosevelt, Dub Taylor, Joe Brockman, Harry Hines, Clem Fuller, Opan Evard, Morgan Brown, Bob Stephenson; D: Andre De Toth; SP: Tom W. Blackburn; S: Kenneth Perkins; P: Ted Sherdeman.

Cattle Queen of Montana (RKO-Radio, 1954) 88 mins.; Barbara Stanwyck, Ronald Reagan, Gene Evans, Lance Ruller, Anthony Caruso, Jack Ingram, Yvette Dugay, Morris Ankrum, Chubby Johnson, Myron Healey, Rodd Redwing, Paul Birch, Byron Foulger, Burt Muslin; D: Allan Dwan; SP: Howard Estabrook, Robert Blees; P: Benedict Bogeaus.

Davy Crockett, King of the Wild Frontier (Buena Vista, 1955) 95 mins.; Fess Parker, Buddy Ebsen, Basil Ruysdael, Hans Conried, William Bakewell, Ken Tobey, Pat Hogan, Helene Stanley, Nick Cravet, Don Megowan, Mike Mazurki, Jeff Thompson, Henry Joyner, Benjamin Hornbuckle, Hall Youngblood, Jim Maddox, Robert Booth, Eugene Brindel, Ray Whitetree, Campbell Brown; D: Norman Foster; SP: Tom Blackburn; P: Bill Walsh.

The Wild Dakotas (Associated, 1956) 73 mins.; Bill Williams, Coleen Gray, Jim Davis, John Litel, Dick Jones, John Miljan, Lisa Montell, I. Stanford Jolley, Wally Brown, Bill Dix, Iron Eyes

Cody, Bill Henry; D: Sam Newfield; SP: Tom W. Blackburn; P: Sigmund Neufeld.

Johnny Tremain (Walt Disney, 1957) 81 mins.; Hal Stalmaster, Luana Patten, Jeff York, Sebastian Cabot, Richard Beymer, Walter Sande; D: Robert Stevenson; SP: Tom W. Blackburn; S: Esther Forbes.

Westward Ho the Wagons! (Disney/Buena Vista, 1957) 90 mins.; Fess Parker, Kathleen Crowley, Jeff York, Karen Pendleton, David Stollery, Leslie Bradley, George Reeves, Sebastian Cabot, John War Eagle, Cubby O'Brien, Jane Liddell, Iron Eyes Cody, Doreen Tracey, Tommy Cole, Barbara Woodell,

Leslie Bradley, Karen Pendleton; D: William Beaudine; SP: Tom W. Blackburn.

Sierra Baron (20th Century–Fox, 1958) 80 mins.; Brian Keith, Rick Jason, Rita Gam, Mala Powers, Allan Lewis, Pedro Calvan, Fernando Wagner, Steve Brodie, Carlos Muzquiz, Lee Morgan, Jose Espinoza, Enrique Lucero, Alberto Mariscal, Lynne Ehrlich, Michael Schmidt, Tommy Riste, Reed Howes, Robin Glattley, Jose Trowe, Armando Saenz, Bob Janis, John Courier, Paul Arnett, Alicia del Lago, Stillam Segar, Marc Lambert, Doris Contreras; D: James B. Clark; SP: Houston Branch; P: Plato A. Skouras.

B. M. Bower

Author Stanley Davidson introduced his excellent article on B. M. Bower and the book *Chip of the Flying U* with these words:

In the first decade of this century, readers of Montana fiction discovered a new ranch in the state. Bearing the alluring name of "The Flying U," it was peopled by a half-dozen personable cowboys, the Happy Family, along with the crusty but agreeable owner, "Old Man" Whitmore. Assorted hired hands, visitors, and neighboring ranchers made up the rest of the cast.

These people and their land were introduced in a series of short stories and serialized novels in Street and Smith magazines, starting in 1904. But it was two years later, with publication of a modest little book called *Chip of the Flying U*, that Montanans became aware of the place. Soon after came *The Lonesome Trail*, made up of a novelette bearing that name, plus six short stories relating adventures of the Happy Family. So smoothly were these tales blended that readers would hardly suspect they had not been written as chapters in this novel. Most were so absorbed by the characters, their conversation and activities, that they had little concern for technicalities of the author's craft.

But they did wonder about a couple of things. Who was the writer B. M. Bower, who could create characters as real as the folks one had known for a lifetime? And where was the Flying U Ranch? It was too real not to exist somewhere in the foothills of North Central Montana.[2]

B. M. Bower's real name was Bertha Muzzey Bower, and the initials were an attempt to conceal the fact that she was a woman. She was born on a farm near Cleveland, Minnesota, on November 15, 1871, and taken as a small child to Montana, where in 1890 she married the first of three husbands, Clayton J. Bower. Most readers were not ready to believe that a woman could write as she did. For two decades there was confusion among literary critics as to her sex. Finally, in 1922 a critic identified her as Mrs. Robert E. Cowan (her third husband). However, the name B. M. Bower still caused some critics to believe she was not a woman, such as this writer in 1926: "B. M. Bower, the president and general manager of a silver-copper mine in Nevada, is a strong but not altogether silent man who, during the intermissions in his professional duties, has found time to write thirty-four books aptly described on the dust jacket of this, his latest, as "rollicking novels of Western adventure."[3] Obviously, the writer had not done his research homework.

Chip of the Flying U came into existence in a series of short stories later to be arranged into a book-length novel in 1906. The story was filmed three times—1914, 1926, and 1939. "The Wolverine" (1921) and "The Taming of the West" (1925) were also popular Bower stories translated into profitable feature-length movies. Bower wrote 14 stories between 1904 and 1916 and continued to write until her death in 1940 at the age of 69.

Averaging two books per year, she was a formula writer, a user of conventions rather than a literary innovator. She had a clear understanding of what her readers wanted. Comedy was always an essential element in the Bower books. She produced essentially formula novels with considerable speed and facility. Quite reticent about her biographical data, certain facts are nevertheless known. At one time or another she lived, among other places, near Glenns Ferry, Idaho; near Las Vegas, Nevada; and at Denoe Bay, Oregon.

Her principal works are as follows: *Chip of the Flying U*, 1904; *the Lure of the Dim Trails*, 1907; *Her Prairie Knight*, 1908; *The Lonesome Trail*, 1909; *The Long Shadow*, 1909; *The Happy Family*, 1910; *The Range Dwellers*, 1910; *Good Indian*, 1912; *Lonesome Land*, 1912; *The Uphill Climb*, 1913; *The Gringos*, 1913; *The Ranch at the Wolverine*, 1914; *Flying U Ranch*, 1914; *Flying U's Last Stand*, 1915; *Jean of the Lazy A*, 1915; *The Phantom Herd*, 1916; *Heritage of the Sioux*, 1916; *The Lookout Man*, 1917; *Starr of the Desert*, 1917; *Cabin Fever*, 1918; *Skyrider*, 1918; *The Thunder Bird*, 1919; *Rim o' the World*, 1920; *The Quirt*, 1920; *Cow Country*, 1921; *Casey Ryan*, 1921; *Trail of the White Mule*, 1922; *The Voice at Johnnywater*, 1923; *The Parowan Bonanza*, 1923; *The Bellehelen Mine*, 1924; *Desert Brew*, 1924; *Meadowlark Basin*, 1925; *Black Thunder*, 1925; *White Wolves*, 1926; *Van Patten*, 1926; *The Adam Chasers*, 1927; *Points West*, 1928; *The Swallowfork Bulls*, 1928; *Rodeo*, 1929; *Fool's Gold*, 1930; *Tiger Eye*, 1930; *The Long Loop*, 1931; *Dark Horse*, 1931; *Laughing Water*, 1932; *Rocking Arrow*, 1932; *Trails Meet*, 1933; *Open Land*, 1933; *The Flying U Strikes*, 1934; *The Haunted Hills*, 1934; *The Dry Ridge Gang*, 1935; *Trouble Rides the Wind*, 1935; *The Five Furies of Leading Ladder*, 1935; *Shadow Mountain*, 1936; *The North Wind Do Blow*, 1936; *Pirates of the Range*, 1937; *The Wind Blows West*, 1938; *Starry Night*, 1938; *The Singing Hill*, 1939; *The Man on Horseback*, 1940; *Sweet Grass*, 1940; *The Spirit of the Range*, 1940; and *The Family Failing*, 1941.

Films Based on B. M. Bower's Writings

The Last of Her Tribe (Selig, 1912) 1 reel; Tom Santschi, William Hutchinson, Wheeler Oakman, Ferdinand Galvez, William Brownlee, Bessie Eyton, Margaret Hall, Eugenie Besserer, Juan Pardee; D: Colin Campbell; SP: B. M. Bower.

The Uphill Climb (Selig, 1914) 2 reels; Wheeler Oakman, Bessie Eyton, Roy Clark; D: Colin Campbell.

Shotgun Jones (Selig, 1914) 2 reels; Bessie Eyton, Wheeler Oakman, Joseph Girard, Hoot Gibson; D: Colin Campbell; SP: B. M. Bower.

When the Cook Fell Ill (Selig, 1914) 1 reel; Tom Mix, Wheeler Oakman, Frank Clark; D: Colin Campbell; SP/S: B. M. Bower.

The Lonesome Trail (Selig, 1914) 1 reel; Wheeler Oakman, Gertrude Ryan.

The Reveler (Selig, 1914) 1 reel; Wheeler Oakman; D: Colin Campbell.

Chip of the Flying U (Selig, 1914) 3 reels; Kathlyn Williams, Tom Mix, Frank Clark, Fred Huntley, Wheeler Oakman, Jack McDonald; D: Colin Campbell; SP: B. M. Bower; S: Peter B. Kyne.

How Weary Went Wooing (Selig, 1915) 1 reel; Tom Mix, Victoria Forde, Sid Jordan, Leo Maloney; D/P: Tom Mix.

Curlew Corliss (Mustang, 1916) 3 reels; Art Acord, Nita Davis, John Gough, Dixie Stratton, Lawrence Peyton, Pete Morrison, Molly Shafer, Joe Massey; D: William Bertram.

North of '53 (Fox, 1917) 5 reels; Dustin Farnum, Winifred Kingston, William Conklin; D: Richard Stanton; SP: Gardner Hunting.

The Galloping Devil (Canyon, 1920) 2 reels; Franklyn Farnum, Vester Pegg; D: Nate Watt; P: William N. Selig.

The Wolverine (Associated Photoplays, 1921) 5 reels; Helen Gibson, Jack Connolly, Leo Maloney, Ivar McFadden, Anne Schaefer, Gus Saville; D: William Bertram; SP: Helen Van Upp.

The Taming of the West (Universal, 1925) 6 reels; Hoot Gibson, Marceline Day, Morgan Brown, Edwin Booth, Herbert Prior, Louise Hippe, Albert J. Smith, Francis Ford, Frona Hale; D: Arthur Rosson; SP: Raymond L. Schrock; S: *The Range Dwellers*.

Ridin' Thunder (Universal, 1925) 5 reels; Jack Hoxie, Katherine Grant, Jack Pratt, Francis Ford, George Connors, Bert De Marc, William McCall; D: Clifford S. Smith; SP: Carl Krusada, Isadore Bernstein; S: *Jean of the Lazy A*.

Chip of the Flying U (Universal, 1926) 7 reels; Hoot Gibson, Virginia Brown Faire, Philo McCullough, Nora Cecil, DeWitt Jennings, Harry Todd, Pee Wee Holmes, Mark Hamilton, Willie Sung; D: Lynn F. Reynolds; SP: Lynn F. Reynolds, Harry Dittmar.

The Flying U Ranch (R-C/FBO, 1927) 5 reels; Tom Tyler, Nora Lane, Bert Hadley, Grace Woods, Frankie Darro, Olin Francis, Barney Furey, Dudley Hendricks, Bill Patton; D: Robert De Lacy; SP: Oliver Drake.

King of the Rodeo (Universal, 1929) 6 reels; Hoot Gibson, Kathryn Crawford, Slim Summerville, Charles K. French, Monty Montague, Joseph W. Girard, Jack Knapp, Harry Todd, Bodil Rosing; D: Henry MacRae; SP: George Morgan.

Points West (Universal, 1929) 6 reels; Hoot Gibson, Alberta Vaughn, Frank Campeau, Jack Raymond, Martha Franklin, Milt Brown, Jim Corey; D: Arthur Rosson; SP: Rowland Brown.

Chip of the Flying U (Universal, 1939) 55 mins.; Johnny Mack Brown, Bob Baker, Fuzzy Knight, Doris

Weston, Karl Hackett, Forrest Taylor, Anthony Warde, Henry Hall, Claire Whitney, Ferris Taylor, Cecil Kellogg, Hank Bell, Harry Tenbrook, Chester Conklin, Vic Potel, Hank Worden, Charles K. French, Al Ward, Budd Buster, Frank Ellis, Kermit Maynard, Jack Shannon, Chuck Morrison; D: Ralph Staub; SP: Larry Rhine, Andrew Bennison.

Max Brand

Undoubtedly, Frederick Faust was the most prolific western writer, penning over 300 western novels under 19 pseudonyms, including his best known, Max Brand. He wrote fast, sometimes turning out a novel in 2 or 3 weeks. Much of his writing, however, was for the pulp magazines, though on occasion his stories appeared in the better-quality ones.

By far his best remembered work, at least by cinemagoers, is *Destry Rides Again*, adapted for the screen four times. He is also responsible for the popular MGM series *Doctor Kildare*.

Brand was born on May 29, 1892, and died in Italy in 1944 while serving as a war correspondent. It is said that during his lifetime he penned more than 25 million words. Probably no one would care to try and verify this statistic. At least 42 films were adapted from his stories. There's a good chance that there were others, but only those that can definitely be identified with Brand are listed in the filmography.

His principal works (incomplete because of the number) are as follows: *The Untamed*, 1918; *The Night Horseman*, 1920; *Trailin'*, 1920; *The Seventh Man*, 1921; *Alcatraz*, 1923; *Dan Barry's Daughter*, 1924; *Fire Brain*, 1926; *Blue Jay*, 1927; *White Wolf*, 1928; *Pleasant Jim*, 1928; *Pillar Mountain*, 1928; *Gun Tamer*, 1929; *Mistral*, 1929; *Destry Rides Again*, 1930; *Mystery Ranch*, 1930, *The Happy Valley*, 1931; *Smiling Charlie*, 1931; *The Jackson Trail*, 1932; *Valley Vultures*, 1932; *Twenty Notches*, 1932; *Longhorn Feud*, 1933; *The Outlaw*, 1933; *Slow Joe*, 1933; *Brothers on the Trail*, 1934; *Crooked Horn*, 1934; *Rancher's Revenge*, 1934; *Timbal Gulch Trail*, 1934; *The Hunted Riders*, 1935; *The Rustlers of Beacon Creek*, 1935; *The Seven of Diamonds*, 1935; *Clung*, 1935; *Tiger*, 1935; *Happy Jack*, 1936; *The King Bird Rides*, 1936; *Harrigan*, 1936; *South of Rio Grande*, 1936; *The Streak*, 1937; *Trouble Trail*, 1937; *The Iron Trail*, 1938; *Dead or Alive*, 1938; *Singing Guns*, 1938; *Lanky for Luck*, 1939; *Fightin' Fool*, 1939; *Gunman's Gold*, 1939; *Marbleface*, 1939; *Six Golden Angels*, 1939; *The Dude*, 1940; *The Secret of Doctor Kildare*, 1940; *Young Doctor Kildare*, 1941; *Doctor Kildare Takes Charge*, 1941; *Long Chance*, 1941; *Silver Tip*, 1942; *Doctor Kildare's Crisis*, 1942.

Faust's pseudonyms included Frank Austin, George Owen Baxter, Lee Bolt, Max Brand, Walter C. Butler, George Challis, Peter Dawson, Martin Dexter, Evin Evan, Evan Evans, John Frederick, Frederick Frost, Dennis

Lawton, David Manning, Peter Henry Morland, Hugh Owen, Nicholas Silver, Henry Uriel, and Peter Ward. He wrote spy novels as Frederick Frost and crime novels as Walter C. Butler.

Faust was especially proud of his two books of poems: *The Village Street and Other Poems* (1922) and *Dionysus in Hades* (1931).

Films Based on Max Brand's Writings

The Adopted Son (Metro, 1917) 6 reels; Francis X. Bushman, Beverly Bayne, Leslie Stowe, J. W. Johnston, John Smiley, Gertrude Norman, Pat O'Malley; D: Charles Brabin; SP: Albert Shelby Levino.

Lawless Love (Fox, 1918) 5 reels; Jewel Carmen, Henry Woodward, Edward Hearn; D: Robert Thornby; SP: Olga Printzlau; S: *Above the Law.*

Kiss or Kill (Universal, 1918) 5 reels; Herbert Rawlinson, Priscilla Dean, Alfred Allen, Harry Carter; D/SP: Elmer Clifton.

The Untamed (Fox, 1920) 5 reels; Tom Mix, Pauline Starke, George Siegmann, Philo McCullough, James O. Barrows, Charles K. French, Pat Chrisman, Sid Jordan, J. A. McGuire, Frank M. Clark, Joe Connelly; D: Emmett J. Flynn; SP: H. P. Keeler.

A Thousand to One (Associated Producers, 1920) 6 reels; Hobart Bosworth, Ethel Grey Terry, Charles West, Landers Stevens, J. Gordon Russell, Fred Kohler, Gus Saville, Monte Collins; D: Rowland V. Lee; SP: Joseph Franklin Poland; S: *Fate's Honeymoon.*

Tiger True (Universal, 1921) 5 reels; Frank Mayo, Fritzi Brunette, Eleanor Hancock, Al Kaufman, Walter Long, Charles Brinley, Herbert Bethew, Henry A. Barrows; D: J. P. McGowan; SP: George C. Hull; S: *Tiger.*

Children of the Night (Fox, 1921) 5 reels; William Russell, Ruth Renick, Lefty Flynn, Ed Burns, Arthur Thalasso, Wilson Hummell, Helen McGin-nis, Edwin Booth Tilton; D: Jack Dillon; SP: John Montagne.

Who Am I? (Selznick/Select, 1921) 5 reels; Claire Anderson, Gertrude Astor, Niles Welch, George Periolat, Josef Swickard, Otto Hoffman; D: Henry Kolker; SP: Katherine Reed.

The Night Horseman (Fox, 1921) 5 reels; Tom Mix, May Hopkins, Harry Lonsdale, Joseph Bennett, Sid Jordan, Bert Sprotte, Cap Anderson, Lon Poff, Charles K. French; D/SP: Lynn F. Reynolds.

Shame (Fox, 1921) 8–9 reels; John Gilbert, Mickey Moore, Frankie Lee, George Siegmann, William V. Mong, George Nicholas, Anna May Wong, Rosemary Theby, Doris Pawn, Red Kirby; D: Emmett J. Flynn; SP: Emmett J. Flynn, Bernard McConville.

Trailin' (Fox, 1921) 5 reels; Tom Mix, Eva Novak, Bert Sprotte, James Gordon, Sid Jordan, William Duvall, Duke Lee, Harry Dunkinson, Al Fremont, Carol Holloway, Bert Handley; D/SP: Lynn F. Reynolds.

His Back Against the Wall (Goldwyn, 1922) 5 reels; Raymond Hatton, Virginia Valli, Will Walling, Gordon Russell, W. H. Bainbridge, Virginia Madison, Fred Kohler, Jack Curtis, Dudley Hendricks, Shannon Day, Raymond Cannon, Louis Morrison; D: Rowland V. Lee; SP: Julien Josephson; S: John Frederick (Max Brand).

The Fighting Streak (Fox, 1922) 5 reels; Tom Mix, Patsy Ruth Miller, Gerald Pring, Al Fremont, Sid Jordan, Bert Sprotte, Robert Fleming; D/SP: Arthur

Rosson; S: George Owen Baxter (Max Brand).

Just Tony (Fox, 1922) 5 reels; Tom Mix, Tony (a horse); Claire Adams, Frank Campeau, J. P. Lockney, Duke Lee, Walt Robbins; D/SP: Lynn F. Reynolds.

Three Who Paid (Fox, 1923) 5 reels; Dustin Farnum, Fred Kohler, Bessie Love, Frank Campeau, Robert Daly, William Conklin, Robert Agnew; D: Colin Campbell; SP: Joseph F. Poland; S: George Owen Baxter (Max Brand).

Mile-a-Minute Romeo (Fox, 1923) 6 reels; Tom Mix, Betty Jewel, Gordon Russell, James Mason, Duke Lee, James Quinn, Tony (a horse); D: Lambert Hillyer; SP: Robert N. Lee; S: *Gun Gentlemen: a Western Story.*

The Gunfighter (Fox, 1923) 5 reels; William Farnum, Doris May, L. C. Shumway, J. Morris Foster, Virginia True Boardman, Irene Hunt, Arthur Morrison, Jerry Campbell; D/SP: Lynn F. Reynolds; S: *Hired Guns.*

Against All Odds (Fox, 1924) 5 reels; Buck Jones, Dolores Rousse, Ben Hendricks, Jr., William Scott, Thais Valdemar, William N. Bailey, Bernard Siegel, Jack McDonald; D: Edmund Mortimer; SP: Frederic Chapin; S: *Cuttle's Hired Man.*

Champion of Lost Causes (Fox, 1925) 5 reels; Edmund Lowe, Barbara Bedford, Walter McGrail, Jack McDonald, Alec Francis; D: Chester Bennett; SP: Thomas Dixon, Jr.

The Best Bad Man (Fox, 1925) 5 reels; Tom Mix, Clara Bow, Buster Gardner, Cyril Chadwick, Tom Kennedy, Frank Beal, Judy King, Tom Wilson, Paul Panzer, Tony (a horse); D: J. G. Blystone; SP: Lillie Hayward; S: *Senor Jingle Bells.*

The Flying Horseman (Fox, 1926) 5 reels; Buck Jones, Gladys McConnell, Bruce Covington, Walter Percival, Hank Mann, Harvey Clark, Vester Pegg, Sil-

ver (a horse); D: Orville O. Dull; SP: Gertrude Orr; S: *Dark Rosaleen.*

The Cavalier (Tiffany-Stahl, 1928) 7 reels; Richard Talmadge, Barbara Bedford, Nora Cecil, David Torrence, David Mir, Stuart Holmes, Christian Frank, Oliver Eckhardt; D: Irvin Willat; SP: Victor Irvin; S: *The Black Rider.*

Fair Warning (Fox, 1931) 74 mins.; George O'Brien, Louise Huntington, Mitchell Harris, George Brent, Nat Pendleton, Ernie Adams, Willard Robertson; D: Alfred Werker; SP: Ernest Pascal; S: *The Untamed.*

A Holy Terror (Fox, 1931) 63 mins.; George O'Brien, Sally Eilers, Rita LaFoy, Humphrey Bogart, James Kirkwood, Stanley Fields, Robert Warwick, Richard Tucker; D: Irving Cummings; SP: Ralph Brock; S: *Trailin.*

Destry Rides Again (Universal, 1932) 61 mins.; Tom Mix, Claudia Dell, ZaSu Pitts, Stanley Fields, Earle Foxe, Edward Piel, Sr., Francis Ford, Frederick Howard, George Ernest, John Ince, Edward J. LeSaint, Charles K. French, Tony, Jr. (a horse); D: Ben Stoloff; SP: Richard Schayer, Isadore Bernstein.

Internes Can't Take Money (Paramount, 1937) 79 mins.; Barbara Stanwyck, Joel McCrea, Lloyd Nolan, Stanley Ridges, Lee Bowman, Barry Macollum, Irving Bacon, Gaylord Pendleton, Pierre Watkin, Charles Lane, James Bush, Nick Lukats, Anthony Nace, Fay Holden, Frank Bruno, Terry Ray (Ellen Drew), Jack Mulhall, Priscilla Lawson; D: Alfred Santell; SP: Rian James; P: Benjamin Glazer.

Young Dr. Kildare (MGM, 1938) 81 mins.; Lew Ayres, Lionel Barrymore, Lynne Carver, Nat Pendleton, Jo Ann Sayers, Samuel S. Hinds, Emma Dunn, Walter Kingsford, Pierre Watkin, Donald Barry, Don Castle, Monty Wooley, Nella Walker, Truman Bradley, Phillip Terry, James Mason; D: Harold S. Bucquet; SP: Willis Goldbeck, Harry Ruskin.

Calling Dr. Kildare (MGM, 1939) 86 mins.; Lionel Barrymore, Laraine Day, Lana Turner, Samuel S. Hinds, Lynne Carver, Nat Pendleton, Emma Dunn, Walter Kingsford, Harlan Briggs, Donald Barry, Aileen Pringle, Ann Todd, Marie Blake, Henry Hunter; D: Harold S. Bucquet; SP: Harry Ruskin, Willis Goldbeck.

The Secret of Dr. Kildare (MGM, 1939) 84 mins.; Lew Ayres, Lionel Barrymore, Lionel Atwill, Laraine Day, Helen Gilbert, Nat Pendleton, Sara Haden, Samuel S. Hinds, Emma Dunn, Walter Kingsford, Donald Barry, Frank Orth, Byron Foulger, Nell Craig, Robert Kerr, Alma Kruger; D: Harold S. Bucquet; SP: Willis Goldbeck, Harry Ruskin.

Destry Rides Again (Universal, 1939) 94 mins.; Marlene Dietrich, James Stewart, Charles Winninger, Mischa Auer, Brian Donlevy, Allen Jenkins, Warren Hymer, Irene Hervey, Una Merkel, Tom Fadden, Samuel S. Hinds, Lillian Yarbro, Billy Gilbert, Edmund McDonald, Virginia Brissac, Ann Todd, Dickie Jones, Jack Carson, Carmen D'Antonio, Joe King, Harry Cording, Dick Alexander, Minerva Urecal, Bob McKenzie, Billy Bletcher, Lloyd Ingraham, Bill Cody, Jr., William Steele, Harry Tenbrook, Bud McClure, Alex Voloshin, Chief Big Tree, Loren Brown; D: George Marshall; SP: Felix Jackson, Gertrude Purcell, Harry Myers.

Dr. Kildare's Strange Case (MGM, 1940) 76 mins.; Lew Ayres, Lionel Barrymore, Laraine Day, Shepperd Strudwick, Samuel S. Hinds, Emma Dunn, Walter Kingsford, Alma Kruger, John Eldredge, Marcia Mae Jones, Frank Orth, Nell Craig, Marie Blake; D: Harold S. Bucquet; SP: Harry Ruskin, Willis Goldbeck.

Dr. Kildare Goes Home (MGM, 1940) 78 mins.; Lew Ayres, Lionel Barrymore, Laraine Day, John Skelton, Gene Lockhart, Samuel S. Hinds, Emma Dunn, Nat Pendleton, Arthur

O'Connell, Donald Briggs, Marie Blake, Nell Craig; D: Harold S. Bucquet; SP: Harry Ruskin, Willis Goldbeck; S: Max Brand, Willis Goldbeck.

Dr. Kildare's Crisis (MGM, 1940) 75 mins.; Lew Ayres, Robert Young, Lionel Barrymore, Laraine Day, Emma Dunn, Nat Pendleton, Bobs Watson, Walter Kingsford, Alma Kruger, Nell Craig, Frank Orth, Marie Blake, Ann Morriss, Frank Sully, Byron Foulger, Eddie Acuff; D: Harold S. Bucquet; SP: Harry Ruskin, Willis Goldbeck; S: Max Brand, Willis Goldbeck.

The People vs. Dr. Kildare (MGM, 1941) 78 mins.; Lew Ayres, Lionel Barrymore, Laraine Day, Bonita Granville, Red Skelton, Tom Conway, Chick Chandler, Grant Withers, Anna Q. Nilsson, Dwight Frye, Alma Kruger, Walter Kingsford, Marie Blake, Eddie Acuff, Diana Lewis; D: Harold S. Bucquet; SP: Willis Goldbeck, Harry Ruskin; S: Max Brand, Lawrence P. Bachmanor.

Powder Town (RKO, 1942) 79 mins.; Victor McLaglen, Edmond O'Brien, June Havoc, Dorothy Lovett, Eddie Foy, Jr., Damian O'Flynn, Marten Lamont, Roy Gordon, Marion Martin, Julie Warren, Mary Gordon, Frances Neal, Jane Woodworth, George Cleveland, John Maguire, Frank Mills; D: Rowland V. Lee; SP: David Boehm, Vicki Baum.

The Valley of Vanishing Men (Columbia, 1942) 15 chapters; Bill Elliott, Slim Summerville, Carmen Morales, Kenneth MacDonald, Jack Ingram, George Chesebro, John Shay, Tom London, Arno Frey, Julian Rivero, Roy Barcroft, Lane Chandler, Ted Mapes, Ernie Adams, Robert Fiske, Lane Bradford, Frank Ellis, Kenne Duncan, Hank Bell, Iron Eyes Cody, Michael Vallon, Tex Palmer; D: Spencer Gordon Bennet; SP: Harry Fraser, Lewis Clay, George Gray.

The Desperadoes (Columbia, 1943) 85 mins.; Randolph Scott, Glenn Ford,

Claire Trevor, Edgar Buchanan, Guinn (Big Boy) Williams, Evelyn Keyes, Raymond Walburn, Porter Hall, Joan Woodbury, Bernard Nedell, Irving Bacon, Glenn Strange, Ethan Laidlaw, Slim Whitaker, Edward Pawley, Chester Clute, Bill Wolfe, Francis Ford, Tom Smith, Jack Kinney, Silver Harr; D: Charles Vidor; SP: Robert Carson; P: Harry Joe Brown.

The Deerslayer (Republic, 1943) 67 mins.; Bruce Kellogg, Jean Parker, Larry Parks, Warren Ashe, Wanda McKay, Yvonne De Carlo, Addison Richards, Robert Warwick, Johnny Michaels, Philip Van Zandt, Trevor Bardette, Chief Many Treaties; D: Lew Landers; SP: P. S. Harrison, E. B. Derr, Max Brand (uncredited); S: James Fenimore Cooper; P: P. S. Harrison, E. B. Derr.

Rainbow Over Texas (Republic, 1946) 65 mins.; Roy Rogers, George (Gabby) Hayes, Dale Evans, Bob Nolan and the Sons of the Pioneers, Sheldon Leonard, Robert Emmett Keane, Gerald Oliver Smith, Minerva Urecal, George J. Lewis, Kenne Duncan, Pierce Lyden, Dick Elliott, Jo Ann Dean, Bud Osborne, George Chesebro, Trigger (a horse); D: Frank McDonald; SP: Gerald Geraghty; AP: Eddy White.

Singing Guns (Republic, 1950) 91 mins.; Vaughn Monroe, Ella Raines, Walter Brennan, Ward Bond, Jeff Corey,

Barry Kelly, Harry Shannon, Tom Fadden, Ralph Dunn, Rex Lease; D: R. G. Springsteen; SP: Dorral and Stuart McGowan; AP: Melville Tucker, Abe Lyman.

Branded (Paramount, 1951) 95 mins.; Alan Ladd, Mona Freeman, Charles Bickford, Robert Keith, Joseph Callem, Peter Hensen, Tom Tully, Milburn Stone, Martin Garralaga, Edward Clark, John Butler, John Berkes; D: Rudolph Mate; SP: Sidney Boehm, Cyril Hume; S: Evan Evans (Max Brand).

My Outlaw Brother (Eagle Lion, 1951) 82 mins.; Mickey Rooney, Wanda Hendrix, Robert Preston, Robert Stack, Carlos Muzquiz, Jose Tervay, Fernando Waggner, Felipe Flores, Hilda Moreno; D: Elliott Nugent; SP: Gene Fowler, Jr.; Albert L. Levitt; S: *South of the Rio Grande*; P: Benedict Bogeaus.

Destry (Universal-International, 1955) 95 mins.; Audie Murphy, Mari Blanchard, Lyle Bettger, Liri Nelson, Thomas Mitchell, Edgar Buchanan, Wallace Ford, Mary Wickes, Alan Hale, Jr., Lee Aaker, Trevor Bardette, Walter Baldwin, Rex Lease, George Wallace, Ralph Peters, Dick Reeves, Frank Richards; D: George Marshall; SP: Felix Jackson, Edmund H. North, D. D. Beauchamp.

William R. Burnett

James Updyke was W. R. Burnett's real name, and some of his works were listed under this. He was born in Springfield, Ohio, in 1899. After his formal education at Miami Military Institute (Germantown, Ohio) and Ohio State University he went to work as a statistician in 1921, after a few miscellaneous jobs, and remained in this field until 1927. During this period he began writing just to offset the boredom of his job. Leaving Ohio for Chicago in 1927, he worked temporarily as a hotel desk clerk. Through a gangster acquaintance he acquired an inside glimpse of the underworld. The outcome was the novel *Little Caesar*. Published in 1929, it was an immediate success and was chosen as a Literary Guild selection.

Randolph Scott, Glenn Ford, and Guinn (Big Boy) Williams, in *The Desperadoes* (Columbia, 1943).

Due to the popularity of this book Warner Brothers offered him $1,000 a week as a consultant and screenwriter, an offer he accepted. He remained in southern California the rest of his life, and at the height of the Depression was earning $3,500 a week, eventually working for all the major studios. In addition to the credited films that follow, he contributed much material to a number of films and television series that went uncredited.

From the 1930s through the 1950s Burnett continued to publish novels on various topics. *The Asphalt Jungle* and *High Sierra* were two of his most popular books and each was filmed several times. Four films have been based, however loosely, on the novel *Saint Johnson*. *Law and Order* was released in 1932 and a second version in 1940. A serial, *Wild West Days*, was also based on the book in 1937. A fourth version of the novel was a 1953 release.

Burnett received the O. Henry Memorial Award for best short story of 1930, "Dressing up"; Academy Award nominations for *High Sierra* and *Wake Island*; and the Writers Guild of America Award for best screen play of 1963, *The Great Escape*.

Burnett died in 1982, after a prolific writing career of more than 50 years in which he published 36 novels and accumulated more than 60 screen credits.

Films Based on William Burnett's Writings

Little Caesar (Warner Brothers, 1930) 77 mins.; Edward G. Robinson, Douglas Fairbanks, Jr., Glenda Farrell, William Collier, Jr., Ralph Ince, George E. Stone, Thomas Jackson, Stanley Fields, Sidney Blackmer; D: Mervyn LeRoy; SP: Francis Faragoh, Robert E. Lee.

The Iron Man (Universal, 1931) 73 mins.; Lew Ayres, Jean Harlow, Robert Armstrong, John Miljan, Eddie Dillon, Ned Sparks; D: Tod Browning; SP: Francis Faragoh.

Beasts of the City (MGM, 1932) 86 mins.; Walter Huston, Jean Harlow, Wallace Ford, Jean Hersholt, Dorothy Peterson, Tully Marshall, John Miljan; D: Charles Brabin; SP: John Lee Mahin.

Law and Order (Universal, 1932) 80 mins.; Walter Huston, Harry Carey, Raymond Hatton, Russell Hopton, Ralph Ince, Russell Simpson, Harry Woods, Dick Alexander, Andy Devine, Alphonz Eithier, Dewey Robinson, Walter Brennan, Nelson McDowell, D'Arcy Corrigan, George Dixon, Arthur Wanzer, Neal Hart, Richard Cramer, Art Mix, Hank Bell; D: Edward Cahn; SP: John Huston, Tom Reed; S: *Saint Johnson.*

Dark Hazard (Warner Brothers, 1934) 72 mins.; Edward G. Robinson, Glenda Farrell, Robert Barrat, Hobart Cavanaugh; D: Alfred E. Green; SP: Ralph Block, Brown Holmes.

Doctor Socrates (Warner Brothers, 1935) 70 min.; Paul Muni, Ann Dvorak, Barton MacLane, Robert Barrat, John Eldridge, Hobart Cavanaugh, Mayo Methot, Samuel S. Hinds, Henry O'Neill; D: William Dieterle; SP: Robert Lord.

The Whole Town's Talking (Columbia, 1936) 88 mins.; Jean Arthur, Edward G. Robinson, Arthur Hohl,

Wallace Ford, Anthony Bryan, Donald Meek, Edward Brophy, Etienne Girardot; D: John Ford; SP: Jo Severling, Robert Riskin.

Wild West Days (Universal, 1937) 13 chapters; Johnny Mack Brown, Lynn Gilbert, Russell Simpson, Frank Yaconelli, George Shelly, Bob Kortman, Walter Miller, Francis McDonald, Frank McGlynn, Jr., Charles Stevens, Al Bridge, Edward J. LeSaint, Bruce Mitchell, Frank Ellis, Chief Thunderbird, Bud Osborne, Jack Clifford, Hank Bell, Lafe McKee, Joe Girard, William Royle, Mike Morita, Robert McClung, Sidney Bracey, Iron Eyes Cody, Chief Thunder Cloud; D: Ford Beebe, Cliff Smith; SP: Wyndham Gittens, Norman S. Hall, Ray Trampe; S: *Saint Johnson.*

King of the Underworld (Warner Brothers, 1938) 69 mins.; Kay Francis, Humphrey Bogart, James Stephenson, John Eldridge; D: Lewis Seiler; SP: George Bricker, Vincent Sherman; S: *Dr. Socrates.*

Law and Order (Universal, 1940) 57 mins.; Johnny Mack Brown, Fuzzy Knight, Nell O'Day, James Craig, Harry Cording, Ethan Laidlaw, Ted Adams, Harry Humphrey, Jimmy Dodd, William Worthington, George Plues, Earle Hodgins, Robert Fiske, Kermit Maynard, Frank McCarroll, Bob Kortman, Frank Ellis, Jim Corey, Lew Meehan, Charles King, The Notables Quartet, Jack Shannon, Scoop Martin, Cliff Parkinson, Bob Reeves, Victor Cox, Al Taylor, Roy Bucko, Herman Hack, Eddie Polo, Wong Chung, Bill Nestell, Cliff Lyons; D: Ray Taylor; SP: Sherman Lowe; S: *Saint Johnson.*

Dark Command (Republic, 1940) 94 mins.; John Wayne, Claire Trevor, Walter Pidgeon, George (Gabby) Hayes, Roy Rogers, Marjorie Main, Porter Hall, Raymond Walburn, Joe Sawyer, Helen MacKellar, J. Farrell MacDonald,

Trevor Bardette, Tom London, Dick Alexander, Yakima Canutt, Hal Taliaferro, Edmund Cobb, Edward Hearn, Ernie Adams, Jack Rockwell, Al Bridge, Glenn Strange, Harry Woods, Harry Cording, Frank Hagney, Dick Rich, John Dilson, Clinton Rosemond, Budd Buster, Howard Hickman, John Merton, Al Taylor, Mildred Gover, Jack Low, Hank Bell, Tex Cooper, Al Haskell, Tom Smith, Bob Woodward, Ferris Taylor, Edward Earle, Joe McCuinn, Harry Strang, Jack Montgomery; D: Raoul Walsh; SP: F. Hugh Herbert, Grover Jones, Lionel Houser.

High Sierra (Warner Brothers, 1941) 96 mins.; Humphrey Bogart, Ida Lupino, Joan Leslie, Alan Curtis, Arthur Kennedy, Henry Hull, Henry Travers, Jerome Cowan; D: Raoul Walsh; SP: John Huston, W. R. Burnett.

Wake Island (Paramount, 1942) 87 mins.; Brian Donlevy, MacDonald Carey, Robert Preston, William Bendix, Albert Dekker, Walter Abel, Mikhail Rasummy, Rod Cameron, Barbara Britton, Bill Goodwin, Richard Loo, Frank Faylen, Angel Cruz, Patti McCarty, Charles Trowbridge, Hugh Beaumont, James Brown, Mary Field, Willard Robertson, Hillary Brooke, Phillip Terry; D: John Farrow; SP: W. R. Burnett, Frank Butler.

Bullet Scars (Warner Brothers, 1942) 59 min.; Regis Toomey, Adele Longmire, Howard De Silva, John Ridgley; D: Ross Lederman; SP: Robert E. Kent; S: *Dr. Socrates.*

Crash Dive (20th Century–Fox, 1943) 105 mins.; Tyrone Power, Anne Baxter, Dana Andrews, James Gleason, Dame May Whitey, Henry (Harry) Morgan, Frank Conroy, Minor Watson; D: Archie Mayo; SP: Jo Swerling.

San Antonio (Warner Brothers, 1945) 111 mins.; Errol Flynn, Alexis Smith, S. Z. Sakall, Victor Francen, Florence Bates, John Litel, Paul Kelly, Robert Shayne, John Alvin, Monte Blue,

Robert Barrat, Pedro De Cordoba, Tom Tyler, Chris-Pin Martin, Charles Stevens, Poodles Hanneford, Doodles Weaver, Dan White, Ray Spikes, Hap Winters, Harry Cording, Chalky Williams, Wallis Clark, Bill Steele, Allen Smith, Howard Hill, Arnold Kent, Wally Wales (Hal Taliaferro), Lane Chandler, James Flavin, Eddy Waller; D: David Butler; SP: Alan Lemay, W. R. Burnett; P: Robert Buckner.

Nobody Lives Forever (Warner Brothers, 1946) 106 mins.; John Garfield, Geraldine Fitzgerald, Walter Brennan, Faye Emerson, George Coulouris, George Tobias; D: Jean Negulesco.

Belle Starr's Daughter (20th Century–Fox, 1947) 85 mins.; George Montgomery, Rod Cameron, Ruth Roman, Wallace Ford, Charles Kemper, William Phipps, Edith King, Chris-Pin Martin, Jack Lambert, Fred Libby, J. Farrell MacDonald, Charles Jewell, Larry Johns; D: Lesley Selander; SP/S: W. R. Burnett; P: Edward L. Aperson.

Yellow Sky (20th Century–Fox, 1948) 98 mins.; Gregory Peck, Anne Baxter, Richard Widmark, Robert Arthur, John Russell, Henry (Harry) Morgan, James Barton, Charles Kemper, Robert Adler, Harry Carter, Victor Kilian, Paul Hurst, Hank Worden, Jay Silverheels, William Gould, Norman Leavitt, Chief Yowlachie, Eula Guy; D: William A. Wellman; SP/P: Lamar Trotti.

Colorado Territory (Warner Brothers, 1949) 94 mins.; Joel McCrea, Virginia Mayo, Dorothy Malone, Henry Hull, John Hull, John Archer, James Mitchell, Morris Ankrum, Basil Ruysdael, Frank Puglia, Ian Wolfe, Harry Woods, Houseley Stevenson, Victor Kilian, Oliver Blake, Monte Blue, Jack Montgomery, Artie Ortego, Charles Horvath, Hallene Hill, Irene Elinor, Jack Daly, Fred Kelsey, Maudie Prickett; D: Raoul Walsh; SP: John Twist, Edmund H. North; S: Adapted from *High Sierra.*

Dance Hall (Warner Brothers, 1950) 80 mins.; Natasha Parry, Donald Houston, Diana Dors, Bonar Colleano, Jane Hylton, Petula Clark, Gladys Henson, Sydney Tafler; D: Charles Crichton; SP: E. V. H. Emmett, Diana Morgan, Alexander Mackendrick; S: Based on *The Giant Swing*.

The Iron Man (Universal, 1951) 81 mins.; Jeff Chandler, Evelyn Keyes, Stephen McNally, Joyce Holden, Rock Hudson, Jim Backus, James Arness; D: Joseph Pevney; SP: George Zuckerman, Borden Chase. Note. Remake of 1931 movie.

Law and Order (Universal, 1953) 80 mins.; Ronald Reagan, Dorothy Malone, Preston Foster, Alex Nichol, Ruth Hampton, Dennis Weaver, Chubby Johnson, Barry Kelly, Buddy Roosevelt, Tris Coffin, Tom Brown, Russell Johnson, Don Garner, Jack Kelly, Richard Garrick, Don Gordon, Valerie Jackson, Gregg Barton, William O'Neal, Wally Cassell; D: Nathan Juran; SP: John and Gwen Bagni, D. D. Beauchamp; S: *Saint Johnson*.

Arrowhead (Paramount, 1953) 105 mins.; Charlton Heston, Jack Palance, Katy Jurado, Brian Keith, Mary Sinclair, Milburn Stone, Richard Shannon, Lewis Martin, Frank de Kava, Robert Wilke, Peter Coe, Kyle James, John Pickard, Pat Hogan, Chick Hannon, Mike Ragan, Judith Ames, Richard Paxton, Frank Cordell, James Burke; D/SP: Charles Marquis Warren; P: Nat Holt.

I Died a Thousand Times (Warner Brothers, 1955) 109 mins.; Jack Palance, Shelley Winters, Lori Nelson, Lon Chaney, Jr., Lee Marvin, Earl Holliman, Perry Lopez, Gonzales Gonzales; D: Stuart Heisler; S: *High Sierra*.

Captain Lightfoot (Universal-International, 1955) 92 mins.; Rock Hudson, Barbara Rush, Jeff Morrow, Kathleen Ryan, Finlay Currie, Denis O'Dea, Geoffrey Toone; D: Douglas Sirk; SP: W. R. Burnett, Oscar Brodney.

Accused of Murder (Republic, 1956) 76 mins.; Vera Ralston, David Brian, Sidney Blackmer, Virginia Grey, Warren Stevens, Lee Van Cleef; D: Joseph Kane; SP: W. R. Burnett, Bob Williams; S: *Vanity Row*.

The Asphalt Jungle (MGM, 1956) 112 mins.; Sterling Hayden, Louis Calhern, Sam Jaffe, Jean Hagen, James Whitmore, John McIntire, Marc Lawrence, Marilyn Monroe, Barry Kelley; D: John Huston; SP: Ben Maddow, John Huston.

Short Cut to Hell (Paramount, 1957) 89 mins.; Robert Ivers, Georgeanne Johnson, William Bishop, Murvyn Vye; D: James Cagney; SP: Ted Berkeman, Ralph Blau, W. R. Burnett; S: Graham Greene.

The Badlanders (MGM, 1958) 85 mins.; Alan Ladd, Ernest Borgnine, Katy Jurado, Claire Kelly, Kent Smith, Nehemiah Persoff, Anthony Caruso, Robert Emhardt, Adam Williams, Ford Rainey, John Day, Gregg Barton, Richard Devon, Henry Wills; D: Delmer Daves; SP: Richard Collins; S: *The Asphalt Jungle*.

September Storm (20th Century–Fox, 1960) 110 mins.; Joanne Dru, Mark Stevens, Robert Strauss; D: Byron Haskin; SP: W. R. Burnett; S: Steve Fisher.

Sergeants 3 (United Artists, 1962) 112 mins.; Frank Sinatra, Dean Martin, Sammy Davis, Jr., Peter Lawford, Joey Bishop, Henry Silva, Ruta Lee, Buddy Lester, Philip Crosby, Dennis Crosby, Lindsay Crosby, Hank Henry, Richard Simmons, Michael Pate, Armand Alzamora, Richard Hale, Mickey Finn, Sonny King, Eddie Little Sky, Rodd Redwing, James Waters, Madge Blake, Dorothy Abbott, Walter Merrill; D: John Sturges; SP: W. R. Burnett; P: Howard W. Koch.

The Great Escape (United Artists, 1963) 173 mins.; James Garner, Steve McQueen, Richard Attenborough,

James Donald, Charles Bronson, Donald Pleasence, James Coburn, David McCollum, Gordon Jackson, John Leyton, Nigel Stork; D: John Sturges; SP: James Clavell, W. R. Burnett; S: Paul Brickhill.

Cairo (MGM, 1963) 91 mins.; George Sanders, Richard Johnson, Faten Hamama, John Meillon, Eric Pohlmann, Walter Rilla; D: Wolf Rilla; SP: Joanne Court; S: *The Asphalt Jungle.*

Illegal (Warner Brothers, 1966) 88 mins.; Edward G. Robinson, Nina Foch, Albert Dekker, Hugh Marlowe, Jayne Mansfield, Howard St. John, Ellen Corby; D: Lewis Allen; SP: W. R. Burnett, James R. Webb; S: Frank J. Collins.

Thunderbolt and Lightfoot (United Artists, 1974) 105 mins.; Clint Eastwood, Jeff Bridges, George Kennedy, Geoffrey Lewis, Catherine Bach; D/SP: Michael Cimino; S: *Captain Lightfoot.*

Borden Chase

Borden Chase wrote "The Chisholm Trail" from which the classic western *Red River* was adapted. He also wrote *The Far Country, Lone Star, Vera Cruz,* and *The Man from Colorado,* all superior westerns. He is equally well known for his screenplays, a good example of which is *Bend of the River.* The screenplay was crafted by Chase to either avoid or freshen the standard ingredients that go with most outdoor dramas. Veering away from the formula kept interest high. In other films he also wrote in such a way as to avoid similar formula situations.

Chase's real name was Frank Fowler, and he was born January 11, 1900, in Brooklyn, New York — hardly an acceptable birthplace for a future western author. In addition to five novels, he wrote or cowrote more than 25 screenplays. Chase had at one time worked as a sandhog in the New York City subways. His first writings were based on his experiences in the tunnels. In 1944 he moved to Hollywood to write screenplays on a full-time basis and to write novels on the side. *Red River* was based on a serial he had written for the *Saturday Evening Post* and this established him as a major motion picture writer. He received an Academy Award nomination for his work on this film. Borden Chase died March 8, 1971.

Films Based on Borden Chase's Writings

The Fighting Seabees (Republic, 1944) 100 mins.; John Wayne, Susan Hayward, Dennis O'Keefe, William Frawley, Addison Richards, Leonid Kinskey, Paul Fix, J. M. Kerrigan, Ben Welden, Grant Withers, Duncan Renaldo; D: Howard Lydecker, Edward Ludwig; SP: Borden Chase, Aeneas MacKenzie; S: Borden Chase; AP: Albert J. Cohen.

Flame of Barbary Coast (Republic, 1945) 91 mins.; John Wayne, Ann Dvorak, Joseph Schildkraut, William Frawley, Virginia Grey, Russell Hicks, Jack Norton, Paul Fix, Manart Kippen, Eve Lynne, Marc Lawrence, Butterfly McQueen, Rex Lease, Jack Mulhall, Hank Bell, Al Murphy, Emmett Vogan, Hugh Prosser, Eddie Parker, Jack O'Shea, Frank Jacquet, Eddie Acuff,

Stuart Hamblen, Frank Hagney, Adele Mara, Tom London, Charlie Sullivan, Bud Geary, Bill Wolfe; D/AP: Joseph Kane; SP: Borden Chase.

Red River (United Artists, 1948) 125 mins.; John Wayne, Montgomery Clift, Joanne Dru, Walter Brennan, Coleen Gray, John Ireland, Noah Beery, Jr., Harry Carey, Jr., Chief Yowlachie, Paul Fix, Hank Worden, Hal Taliaferro, Glenn Strange, Tom Tyler, Lane Chandler, Shelley Winters, Billy Self, Paul Fiero, Ivan Parry, Mickey Kuhn, George Lloyd, Pierce Lyden, John Merton; D: Howard Hawks; SP: Borden Chase, Charles Schnee; S: *The Chisholm Trail.*

Man from Colorado (Columbia 1948) 99 mins.; Glenn Ford, William Holden, Ellen Drew, Ray Collins, Edgar Buchanan, Jerome Courtland, James Millican, Jim Bannon, Bill Phillips, Denver Pyle, James Bush, Mikel Conrad, David Clarke, Ian MacDonald, Clarence Chase, Stanley Andrews, Myron Healey, Craig Reynolds, David York, Ray Teal, Fred Coby, Ben Corbett, Ray Hyke, Walter Baldwin, Symona Boniface, Pat O'Malley, Fred Graff, Eddie Fetherstone, Fred Sears; D: Henry Levin; SP: Robert D. Andrews, Ben Maddow.

Montana (Warner Brothers, 1950) 76 mins.; Errol Flynn, Alexis Smith, S. Z. Sakall, Douglas Kennedy, Ian MacDonald, James Brown, Charles Irwin, Paul E. Burns, Tudor Owen, Lester Matthews, Nacho Galindo, Lane Chandler, Monte Blue, Billy Vincent, Warren Jackson, Jack Perrin; D: Ray Enright; SP: James R. Webb, Borden Chase, Charles O'Neal; S: Ernest Haycox.

Winchester 73 (Universal, 1950) 92 mins.; James Stewart, Shelley Winters, Dan Duryea, Stephen McNally, Millard Mitchell, Charles Drake, John McIntyre, Will Geer, Jay C. Flippen, Rock Hudson, John Alexander, Steve Brodie, James Millican, Abner Biberman, Tony Curtis, James Best, Ray Teal, Guy Wilkerson, Chief Yowlatchie, Gregg Martell,

Frank Chase, Chuck Roberson, Carol Henry, Virginia Mullens, Edmund Cobb, Forrest Taylor, Ethan Laidlaw, Bud Osborne, John War Eagle, Bonnie Kay Eddy, Jennings Miles, John Doucette, Steve Darrell, Frank Conlon, Ray Bennett, Bob Anderson, Larry Olsen; D: Anthony Mann; SP: Robert L. Richards, Borden Chase.

Lone Star (MGM, 1952) 94 mins.; Clark Gable, Ava Gardner, Broderick Crawford, Lionel Barrymore, Beulah Bondi, Ed Begley, James Burke, William Farnum, Lowell Gilmore, Lucius Cook, Ralph Reed, Rick Roman, Victor Sutherland, Jonathan Cott, Charles Kane, Nacho Galindo, Trevor Bardette, Harry Woods, Dudley Sadler, Emmett Lynn, Earle Hodgins; D: Vincent Sherman; SP/S: Borden Chase.

Bend of the River (Universal, 1952) 91 mins.; James Stewart, Arthur Kennedy, Julia Adams, Rock Hudson, Jay C. Flippen, Stepin Fetchit, Lori Nelson, Henry (Harry) Morgan, Chubby Johnson, Howard Petrie, Frances Bavier, Jack Lambert, Royal Dano, Cliff Lyons, Frank Ferguson, Jennings Miles, Frank Chase, Lillian Randolph, Britt Wood, Gregg Barton, Hugh Prosser, Donald Kerr, Henry Arnie; D: Anthony Mann; SP: Borden Chase; S: Bill Bulick.

Sea Devils (RKO-Radio, 1953) 90 mins.; Yvonne De Carlo, Rock Hudson, Maxwell Reed, Denis O'Dean, Michael Goodliffe, Bryan Forbes, Jacques Brunius, Ivor Barnard, Arthur Wontner, Gerard Oury; D: Raoul Walsh; SP/S: Borden Chase; P: David E. Rose.

Vera Cruz (United Artists, 1954) 94 mins.; Gary Cooper, Burt Lancaster, Denise Darcel, Cesar Romero, Sarita Monteil, George Macready, Ernest Borgnine, Morris Andrum, James McCallion, Jack Lambert, Henry Brandon, Charles Buchinsky (Bronson), Jack Elam, James Seay, Archie Savage, Charles Horvath, Juan Garcia; D: Robert Aldrich; SP: Roland Kibbee, James R. Webb.

Man Without a Star (Universal, 1955) 89 mins.; Kirk Douglas, Jeanne Craine, Claire Trevor, William Campbell, Jay C. Flippen, Myrna Hansen, Mara Corday, Eddy C. Waller, Richard Boone, Frank Chase, Roy Barcroft, Millicent Patrick, Casey MacGregor, Jack Ingram, Ewing Mitchell, George Wallace, William Challee, Sheb Wooley, William Phipps, James Hayward, Malcolm Atterbury, Paul Birch, Myron Healey, Mark Hanna, Lee Roberts, Jack Elam; D: King Vidor; SP: Borden Chase, D. D. Beauchamp; S: Dee Linford; P: Aaron Rosenberg.

The Far Country (Universal, 1955) 97 mins.; James Stewart, Ruth Roman, Corinne Calvet, Walter Brennan, John McIntire, Jay C. Flippen, Henry (Harry) Morgan, Steve Brodie, Royal Dano, Gregg Barton, Chubby Johnson, Robert Foulk, Eugene Borden, Allan Ray, Connie Gilchrist, Damian O'Flynn, Kathleen Freeman, Bob Wilke, Jack Elam, Guy Wilkerson, Stuart Randall, Chuck Roberson, Gene Holland, Don Harvey, Carl Harbaugh, Jack Dixon, Dick Taylor, John Doucette, Terry Frost, Marjorie Stapp, Eddie Parker, Ted Mapes; D: Anthony Mann; SP/S: Borden Chase.

Backlash (Universal, 1956) 84 mins.; Richard Widmark, Donna Reed, William Campbell, John McIntire, Barton MacLane, Edward C. Platt, Harry Morgan, Bob Wilke, Reg Parton, Robert Foulk, Roy Roberts, Jack Lambert, Glenn Strange, Rex Lease, Phil Chambers, Gregg Barton, Fred Graham, Frank Chase, Lee Roberts, I. Stanford Jolley, Kermit Maynard; D: John Sturges; SP: Borden Chase.

Night Passage (Universal, 1957) 90 mins.; James Stewart, Audie Murphy, Dan Duryea, Dianne Foster, Elaine Stewart, Brandon de Wilde, Jay C. Flippen, Herbert Anderson, Robert J. Wilke, Hugh Beaumont, Boyd Stockman, Olive Carey, Harold Hart, Polly Burson, Patsy Novak, Jack Elam, Tommy Cook, Ellen Corby, Harold

Goodwin, Chuck Roberson, Ted Mapes, Donald Curtis, Paul Fix, Kenne Duncan, Jack Lowell, John Davis, Paul Spahn, Herman Pulver; D: James Neilson; SP: Borden Chase.

Ride a Crooked Trail (Universal, 1958) 87 mins.; Audie Murphy, Gia Scala, Walter Matthau, Henry Silva, Bill Walker, Ned Weaver, Richard Cutting, Morgan Woodward, Henry Wills, Joanna Moore, Eddie Little, Mary Field, Leo Gordon, Mort Mills, Frank Chase, Rayford Barnes, Eddie Parker; D: Jesse Hibbs; SP: George Bruce.

Gunfighters of Casa Grande (MGM, 1965) 92 mins.; Alex Nicol, George Mistral, Dick Bentley, Steve Rowland, Phil Posner, Mercedes Alonso, Diana Lorys, Maria Granada, Roberto Rey, Aldo Sambrell, Antonio Fuentes, Emilio Rodriguez, Ana Maria Custodio, Angel Solano, Jose Manuel Martin, Jim Gillen, Simon Arriaga, Maria Jose Collado; D: Roy Rowland; SP: Borden Chase, Clarke Reynolds, Patricia Chase; S: Borden Chase, Patricia Chase.

Backtrack (MCA-TV/Universal, 1969) 95 mins.; Neville Brand, James Drury, Doug McClure, Peter Brown, William Smith, Philip Carey, Ida Lupino, Rhonda Fleming, Fernando Lamas, Royal Dano, Gary Clarke, Randy Boone, L. Q. Jones, Carol Byron, Ross Elliott, Priscilla Garcia, Ruben Moreno; D: Earl Bellamy; SP: Borden Chase; P: David J. O'Connell.

Red River (Catalina Prod./MGM-UA TV, April 10, 1988) 2 hrs.; James Arness, Bruce Boxleitner, Gregory Harrison, Ray Walston, Stan Shaw, Laura Johnson, Zachary Ansley, Ty Hardin, Robert Horton, John Lupton, Guy Madison, L. Q. Jones, Burton Gilliam, Jerry Potter, Johnmark Bradley, Donnie Jeffcoat, James Oscar Lee, Bud Stout, Travis Swords, Bob Terhune, Temple Williams; D: Richard Michaels; TP: Richard Fielder; S: Borden Chase and the 1948 screenplay by Chase and Charles Schnee.

Walt Coburn

Walt Coburn, a true westerner, was born and raised in the cattle business. He was born October 13, 1889, in White Sulphur Springs, Montana. World War I interrupted his life as a cowboy; he served in the U.S. Army Air Service, Signal Corps, 1917–19, attaining the rank of sergeant first class. His writing career began in 1922, but for two years all he got was rejection slips. Finally, his luck changed. He sold nearly 900 novelettes in the years 1924–50 to 37 different magazines and had the feature story and cover in each magazine over a number of years. By 1950 most of these pulps had ceased to exist, so he concentrated on writing novels. Six of his stories have been made into movies, but as was true with other popular writers, his name would sometimes be used as the story writer when he had nothing to do with the films.

He was once quoted as saying "I have never read another western writer's books in my lifetime of writing," also saying that he did not do research, since he knew the cow country and time about which he wrote.

The following is a list of his principal works: *The Ringtailed Rannyhans*, 1927; *Mavericks*, 1929; *Barb Wire*, 1931; *Walt Coburn's Action Novels*, 1931; *Law Rides the Range*, 1935; *Pardners of the Dim Trails*, 1951; *The Way of a Texan*, 1953; *Drift Fence*, 1953; *The Burnt Ranch*, 1954; *Gun Grudge*, 1955; *Wet Cattle*, 1955; *The Square Shooter*, 1955; *Cayuse*, 1956; *Border Jumper*, 1956; *Beyond the Wild Missouri*, 1956; *One Step Ahead of the Posse*, 1956; *The Night Branders*, 1956; *Violent Maverick*, 1957; *Stirrup High*, 1957; *Fear Branded*, 1957; *Buffalo Run*, 1958; *Free Rangers*, 1959; *Invitation to a Hanging*, 1959; *La Jornada*, 1960; *Feud Valley*, 1960; *Guns Blaze on Spiderweb Range*, 1961; and *Pioneer Cattleman: The Story of the Circle C Ranch*, 1968.

Two pulp magazines were at one time published as *Walt Coburn's Action Novels* and *Walt Coburn's Western Magazine*.

Films Based on Walt Coburn's Writings

Fighting Fury (Universal, 1924) 5 reels; Jack Hoxie, Helen Holmes, Fred Kohler, Duke R. Lee, Bert DeMarc, Al Jennings, George (Buck) Connors, Pat Harmon, Scout (a horse); D: Cliff Smith; SP: Isadore Bernstein; S: *Triple Cross for Danger.*

The Fightin' Comeback (Action/Pathe, 1927) 5 reels; Buddy Roosevelt, Clara Horton, Sidney M. Goldin, Richard Neill, Robert Homans, Charles Thurston, Richard Alexander; D: Tenny Wright; S: *The Sun Dance Kid*; P: Lester F. Scott, Jr.

Between Dangers (Action/Pathe, 1927) 5 reels; Buddy Roosevelt, Alma Rayford, Rennie Young, Al Taylor, Charles Thurston, Allen Sewall, Edward W. Borman, Hank Bell; D/SP: Richard Thorpe; S: *Ride 'Em Cowboy*; P: Lester F. Scott, Jr.

Rusty Rides Alone (Columbia, 1933) 58 mins.; Tim McCoy, Barbara Weeks, Dorothy Burgess, Wheeler Oakman, Ed Burns, Rockcliffe Fellows, Edmund Cobb, Clarence Geldert, Wally Wales, Buffalo Bill, Jr. (Jay Wilsey), Silver King (a horse); D: D. Ross Lederman; SP: Robert Quigley.

The Westerner (Columbia, 1934) 58 mins.; Tim McCoy, Marion Shilling, Joseph Sauers (Joe Sawyer), Hooper Atchley, Edward J. LeSaint, Edmund Cobb, John Dilson, Bud Osborne, Albert Smith, Harry Todd, Slim Whitaker, Lafe McKee, Merrill McCormack, Steve Clark, Art Mix, Edmund Cobb, Hank Bell; D: David Sellman; SP: Harold Shumate.

The Return of Wild Bill (Columbia, 1940) 60 mins.; Bill Elliott, Iris Meredith, Dub Taylor, Luana Walters, George Lloyd, Edward J. LeSaint, Frank LaRue, Francis Walker, Chuck Morrison, Buel Bryant, William Kellogg, John Ince, Jack Rockwell, Jim Corey, John Merton, Donald Haines; D: Joseph H. Lewis; SP: Robert Lee Johnson, Fred Myton; P: Leon Barsha.

James Fenimore Cooper

Mention James Fenimore Cooper and *The Last of the Mohicans* comes to mind. The book is often required reading for students, and it can be found in most libraries. It has been filmed seven times: six times as *Last of the Mohicans* and once as *Last of the Redmen.* The 1920 version starring Wallace Beery and Barbara Bedford was probably the best, though many filmgoers would hold out for the 1936 version starring Randolph Scott.

Cooper was born in Burlington, New Jersey, on September 14, 1789, as the eleventh child of Judge William Cooper and Elizabeth Fenimore Cooper. The family moved into the wilderness area around Lake Otsego, New York, and James grew up there, learning much about wilderness and the many Indians who were in that region.

In 1802 he became a student at Yale but was expelled after two years for misconduct. He returned home to Cooperstown (the town his father had founded) for a period and then signed on as a seaman on a sailing ship bound for England. A year later, on his return to America, he was given a commission in the navy. A few years later his father died leaving the estate to his children, but Cooper and his brothers soon spent all the money that could be raised from their inheritance. On January 1, 1811, he married Susan De Lancey, who was responsible for him leaving the navy and settling down on a farm near Scarsdale, New York.

In 1819, on a dare, he penned his first book, *Precaution,* even though he hated writing. The experience changed his perspective and provided the impetus to try a second novel, which was published as *The Spy.* Now considering himself an author, he began to write seriously. He spent seven years in France, an experience that gave him a different outlook on life, and he became a critic of his own country, although he would return home and settle around Cooperstown. At one time he was earning around $20,000 a year in royalties, an extremely large amount of money at that time. However, he was a poor manager and in his later years he was writing primarily to keep food on the table and creditors off his back. He died of sclerosis of the liver in 1851, just short of his sixty-second birthday.

The following is a list of his principal works: *Precaution*, 1820; *The Spy*, 1821; *The Pioneers*, 1823; *The Pilot*, 1823; *Lionel Lincoln*, 1825; *The Last of the Mohicans*, 1826; *The Prairie*, 1827; *The Red Rover*, 1827; *Notions of the Americans: Picked Up by a Traveling Bachelor*, 1828; *The Wept of Wish-ton-Wish*, 1829; *The Water Witch*, 1830; *The Bravo*, 1831; *The Heidenmauer*, 1832; *The Headsman*, 1833; *A Letter to His Countrymen*, 1834; *The Monikins*, 1835; *Sketches of Switzerland*, 1836; *Gleanings in Europe*, 1837–38; *The American Democrat*, 1838; *The Chronicles of Cooperstown*, 1838; *Homeward Bound*, 1838; *Home as Found*, 1838; *The History of the Navy of the United States of America*, 1839; *The Pathfinder*, 1840; *Mercedes of Castile*, 1840; *The Deerslayer*, 1841; *The Two Admirals*, 1842; *The Wing-and-Wing*, 1842; *Wyandotté*, 1843; *Ned Myers*, 1843; *Afloat and Ashore*, 1844; *Miles Wallingford*, 1844; *Satanstoe*, 1845; *The Chainbearer*, 1845; *Lives of Distinguished American Naval Officers*, 1846; *The Redskins*, 1846; *The Crater*, 1847; *Jack Tier*, 1848; *The Oak Openings*, 1848; *The Sea Lions*, 1849; and *The Ways of the Hour*, 1850.

Films Based on James Fenimore Cooper's Writings

Leather Stocking (Biograph, 1909) 1 reel; James Kirkwood, Linda Arvidson, Marion Leonard, Mack Sennett, Billy Quirk, Verner Clarges, Owen Moore, Adele DeGarde; D: D. W. Griffith; SP: Stanner E. V. Taylor.

Last of the Mohicans (Powers, 1911) 1 reel; Cast unknown.

Last of the Mohicans (Thanhouser, 1911) Frank Crane, William Russell, Alphonse Ethier; D/SP: Theodore Marston.

The Deerslayer (Vitagraph, 1913) 2 reels; Hal Reid, Wallace Reid, Florence Turner, Harry T. Morey, Walter Long, Ethel Dunn, Ed Thomas, Evelyn Dominicus, William F. Cooper; D: Hal Reid, Larry Trimble; SP: Eugene Mullin.

The Last of the Mohicans (Associated Producers, 1920) 6 reels; Wallace Beery, Barbara Bedford, Albert Roscoe, Lillian Hall, Henry Woodward, James Gordon, George Hackathorne, Nelson McDowell, Harry Lorraine, Theodore Lorch, Jack F. Mcdonald, Sydney

Deane, Joseph Singleton; D: Maurice Tourneur, Clarence L. Brown; SP: Robert A. Dillon.

The Last of the Mohicans (Mascot, 1932) 12 chapters; Harry Carey, Hobart Bosworth, Junior Coghlan, Edwina Booth, Lucile Browne, Walter Miller, Bob Kortman, Walter McGrail, Nelson McDowell, Edward Hearn, Mischa Auer, Yakima Canutt, Chief Big Tree, Joan Gale, Tully Marshall, Al Craven, Jewel Richford; D: B. Reeves Eason, Ford Beebe; SP: Colbert Clark, Jack Natteford, Ford Beebe, Wyndham Gittens; P: Nat Levine.

The Last of the Mohicans (United Artists, 1936) 91 mins.; Randolph Scott, Binnie Barnes, Henry Wilcoxon, Bruce Cabot, Heather Angel, Phillip Reed, Robert Barrat, Hugh Buckler, Willard Robertson, Frank McGlynn, Sr., Will Stanton, William V. Mong, Olaf H. Hare, Reginald Barlow, Lionel Belmore; D: George B. Seitz; SP: Philip Dunne.

The Pioneers (Monogram, 1941) 58 mins.; Tex Ritter, Red Foley and his

Saddle Pals, Arkansas Slim Andrews, Wanda McKay, Doye O'Dell, George Chesebro, Del Lawrence, Post Park, Karl Hackett, Lynton Brent, Chick Hannon, Gene Alsace, Jack C. Smith, Chief Many Treaties, Chief Soldani, Art Dillard; D: Al Herman; SP: Charles Alderson.

The Deerslayer (Republic, 1943) 67 mins.; Bruce Kellogg, Jean Parker, Larry Parks, Warren Ashe, Wanda McKay, Yvonne De Carlo, Addison Richards, Johnny Michaels, Phil Van Zandt, Clancy Cooper, Trevor Bardette, Robert Warwick, Chief Many Treaties, Princess Whynemah, William Edmunds; D: Lew Landers; SP: P. S. Harrison, E. B. Derr; P: E. B. Derr.

Last of the Redmen (Columbia, 1947) 77 mins.; Jon Hall, Michael O'Shea, Evelyn Ankers, Julie Bishop, Buster Crabbe, Rick Vallin, Buzz Henry, Guy Hedlund, Frederick Worlock, Emmett Vogan, Chief Many Treaties; D: George Sherman; SP: Herbert Dalmas, George H. Plympton; S: *The Last of the Mohicans*.

Last of the Mohicans (Schick Sunn, November 27, 1977) 90 mins.; Steve Forrest, Ned Romero, Andrew Prine, Don Shanks, Robert Turner, Jane Actman, Michele Marsh, Robert Eastman, Whit Bissell, Dehi Berti, John G. Bishop; D: James L. Conway; TP: Stephen Lord.

Last of the Mohicans (Fox, 1992) 122 mins.; Daniel Day-Lewis, Madeleine Stowe, Russell Means, Eric Schweig, Jodhi May, Steven Waddington, Wes Studi, Maurice Roëves, Patrice Chereau, Colm Meaney, Peter Postlethwaite; D: Michael Mann; SP: Michael Mann, Christopher Crowe.

John M. Cunningham

John M. Cunningham was a minor writer who produced three good stories brought to the screen as *High Noon*, *The Stranger Wore a Gun*, and *Day of the Badman*. All were great pictures, especially *High Noon*, in which Gary Cooper plays the marshal going up against superior forces as the townspeople duck their tails and hide.

Cunningham's novels include *The Rainbow*, *Starfall*, and *Warhorse*.

Films Based on John Cunningham's Writings

High Noon (United Artists, 1952) 85 mins.; Gary Cooper, Thomas Mitchell, Grace Kelly, Lloyd Bridges, Katy Jurado, Otto Kruger, Lon Chaney, Jr., Harry Morgan, Lee Van Cleef, Robert Wilke, Ralph Reed, Virginia Christine, Virginia Farmer, Tom London, Ted Stanhope, William Phillips, Jeanie Farmer, Ian MacDonald, Larry Blake, Harry Shannon, Cliff Clark, James Millican; D: Fred Zinnemann; SP: Carl Foreman; P: Stanley Kramer.

The Stranger Wore a Gun (Scott-Brown, 1953) 83 mins.; Randolph Scott, Claire Trevor, Joan Weldon, George McCready, Lee Marvin, Pierre Watkin, Roscoe Ates, Terry Frost, Joseph Vitale, Guy Wilkerson, Al Haskell, Yakima Canutt, Mary Newton, Mary Lou Holloway, Tap Canutt, Edward Earle, Ernest Borgnine, Harry Semour, Diana Dawson; D: Andre De Toth; SP: Kenneth Gamet; S: *Yankee Gold*; P: Harry Joe Brown, Randolph Scott.

Day of the Bad Man (Universal-International, 1958) 81 mins.; Fred MacMurray, Joan Weldon, John Ericson, Robert Middleton, Marie Windsor,

Edgar Buchanan, Eduard Franz, Ann
Doran, Peggy Converse, Skip Homeier,
Robert Foulk, Lee Van Cleef, Eddy

Waller, Don Haggerty, Chris Alcaide;
D: Harry Keller; SP: Lawrence Roman;
S: *Raiders Die Hard*; P: Gordon Kay.

Harry Sinclair Drago/Bliss Lomax (Will Ermine/J. Wesley Putnam)

Harry Sinclair Drago was a fine writer who wrote the stories for a number of B westerns that sent chills through young movie fans converging on
the Saturday matinees. There are few classics among his writings, but the stories brought to the screen by cowboy favorites provided an hour's great entertainment.

Drago was born March 20, 1888, in Toledo, Ohio. He was the author
of more than 100 novels, some under the pseudonyms Will Ermine, Bliss
Lomax, and J. Wesley Putnam. He began his writing career as a columnist
for the *Toledo Bee*, but left the journalism field after the publication of his first
novel, *Out of the Silent North*. After five years as a scriptwriter in Hollywood,
Drago moved to New York in 1933. He became a prolific writer in the following years, turning out 1,000 words a day, an average of three books a year,
and in one case wrote a 60,000-word novel, *Oh, Susannah*, in 11 days.

His fiction included *Whispering Sage, Buckskin Affair, Fenced Off*, and
Decision at Broken Butte. Among his histories of the old west are *Great American Cattle Trails, Road Agents and Train Robbers*, and *The Great Range Wars*,
for which he received the Western Heritage Award for the most outstanding
western nonfiction book of 1970.

Harry Sinclair Drago died on October 25, 1979, in White Plains, New
York.

Films Based on the Writings of Harry Sinclair Drago/ Bliss Lomax/J. Wesley Putnam

Whoso Findeth a Wife (U.S. Amuse-
ment Corporation, 1917) Note. Cast
information is unavailable. SP: Rudolph
de Cordova; S: J. Wesley Putnam (pseudonym of Harry Sinclair Drago); P:
Frank Crane.

Out of the Silent North (Universal,
1922) 5 reels; Frank Mayo, Barbara Bed-
ford, Frank Leigh, Harris Gordon,
Christian J. Frank, Louis Rivero, Dick
La Reno; D: William Worthington; SP:
Wallace Clifton, George Hull; S: Harry
Sinclair Drago, Joseph Noel.

Playthings of Desire (Jans Produc-
tions, 1924) 7 reels; Estelle Taylor,
Mahlon Hamilton, Dagmar Godowsky,
Mary Thurman, Lawrence Davidson,
Walter Miller, Edmund Breese, Bradley
Barker, Lee Beggs, Ida Pardee; D: Bur-
ton King; SP: William B. Laub; S: J.
Wesley Putnam (pseudonym of Harry
Sinclair Drago).

Whispering Sage (Fox, 1927) 5 reels;
Buck Jones, Natalie Joyce, Emile Chau-
tard, Carl Miller, Albert J. Smith,
Joseph Girard, William A. Steele, Ellen

Winston, Hazel Keener, Enrique Acosta, Joe Rickson; D: Scott R. Dunlap; SP: Harold Shumate; S: Harry Sinclair Drago, Joseph Noel.

Silver Valley (Fox, 1927) 5 reels; Tom Mix, Dorothy Dwan, Philo McCullough, Jocky Hoefli, Tom Kennedy, Lon Poff, Harry Dunkinson, Clark Comstock, Tony (a horse); D: Ben Stoloff; SP: Harold B. Lipsitz.

A Horseman of the Plains (Fox, 1928) 5 reels; Tom Mix, Sally Blane, Heinie Conklin, Charles Byer, Lew Harvey, Grace Marvin, William Ryno, Tony (a horse); D: Benjamin Stoloff; SP: Fred Kennedy Myton.

Hello Cheyenne (Fox, 1928) 5 reels; Tom Mix, Caryl Lincoln, Jack Baston, Martin Faust, Joseph Girard, Al St. John, William Caress, Tony (a horse); D: Eugene Forde; SP: Fred Kennedy Myton.

Painted Post (Fox, 1928) 5 reels; Tom Mix, Natalie Kingston, Philo McCullough, Al St. John, Fred Gamble, Tony (a horse); D: Eugene Forde; SP: Buckleigh F. Orford.

The Cowboy Kid (Fox, 1928) 5 reels; Rex Bell, Mary Jane Temple, Brooks Benedict, Alice Belcher, Joseph De Grasse, Syd Crossley, Billy Bletcher; D: Clyde Carruth; SP: James J. Tynan; S: Harry Sinclair Drago, Seton I. Miller.

The Overland Telegraph (MGM, 1929) 6 reels; Tim McCoy, Dorothy Janis, Frank Rice, Lawford Davidson, Clarence Geldert, Chief Big Tree; D: John Waters; SP: George C. Hull, Edward Meagher, Harry Sinclair Drago; S: Ward Wing.

Sioux Blood (MGM, 1929) 6 reels; Tim McCoy, Robert Frazer, Marion Douglas (Ena Gregory), Clarence Geldert, Chief Big Tree, Sidney Bracy; D: John Waters; SP: George C. Hull.

Where East Is East (MGM, 1929) 7 reels; Lon Chaney, Lupe Velez, Estelle Taylor, Lloyd Hughes, Louis Stern,

Mrs. Wong Wing; D: Tod Browning; SP: Richard Schayer; S: Tod Browning, Harry Sinclair Drago.

The Desert Rider (MGM, 1929) 6 reels; Tim McCoy, Raquel Torres, Bert Roach, Edward Connelly, Harry Woods, Jess Cavin; D: Nick Grinde; SP: Oliver Drake, Harry Sinclair Drago; S: Ted Shane.

King of the Kongo (Mascot, 1929) 10 chapters; Jacqueline Logan, Walter Miller, Richard Tucker, Larry Steers, Boris Karloff, Harry Todd, Richard Neill, Lafe McKee, J. P. Lockney, William Bert, Gordon Russell, Robert Frazer, Ruth Davis, Joe Bonomo; D: Richard Thorpe; SP: Harry Sinclair Drago.

Secret of the Wasteland (Paramount, 1941) 66 mins.; William Boyd, Andy Clyde, Brad King, Barbara Britton, Douglas Fowley, Keith Richards, Soo Yong, Richard Loo, Lee Tung Foo, Gordon Hart, Hal Price, Jack Rockwell, John Rawlings, Earl Guinn, Roland Got, Ian MacDonald; D: Derwin Abrahams; SP: Gerald Geraghty; S: Bliss Lomax (Harry Sinclair Drago).

Buckskin Frontier (United Artists, 1943) 74 mins.; Richard Dix, Jane Wyatt, Albert Dekker, Lee J. Cobb, Victor Jory, Lola Lane, Max Baer, Joe Sawyer, George Reeves, Henry Allen, Francis McDonald, Bill Nestell; D: Lesley Selander; SP: Norman Houston; P: Harry Sherman.

The Leatherburners (United Artists, 1943) 58 mins.; William Boyd, Andy Clyde, Jay Kirby, Victor Jory, George Reeves, Shelley Spencer, George Givot, Bobby Larson, Hal Taliaferro (Wally Wales), Forbes Murray, Robert Mitchum, Bob Kortman, Herman Hack, Merrill McCormick, Bob Burns, George Morrell, Roy Bucko; D: Joseph E. Henabery; SP: Jo Pagano; S: Bliss Lomax (Harry Sinclair Drago); P: Harry Sherman.

Colt Comrades (United Artists,

1943) 67 mins.; William Boyd, Andy Clyde, Jay Kirby, George Reeves, Gayle Lord, Earle Hodgins, Victor Jory, Douglas Fowley, Herbert Rawlinson, Robert Mitchum, Russell Simpson, Fred Kohler, Jr., William Gould, Art Dillard, Jack Shannon, Tex Cooper, Henry Wills, Jack Mulhall, Dewey Robinson, Blackjack Ward, Roy Bucko; D: Lesley Selander; SP: Michael Wilson; P: Harry Sherman.

Lauri York Erskine

Lauri York Erskine authored the "Renfrew of the Mounties" stories that Monogram brought to the screen in a series starring James Newill. His stories contained no complicated plots and appealed to younger readers. The films were standard B outdoor dramas.

Erskine is believed to have been born in 1894 in England of American parents. He served in both world wars and was cofounder of a prep school in New Hope, Pennsylvania, where he died on December 3, 1976.

Films Based on Lauri York Erskine's Writings

Fighting Mad (Monogram, 1939) 60 mins.; James Newill, Dave O'Brien, Sally Blane, Benny Rubin, Walter Long, Warner Richmond, Ted Adams, Chief Thunder Cloud, Ole Olson, Horace Murphy; D: Sam Newfield; S: *Renfred Rides Again*; P:Philip Krasne.

Crashing Thru (Monogram, 1939) 65 mins.; James Newill, Jean Carmen, Warren Hull, Iron Eyes Cody, Milburn Stone, Walter Byron, Stanley Blystone, Robert Frazer, Joseph Girard, Dave O'Brien, Earl Douglas, Ted Adams, Roy Barcroft; D: Elmer Clifton; SP: Sherman L. Lowe; P: Philip N. Krasne.

Yukon Flight (Monogram, 1940) 57 mins.; James Newill, Louise Stanley, Warren Hull, Dave O'Brien, William Pawley, Karl Hackett, Roy Barcroft, Jack Clifford, Bob Terry, Earl Douglas, Reed Howes, Forrest Taylor, Budd Buster, Wally West, Carl Mathews, Jack Ingram; D: Sam Newfield; SP: Joseph O'Donnell, Basil Dickey; S: *Renfrew Rides North*; P: Sam Katzman.

Murder on the Yukon (Monogram, 1940) 58 mins.; James Newill, Polly Ann Young, Dave O'Brien, Al St. John, William Royle, Chief Thunder Cloud, Budd Buster, Karl Hackett, Snub Pollard, Kenne Duncan, Earl Douglas, Jack Clifford; D: Louis Gasnier; SP: Milton Raison; S: *Renfrew Rides North*; P: Philip N. Krasne.

Danger Ahead (Monogram, 1940) 60 mins.; James Newill, Dorothea Kent, Dave O'Brien, Guy Usher, Maude Allen, Harry Depp, John Dilson, Al Shaw, Dick Rich, Bob Terry, Dave Sharpe, Earl Douglas, Lester Dorr; D: Ralph Staub; SP: Edward Halperin; S: *Renfrew's Long Trail*; P: Philip N. Krasne.

Sky Bandits (Monogram, 1940) 62 mins.; James Newill, Dave O'Brien, Louise Stanley, Ted Adams, William Pawley, Bob Terry, Joseph Stefani, Dwight Frye, Dewey Robinson, Jack Clifford, Kenne Duncan; D: Ralph Staub; SP: Edward Halperin; S: *Renfrew Rides the Sky*; P: Phil Goldstein.

Louise Stanley, Dave O'Brien, and James Newill in *Yukon Flight* (Monogram, 1939).

Hal G. Evarts

Hal G. Evarts was born in Topeka, Kansas, on August 24, 1887. Before finishing high school, he took a job surveying in Indian territory and fell in love with the West. In his earlier years he lived in Wyoming and other parts of the West as rancher, trapper, licensed guide, and raiser of fur-bearing animals. He was recognized as an authority on hunting and trapping, and he was the outdoor editor of the *Saturday Evening Post* for several years, contributing many articles on hunting.

In World War I he spent several months in the Officers Training Corps, receiving his commission as second lieutenant shortly before the armistice.

In his later years he suffered several heart attacks. To try to regain his health, he took a cruise bound for South America. He died from a heart attack as the steamship neared Rio de Janeiro on October 18, 1934, at the age of 57.

For the most part Evarts wrote romantic westerns adhering to the accepted formula. The thrust of his work was great, sweeping events. *Tumbleweeds* (1925) and *The Big Trail* (1930) are the best examples of this trait. *Tumbleweeds* deals with the Cherokee land rush in Oklahoma and its aftermath, whereas *The Big Trail* concerns a wagon train of Eastern pioneers who leave from Westport, Mississippi, to travel the Oregon Trail and to extend the boundaries of the American republic to the Pacific northwest.

Like James Oliver Curwood and Jack London, Evarts's thrillers found favor in France. Although a popular author in his own time, his books have not worn well with age, and most of his work is forgotten today.

The following are his principal works: *The Cross Pull*, 1920; *The Bald Face*, 1921; *The Passing of the Old West*, 1921; *The Yellow Horde*, 1921; *The Settling of the Sage*, 1922; *Fur Sign*, 1922; *Tumbleweeds*, 1923; *Spanish Acres*, 1925; *The Painted Stallion*, 1926; *The Moccasin Telegraph*, 1927; *Fur Brigade*, 1928; *Tomahawk Rights*, 1929; *The Shaggy Legion*, 1930; *Shortgrass*, 1932; and *Wolf Dog*, 1935.

Films Based on Hal Evarts's Writings

The Silent Call (Associated First National, 1921) 7 reels; Strongheart (dog), John Bowers, Kathryn McGuire, William Dyer, James Mason, Nelson McDowell, Edwin J. Brady, Robert Bolder; D: Lawrence Trimble; SP: Jane Murfin; S: *The Cross Pull*.

Tumbleweeds (United Artists, 1925) 89 mins.; William S. Hart, Barbara Bedford, Lucien Littlefield, Richard R. Neill, Jack Murphy, Lillian Leighton, Gertrude Claire, George Marion, James Gordon, Al Hoxie, Fred Gamble, T. E. Duncan, Turner Savage, Monte Collins; D: King Baggot; SP: C. Gardner Sullivan.

The Big Trail (Fox, 1930) 158 mins.; John Wayne, Marguerite Chur-chill, Ian Keith, Tyrone Power, Sr., Ward Bond, El Brendel, Tully Marshall, Charles Stevens, Andy Shuford, David Rollins, Jack Prabody, Russ Powell, Helen Parrish, Marjorie Leet, Louise Carver, Chief Big Tree, Pete Morrison, Iron Eyes Cody, Don Coleman, Alphonz Ethier, Lucille Van Lent, Gertrude Van Lent; D: Raoul Walsh; SP: Marie Boyle, Jack Peabody, Florence Postal.

The Santa Fe Trail (Paramount, 1930) 6 reels; Richard Arlen, Rosita Moreno, Eugene Pallette, Mitzi Green, James Durkin, Hooper Atchley, Luis Alberni, Lee Shumway, Chief Yow-latchi, Blue Cloud, Chief Standing Bear, Jack Byron; D: Edwin Knopf, Otto Brower; SP: Sam Mintz; S: *Spanish Acres*.

Edna Ferber

Edna Ferber was a novelist, short story writer, and playwright, born on August 15, 1887, in Kalamazoo, Michigan. At age 17 she was a full-time reporter for the *Appleton Daily Crescent*, later working for the *Milwaukee Journal* as a writer and reporter. She is said to have written 1,000 words a day, 350 days a year. *Cimarron* was the first of her two western books, and the movie version in 1931 was an example of super filmmaking and a big money-maker. Likewise, the 1960 remake was a winner for MGM.

Giant was a powerful Texas saga of cattle, oil, and race bias. The film registered strongly on all levels. Many elements were fused to make *Giant* work. Producers George Stevens and Henry Ginsberg spent freely to capture the mood of the Ferber novel, and the picture is saturated with the feeling of the vastness, the mental narrowness, the wealth, the poverty, the pride, and the prejudice that make up the Texas of today.

Ferber wrote her first novel, *Dawn O'Hara* during a long illness. She earned sudden success and popularity with her stories of Emma McChesney, a traveling saleswoman.

She won the Pulitzer Prize for *So Big*, considered by many to be her best novel. In the book Selina Peake, the daughter of a gambler, is forced to make her own way in the world after her father is accidentally killed. She moves to a farming community and eventually marries, but on the death of her husband she is left to raise their son Dirk, a rebellious youth, alone.

Cimarron is Ferber's most feminist novel. In the story Sabra's husband, Yancy, is a dreamer, while Sabra is the practical one who gets things done. She becomes Oklahoma's first U.S. congresswoman.

Ferber's work deserves serious consideration for her treatment of the land, her feminism, and her egalitarianism, although her work never appreciably evolved in terms of style, content, or structure. She died in New York City on April 16, 1968.

The following is a list of her principal works: *Dawn O'Hara: The Girl Who Laughed*, 1911; *Buttered Side Down*, 1912; *Roast Beef, Medium: The Business Adventures of Emma McChesney*, 1913; *Personality Plus: Some Experiences of Emma McChesney and Her Son, Jack*, 1914; *Emma McChesney and Company*, 1915; *Fanny Herself*, 1917; *Cheerful by Request*, 1918; *Half Portions*, 1920; *$12 a Year*, 1920; *The Girls*, 1921; *Gigolo*, 1922; *So Big*, 1924; *Eldest*, 1925; *Minick* (with G. S. Kaufmann), 1925; *Show Boat*, 1926; *Mother Knows Best: A Fiction Book*, 1927; *Royal Family* (with G. S. Kaufmann), 1928; *Cimarron*, 1929; *American Beauty*, 1931; *Dinner at Eight* (with G. S. Kaufmann), 1931; *They Brought Their Women: A Book of Short Stories*, 1933; *Come and Get It*, 1935; *Stage Door* (with G. S. Kaufmann), 1936; *Nobody's in Town*, 1938; *A Peculiar Treasure*, 1939; *The Land Is Bright* (with G. S. Kaufmann), 1941; *Saratoga Trunk*, 1941; *Great Son*, 1945; *One Basket: Thirty-One Short Stories*, 1947; *Bravo!* (with G. S. Kaufmann), 1949; *Giant*, 1952; *Ice Palace*, 1958; and *A Kind of Magic*, 1963.

Films Based on Edna Ferber's Writings

So Big (First National, 1924) 9 reels; Colleen Moore, Joseph De Grasse, John Bowers, Ben Lyon, Wallace Beery, Gladys Brockwell, Jean Hersholt, Charlotte Merriam, Ford Sterling, Frankie Darrow, Phyllis Haver, Henry Herbert; D: Charles Brabin; SP: Adelaide Heilbron.

Classified (First National, 1925) 7 reels; Corinne Griffith, Jack Mulhall, Ward Crane, Carroll Nye, Charles Murray, Edythe Chapman, Jacqueline Wells, George Sidney, Bernard Randall; D: Alfred Santell; SP: June Mathis.

Gigolo (DeMille Pictures/Producers

Distributing Corporation, 1926) 7 reels; Rod La Rocque, Jobyna Ralston, Louise Dresser, Cyril Chadwick, George Nichols, Ina Anson, Sally Rand; D: William K. Howard; Cont.: Marion Orth; Adapt: Garrett Fort.

Show Boat (Universal, 1927) 12 reels; Laura La Plante, Joseph Schildkraut, Otis Harlan, Emily Fitzroy, Alma Rubens, Elsie Bartlett, Jack McDonald, Jane La Verne, Neely Edwards, Theodore Larch, Gertrude Howard, Ralph Yearsley, George Chesebro, Harry Holden, Max Asher, Jim Coleman, Carl Herlinger; D: Harry Pollard; SP: Charles Kenyon.

Mother Knows Best (Fox, 1928) 9 reels; Madge Ballamy, Louise Dresser, Barry Norton, Albert Gron, Joy Auburn, Annette De Kirby, Stuart Erwin, Lucien Littlefield, Ivor De Kirby, Dawn O'Day; D: John Blystone; SP: Marion Orth.

Cimarron (RKO, 1930) 124 mins.; Richard Dix, Irene Dunne, Estelle Taylor, William Collier, Jr., Nance O'Neil, Edna May Oliver, Roscoe Ates, George E. Stone, Stanley Fields, Robert McWade, Helen Parrish, Douglas Scott, Ann Lee, Bob McKenzie, Henry Rocquemore, Otto Loffman; D: Wesley Ruggles; SP: Howard Estabrook; P: Wesley Ruggles.

The Royal Family of Broadway (Paramount, 1931) 82 mins.; Ina Claire, Fredric March, Mary Brian, Henrietta Crosman, Charles Starret, Frank Conroy, Arnold Korff, Royal C. Stout, Elsie Emond, Murray Alper, Wesley Stark, Hershal Mayall; D: George Cukor, Cyril Gardner; SP: Herman Mankiewicz, Gertrude Purcell; S: Edna Ferber and George S. Kaufman.

The Expert (Warner Brothers, 1932) 69 mins.; Charles "Chic" Sale, Lois Wilson, Dickie Moore, Earle Foxe, Ralf Harolde, May Boley, Adrienne Ames, Noel Francis, Dorothy Wolbert, Louise Beavers, Ben Holmes, William Robyns, Charles Evans, Walter Catlett, Clara

Blandick, Zeta Moulton, Elea Peterson; D: Archie Mayo; SP: Julian Josephson, Maude Howell.

So Big (Warner Brothers, 1932) 90 mins.; Barbara Stanwyck, George Brent, Dickie Moore, Guy Kibbee, Mae Madison, Hardie Albright, Robert Warwick, Arthur Stone, Earle Foxe, Alan Hale, Dorothy Patterson, Dick Winslow, Dawn O'Day (Anne Shirley), Harry Beresford, Elizabeth Patterson, Rita LeRoy, Willard Robertson, Martha Mattox, Emma Ray, Olin Howland, Harry Holman, Lionel Belmore; D: William A. Wellman; SP: Grubb Alexander, Joseph Jackson; P: Jack L. Warner.

Dinner at Eight (MGM, 1933) 110 mins.; Marie Dressler, John Barrymore, Wallace Beery, Jean Harlow, Lionel Barrymore, Lee Tracy, Edmund Lowe, Billie Burke, Madge Evans, Jean Hersholt, Karen Morley, Louise Closser Hale, Phillips Holmes, May Robson, Grant Mitchell, Phoebe Foster, Hilda Vaughn, Elizabeth Patterson, Harry Beresford, Edwin Maxwell, John Davidson, George Baxter, Herman Bing, Anna Duncan; D: George Cukor; SP: Frances Marion, Herman Mankiewicz, Donald Ogden.

Glamour (Universal, 1934) 74 mins.; Constance Cummings, Paul Lukas, Phillip Reed, Joseph Cowthorn, Doris Lloyd, Alice Lake, Olaf Hylton, Jessie McAllister, Lita Chevet, Luis Alberni, Yola D'Avril, Grace Hale, Louise Beavers, Wilson Benge, Lyman Williams, Peggy Campbell, David Dickinson; D: William Wyler; SP: Gladys Unger, Doris Anderson.

Show Boat (Universal, 1936) 110 mins.; Irene Dunne, Allan Jones, Charles Winninger, Helen Westley, Paul Robeson, Helen Morgan, Donald Cook, Sammy White, Queenie Smith, Barbara Pepper, J. Farrell MacDonald, Eddie Anderson, Charles Middleton, Edmund Cobb, Jack Mulhall, Al Ferguson, Flora Finch, Harry Barris, Patti Patterson, Selmer Jackson; D: James Whale; SP: Oscar Hammerstein, Jerome Kern.

Come and Get It (Goldwyn, 1936) 99 mins.; Edward Arnold, Joel McCrea, Frances Farmer, Walter Brennan, Andrea Leeds; D: Howard Hawks, William Wyler; SP: John Furthman, Jane Murfin.

Stage Door (RKO-Radio, 1937) 92 mins.; Katharine Hepburn, Ginger Rogers, Adolphe Menjou, Gail Patrick, Constance Collier, Andrea Leeds, Eve Arden, Ann Miller, Frances Gifford, Phyllis Kennedy, Jack Carson, Franklin Pangborn, Grady Sutton, Jean Rouverol, Theodore Von Eltz, Jack Rice, Ralph Forbes; D: Gregory La Cava; SP: Morris Ryskind, Anthony Veiller.

No Place to Go (First National, 1939) 57 mins.; Fred Stone, Dennis Morgan, Gloria Dickson, Sammy Bupp, Aldrich Bowker, Charles Hilton, Georgia Caine, Dennis Moore, Frank Faylen, Alan Bridge; D: Terry Motse; SP: Lee Katz, Lawrence Kimble, Fred Noble, Jr.

Saratoga Trunk (Warner Brothers, 1943) 136 mins.; Ingrid Bergman, Gary Cooper, Flora Robson, Jerry Austin, Florence Bates, John Warburton, John Abbott, Curt Bois, Ethel Griffies; D: Sam Wood; SP: Casey Robinson.

Show Boat (MGM, 1951) 106 mins.; Kathryn Grayson, Howard Keel, Ava Gardner, William Warfield, Joe E. Brown, Robert Sterling, Marge and Gower Champion, Agnes Moorhead; D: George Sidney; SP: John Lee Makin.

Giant (Warner Brothers, 1956) 201 mins.; Rock Hudson, Elizabeth Taylor, James Dean, Carroll Baker, Chill Wills, Ray Whitley, Monte Hale, Paul Fix, Rod Taylor, Max Terhune, Earl Holliman, Noreen Nash, Tina Minard; D: George Stevens; SP: Fred Guiol, Ivan Moffat.

Ice Palace (Warner Brothers, 1960) 143 mins.; Richard Burton, Robert Ryan, Martha Hyer, Carolyn Jones, Jim Backus, Ray Danton, Diane McBain, Karl Swenson; D: Vincent Sherman; SP: Harry Kleiner.

Cimarron (MGM, 1960) 147 mins.; Glenn Ford, Maria Schell, Anne Baxter, Arthur O'Connell, Russ Tamblyn, Lili Darvas, Henry (Harry) Morgan, David Opatoshu, Charles McGraw, Aline MacMahon, Edgar Buchanan, Mercedes McCambridge, Vic Morrow, Robert Keith, John Cason, Mary Wickes, Royal Dano, Vladimir Sokoloff; D: Anthony Mann; SP: Arnold Schulman.

Norman Fox

Norman Fox was born on May 26, 1911, in Michigan and died March 24, 1960. He was an accountant from 1929 until 1938, at which time he became a freelance writer of western novels and short stories. He contributed more than 400 short stories to periodicals and authored 33 novels.

Fox authored four stories that were made into movies. *Tall Man Riding* was a good vehicle for Randolph Scott and *Night Passage* a good one for James Stewart and Audie Murphy. *Gunsmoke* was typical of Audie Murphy westerns and *The Rawhide Years* was average western fare.

Films Based on Norman Fox's Writings

Gunsmoke (Universal-International, 1953) 70 mins.; Audie Murphy, Susan Cabot, Paul Kelly, Charles Drake, Mary Castle, Jack Kelly, William Reynolds, Forrest Taylor, Chubby Johnson, Al Haskell, Edmund Cobb, Denver Pyle,

Gregg Barton, Donald Randolph, Clem Fuller, George Eldridge; D: Nathan Juran; SP: D. D. Beauchamp; P: Aaron Rosenberg.

Tall Man Riding (Warner Brothers, 1955) 83 mins.; Randolph Scott, Dorothy Malone, Peggie Castle, William Ching, Robert Barrat, John Dehner, Mickey Simpson, Carl Andre, Bill Faucett, Patrick Henry, Joe Brooks, Vernon Rich, Buddy Roosevelt, Dub Taylor, Mike Ragan, Nolan Leary, Phil Rick; D: Lesley Selander; SP: Joseph Hoffman; P: David Weisbart.

The Rawhide Years (Universal-International, 1956) 85 mins.; Tony Curtis, Colleen Miller, Arthur Kennedy, William Demarest, William Gargan, Peter Van Eyck, Minor Watson, Bob Wilke, Chubby Johnson, Donald Randolph, Don Beddoe, Robert Foulk, James Anderson, Leigh Snowden, Clarence Long, Trevor Bardette; D: Rudolph Maté; SP: Earl Felton, Robert Presnell, Jr., D. D. Beauchamp; P: Stanley Rubin.

Night Passage (Universal-International, 1957) 90 mins.; James Stewart, Audie Murphy, Dan Duryea, Dianne Foster, Elaine Stewart, Jay C. Flippen, Patsy Novac, Polly Burson, James Flavin, Harold Goodwin, Henry Wills, Donald Curtis, Ellen Corby, Henry Wills, Brandon De Wilde; D: James Neilson; SP: Borden Chase; P: Aaron Rosenberg.

Hamlin Garland

Hamlin Garland had a patronizing attitude toward the Midwest and small towns, a fact reflected in some of his books. His writings make it clear that he was capable of seeing mostly the drab and dull in the small towns he lived in before encountering the good life of Chicago, Boston, New York, and London. The five films based on his books are routine westerns without any particular outstanding features to set them apart from other similar movies.

Garland was born September 14, 1860, in West Salem, Wisconsin. He spent his youth in Wisconsin, Iowa, and South Dakota. Garland's early exposure to the poverty and drudgery of agrarian life directed much of his writing, in which he sought to shatter the myth of utopian rural America.

During the early 1900s Garland strayed from his commitment to realism and wrote several romantic novels set in the Rocky Mountains. Such books as *The Captain of the Gray Horse Troop* (1902) and *Cavanagh, Forest Ranger: A Romance of the Mountain West* (1910) proved to be popular ones. His *Middle Border* was also highly acclaimed, and he won a Pulitzer Prize for *A Daughter of the Middle Border* (1921).

Garland died on March 4, 1940, in Los Angeles.

Films Based on Hamlin Garland's Writings

Hesper of the Mountains (Vitagraph, 1916) 5 reels; Lillian Walker, Donald Hall, Evart Overton, Donald MacBride, Denton Vane, Robert Gaillard, Rose E. Tapley, Templer Saxe, Josephine Earle; D: Wilfrid North; SP: Joseph F. Poland; S: *Hesper: A Novel.*

Money Magic (Vitagraph, 1917) 5 reels; Antonio Moreno, Laura Winston, Edith Storey, William Duncan, Florence Dye; D: William Wolbert; SP: A Van Buren Powell.

The Captain of the Gray Horse Troop (Vitagraph, 1917) 5 reels; Antonio Moreno, Edith Storey, Otto Lederer, Al Jennings, Neola May, Robert Burns, H. A. Barrows; D: William Wolbert; SP: A. Van Buren Powell.

Cavanagh of the Forest Rangers (Vitagraph, 1918) 5 reels; Nell Shipman, Alfred Whitman, Otto Lederer, Laura Winston, R. Bradbury, Rex Downs, Joe Rickson, Hal Wilson, Hattie Buskirk; D: William Wolbert; S: *Cavanagh, Forest Ranger.*

Ranger of the Big Pines (Vitagraph, 1925) 7 reels; Kenneth Harlan, Helene Costello, Eulalie Jensen, Will Walling, Lew Harvey, Robert Graves; D: William S. Van Dyke; SP: Hope Loring, Louis D. Lighton; S: *Cavanagh, Forest Ranger.*

Jackson Gregory

Jackson Gregory was one of the better western writers of his time. He wrote a number of well-plotted traditional westerns, 17 of which were adapted to the screen. Popular cowboy star Buck Jones starred in four of them. Gregory was adept at plotting and sometimes went overboard on sentimentality. Although the films based on his books never rose above the B level, both his books and the film adaptations proved immensely popular with the public.

Gregory was born March 12, 1882, in Salinas, California. After graduation from the University of California he went into teaching, and later became a newspaper reporter. He published his first novel early in World War I and before the war was over had published five more. Before his death on June 12, 1943, he had written over 40 books, as here listed: *Under Handicap,* 1914; *The Outlaw,* 1916; *The Short Cut,* 1916; *Wolf Breed,* 1917; *The Joyous Trouble Maker,* 1918; *Six Feet Four,* 1918; *Judith of Blue Lake Ranch,* 1919; *The Bells of San Juan,* 1919; *Ladyfingers,* 1920; *Man to Man,* 1920; *Desert Valley,* 1921; *The Everlasting Whisper,* 1922; *Timber Wolf,* 1923; *The Maid of the Mountain,* 1925; *The Desert Thoroughbred,* 1926; *Captain Cavalier,* 1927; *Redwood and Gold,* 1928; *Sentinel of the Desert,* 1929; *Mystery at Spanish Hacienda,* 1929; *The Trail to Paradise,* 1930; *The Silver Star,* 1931; *The House of the Opal,* 1932; *Splendid Outlaw,* 1932; *A Case for Mr. Paul Savoy,* 1933; *Red Rivals,* 1933; *The Shadow on the Mesa,* 1933; *Ru, the Conquerer,* 1933; *Riders Across the Border: Second Case for Mr. Paul Savoy,* 1933; *High Courage,* 1934; *Emerald Murder Trap,* 1934; *Island of Allure,* 1934; *Valley of Adventure,* 1935; *Lords of the Coast,* 1935; *White Water Valley,* 1935; *Into the Sunset,* 1936; *Mountain Men,* 1936; *Third Case of Mr. Paul Savoy,* 1936; *Sudden Bill Dorn,* 1937; *Dark Valley,* 1937; *Powder Smoke on Wandering River,* 1938; *The Secret of Secret Valley,* 1939; *Girl at the Crossroads,* 1940; *The Far Call,* 1940; *Guardians of the Trail,* 1940; *Ace in the Hole,* 1941; *Red Law,* 1941; *Border Law,* 1942; and *Two in the Wilderness,* 1942.

Films Based on Jackson Gregory's Writings

Under Handicap (Metro, 1917) 7 reels; Harold Lockwood, Anna Little, William Clifford, Lester Cuneo, W. H. Bainbridge; D: Fred J. Balshofer; SP: Fred J. Balshofer, Richard V. Spencer.

The Secret of Black Mountain (Falcon, 1917) 4 reels; Vola Vale, Philo McCullough, Charles Dudley, George Austin, Henry Crawford, Mignon LeBrun, James Warner, Louis King, Jack McLaughlin, T. H. Gibson Gowland, H. C. Russell; D: Otto Hoffman.

The Man from Painted Post (Paramount, 1917) 5 reels; Douglas Fairbanks, Eileen Percy, Frank Campeau, Fred Clark, Herbert Standing, W. E. Lowery, Rhea Haines, Charles Stevens, Monte Blue; D: Joseph Henabery; SP: Douglas Fairbanks; S: *Silver Slippers.*

Six Feet Four (American/Pathe, 1919) 6–7 reels; William Russell, Vola Vale, Charles K. French, Harvey Clark, Clarence Burton, Al Garcia, Jack Collins, Jack Brammall, Calvert Carter, Perry Banks, John Gough, Anne Schaefer; D: Henry King; SP: Stephen Fox.

The Joyous Troublemakers (Fox, 1920) 6 reels; William Farnum, Louise Lovely, Henry J. Hebert, Harry De Vere, G. Raymond Nye, Clarence Morgan, George Nichols, Sedley Brown, John Underhill, Harry Archer, Al Fremont, Earl Crain, Chick Leyva, Pedro De Leon, Claire De Lorez, Molly Bishop; D: J. Gordon Edwards; SP: Charles Kenyon.

Alias Lady Fingers (Metro, 1921) 6 reels; Bert Lytell, Ora Carew, Frank Elliott, Edythe Chapman, DeWitt Jennings; D: Bayard Veiller; SP: Lenore J. Coffee; S: *Ladyfingers.*

Two Kinds of Women (R-C, 1922) 6 reels; Pauline Frederick, Tom Santschi, Charles Clary, Dave Winter, Eugene Pallette, Billy Elmer, Jack Curtis, Jim Barley, Tom Bates, Lydia Yeamans

Titus, Sam Appel, Billy Elmer; D: Colin Campbell; SP: Winifred Dunn; S: *Judith of Blue Lake Ranch.*

Billy Jim (R-C, 1922) 5 reels; Fred Stone, Millicent Fisher, George Hernandez, William Bletcher, Marion Skinner, Frank Thorne; D: Frank Borzage; SP: Frank Howard.

Man to Man (Universal, 1922) 6 reels; Harry Carey, Lillian Rich, Charles Le Moyne, Harold Goodwin; D: Stuart Paton; SP: George C. Hull.

Bells of San Juan (Fox, 1922) 5 reels; Buck Jones, Fritzi Brunette, Claude Peyton, Harry Todd, Kathleen Key, William Steele, Otto Matieson; D: Scott Dunlap; SP: Rex Taylor.

Luck (Mastodon Films, 1923) 7 reels; Johnny Hines, Robert Edeson, Edmund Breese, Violet Mersereau, Charles Murray, Flora Finch, Polly Moran, Matthew Betts; SP: Doty Hobart; P: C. C. Burr.

Hearts and Spurs (Fox, 1925) 5 reels; Buck Jones, Carole Lombard, William Davidson, Freeman Wood, Jean LaMotte, J. Gordon Russell, Walt Robbins, Charles Eldridge; D: W. S. Van Dyke; SP: John Stone; S: *The Outlaw.*

Timber Wolf (Fox, 1925) 5 reels; Buck Jones, Elinor Fair, David Dyas, Sam Allen, William Walling, Jack Craig, Robert Mack; D: W. S. Van Dyke; SP: John Stone.

The Everlasting Whisper (Fox, 1925) 6 reels; Tom Mix, Alice Calhoun, Robert Cain, George Berrell, Walter James, Virginia Madison, Karl Dane; D: J. G. Blystone; SP: Wyndham Gittens.

Desert Valley (Fox, 1926) 5 reels; Buck Jones, Virginia Brown Faire, Eugene Pallette, J. W. Johnston, Malcolm Waite, Charles Brinley; D: Scott R. Dunlap; SP: Randall H. Faye.

Sudden Bill Dorn (Universal, 1937)

60 mins.; Buck Jones, Noel Francis, Evelyn Brent, Frank McGlynn, Harold Hodge, Ted Adams, William Lawrence, Lee Phelps, Tom Chatterton, Carlos Valdez, Ezra Paulette, Red Hightower, Charles LeMoyne, Adolph Milar; D: Ray Taylor; SP: Frances Guihan; P: Buck Jones.

The Laramie Trail (Republic, 1944) 55 mins.; Robert Livingston, Smiley Burnette, Linda Brent, Emmett Lynn, John James, George J. Lewis, Leander De Cordova, Slim Whitaker, Bud Osborne, Bud Geary, Roy Barcroft, Kenne Duncan, Marshall Reed; D: John English; SP: J. Benton Chaney; S: *Mystery at Spanish Hacienda.*

Frank Gruber

Frank Gruber has written 14 stories adapted to the screen; in addition he wrote or cowrote the screenplays for 11 movies. Nearly all of the films rated the A status.

Films Based on Frank Gruber's Writings

The Kansan (United Artists, 1943) 79 mins.; Richard Dix, Jane Wyatt, Victor Jory, Albert Dekker, Eugene Pallette, Robert Armstrong, Clem Bevans, Rod Cameron, Francis McDonald, Willie Best, Glenn Strange, Douglas Fowley, Jack Norton, Eddy Waller, Ray Bennett, Sam Flint, Merrill McCormack, Jack Mulhall; D: George Archainbaud; SP: Harold Shumate; S: *Peace Marshal*; P: Harry Sherman.

Accomplice (PRC, 1946) 67 mins.; Richard Arlen, Veda Ann Borg, Michael Brandon, Earle Hodgins, Edward Earle, Tom Dugan, Herbert Rawlinson, Sherry Hall; D: Walter Colmes; SP: Irving Elman, Frank Gruber; S: *Simon Lash, Private Detective*; P: John E. Teaford.

In Old Sacramento (Republic, 1946) 89 mins.; William (Bill) Elliott, Constance Moore, Hank Daniels, Ruth Donnelly, Eugene Pallette, Lionel Stander, Jack LaRue, Grant Withers, Bobby Blake, Charles Judels, Paul Hurst, Victoria Horne, Dick Wessel, Hal Taliaferro (Wally Wales), Jack O'Shea, H. T. Tsiang, Marshall Reed, Wade Crosby, Eddy Waller, William Haade, Ethel Wales, Boyd Irwin, William B. David-

son, Ellen Corby, Fred Burns; D/AP: Joseph Kane; SP: Frances Lyland, Frank Gruber; S: Jerome Odlum.

Fighting Man of the Plains (20th Century–Fox, 1949) 94 mins.; Randolph Scott, Bill Williams, Victor Jory, Jane Nigh, Dale Robertson, Douglas Kennedy, Joan Taylor, Barry Kroeger, Rhys Williams, Barry Kelly, James Todd, James Millican, Burk Symon, Herbert Rawlinson, J. Farrell MacDonald, Harry Cheshire, James Griffith, Tony Hughes, Kermit Maynard; D: Edwin L. Marin; SP/S: *Fighting Men*; P: Nat Holt.

Dakota Lil (20th Century–Fox, 1950) 88 mins.; George Montgomery, Marie Windsor, Rod Cameron, John Emery, Wallace Ford, Jack Lambert, Larry Johns, Marion Martin, James Flavin, J. Farrell MacDonald, Jack Perrin, Kenneth MacDonald, Clancy Cooper, Frank Lackteen, Bob Morgan, Nacho Galindo, Rosa Turich, Walter Sande, Bill Perrott, Joel Friedkin; D: Leslie Selander; SP: Maurice Selander, Frank Gruber; P: Edward L. Alperson.

The Cariboo Trail (20th Century–Fox, 1950) 81 mins.; Randolph Scott, George F. (Gabby) Hayes, Bill

Williams, Karin Booth, Victor Jory, Douglas Kennedy, Jim Davis, Dale Robertson, Mary Stuart, James Griffith, Lee Tung Foo, Tony Hughes, Mary Kent, Ray Hyke, Kansas Moehring, Dorothy Adams, Jerry Root, Kermit Maynard, Smith Ballew, Cliff Clark, Tom Monroe, Michael Barret, Fred Libby; D: Edwin L. Marin; SP: Frank Gruber; S: John Rhodes Sturdy; P: Nat Holt.

The Great Missouri Raid (Paramount, 1951) 83 mins.; Wendell Corey, MacDonald Carey, Ellen Drew, Ward Bond, Bruce Bennett, Bill Williams, Anne Revere, Edgar Buchanan, Louis Chastland, Louis Jean Heydt, Barry Kelly, James Millican, Guy Wilkerson, Ethan Laidlaw, Tom Tyler, Paul Fix, Paul Lees, Bob Brey, Alan Wells, Steve Pendleton, Whit Bissell, James Griffith; D: Gordon Douglas; SP/S: Frank Gruber; P: Nat Holt.

The Texas Rangers (Columbia, 1951) 74 mins.; George Montgomery, Gale Storm, Jerome Courtland, Noah Beery, Jr., John Litel, William Bishop, Douglas Kennedy, John Dehner, Ian MacDonald, John Doucette, Jock O'Mahoney, Jim Bannon, George Chesebro, Dick Curtis, Trevor Bardette, Julian Rivero, Stanley Andrews, Edward Earle, Myron Healey, Joseph Fallon, John Cason, William Haade, Kenne Duncan; D: Phil Karlson; SP: Richard Schayer; S: Frank Gruber; P: Edward Small.

Warpath (Paramount, 1951) 95 mins.; Edmond O'Brien, Dean Jagger, Forrest Tucker, Harry Carey, Jr., Polly Bergen, James Millican, Wallace Ford, Paul Fix, Louis Jean Heydt, Paul Lees, Walter Sande, Charles Dayton, Robert Bray, Douglas Spencer, James Burke, Chief Yowlachie, John Mansfield, Monte Blue, Frank Ferguson, Cliff Clark, Paul Burns, Charles Stevens, John Hart; D: Byron Haskin; SP/S: Frank Gruber; P: Nat Holt.

Silver City (Paramount, 1951) 90 mins.; Edmond O'Brien, Yvonne De

Carlo, Richard Arlen, Barry Fitzgerald, Gladys George, Laura Elliott, Edgar Buchanan, Michael Moore, John Dierkes, Myron Healey, Frank Fenton, Paul E. Burns, Harvey Parry, Slim Gaut, Frank Cordell, Don Dunning, Howard Negley, Cliff Clark; D: Byron Haskins; SP: Frank Gruber; S: Luke Short; P: Nat Holt.

Flaming Feather (Paramount, 1952) 78 mins.; Sterling Hayden, Forrest Tucker, Arleen Whelan, Barbara Rush, Victor Jory, Richard Arlen, Edgar Buchanan, Carol Thurston, Ian MacDonald, George Cleveland, Bob Kortman, Ethan Laidlaw, Don Dunning, Paul Burns, Ray Teal, Nacho Galindo, Frank Lackteen, Gene Lewis, Larry McGrath, Herman Newlin, Bryan Hightower, Donald Kerr; D: Ray Enright; SP: Gerald Drayson Adams, Frank Gruber; S: Gerald Drayson Adams; P: Nat Holt.

Denver and the Rio Grande (Paramount, 1952) 89 mins.; Edmond O'Brien, Sterling Hayden, Dean Jagger, Laura Elliott, Lyle Bettger, J. Carroll Naish, ZaSu Pitts, Tom Powers, Robert Barrat, Paul Fix, Don Haggerty, James Burke; D: Byron Haskin; S/SP: Frank Gruber; P: Nat Holt.

Hurricane (Paramount, 1952) 90 mins.; Yvonne De Carlo, John Ireland, James Craig, Forrest Tucker, Lyle Bettger, Richard Arlen, Mike Kellin, Murray Matheson, Henry Brandon, Emile Meyer, Stuart Randall, Ralph Dumke, Kim Spaulding; D: Jerry Hopper; SP: Frank Gruber; S: Gordon Ray Young.

Pony Express (Paramount, 1953) 101 mins.; Charlton Heston, Rhonda Fleming, Jan Sterling, Forrest Tucker, Michael Moore, Porter Hall, Richard Shannon, Henry Brandon, Stuart Randall, Lewis Martin, Pat Hogan, Eric Alden, Howard Joslin, LeRoy Johnson, Jimmy H. Burke, Robert J. Miles, Robert Scott, Bob Templeton, Willard Willingham, John Mansfield, Frank Wilcox; D: Jerry Hopper; SP: Charles

Marquis Warren; S: Frank Gruber; P: Nat Holt.

Rage at Dawn (RKO, 1955) 87 mins.; Randolph Scott, Forrest Tucker, Mala Powers, J. Carroll Naish, Edgar Buchanan, Myron Healey, Howard Petrie, Ray Teal, William Forrest, Denver Pyle, Trevor Bardette, Kenneth Tobey, Chubby Johnson, Richard Garland, Ralph Moody, Guy Prescott, Mike Ragan, Phil Chambers, Dennis Moore, Jimmy Lyden, Arthur Space, George Wallace, Bill Phipps, Dan White, Henry Wills; D: Tim Whelan; SP: Horace McCoy; S: Frank Gruber; P: Nat Holt.

Tension at Table Rock (RKO, 1956) 93 mins.; Richard Egan, Dorothy Malone, Cameron Mitchell, Billy Chapin, Royal Dano, Edward Andrews, John Dehner, DeForrest Kelly, Angie Dickinson, Joe DeSantis, Harry Lauter, Tom Steele; D: Charles Marquis Warren; SP: Winston Miller; S: *Bitter Sage*; P: Sam Wiesenthal.

The Big Land (Warner Brothers, 1957) 93 mins.; Alan Ladd, Virginia Mayo, Edmond O'Brien, Anthony Caruso, Julie Bishop, John Qualen, Don Castle, David Ladd, Jack Wrather, Jr., George J. Lewis, James Anderson, Don Kelly, Charles Watts; D: Gordon Douglas; SP:

David Dortort, Martin Rackin; S: *Buffalo Grass*; AP: George C. Bertholon.

Twenty Plus Two (Allied Artists, 1961) 102 mins.; David Janssen, Jeanne Crain, Dina Merrill, Agnes Moorehead, Brad Dexter, Robert Strauss, Jacques Aubuchon, William Demarest, George Neise, Fred Wayne, Carleton Young, Robert H. Harris, Billy Varga, Teri Janssen, Ellie Kent, Mort Mills, Robert Gruber, Will Wright; D: Joseph M. Newman; SP/S/P: Frank Gruber.

Arizona Raiders (Columbia, 1965) 88 mins.; Audie Murphy, Michael Dante, Ben Cooper, Buster Crabbe, Gloria Talbott, Red Morgan, Ray Stricklyn, George Keymas, Fred Krone, Willard Willingham, Fred Graham; D: William Witney; SP: Alex Gottlieb, Mary and Willard Willingham; S: Frank Gruber, Richard Schayer; P: Grant Whytock.

Town Tamer (Paramount, 1965) 89 mins.; Dana Andrews, Terry Moore, Pat O'Brien, Lon Chaney, Bruce Cabot, Lyle Bettger, Coleen Gray, Richard Arlen, Barton MacLane, Richard Jaeckel, Philip Carey, DeForest Kelley, Sonny Tufts, Roger Torres, James Brown, Richard Webb, Jeanne Cagney, Donald Barry, Bob Steele; D: Lesley Selander; S/SP: Frank Gruber; P: A. C. Lyles.

Bill Gulick

Bill Gulick has authored three excellent stories that translated effectively to the screen. *Bend of the River* is a picturesque and romantic film without sacrificing action. *The Road to Denver* is a first-rate western sure to please in the outdoor market and where soundly developed story values, good direction, and credible performances count for pleasing entertainment. And *The Hallelujah Trail* is a lusty, gusty comedy with screwball situations. It is one of the nuttiest cinematic mishmashes ever seen, in which thirsty miners, a worried U.S. Cavalry, a band of whiskey-mad Sioux, a crusading temperance group, and a train of 40 wagons carrying 600 barrels of hard liquor become so thoroughly involved that even the off-screen narrator has a hard time trying to keep track of them all and the correct logistics.

Principal writings include *Distant Trails*, *Gathering Storm*, and *River's End*.

Films Based on Bill Gulick's Writings

Bend of the River (Universal-International, 1952) 91 mins.; James Stewart, Arthur Kennedy, Julia Adams, Rock Hudson, Jay C. Flippen, Stepin Fetchit, Lori Nelson, Henry (Harry) Morgan, Chubby Johnson, Howard Petrie, Frances Bavier, Jack Lambert, Royal Dano, Cliff Lyons, Frank Chase, Lillian Randolph, Frank Ferguson, Gregg Barton, Hugh Prosser; D: Anthony Mann; P: Aaron Rosenberg.

The Road to Denver (Republic, 1955) 90 mins.; John Payne, Mona Freeman, Lee J. Cobb, Ray Middleton, Skip Homeier, Andy Clyde, Lee Van Cleef, Karl Davis, Glenn Strange, Buzz Henry, Dan White, Anne Carroll, Tex Terry; D: Joseph Kane; SP: Horace McCoy, Allen Rivkin; P: Herbert J. Yates.

The Hallelujah Trail (United Artists, 1965) 156 mins.; Burt Lancaster, Lee Remick, Jim Hutton, Pamela Tiffin, Donald Pleasence, Brian Keith, Martin Landau, John Anderson, Tom Stern, Robert J. Wilke, Dub Taylor, James Burke, Larry Doran; D: John Sturges; S: *The Hallelujah Trail*; SP: John Gay; P: John Sturges.

Bret Harte

The medium in which Harte worked — the short story — was the best for capturing the transient, kaleidoscopic life of the mining camps that he wrote about. His best short stories included "The Luck of Roaring Camp," "The Outcast of Poker Flat," "Tennessee's Partner," "A Waif of the Plains," "Cressy," and "In a Hollow of the Hills." The first significant story that Harte published was "An Idyl of Red Mountain" more commonly known as "M'liss." It has been filmed three times.

In 1868 Harte published his extremely popular *The Luck of Roaring Camp* and in the same volume was "The Outcasts of Poker Flat." To date, 34 films have been based on Harte's stories, but only five have been made in the sound era.

G. K. Chesterton, writing in *Varied Types* (1903), says this of Bret Harte:

> He discovered the intense sensibility of the primitive man. To him we owe the realization of the fact that while modern barbarians of genius like Mr. [William Ernest] Henley, and in his weaker moments Mr. Rudyard Kipling, delight in describing the coarseness and crude cynicism and fierce humor of the unlettered classes, the unlettered classes are in reality highly sentimental and religious, and not in the least like the creations of Mr. Henley and Mr. Kipling. Bret Harte tells the truth about the wildest, the grossest, the most rapacious of all the districts of the earth — the truth that, while it is very rare indeed in the world to find a thoroughly good man, it is rarer still, rare to the point of monstrosity, to find a man who does not either desire to be one, or imagine that he is one already.

The following is a list of Harte's principal works: *Condensed Novels and Other Papers*, 1867; *The Luck of Roaring Camp and Other Stories*, 1870; *An*

Idyll of Red Mountain, 1873; Mrs. *Skagg's Husbands and Other Sketches*, 1873; "Idylls of the Foothills," 1875; *Tales of the Argonauts and Other Sketches*, 1875; "Gabriel Conroy," 1876; *Thankful Blossoms*, 1877; "Drift from Two Shores," 1878; "Story of Mine," 1878; *The Twins of Table Mountain and Other Stories*, 1879; *Jeff Briggs's Love Story and Others*, 1880; *Flip and Found at Blazing Star*, 1882; *In the Carquinez Woods*, 1884, *On the Frontier*, 1884; *Maruja*, 1885; *By Shore and Sedge*, 1885; *Snow Bound at Eagle's*, 1886; *The Crusade of the Excelsior*, 1887; *Frontier Stories*, 1887; *A Millionaire of Rough-and-Ready, and Devil's Ford*, 1887; *Argonauts of North Liberty*, 1888; *A Phyllis of the Sierras*, 1888; *Cressy and Other Tales*, 1889; *The Heritage of Dedlow Marsh and Other Tales*, 1889; *A Waif of the Plains*, 1890; *A Ward of the Golden Gate*, 1890; *A Sappho of Green Springs and Other Tales*, 1891; *Colonel Starbottle's Client, and Some Other People*, 1892; *Sally Downs and Other Stories*, 1893; *Susy, A Story of the Plains*, 1893; *The Bell-Ringer of Angel's and Other Stories*, 1894; *A Protege of Jack Hamlin's, and Other Stories*, 1894; *Clarence*, 1895; *In a Hollow of the Hills*, 1895; *Baker's Luck and Other Stories*, 1896; *Three Partners or the Big Strike on Henry Tree Hill*, 1897; *Stories in Light and Shadow*, 1898; *Tales of Trail and Town*, 1898; *Mr. Jack Hamlin's Meditation and Other Stories*, 1899; *From Sand Hill to Pine*, 1900; *Under the Redwoods*, 1901; and *Openings in the Old Trail*, 1902.

Films Based on Bret Harte's Writings

The Heart of O Yama (Biograph, 1908) 1 reel; Florence Lawrence, D. W. Griffith, Harry Salter; D/SP; D. W. Griffith.

Bradford's Claim (Edison, 1910) ½ reel; J. Barney Sherry; D/SP: Edwin S. Porter.

Ononko's Vow (Edison, 1910) 1 reel; Mary Fuller; D/SP: Edwin S. Porter.

The Stolen Claim (Edison, 1910) 1 reel; J. Barney Sherry; D/SP: Edwin S. Porter.

The White Rose of the Wilds (Biograph, 1911) 1 reel; Blanche Sweet, Wilfred Lucas, Mack Sennett, Robert Harron, Joe Graybill, W. Chrystie Miller, Donald Crisp, Edwin August; D: D. W. Griffith; SP: Frank Woods.

The Last Drop of Water (Biograph, 1911) 1 reel; Blanche Sweet, Charles West, Joe Graybill, Jeanie Macpherson, W. Chrystie Miller, William J. Butler, Robert Harron, Mack Sennett; D:

D. W. Griffith; SP: Stanner E. V. Taylor.

In the Aisles of the Wild (Biograph, 1912) 1 reel; Henry B. Walthall, Harry Carey, Claire McDowell, Lillian Gish, Elmer Booth; D: D. W. Griffith; SP: Stanner E. V. Taylor.

Breed o' the North (Broncho, 1914) 2 reels; Walter Edwards, Clara Williams, Harry Keenan; D: Walter Edwards; SP: C. Gardner Sullivan.

Salomy Jane (California Motion Picture Company, 1914) 6 reels; Beatriz Micheleana, House Peters, Sr., Mabel Hilliard, Fred W. Snook, William Nigh, Ernest Joy, Bill Pike, Forrest Halsey, Jack Holt; D: William Nigh; SP: Paul Armstrong.

M'Liss (World, 1915) 5 reels; Barbara Tennant, Howard Estabrook, O. A. C. Lund, Anita Navarro; D/SP: O. A. C. Lund.

The Lily of Poverty Flat (California

Motion Picture Company, 1915) 5 reels; Beatriz Michelena, Frederick Lewis, Andrew Robson, D. Mitsoras, Clarence Arper, Nat Snyder, Clara Beyers; D: George E. Middleton; SP: Charles Kenyon; S: *Her Letter, His Answer, Her Last Letter.*

The "Bad Buck" of Santa Ynez (KB, 1915) 2 reels; William S. Hart, Thelma Salter, Fanny Midgley; D: William S. Hart; SP: J. G. Hawks.

A Phyllis of the Sierras (California Motion Picture Company/World, 1915) 5 reels; Beatriz Michelena, William Pike, Andrew Robson, Carl Emlay; D: George E. Middleton; SP: Charles Kenyon.

Tennessee's Pardner (Paramount, 1916) 5 reels; Fannie Ward, Jack Dean, Charles Clary, Jesse Arnold, Robert Bradbury, Raymond Hatton, James Neill; D: George Melford; SP: Marion Fairfax.

Two Men of Sandy Bar (Universal, 1916) 5 reels; Hobard Bosworth, Emory Johnson, Gretchen Lederer, Frank Mac-Quarrie, Charles Hickman, William Mong, A. E. Whitting, Jack Curtis, Jean Taylor, Yona Landowska; D: Lloyd B. Carleton; SP: Olga Printzlau.

The Half Breed (Triangle, 1916) 5 reels; Douglas Fairbanks, Alma Rubens, Jewel Carmen, Sam De Grasse, Frank Brownlee, George Beranger, Tom Wilson; D: Allan Dwan; SP: Anita Loos; S: *In the Carquinez Woods.*

The Luck of Roaring Camp (Edison, 1917) 2 reels; Ivan Christy, Eugene Field, Robert Chandler, William Wadsworth, J. C. O'Loughlin, Betty Young, Thomas Trenor, Florence Adams, Al Stewart; D: Floyd France; SP: Edward H. Griffith.

M'Liss (Famous Players–Lasky, 1918) 5 reels; Mary Pickford, Theodore Roberts, Thomas Meighan, Tully Marshall, Charles Ogle, Monte Blue, Winifred Greenwood, Helen Kelly, Val Paul, W. H. Brown, John Burton, Bud

Post, Guy Oliver; D: Marshall Neilan; SP: Frances Marion.

The Dawn of Understanding (Vitagraph, 1918) 5 reels; Bessie Love, Jack Gilbert, Frank Glendon, George A. Williams, George Kunkel, Bob McKenzie, Dorothea Wolbert, Jake Abraham; D: David Smith; SP: Edward J. Montagne; S: *The Judgment of Bolinas Plains.*

Tongues of Flame (Universal, 1918) 5 reels; Marie Walcamp, Al Whitman, Alfred Allen, Hugh Sutherland, J. P. Wilde, Lilly Clarke; D: Colin Campbell; SP: Lanier Bartlett; S: *In the Carquinez Woods.*

The Outcasts of Poker Flat (Universal, 1919) 6 reels; Harry Carey, Cullen Landis, Gloria Hope, J. Farrell Mac-Donald, Charles Hill Mailes, Victor Potel, Joseph Harris, Louise Lester, Virginia Chester, Duke Lee, Vester Pegg; D: John Ford; SP: H. Tipton Steck.

The Gray Wolf's Ghost (Robertson-Cole, 1919) 5 reels; Lurline Lyons, Rita Stanwood, Hector V. Sarno, Violet Schram, H. B. Warner, Lloyd Whitlock, George Field; D: Park Frame; SP: Fred Myton; S: *Maruja.*

Fighting Cressy (Pathe, 1919) 6 reels; Blanche Sweet, Russell Simpson, Edward Peil, Pell Trenton, Antrim Short, Frank Lanning, Billie Bennett, Georgie Stone, Walter Perry, Eunice Moore; D: Robert T. Thornby; SP: Fred Myton; S: *Cressy.*

The Girl Who Ran Wild (Universal, 1922) 5 reels; Gladys Walton, Marc Robbins, Vernon Steele, Al Hart, Nelson McDowell, Lloyd Whitlock, Lucille Rickson; D: Rupert Julian; SP: Rupert Julian, George C. Hull; S: *An Idyl of Red Mountain.*

Salomy Jane (Paramount, 1923) 7 reels; Jacqueline Logan, George Fawcett, Maurice B. Flynn, William Davidson, Charles Ogle, William Quirk, G. Raymond Nye, Louise Dresser, James Neill, Tom Carrigan, Clarence Burton, Barbara Brower, Milton Ross; D: George Melford; SP: Waldemar Young; S: *Salomy Jane's Kiss.*

The Flaming Forties (PDC, 1924) 6 reels; Harry Carey, William Norton Bailey, Jacqueline Gadson, James Mason, Frank Norcross, Wilbur Higby; D: Tom Forman, SP: Elliott J. Clawson, Harvey Gates; S: *Tennessee's Pardner.*

The Golden Princess (Paramount, 1925) 9 reels; Betty Bronson, Neil Hamilton, Rockliffe Fellowes, Phyllis Haver, Joseph Dowling, Edgar Kennedy, George Irving, Norma Willis; D: Clarence Badger, SP: Frances Agnew.

The Man from Red Gulch (PDC, 1925) 6 reels; Harry Carey, Harriet Hammond, Frank Campeau, Mark Hamilton, Lee Shumway, Doris Lloyd, Frank Norcross; D: Edmund Mortimer; SP: Elliott J. Clawson; S: *The Idyll of Red Gulch.*

Taking a Chance (Fox, 1928) 5 reels; Rex Bell, Lola Todd, Richard Carle, Betty Butts, Jack Byron, Martin Cichy, Jack Henderson; D: Norman Z. McLeod; SP: A. H. Halpin; S: *The Saint of Calamity Gulch.*

M'Liss (RKO-Radio, 1936) 66 mins.; Anne Shirley, John Beal, Guy Kibbee, Moroni Olsen, Douglas Dumbrille, Frank M. Thomas, Ray Mayer, Barbara Pepper, William Benedict, Arthur Hoyt, Margaret Armstrong, Esther Howard, James Bush; D: George Nicholls, Jr.; SP: Dorothy Yost.

The Outcasts of Poker Flat (RKO-Radio, 1937) 68 mins.; Preston Foster, Jean Muir, Van Heflin, Virginia Weidler, Margaret Irving, Barbara Pepper, Si Jenks, Frank M. Thomas, Bradley Page, Monte Blue, Al Ferguson, Richard Lane, Billy Gilbert, Al St. John, George Irving, Dudley Clements, Dick Elliott; D: Christy Cabanne; P: Robert Sisk.

The Luck of Roaring Camp (Monogram, 1937) 58 mins.; Owen Davis, Jr., Joan Woodbury, Charles Brokaw, Forrest Taylor, Bob Kortman, Charles King, Byron Foulger, Bob McKenzie, John Wallace; D: Irvin Willat; SP: Harvey Gates; P: Scott R. Dunlap.

The Outcasts of Poker Flats (20th Century-Fox, 1952) 81 mins.; Anne Baxter, Dale Robertson, Miriam Hopkins, Cameron Mitchell, Craig Hill, Barbara Bates, Bill Lynn, Dick Rich, Tom Greenway, Russ Conway, John Midgley, Harry T. Shannon, Harry Harvey, Jr. D: Joseph M. Newman; SP: Edmund H. North; P: Julian Blaustein.

Tennessee's Partner (RKO-Radio, 1955) 86 mins.; John Payne, Ronald Reagan, Rhonda Fleming, Coleen Gray, Tony Caruso, Morris Ankrum, Leo Gordon, Chubby Johnson, Myron Healey, Joe Devlin, John Mansfield, Angie Dickinson; D: Allan Dwan; SP: Milton Krims, D. D. Beauchamp, Gram Baker, Teddi Sherman; P: Benedict Bogeaus.

Ernest Haycox

Ernest Haycox wrote over 20 novels and hundreds of short stories, but to date only 12 films have been based on his stories. By far the most remembered film is *Stagecoach* (1939), based on the short story "Stage to Lordsburg." *Union Pacific*, also a box office success, was an adaptation of one of his stories.

Haycox was born in Portland, Oregon, on October 1, 1899. During his boyhood he spent much time around logging camps, shingle mills, and on ranches and in small towns. He served on the Mexican border in 1916 as a

John Wayne and Claire Trevor in *Stagecoach* (UA, 1939).

member of a National Guard regiment. Later he was in France with the American Expeditionary Forces for over a year. After the war he attended college and graduated from the University of Oregon in 1923 with a major in journalism. His first book, *Free Grass* was published in 1929. The *New York Times*, on October 14, 1950, listed the following as his principal works: *Free Grass*, 1929; *Chaffee of Roaring Horse*, 1930; *All Trails Cross*, 1931; *Whispering Range*, 1931; *Starlight Rider*, 1933; *Rough Air*, 1934; *Smoky Pass*, 1934; *Riders West*, 1937; *Silver Desert*, 1935; *Trail Smoke*, 1936; *Deep West*, 1937; *Trouble Shooter*, 1937; *Man in the Saddle*, 1938; *Sundown Jim*, 1938; *Border Trumpet*, 1939; *Saddle and Ride*, 1940; *Rim of the Desert*, 1941; *Trail Town*, 1941; *Alder Gulch*, 1942; *Action by Night*, 1943; *Wild Bunch*, 1943; *Bugles in the Afternoon*, 1944; *Canyon Passage*, 1945; *Long Storm*, 1947; *Rough Justice*, 1950; *By Rope and Lead*, 1951; *The Earthbreakers*, 1952; and *The Adventurers*, 1954.

Haycox died from cancer on October 13, 1950, one of the most under-rated of contemporary novelists. Among his later books, published after his death, are *Man in the Saddle*, *Saddle and Ride*, and *Riders West*.

Films Based on Ernest Haycox's Writings

Stagecoach (United Artists, 1939) 96 mins.; John Wayne, Claire Trevor, Thomas Mitchell, George Bancroft, Andy Devine, John Carradine, Louise

Platt, Donald Meek, Berton Churchill, Tom Tyler, Tim Holt, Chris-Pin Martin, Elvira Rios, Bill Cody, Buddy Roosevelt, Yakima Canutt, Paul McVay, Joe Rickson, Harry Tenbrook, Jack Pennick, Kent Odell, William Hopper, Vester Pegg, Ted Lorch, Artie Ortego, Merrill McCormack, Franklyn Farnum, James Mason, Si Jenks, Robert Homans, Chief White Horse, Bryant Washburn, Walter McGrail, Francis Ford, Chief Big Tree, Marga Daighton, Florence Lake, Duke Lee, Cornelius Keefe, Nora Cecil, Lou Mason, Mary Walker, Ed Brady, Eva Novak; D: John Ford; SP: Dudley Nichols; S: *Stage to Lordsburg*; P: Walter Wanger.

Union Pacific (Paramount, 1939) 125 mins.; Barbara Stanwyck, Joel McCrea, Akim Tamiroff, Robert Preston, Lynne Overman, Brian Donlevy, Anthony Quinn, Evelyn Keyes, Stanley Ridges, Regis Toomey, J. M. Kerrigan, Syd Saylor, Julia Faye, Ruth Warren, Fuzzy Knight, Lane Chandler, Si Jenks, Robert Barrat, Lon Chaney, Jr., Joe Sawyer, Henry Kolker; D: Cecil B. DeMille; SP: Walter DeLeon, Gardiner Sullivan, Jesse Lasky, Jr.; P: Cecil B. DeMille.

Sundown Jim (20th Century–Fox, 1942) 63 mins.; John Kimbrough, Virginia Gilmore, Arleen Whelan, Moroni Olson, Paul Hurst, Joe Sawyer, Don Costello, Tom Fadden, Frank McGrath, LeRoy Mason, James Bush, Lane Chandler, Charles Tanner, Cliff Edwards, Paul Sutton, Eddy Waller, Glenn Strange, Kermit Maynard, Syd Saylor; D: James Tinling; SP: Robert F. Metzler, William Bruckner; P: Sol M. Wurtzel.

Apache Trail (MGM, 1943) 66 mins.; Lloyd Nolan, Donna Reed, William Lundigan, Ann Ayars, Connie Gilchrist, Chill Wills, Miles Mander, Gloria Holden, Ray Teal, Grant Withers, Fuzzy Knight, Trevor Bardette, Tito Renaldo, Frank M. Thomas, George Watts; D: Richard Thorpe; SP: Maurice Geraghty; P: Samuel Marx.

Abilene Town (United Artists, 1946) 89 mins.; Randolph Scott, Ann Dvorak, Edgar Buchanan, Rhonda Fleming, Lloyd Bridges, Helen Boyce, Howard Freeman, Richard Hale, Jack Lambert, Hank Patterson, Dick Curtis, Eddy Waller, Buddy Roosevelt; D: Edwin L. Marin, SP: Harold Shumate; S: *Trail Town*; P: Jules Levey.

Canyon Passage (Universal, 1946) 90 mins.; Dana Andrews, Brian Donlevy, Susan Hayward, Patricia Roc, Ward Bond, Andy Devine, Rose Hobart, Halliwell Hobbes, Lloyd Bridges, Stanley Ridges, Dorothy Peterson, Vic Cutler, Fay Holden, Tad Devine, Dennis Devine, Hoagy Carmichael, Karl Hackett, Onslow Stevens, Roy Teal, Gene Roth, Jack Clifford, Jack Ingram, Jack Rockwell, Rex Lease, Harry Shannon, Dick Alexander, Frank Ferguson; D: Jacques Tourneur; SP: Ernest Pascal; P: Walter Wanger.

Heaven Only Knows (United Artists, 1947) 98 mins.; Robert Cummings, Brian Donlevy, Marjorie Reynolds, Jorja Cartright, Bill Goodwin, John Litel, Stuart Erwin, Gerald Mohr, Edgar Kennedy; D: Albert S. Rogell; SP: Ernest Haycox, Art Arthur, Rowland Leigh; P: Seymour Nebenzal.

Montana (Warner Brothers, 1950) 76 mins.; Errol Flynn, Alexis Smith, S. Z. Sakall, Douglas Kennedy, Ian MacDonald, James Brown, Charles Irwin, Paul E. Burns, Tudor Owen, Lester Matthews, Nacho Galindo, Lane Chandler, Monte Blue, Billy Vincent, Warren Jackson, Jack Perrin; D: Ray Enright; SP: James R. Webb, Borden Chase, Charles O'Neal; P: William Jacobs.

Man in the Saddle (Columbia, 1951) 87 mins.; Randolph Scott, Joan Leslie, Ellen Drew, Alexander Knox, Richard Rober, John Russell, Alfonso Bedoya, Guinn (Big Boy) Williams, Clem Bevins, Cameron Mitchell, Richard Crane, Frank Sully, George Lloyd, James Kirkwood, Frank Hagney, Don Beddoe, Tennessee Ernie Ford, Frank Ellis,

George Wallace; D: Andre de Toth; SP: Kenneth Gamet; P: Harry Joe Brown.

Bugles in the Afternoon (Warner Brothers, 1952) 85 mins.; Ray Milland, Helena Carter, Hugh Marlowe, Forrest Tucker, Barton MacLane, George Reeves, James Millican, Gertrude Michael, Stuart Randall, William Phillips, Sheb Wooley, John Pickard; D: Roy Rowland; SP: Geoffrey Homes, Harry Brown; P: William Cagney.

Apache War Smoke (MGM, 1952) 67 mins.; Gilbert Roland, Glenda Farrell, Robert Horton, Barbara Ruick, Gene Lockhart, Henry (Harry) Morgan, Patricia Tiernan, Hank Worden, Myron Healey, Emmett Lynn, Argentina Brunetti, Bobby Blake, Douglas Dumbrille, Iron Eyes Cody, Chubby Johnson; D: Harold Kress; SP: Jerry Davis; P: Hayes Goetz.

Stagecoach (20th Century–Fox, 1966) 114 mins.; Ann-Margret, Red But-tons, Michael Connors, Alex Cord, Bing Crosby, Robert Cummings, Van Heflin, Slim Pickens, Stefanie Powers, Keenan Wynn, Brad Weston, Joseph Hoover; D: Gordon Douglas; SP: Joseph Landon, Dudley Nichols; S: *Stage to Lordsburg*; P: Martin Rackin.

Stagecoach (Raymond Katz Productions/Plantation Productions/Heritage Entertainment, May 18, 1986) 120 mins.; Willie Nelson, Kris Kristofferson, Johnny Cash, Waylon Jennings, Elizabeth Ashley, Mary Crosby, John Schneider, Anthony Franciosa, Anthony Newley, Alex Kubic, June Carter Cash, Lash LaRue, Merritt Butrick, Jessie Colter, David Allen Coe, Bob McLean, Norman Stone, Dave Adams, Jack Dunlap, Bob Cosa, Anthony Russell, Joe Unger, Glen Clark, Ed Adams, Tim Gilbert; D: Ted Post; TP: James Lee Barrett; S: Based on original screenplay by Dudley Nicholls and *Stage to Lordsburg* by Ernest Haycox.

James B. Hendryx

James B. Hendryx had only four of his works turned into film; there should have been more. He was a good writer and his stories about Halfaday Creek and its inhabitants would have made excellent B movies in series form.

Films Based on James Hendryx's Writings

The Promise (Metro, 1917) 5 reels; Harold Lockwood, May Allison, Lester Cuneo, Paul Willis, Lillian Hayward, W. H. Bainbridge, George Fisher, Leota Lorraine, John Steppling, Doc Pomeroy; D: Jay Hunt; SP: Fred J. Balshofer, Richard V. Spencer.

Mints of Hell (R–C, 1919) 5 reels; William Desmond, Vivian Rich, Edward Jobson, Charles French, Jack Richardson, Mary McIvor, Frank Lanning, J. J. Franz, Walter Perry, Tom O'Brien; D: Park Frame; SP: George Elwood Jenks.

The Texan (Fox, 1920) 5 reels; Tom Mix, Gloria Hope, Pat Chrisman, Sid Jordan, Robert Walker; D: Lynn F. Reynolds; SP: Lynn F. Reynolds, Julius Furthman.

Prairie Trails (Fox, 1920) 5 reels; Tom Mix, Kathleen O'Connor, Gloria Hope, Charles K. French, Robert Walker, Sid Jordan, Harry Dunkinson, William Elmer; D: George Marshall; SP: Frank Howard Clark.

The Fourth Horseman, 1954; *Who Rides with Wyatt*, 1956; *The North Star*, 1956; *The Texas Rangers*, 1957; *Orphans of the North*, 1958; *Reckoning at Yankee Flat*, 1958; *The Seven Men at Mimbres Springs*, 1958; *From Where the Sun Now Stands*, 1960; *Journey to Shiloh*, 1960; *San Juan Hill*, 1962; *The Feleen Brand*, 1962; *The Gates of the Mountains*, 1963; *Mackenna's Gold*, 1963; *In the Land of the Mandans*, 1965; *Sons of the Western Frontier*, 1966; *The Last Warpath*, 1966; *Custer's Last Stand*, 1966; *One More River to Cross*, 1967; *Alias Butch Cassidy*, 1967; *Maheo's Children*, 1968; *The Day Fort Larking Fell*, 1969; *The Bear Paw Horses*, 1973; *I, Tom Horn*, 1975; and *Summer of the Gun*, 1978.

Other writings of Allen include *Genesis Five*, 1968; *Tayopa!* 1970; *See How They Run*, 1970; *The Winter of Mrs. Dorion*, and *Dark River*.

Films Based on Will Henry/Clay Fisher's Writings

Santa Fe Passage (Republic, 1955) 90 mins.; John Payne, Faith Domergue, Rod Cameron, Slim Pickens, Leo Gordon, Irene Tedrow, Anthony Caruso; D: William Witney; S: Clay Fisher; SP: Lillie Hayward.

The Tall Men (20 Century–Fox, 1955) 121 mins.; Clark Gable, Jane Russell, Robert Ryan, Cameron Mitchell, Juan Garcia, Harry Shannon, Emile Meyer, Steve Darrell, Will Wright, Robert Adler, J. Lewis Smith, Mae Marsh, Russell Simpson, Gertrude Graner, Tom Wilson, Tom Fadden, Dan White, Argentina Brunetti, Doris Kemper, Carl Harbaugh; D: Raoul Walsh; SP: Sidney Boehm, Frank Nugent; S: Clay Fisher; P: William A. Bacher, William B. Hawks.

Pillars of the Sky (Universal, 1956) 95 mins.; Jeff Chandler, Dorothy Malone, Ward Bond, Keith Andes, Lee Marvin, Sidney Chaplin, Willis Bouchey, Michael Ansara, Olive Carey, Charles Horvath, Orlando Rodriguez, Glen Kramer, Floyd Simmons, Pat Hogan, Felix Noriego, Paul Smith, Martin Milner, Robert Ellis, Ralph J. Votrian, Walter Coy, Alberto Motin, Richard Hale, Frank De Kova, Terry Wilson; D: George Marshall; SP: Sam Rolfe; S: Will Henry, *Frontier Fury*.

Yellowstone Kelly (Warner Brothers, 1959) 91 mins.; Clint Walker, Edward Byrnes, John Russell, Ray Danton, Claude Akins, Rhodes Reason, Andra Martin, Gary Vinson, Warren Oates; D: Gordon Douglas; SP: Burt Kennedy; S: Clay Fisher.

Journey to Shiloh (Universal, 1968) 101 mins.; James Caan, Michael Sarrazin, Brenda Scott, Don Stroud, Paul Peterson, Michael Burns, Michael Vincent, Tisha Sterling, Harrison Ford, John Doucette, Noah Beery, Jr., James Gammon, Brian Avery, Clark Gordon, Robert Pine, Sean Kennedy, Wesley Lau, Chet Stratton, Bing Russell, Lane Bradford, Rex Ingram, Myron Healy, Eileen Wesson, Albert Popwell; D: William Hale; SP: Gene Coon; S: Will Henry.

Mackenna's Gold (Columbia, 1969) 138 mins.; Gregory Peck, Omar Sharif, Telly Savalas, Camilla Sparv, Keenan Wynn, Julie Newmar, Ted Cassidy, Eduardo Cianelli, Dick Peabody, Rudy Diaz, Robert Phillips, Eli Wallach, Burgess Meredith, Victor Jory (narrator); D: J. Lee Thompson; SP: Carl Foreman; S: Will Henry.

Young Billy Young (United Artists, 1969) 88 mins.; Robert Mitchum, Angie Dickinson, Robert Walker, Jr., David Carradine, Jack Kelly, Paul Fix, John Anderson, William Bouchey, Rodolfo Acosta, Deana Martin; D/SP: Burt Kennedy; S: Will Henry, *Who Rides with Wyatt?*

Emerson Hough

The *Covered Wagon* was Emerson Hough's most popular story, and the film adaptation was a box-office success. *North of '36* was probably his second most popular work. In the sound era only two Hough stories have been made into movies: *The Conquering Horde* and *The Texans*, the latter a remake of *North of '36*.

Hough was born on June 28, 1857, in Newton, Iowa. He taught school for a while after graduation from high school, then went to the University of Iowa to major in law. Receiving his degree, he set up practice in White Oaks, New Mexico. While still in college he had started to sell stories to the popular magazines and his life was actually devoted to what he called "professional out-of-door journalism": camping out, roughing it throughout the United States and Canada, and writing about his experiences.

It wasn't until he was 42 that he sold his first novel. For a number of years he edited a section called "Out-of-doors" for the *Saturday Evening Post.*

His constant wandering and his incessant need to get away from the cities and renew his contact with nature actually came extremely close to nomadism.

Hough's historical fiction dealing with the building of the West was his special field. His work had a certain force, but it was conventional and what he wrote was often awkwardly worded. However, his novels were ideally suited for motion pictures. He wrote over 30 novels before his death on April 30, 1923.

His principal works were as follows: *The Singing Mouse Stories*, 1895; *The Story of the Cowboy*, 1897; *The Girl at the Halfway House*, 1900; *The Mississippi Bubble*, 1902; *The Way to the West*, 1903; *The Law of the Land*, 1905; *The King of Gee-Whiz*, 1906; *Story of the Outlaw*, 1907; *The Way of a Man*, 1907; *54–40 or Fight*, 1909; *The Sowing*, 1909; *The Purchase Price*, 1910; *The Young Alaskans*, 1911; *Young Alaskans on the Trail*, 1911; *John Rawn, Prominent Citizen*, 1912; *The Lady and the Pirate*, 1913; *The Let Us Go Afield*, 1916; *The Magnificent Adventure*, 1916; *The Man Next Door*, 1917; *The Broken Gate*, 1917; *Young Alaskans in the Far North*, 1918; *The Way Out*, 1918; *The Sagebrusher*, 1919; *The Web*, 1919; *The Covered Wagon*, 1922; *The Young Alaskans on the Missouri*, 1922; *North of 36*, 1923; *Mother of Gold*, 1924; and *The Ship of Souls*, 1925.

Films Based on Emerson Hough's Writings

The Broken Coin (Universal, 1915) 22 chapters; Francis Ford, Grace Cunard, Harry Mann, Eddie Polo, John Ford, Mina Cunard, Harry Schumm, Ernest Shields, Jack Holt; D: Francis Ford; SP: Grace Cunard.

The Campbells Are Coming (Universal, 1915) 4 reels; Francis Ford, Grace Cunard, Duke Worne, Harry Schumm, M. Denecke, Jack Holt, Lew Short; D/P: Francis Ford; SP: Grace Cunard.

The Sagebrusher (Hodkinson, 1919)

Jack Holt and Lois Wilson in *North of '36* (Paramount, 1924).

7 reels; Roy Stewart, Marguerite De La Motte, Noah Beery, Sr., Betty Brice, Arthur Morrison, Gordon Russell, Edwin Wallock, Thomas O'Brien, Aggie Herring; D: Edward Sloman; SP: William H. Clifford.

The Broken Gate (Hodkinson, 1920) 6 reels; Bessie Barriscale, Joseph Kilgour, Marguerite De La Motte, Sam De Grasse, Arnold Gregg, Lloyd Bacon, Evelyn Selbie, Alfred Allen, Lon Poff; D: Paul Scardon; SP: Jack Cunningham.

The Man Next Door (Vitagraph, 1923) 7 reels; David Torrence, Frank Sheridan, James Morrison, Alice Calhoun, John Steppling, Adele Farrington, Mary Culver, Bruce Boteler; D: Victor Schertzinger; SP: C. Graham Baker.

Way of a Man (Pathe, 1924) 10 chapters; Allene Ray, Harold Miller, Bud Osborne, Lillian Gale, Whitehorse, Kathryn Appleton, Florence Lee, Chet

Ryan, Lillian Adrian; D/SP: George B. Seitz.

The Covered Wagon (Paramount, 1924) 10 reels; Lois Wilson, J. Warren Kerrigan, Ernest Torrence, Alan Hale, Ethel Wales, Tully Marshall, Guy Oliver, John Fox; D: James Cruze; SP: Jack Cunningham.

North of '36 (Paramount, 1924) 8 reels; Jack Holt, Ernest Torrence, Lois Wilson, Noah Beery, Sr., Guy Oliver, Ella Miller, Clarence Geldert; D: Irvin Willat; SP: James Shelley Hamilton.

Ship of Souls (Associated Exhibitors, 1925) 6 reels; Bert Lytell, Lillian Rich, Gertrude Astor, Earl Metcalf, Russell Simpson, Ynez Seabury, Cyril Chadwick, Jean Perry, Pete Mauer, W. J. Miller, Jack Irwin; D: Charles Miller; SP: Frank P. Donovan.

One Hour of Love (Tiffany, 1927) 7 reels; Jacqueline Logan, Robert Frazer,

Montagu Love, Taylor Holmes, Mildred Harris; D: Robert Florey; SP: Sarah Y. Mason; S: *The Broken Gate*.

The Broken Gate (Tiffany, 1927) 6 reels; Dorothy Phillips, William Collier, Jr., Jean Arthur, Phillips Smalley, Gibson Gowland, Jack McDonald, Charles Thurston, Adele Watson, Florence Turner, Charles A. Post; D: James C. McKay; SP: John Francis Natteford.

The Conquering Horde (Paramount, 1931) 75 mins.; Richard Arlen, Fay Wray, George Mendoza, Ian MacLaren, Charles Stevens, Claire Ward, Claude Gillingwater, Arthur Stone, Frank Rice, James Durkin, Ed Brady, Bob Kortman, Harry Cording, John Elliott, Chief Standing Bear; D: Edward Sloman; SP: Grover Jones, William McNutt.

The Texans (Paramount, 1938) 92 mins.; Randolph Scott, Joan Bennett, May Robson, Walter Brennan, Robert Cummings, Robert Barrat, Harvey Stephens, Francis Ford, Raymond Hatton, Clarence Wilson, Jack Moore, Chris-Pin Martin, Anna Demetrio, Richard Tucker, Ed Gargan, Otis Harlan, Spencer Charters, Archie Twitchell, William Haade, Irving Bacon, Bill Roberts, Francis MacDonald, Jack Perrin, Ernie Adams, John Qualen, Wheeler Oakman, Edward J. LeSaint, Richard Denning, Laurie Lane, Everett Brown, Whitey Sovern, Ed Brady, Frank Cordell, Slim Talbot, John Quinn, Harry Woods, James Burtis, Esther Howard, Lon Poff, Kay Whitehead; D: James Hogan; SP: Bertrand Millhauser, Paul Sloane, William Wister Haines; S: *North of '36*; P: Lucien Hubbard.

Clair Huffaker

Clair Huffaker is responsible for five stories and screenplays, perhaps more. In addition, she wrote the screenplay for Paul I. Wellman's *The Comancheros*, a popular John Wayne film.

Films Based on Clair Huffaker's Writings

Seven Ways from Sundown (Universal, 1960) 86 mins.; Audie Murphy, Barry Sullivan, John McIntire, Venetia Stevenson, Kenneth Tobey, Mary Field, Teddy Rooney, Suzanne Lloyd, Ken Lynch, Wade Ramsey, Don Collier, Jack Kruschen, Claudia Barrett, Dale Van Sickel, Fred Graham, Don Haggerty, Robert Burton; D: Harry Keller; SP/S: Clair Huffaker.

Flaming Star (20th Century–Fox, 1960) 101 mins.; Elvis Presley, Barbara Eden, Steve Forrest, Dolores Del Rio, John McIntire, Rodolfo Ascota, Karl Swensen, Ford Rainey, Richard Jaeckel, Anne Benton, L. Q. Jones, Douglas Dick, Tom Reese, Rodd Redwing, Ted Jacques, Monte Burkhart, Marion Cold-

ina, Sharon Bercutt, The Jordanaires; D: Don Siegel; SP: Clair Huffaker, Nunnally Johnson; S: Clair Huffaker.

Posse from Hell (Universal, 1961) 89 mins; Audie Murphy, John Saxon, Zohra Lampert, Vic Morrow, Robert Keith, Ward Ramsey, Rodolfo Acosta, Royal Dano, Frank Overton, James Bell, Paul Carr, Lee Van Cleef, Ray Teal, Forrest Lewis, Charles Horvath, Harry Lauter, Allan (Rocky) Lane, Rand Brooks, I. Stanford Jolley, Kenneth MacDonald, Steve Darrell; D: Herbert Coleman; SP/S: Clair Huffaker.

The Comancheros (20th Century–Fox, 1961) 107 mins.; John Wayne, Stuart Whitman, Ina Balin, Nehemiah Persoff, Lee Marvin, Michael Ansara,

Pat Wayne, Bruce Cabot, Joan O'Brien, Jack Elam, Edgar Buchanan, Henry Daniell, Richard Devon, Steve Taylor, John Dierkes, Roger Mobley, Bob Steele, Luisa Triana, Don Brodie, Greg Paumer, George J. Lewis, Aissa Wayne, Jon Lormer, Phil Arnold, Alan Carney, Dennis Cole; D: Michael Curtiz; S: Paul I. Wellman; SP: Clair Huffaker, James Edward Grant.

Rio Conchos (20th Century–Fox, 1964) 107 mins.; Richard Boone, Stuart Whitman, Tony Franciosa, Wende Wagner, Warner Anderson, Jim Brown, Rodolfo Acosta, Barry Kelly, Vito Scotti, House Peters, Jr., Kevin Hagen, Edmund O'Brien; D: Gordon Douglas; S: *Guns of the Rio Conchos*; SP: Clair Huffaker.

Flap (Warner Brothers, 1970) 106 mins.; Anthony Quinn, Claude Akins, Tony Bill, Victor Jory, Don Collier, Shelley Winters, Susana Miranda, William Mims, Rudy Diaz, Pedro Regas, John War Eagle; D: Carol Reed; SP: Clair Huffaker; S: *Nobody Loves a Drunken Indian*.

Chino (Dino De Laurentis–Coral, 1973) 97 mins.; Charles Bronson, Jill Ireland, Vincent Van Patten, Marcel Bozzuffi, Melissa Chimenti, Fausto Tozzi, Diana Lorys, Ettore Manni; D: John Sturges; SP: Clair Huffaker, Dino Maiuri, Massimo DeRita; S: Lee Hoffman.

Peter B. Kyne

Peter B. Kyne was born on October 12, 1880, in San Francisco and died there from cancer at the age of 77.

Kyne was fond of saying that he had written more best-selling novels in a row — 12 — than any other writer. He made and spent a fortune with his 25 novels and 1,000 or so short stories. In addition to his westerns he created the temper prone, softhearted, trouble-seeking old sea dog, Cappy Ricks.

Kyne is best known for the several versions of *The Three Godfathers*, which was filmed three times under that title and one time each as *Three Badmen*, *Hell's Heroes*, and *Marked Men*. The regeneration of three outlaws through the adoption of an infant born in the desert and left in their care by a dying mother forms the theme of Kyne's story. Each of the six versions proved to be moneymakers.

Many films from the 1920s and 1930s credit Kyne as their source. This was a common practice of the time. James Oliver Curwood is another author whose name was attached to the title in order to give it drawing power.

There is nothing polished, profound, or durable about Kyne's writings; but his stories are well paced and charged with sentimental values. For 75 years they have found a large and constant reading public.

Kyne attended public schools in San Francisco, as well as business college. After spending a few months as a clerk in a general store, he joined the army and saw service in the Philippine Rebellion. After his brief army stint he went to work in a lumber and shipping office for seven years.

He then opened a haberdashery store on the San Francisco waterfront, and a little later became a lumber broker. In 1910 he was married and shortly thereafter started his writing career, one that was interrupted by World War I. He served in France as captain of the 144th Field Artillery. Returning home, he settled down to serious writing of both novels and short stories.

His principal works are as follows: *Three Godfathers*, 1913; *Cappy Ricks*, 1916; *The Valley of the Giants*, 1918; *Kindred of the Dust*, 1920; *The Pride of Palomar*, 1921; *Never the Twain Shall Meet*, 1923; *The Understanding Heart*, 1926; *They Also Serve*, 1927; *Comrades of the Storm*, 1933; *Cappy Ricks Comes Back*, 1934; and *Dude Woman*, 1940.

Films Based on Peter Kyne's Writings

Broncho Billy and the Baby (Essanay, 1915) 1 reel; Broncho Billy Anderson.

It Happened While He Fished (Nestor, 1915); Jack Dillon, Neal Burns, Billie Rhodes, Jane Waller; D/SP: Horace Davey.

Judge Not, or the Woman of Mona Diggins (Universal, 1915) 6 reels; Julia Dean, Harry Carter, Harry Carey, Marc Robbins, Kingsley Benedict, Joe Singleton, Lydia Yeamans Titus, Walter Belasco; D: Robert Leonard; SP: Robert Leonard, Harvey Gates; S: *Renunciation*.

The Long Chance (Universal, 1915) 6 reels; Frank Keenan, Fred Church, Harry Blaising, Walter Newman, Beryl Boughton, Stella Razeto, Clyde Benson, Jack Nelson; D: Edward J. LeSaint; SP: Harvey Gates.

What the River Foretold (Universal, 1915) 3 reels; Edythe Sterling, Jack Holt, Sherman Bainbridge; D: William Franey, Joseph Franz; P: Joseph Franz.

The Three Godfathers (Universal, 1916) 6 reels; Harry Carey, Stella Razetto, George Berrell, Frank Lanning, Joe Rickson, Hart (Jack) Hoxie; D: Edward J. LeSaint; SP: Harvey Gates.

The Committee on Credentials (Bison, 1916) 3 reels; Harry Carey, George Berrell, Neal Hart, Joe Rickson, Olive Fuller Golden, Elizabeth Janes; D: Harry Carey; SP: Harvey Gates.

The Parson of Panamint (Pallas,

1916) 5 reels; Dustin Farnum, Winifred Kingston, Pomeroy Cannon, Howard Davies, Colin Chase, Ogden Crane, Jane Keckley, Tom Bates; D: William D. Taylor; SP: Julia Crawford.

Humanizing Mr. Winsby (Unity Sales, 1916) 5 reels; George Chesebro, Julius Frankenberg, Arthur Millett, Alice Neice.

The Resurrection of Dan Packard (Edison, 1916) 2 reels; Otis Harlan, William Wadsworth, Raymond McKee, Marcia Harris; D: Frank Smithson; SP: Edward H. Griffith; S: *The Handshake Agreement*.

The Land Just Over Yonder (1916) 6 reels; George Chesebro, Arthur N. Millett, George Best, Elsa Fox, Charles Eichman, Julius Frankenberg, Sidney Lang.

A Man's Man (Paralta, 1917) 7 reels; J. Warren Kerrigan, Lois Wilson, Kenneth Harlan, Ed Coxen, Ida Lewis, Eugene Pallette, Joseph J. Dowling, John Steppling, Harry Von Meter, Ernest Pasque, Arthur Allardt, Wallace Worsley, Walter Perry; D: Oscar Apfel; SP: Thomas Geraghty; P: J. Warren Kerrigan.

Light in Darkness (Edison, 1917) 5 reels; Shirley Mason, Frank Morgan, William Tooker, J. Frank Glendon, George Trimble, Bigelow Cooper, William Wadsworth, Charles Martin, Sam Niblack, Nellie Grant, Betty Young; D/SP: Alan Crosland.

One Touch of Nature (Edison/K-E-S-E Service, 1917) 5 reels; John Drew Bennett, Viola Cain, Edward O'Connor, George Henry, Helen Strickland, John J. McGraw, Edward Lawrence; D: Edward H. Griffith.

Salt of the Earth (Edison/George Kleine System/Perfection, 1917) 5 reels; Peggy Adams, Chester Barnett, Russell Simpson, William Wadsworth, William Chatterton, Ivan Christie; D: Saul Harrison; SP: Raymond E. Dakin.

Valley of the Giants (Paramount, 1919) 5 reels; Wallace Reid, Grace Darmond, Will Brunton, Charles Ogle, Alice Taafe (Terry), Ralph Lewis, Kay Laurel, Hart (Jack) Hoxie, Noah Beery, Sr., Guy Oliver, William H. Brown, Richard Cummings, Virginia Foltz, Ogden Crane, Lillian Mason, Speed Hansen; D: James Cruze; SP: Marion Fairfax.

Marked Men (Universal, 1919) 5 reels; Harry Carey, J. Farrell MacDonald, Joe Harris, Ted Brooks, Winifred Westover, Charles Le Moyne, David Kirby; D: John Ford; SP: H. Tipton Steck; S: *The Three Godfathers.*

The Ten Dollar Raise (Associated Producers, 1921) 6 reels; William V. Mong, Marguerite De La Motte, Pat O'Malley, Helen Jerome Eddy, Hal Cooley, Lincoln Plumer, Charles Hill Mailes; D: Edward Sloman; SP: Albert S. Le Vino.

Cappy Ricks (Paramount, 1921) 6 reels; Thomas Meighan, Charles Abbe, Agnes Ayres, Hugh Cameron, John Sainpolis, Paul Everton, Tom O'Malley, Ivan Linow, Jack Dillon; D: Tom Forman; SP: Albert S. LeVino.

Red Courage (Universal, 1921) 5 reels; Hoot Gibson, Joel Day, Molly Malone, Joseph Girard, Merrill McCormick, Charles Newton, Arthur Hoyt, Joe Harris, Dick Cummings, Mary Philbin, Jim Corey, Mac V. Wright; D: Reaves Eason; SP: Harvey Gates; S: *The Sheriff of Cinnabar.*

A Motion to Adjourn (Arrow, 1921) 6 reels; Harry Rattenberry, Roy Stewart, Sidney D'Albrook, Evelyn Nelson, Marjorie Daw, Peggy Blackwood; D/SP: Roy Clements; P: Ben Wilson.

The Innocent Cheat (Arrow, 1921) 6 reels; Roy Stewart, Sidney DeGray, George Hernandez, Rhea Mitchell, Kathleen Kirkham; D/P: Ben Wilson; SP: J. Grubb Alexander.

Kindred of the Dust (Associated First National, 1922) 8 reels; Miriam Cooper, Ralph Graves, Lionel Belmore, Eugénie Besserer, Maryland Morne, Elizabeth Waters, W. J. Ferguson, Caroline Rankin, Pat Rooney, John Herdman; D: R. H. Walsh; SP: James T. O'Donohue.

Back to Yellow Jacket (Arrow, 1922) 6 reels; Roy Stewart, Kathleen Kirkham, Earl Metcalfe, Jack Pratt; D/P: Ben Wilson; SP: J. Grubb Alexander.

One Eighth Apache (Berwilla/Arrow, 1922) 6 reels; Roy Stewart, Kathleen Kirkham, Wilbur McGaugh, George M. Daniel, Dick La Reno; D/P: Ben Wilson; SP: J. Grubb Alexander.

The Long Chance (Universal, 1922) 5 reels; Henry B. Walthall, Marjorie Daw, Ralph Graves, Jack Curtis, Leonard Clapham (Tom London), Boyd Irwin, William Bertram, Grace Marvin, George A. William; D: Jack Conway; SP: Raymond Schrock.

Brothers Under the Sun (Goldwyn, 1922) 6 reels; Pat O'Malley, Helene Chadwick, Mae Busch, Norman Kerry, Claire Windsor; D: E. Mason Hopper; SP: Grant Carpenter.

The Pride of Palomar (Paramount, 1922) 8 reels; Forrest Stanley, Marjorie Daw, Tote Du Crow, James Barrows, Joseph Dowling, Alfred Allen, Percy Williams, George Nichols; D: Frank Borzage; SP: Grant Carpenter, John Lynch.

Making a Man (Paramount, 1922) 6 reels; Jack Holt, J. P. Lockney, Eva

John Wayne in *Three Godfathers* (MGM, 1948).

Novak, Bert Woodruff, Frank Nelson, Robert Dudley; D: Joseph Henabery; SP: Albert S. LeVino; S: *Humanizing Mr. Winsby.*

The Go-Getter (Paramount, 1923) 8 reels; T. Roy Barnes, Seena Owen, William Norris, Tom Lewis, Louis Wolheim, Fred Huntley, John Carr, Frank Currier, William J. Sorrelle, William J. MacMillan, Jane Jennings; D: E. H. Griffith; SP: John Lynch.

A Man's Man (FBO, 1923) 5 reels; J. Warren Kerrigan, Lois Wilson, Kenneth Harlan, Edward Coxen, Ida Lewis, Harry van Meter, Eugene Pallette, Joseph J. Dowling; D: Oscar Apfel; SP: Thomas J. Geraghty. Note. This is a 5-reel version of the 7-reel film released by Hodkinson in January 1918.

Homeward Bound (Paramount, 1923) 7 reels; Thomas Meighan, Lila Lee, Charles Abbe, William P. Carleton, Hugh Cameron, Gus Weinberg, Maude Turner Gordon, Cyril Ring, Katherine Spencer; D: Ralph Ince; SP: Jack Cunningham, Paul Sloane.

Loving Lies (Associated Authors/ Allied Producers, 1924) 7 reels; Evelyn Brent, Monte Blue, Joan Lowell, Charles Gerrard, Ralph Faulkner, Ethel Wales, Andrew Waldron, Tom Kennedy; D: W. S. Van Dyke; SP: Thompson Buchanan; S: *The Harbor Bar.*

Beauty and the Bad Man (Peninsula Studios, 1925) 6 reels; Mabel Ballin, Forrest Stanley, Russell Simpson, Andre de Beranger, Edna Mae Cooper, James Gordon; D: William Worthington; SP: Frank E. Woods; S: *Cornflower Cassie's Concert.*

The Beautiful Gambler (Universal, 1925) 5 reels; Grace Darmond, Jack Mower, Harry van Meter, Charles Brinley, Herschel Mayall, Willis Marks; D: William Worthington; SP: Hope Loring.

Never the Twain Shall Meet (Cosmopolitan/MGM, 1925) 8 reels; Anita Stewart, Bert Lytell, Huntley Gordon, Justine Johnstone, George Siegmann, Lionel Belmore, William Norris, Emily Fitzroy, Princess Marie de Bourbon, Florence Turner, James Wang, Ben Deeley, Roy Coulson, Thomas Ricketts, Ernest Butterworth; D: Maurice Tourneur; SP: Eugene Mullin.

The Golden Strain (Fox, 1925) 6 reels; Hobart Bosworth, Kenneth Harlan, Madge Bellamy, Lawford Davidson, Ann Pennington, Frank Beal, Frankie Lee, Coy Watson, Robert Frazer, Oscar Smith, George Reed, Grace Morse, Frank McGlynn, Jr., Larry Fisher, Lola Mackey; D: Victor Schertzinger; SP: Eve Unsell; S: *Thoroughbreds.*

The Enchanted Hill (Paramount, 1926) 7 reels; Jack Holt, Florence Vidor, Noah Beery, Sr., Mary Brian, Richard Arlen, George Bancroft, Ray Thompson, Brandon Hurst, Henry Hebert, George Kuwa, Mathilde Comont, Willard Cooley, George Magrill; D: Irvin Willat; SP: James Shelley Hamilton.

Rustling for Cupid (Fox, 1926) 5

reels; George O'Brien, Anita Stewart, Russell Simpson, Edith Yorke, Herbert Prior, Frank McGlynn, Jr., Sid Jordan; D: Irving Cummings; SP: L. G. Rigby.

The Shamrock Handicap (Fox, 1926) 6 reels; Janet Gaynor, Leslie Fenton, J. Farrell MacDonald, Louis Payne, Claire McDowell, Willard Louis, Andy Clark, Georgie Harrie, Brandon Hurst, Ely Reynolds; D: John Ford; SP: John Stone.

More Pay—Less Work (Fox, 1926) 6 reels; Albert Gran, Mary Brian, E. J. Ratcliffe, Charles Rogers, Otto Hoffman, Charles Conklin; D: Albert Ray; SP: Rex Taylor.

War Paint (MGM, 1926) 6 reels; Tim McCoy, Pauline Starke, Charles French, Chief Yowlachie, Whitehorse, Karl Dane; D: W. S. Van Dyke; SP: Charles Maigne.

Breed of the Sea (R-C/FBO, 1926) 6 reels; Ralph Ince, Margaret Livingston, Pat Harmon, Alphonz Ethier, Dorothy Dunbar, Shannon Day; D: Ralph Ince; SP: J. Grubb Alexander, J. G. Hawks; S: *Blue Blood and the Pirates.*

The Buckaroo Kid (Universal, 1926) 6 reels; Hoot Gibson, Ethel Shannon, Burr McIntosh, Harry Todd, James Gordon, Joe Rickson, Newton House, Clark Comstock; D/SP: Lynn F. Reynolds; S: *Oh, Promise Me.*

The Understanding Heart (Cosmopolitan/MGM, 1927) 7 reels; Joan Crawford, Rockliffe Fellowes, Francis X. Bushman, Jr., Carmel Myers, Richard Carle, Jerry Miley, Harvey Clark; D: Jack Conway; SP: Edward T. Lowe, Jr.

California (MGM, 1927) 5 reels; Tim McCoy, Dorothy Sebastian, Marc MacDermott, Frank Currier, Fred Warren, Lillian Leighton, Edwin Terry; D: W. S. Van Dyke; SP: Frank Davis.

A Hero on Horseback (Universal, 1927) 6 reels; Hoot Gibson, Ethlyne Clair, Edwards Davis, Edward Hearn, Dan Mason; D: Del Andrews; SP:

Mary Alice Scully; S: *Bread Upon the Waters.*

Foreign Devils (MGM, 1927) 5 reels; Tim McCoy, Claire Windsor, Cyril Chadwick, Frank Currier, Emily Fitzroy, Lawson Butt, Sojin, Frank Chew; D: W. S. Van Dyke; SP: Marian Ainslee.

Galloping Fury (Universal, 1927) 6 reels; Hoot Gibson, Otis Harlan, Sally Rand, Frank Beal, Pee Wee Holmes, Max Asher, Edward Coxen, Duke R. Lee; D: Reaves Eason; SP: Arthur Statter; S: *Tidy Toreador.*

The Valley of the Giants (First National, 1927) 7 reels; Milton Sills, Doris Kenyon, Arthur Stone, George Faucett, Paul Hurst, Charles Sellon, Yola D'Avril, Phil Brady; D: Charles J. Brabin; SP: L. G. Rigby.

The Rawhide Kid (Universal, 1928) 6 reels; Hoot Gibson, Georgia Hale, Frank Hagney, William H. Strauss, Harry Todd, Tom Lingham; D: Del Andrews; SP: Arthur Statter.

The Man in Hobbles (Tiffany-Stahl, 1928) 6 reels; John Harron, Lila Lee, Lucien Littlefield, Sunshine Hart, Betty Egan, Eddie Nugent, William Anderson, Vivian Oakland; D: George Archainbaud; SP: J. F. Natteford.

Freedom of the Press (Universal, 1928) 7 reels; Lewis Stone, Marceline Day, Malcolm McGregor, Henry B. Walthall, Robert E. O'Connor, Thomas Ricketts, Hayden Stevenson, Robert Ellis, Boris Baronoff, Morgan Thorpe, Evelyn Selbie, Bernard Siegel, Wilson Benge; D: George Melford; SP: J. Grubb Alexander, J. G. Hawks, Curtis Benton.

Tide of Empire (MGM, 1929) 8 reels; Renee Adoree, George Duryea, George Faucett, William Collier, Jr., Fred Kohler, James Bradbury, Sr., Harry Gribbon, Paul Hurst; D: Allan Dwan, SP: Waldemar Young.

Hell's Heroes (Universal, 1930) 7

reels; Charles Bickford, Raymond Hatton, Fred Kohler, Fritzi Ridgeway, Marie Alba, Jose De La Cruz, Buck Connors, Walter James; D: William Wyler; SP: Tom Reed; *The Three Godfathers*.

Wild Horse (Allied, 1931) 77 mins.; Hoot Gibson, Alberta Vaughn, Stepin Fetchit, Neal Hart, Edmund Cobb, Skeeter Bill Robbins, George Bunny, Edward Piel, Sr., Joe Rickson, Glenn Strange; D: Richard Thorpe, Sidney Algier; SP: Jack Natteford.

The Local Bad Man (Allied, 1932) 59 mins.; Hoot Gibson, Sally Blane, Edward Piel, Sr., Hooper Atchley, Milt Brown, Edward Hearn, Skeeter Bill Robbins, Jack Clifford, Bud Osborne, Lew Meehan; D: Otto Brower; SP: Philip White; P: M. H. Hoffman.

Heroes of the West (Universal, 1932) 12 chapters; Onslow Stevens, Diane Duval (Jackqueline Wells/Julie Bishop), Noah Beery, Jr., William Desmond, Martha Mattox, Francis Ford, Philo McCullough, Harry Tenbrook, Frank Lackteen, Edmund Cobb, Jules Cowles, Grace Cunard, Chief Thunderbird, Lafe McKee; D: Ray Taylor; P: Henry MacRae.

The Pride of the Legion (Mascot, 1932) 70 mins.; Sally Blane, Barbara Kent, Victor Jory, Tom Dugan, Ralph Ince, Lucien Littlefield, J. Farrell MacDonald, Matt Moore, Jason Robards, Glenn Tyron; D/SP: Ford Beebe; P: Nat Levine.

Flaming Guns (Universal, 1932) 57 mins.; Tom Mix, Ruth Hall, William Farnum, George Hackathorne, Clarence Wilson, Bud Osborne, Duke Lee, Pee Wee Holmes, Jimmy Shannon, William Steele, Walter Patterson, Fred Burns, Slim Whitaker, Clyde Kinney, Tony, Jr. (a horse); D: Arthur Rosson; SP: Jack Cunningham.

Self Defense (Monogram, 1932) 68 mins.; Pauline Frederick, Claire Windsor, Theodore Von Eltz, Barbara Kent,

Robert Elliott, Henry B. Walthall, Jameson Thomas, George Hackathorne, Willie Fung, Lafe McKee, Si Jenks, George F. Hayes; D: Phil Rosen; SP: Tristram Tupper; S: "The Just Judge"; P: William T. Lackey.

Gordon of Ghost City (Universal, 1933) 12 chapters; Buck Jones, Madge Bellamy, Walter Miller, William Desmond, Tom Ricketts, Francis Ford, Edmund Cobb, Hugh Enfield (Craig Reynolds), Bud Osborne, Ethan Laidlaw, Dick Rush, Jim Corey, William Steele, Bob Kerrick, Cecil Kellogg, Artie Ortego, Silver (a horse); D: Ray Taylor; SP: Ella O'Neill, Basil Dickey, George H. Plympton, Harry O. Hoyt, Het Mannheim; S: "Oh, Promise Me!"; P: Henry MacRae.

Galland Defender (Columbia, 1935) 60 mins.; Charles Starrett, Joan Perry, Harry Woods, Edward J. LeSaint, Jack Clifford, Al Bridge, George Billings, George Chesebro, Edmund Cobb, Frank Ellis, Jack Rockwell, Tom London, Stanley Blystone, Lew Meehan, Merrill McCormack, Glenn Strange, Al Ferguson, Slim Whitaker, Bud Osborne, Sons of the Pioneers (Roy Rogers, Bob Nolan, Tim Spencer, Hugh and Carl Farr), Roy Jones, Buck Connors, Jack Kirk, Oscar Gahan, Chuck Baldra, Pascale Perry, Bud McClure, Dick Botiller, Bob Card, Al Haskell, Tom Smith; D: David Selman; SP: Ford Beebe; S: "All for Love."

Valley of Wanted Men (Conn, 1935) 62 mins.; Frankie Darro, Grant Withers, Dru Layron, Roy (LeRoy) Mason, Paul Fix, Russell Hopton, Walter Miller, Fred Toones, Al Bridge, William Gould, Jack Rockwell, Slim Whitaker, Irene Crane; D: Alan James; SP: Barry Barringer, Forrest Barnes; S: "All for Love"; P: Maurice Conn.

Men of Action (Conn, 1935) 61 mins.; Frankie Darro, Roy (LeRoy) Mason, Barbara Worth, Fred Kohler, Gloria Shea, Edwin Maxwell, Arthur Hoyt, Syd Saylor, John Ince; D: Alan

James; SP: Forrest Sheldon, John W. Krafft, Barry Barringer.

Cappy Ricks Returns (Republic, 1935) 67 mins.; Robert McWade, Ray Walker, Florine McKinney, Lucien Littlefield, Bradley Page, Lois Wilson, Oscar Apfel, Kenneth Harlan; D: Mack Wright; SP: George Wassner; P: Trem Carr.

The Mysterious Avenger (Columbia, 1936) 5 reels; Charles Starrett, Joan Perry, Wheeler Oakman, Edward J. LeSaint, Lafe McKee, Hal Price, Charles Locher (Jon Hall), George Chesebro, Jack Rockwell, Dick Botiller, Edmund Cobb, Sons of the Pioneers (Roy Rogers, Bob Nolan, Hugh Farr, Karl Farr, Tim Spencer); D: David Selman; SP: Ford Beebe.

Three Godfathers (MGM, 1936) 82 mins.; Chester Morris, Lewis Stone, Walter Brennan, Irene Hervey, Sidney Toler, Dorothy Tree, Roger Imhoff, Robert Livingston, Willard Robertson, John Sheehan, Victor Potel, Harvey Clark, Joseph Marievsky, Helen Brown, Virginia Brissac; D: Richard Boleslawski; SP: Edward E. Paramore, Jr., Manuel Seff.

Rio Grande Romance (Victory, 1936) 70 mins.; Eddie Nugent, Maxine Doyle, Fuzzy Knight, Forrest Taylor, Ernie Adams, George Cleveland, Lucille Lund, Nick Stuart, Don Alvarado, George Walsh, Joyce Kay; D: Robert Hill; SP: AL Martin; P: Sam Katzman.

Secret Patrol (Columbia, 1936) 60 mins.; Charles Starrett, Finis Barton, J. P. McGowan, Henry Mollinson, LeStrange Millman, Arthur Kerr, Reginald Hincks, Ted Mapes, James McGrath; D: David Selman; SP: J. P. McGowan, Robert Watson.

Kelly of the Secret Service (Victory, 1936) 69 mins.; Ted Kelly, Lloyd Hughes, Sheila Mannors, Fuzzy Knight, Syd Saylor, Jack Mulhall, Forrest Taylor, John Elliott, Miki Morita, Jack Corwell;

D: Bob Hill; SP: Al Martin; P: Sam Katzman.

Code of the Range (Columbia, 1936) 55 mins.; Charles Starrett, Mary Blake, Ed Coxen, Allan Cavan, Edward Piel, Sr., Edmund Cobb, Edward J. LeSaint, Ralph McCullough, George Chesebro, Art Mix, Albert J. Smith; D: C. C. Coleman, Jr.; SP: Ford Beebe.

Stampede (Columbia, 1936) 58 mins.; Charles Starrett, Finis Barton, J. P. McGowan, LeStrange Millman, James McGrath, Arthur Kerr, Jack Atkinson, Mike Heppell, Ted Mapes; D: Ford Beebe; SP: Robert Watson, Ford Beebe.

The Fighting Coward (Victory, 1936) 60 mins.; Ray Walker, Joan Woodbury, William Farnum, Clara Kimball Young, Syd Saylor, Reed Howes, Earl Dwire, Matthew Betz, Roger Williams; D: Dan Milner; SP: Al Martin; S: "The Last Assignment."

Born to Fight (Conn/Ambassador, 1936) 69 mins.; Frankie Darro, Kane Richmond, Frances Grant, Jack LaRue, Monte Collins, Sheila Mannors (Bromley), Eddie Phillips, Fred (Snowflake) Toones; D: Charles Hutchinson; SP: Stephen Norris; P: Maurice Conn.

Headline Crasher (Conn, 1937) 6 reels; Frankie Darro, Kane Richmond, Muriel Evans, John Merton, Richard Tucker, Edward Earle, Jack Ingram, Charles King, Dick Curtis, Eddie Kane, Eleanor Stewart, John Ward, Harry Harvey, Walter Clinton, Henry Hall, Wayne Bumpus, Bunny Bronson, Ray Martin; D: Les Goodwins; SP: Harry C. Hoyt, Sherman Lowe; P: Maurice Conn.

Flaming Frontiers (Universal, 1938) 15 chapters; Johnny Mack Brown, Eleanor Hansen, Ralph Bowman (John Archer), Charles Middleton, Chief Thunder Cloud, Horace Murphy, Charles King, James Blaine, Roy Barcroft, Charles Stevens, William Royle, John Rutherford, Eddy Waller, Edward

Cassidy, Michael Slade, Karl Hackett, Iron Eyes Cody, Pat O'Brien, Earle Hodgins, J. P. McGowan, Frank Ellis, Jim Toney, Hank Bell, Horace B. Carpenter, Tom Steele, Slim Whitaker, Frank LaRue, Al Bridge, Blackjack Ward, Ferris Taylor, Jim Farley, Jim Corey, Bob Woodward, Frank Straubinger, Helen Gibson, Sunni Chorre, George Plues, Jack Saunders, Jack Roper, Bill Hazelett; D: Ray Taylor, Alan James; SP: Wyndham Gittens, Paul Perez, Basil Dickey, George H. Plympton, Ella O'Neill; S: "The Tie That Binds"; P: Henry MacRae.

Valley of the Giants (Warner Brothers, 1938) 79 mins.; Wayne Morris, Claire Trevor, Frank McHugh, Alan Hale, Donald Crisp, Charles Bickford, Jack LaRue, John Litel, Dick Purcell, El Brendel, Russell Simpson, Cy Kendall, Harry Cording, Wade Boteler, Helen MacKellar, Addison Richards, Jerry Colonna; D: William Keighley; SP: Seton I. Miller, Michael Fessier.

The Parson of Panamint (Paramount, 1941) 84 mins.; Charlie Ruggles, Ellen Drew, Phillip Terry, Joseph Schildkraut, Porter Hall, Henry Kolker, Janet Beecher, Paul Hurst, Clem Bevins, Douglas Fowley, Frank Puglia, Minor Watson, Harry Hayden, Russell Hicks, Hal Price; D: William McGann; SP: Harold Shumate, Adrian Scott; P: Harry Sherman.

Three Godfathers (Argosy/MGM, 1948) 106 mins.; John Wayne, Pedro Armendariz, Harry Carey, Jr., Ward Bond, Jane Darwell, Mae Marsh, Mildred Natwick, Guy Kibbee, Dorothy Ford, Ben Johnson, Charles Halton, Hank Worden, Jack Pennick, Fred Libby, Michael Dugan, Don Summers, Francis Ford, Eva Novak, Gertrude Astor, Ruth Clifford, Emilia Grace Yelda, Cliff Lyons, Frank McGrath, Richard Hagemen; D: John Ford; SP: Laurence Stallings, Frank S. Nugent; P: John Ford, Merian C. Cooper.

Belle Le Grande (Republic, 1951) 90 mins.; Vera Ralston, John Carroll, William Ching, Muriel Lawrence, Hope Emerson, John Qualen, Henry (Harry) Morgan, Stephen Chase, Charles Cane, Marietta Cantry, Andrew Tombes, Russell Hicks, Isabel Randolph, Frank Wilcox, Grant Withers, Thurston Hall, Sam Flint, Edward Cassidy, John Hart, Hal Price, James Arness, Don Beddoe, Pierce Watkin, Eduard Keane, Russell Hicks, John Hamilton, Carl Switzer, Giro Carrado, Fred Hoose, Emory Parnell; D: Allan Dwan; SP: D. D. Beauchamp; P: Herbert J. Yates.

The Godchild (MGM, November 1974) 90 mins.; Jack Palance, Jack Warden, Keith Carradine, Ed Lauter, Jose Perez, Bill McKinney, Jesse Vint, Simon Dechard, Fionnula Flangan, John Quade, Ed Bakey; D: John Badham; TP: Ron Bishop.

Louis L'Amour/Tex Burns

Louis L'Amour is the most successful of all western writers, even surpassing Zane Grey. Over 85 million copies of his novels have been printed, and at least 16 of these novels have been made into motion pictures. At last count he was the author of about 400 short stories in some 80 magazines, both in the United States and abroad. He has written approximately 90 novels, and nearly all of them have been translated into various foreign languages. Though self-educated, he has lectured at many universities and has received numerous awards for his writing. In 1972 Jamestown College bestowed upon him an honorary LL.D.

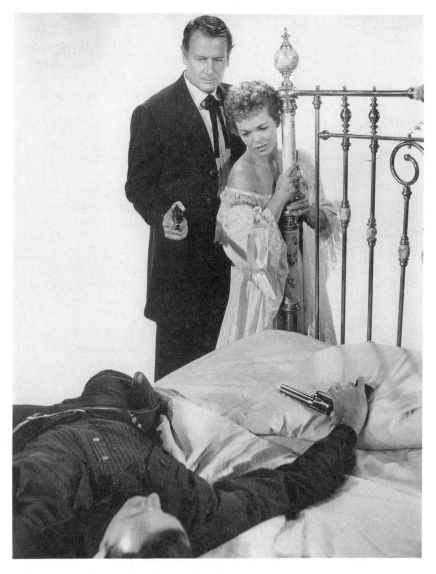

Joel McCrea and Nancy Gates in *Stranger on Horseback* (United Artists, 1955).

L'Amour was born in Jamestown, North Dakota, in 1908. Before becoming a successful writer, he worked at numerous jobs — hay shocker, flume builder, boxer, longshoreman, lumberjack, fruit picker, miner, and elephant handler, to name a few. During World War II he served in the U.S. Army (1942–46) and rose to the rank of first lieutenant.

Among his achievements has been the writing of film and television scripts. Under the pseudonym Tex Burns he has published several Hopalong Cassidy novels, all originally published by Doubleday. Many critics suggest the great success of L'Amour's novels is because of his devotion to authenticity and accuracy — due to his careful research and special attention to details — and because his books are fast moving, contain much action, and are easy to read.

The following are his principal writings as Tex Burns: *Hopalong Cassidy and the Riders of High Rock*, 1951; *Hopalong Cassidy and the Rustlers of West Fork*, 1951; *Hopalong Cassidy and the Trail to Seven Pines*, 1951; and *Hopalong Cassidy: Trouble Shooter*, 1952.

As Louis L'Amour his principal works are as follows: *Smoke from This Altar*, 1939; *Hondo*, 1953; *Showdown at Yellow Butte*, 1954; *Crossfire Trail*, 1954; *Heller with a Gun*, 1954; *Utah Blaine*, 1954; *Kilkenny*, 1954; *To Tame a Land*, 1955; *Guns of the Timberlands*, 1955; *The Burning Hills*, 1956; *Silver Canyon*, 1956; *Last Stand at Papago Wells*, 1957; *The Tall Stranger*, 1957; *Sitka*, 1957; *Radigan*, 1958; *The First Fast Draw*, 1959; *Taggart*, 1959; *The Daybreakers*, 1960; *Flint*, 1960; *Sackett*, 1961; *Shalako*, 1962; *Killoe*, 1962; *High Lonesome*, 1962; *Lando*, 1962; *How the West Was Won*, 1963; *Fallon*, 1963; *Catlow*, 1963; *Dark Canyon*, 1963; *Mojave Crossing*, 1964; *Hanging Woman Creek*, 1964; *Kiowa Trail*, 1965; *The High Graders*, 1965; *The Sackett Brand*, 1965; *The Key-Lock Man*, 1965; *Kid Rodelo*, 1966; *Mustang Man*, 1966; *Kilrone*, 1966; *The Broken Gun*, 1966; *The Skyliners*, 1967; *Matagorda*, 1967; *Down the Long Hills*, 1968; *Chaney*, 1968; *Conagher*, 1969; *The Empty Land*, 1969; *The Lonely Men*, 1969; *The Man Called Noon*, 1970; *Galloway*, 1970; *Reilly's Luck*, 1970; *Brionne*, 1971; *Under the Sweetwater Rim*, 1971; *Tucker*, 1971; *North to the Rails*, 1971; *Callaghen*, 1972; *Treasure Mountain*, 1972; *Ride the Dark Trail*, 1972; *The Ferguson Rifle*, 1973; *The Man from Skibbereen*, 1973; *The Quick and the Dead*, 1973; *The Californios*, 1973; *Rivers West*, 1974; *Sackett's Land*, 1974; *Over the Dry Side*, 1975; *The Man from the Broken Hills*, 1975; *War Party*, 1975; *The Rider of the Lost Creek*, 1976; *To the Far Blue Mountains*, 1976; *Where the Long Grass Blows*, 1976; *Westward the Tide*, 1977; *Sackett's Gold*, 1977; *Borden Chantry*, 1977; *The Mountain Valley War*, 1978; *Bendigo Shafter*, 1978; *The Proving Trail*, 1979; *The Iron Marshall*, 1979; *The Warrior's Path*, 1980; *Yondering*, 1980; *The Strong Shall Live*, 1980; *Lonely on the Mountain*, 1980; *Comstock Lode*, 1981; *Buckskin Run*, 1981; *Milo Talon*, 1981; *The Tall Stranger*, 1982; *The Cherokee Trail*, 1982; *The Shadow Riders*, 1982; *The Lonesome Gods*, 1983; *Bowdrie*, 1983; *Law of the Desert Born*, 1983; *Ride the River*, 1983; *The Hills of Homicide*, 1984; *Son of a Wanted Man*, 1984; *Frontier*, 1984; *The Walking Drum*, 1984; *Bowdrie's Law*, 1984; *Jubal Sackett*, 1985; *Riding for the Brand*, 1986; *Dutchman's Flat*, 1986; *Night over the Solomons*, 1986; *The Trail to Crazy Man*, 1986; *The Haunted Mesa*, 1987; and *Lonigan*, 1988.

Louis L'Amour passed away on June 10, 1988, at the age of 80. Cause of death was attributed to lung cancer, though he had never been a smoker.

In addition to Tex Burns, L'Amour used another pseudonym in his early writing years. Both *Showdown at Yellow Butte* and *Utah Blaine* were written under the name Jim Mayo.

Films Based on Louis L'Amour/Tex Burns's Writings

Hondo (Warner Brothers, 1953) 83 mins.; John Wayne, Ward Bond, Geraldine Page, Michael Pate, James Arness, Rodolfo Acosta, Leo Gordon, Tim Irish, Lee Aaker, Paul Fix, Rayford Barnes; D: John Farrow; SP: James Edward Grant; P: Robert Fellows.

Four Guns to the Border (Universal-International, 1954) 82 mins.; Rory Calhoun, Colleen Miller, George Nader, Walter Brennan, Nina Foch, John McIntire, Charles Drake, Jay Silverheels, Nestor Paiva, Mary Field, Bob Herron, Bob Hoy, Reg Parton; D: Richard Carlson; SP: George Van Martin, Franklin Coen.

Stranger on Horseback (United Artists, 1955) 66 mins.; Joel McCrea, Miroslava, Kevin McCarthy, John McIntire, John Carradine, Emile Meyer, Robert Cornthwaite, James Bell, Jadynne, Walter Brennan; D: Jacques Tourneur; SP: Herb Meadow, Don Martin.

Treasure of the Ruby Hills (Allied Artists, 1955) 71 mins.; Zachary Scott, Carole Matthews, Barton MacLane, Dick Foran, Lola Albright, Lee Van Cleef, Raymond Hatton, Gordon Jones, Steve Darrell, Charles Fredricks, Stanley Andrews, James Alexander, Rick Vallin, Glenn Strange, Ray Jones, Evelyn Finley, Carl Matthews, John Cason; D: Frank McDonald; SP: Tom Hubbard, Fred Eggers; S: *Rider of the Ruby Hills*; P: William F. Broidy.

Apache Territory (Columbia, 1956) 75 mins.; Rory Calhoun, Barbara Bates, John Dehner, Carolyn Craig, Thomas Pittman, Leo Gordon, Myron Healey, Francis de Dales, Frank de Kova, Reg Parton, Bob Woodward, Fred Krone; D: Ray Nazzaro; SP: Charles R. Marion,

George W. George; S: *Last Stand at Papago Wells*.

Blackjack Ketchum, Desperado (Columbia, 1956) 76 mins.; Howard Duff, Victor Jory, Maggie Mahoney, Angela Stevens, David Orrick, William Tannen, Ken Christy, Martin Garralaga, Robert Roark, Don C. Harvey, Pat O'Malley, Jack Littlefield, Sidney Mason, Ralph Sanford, George Edward Mather, Charles Wagenheim, Wes Hudman; D: Earl Bellamy; SP: Luci Ward, Jack Netteford; S: *Kilkenny*; P: Sam Katzman.

The Burning Hills (Warner Brothers, 1956) 94 mins.; Tab Hunter, Natalie Wood, Skip Homeier, Edward Franz, Earl Holliman, Claude Akins, Ray Teal, Frank Puglia, Hal Baylor, Tyler MacDuff, Rayford Barnes, Tony Terry; D: Stuart Heisler; SP: Irving Wallace; P: Richard Whorf.

The Tall Stranger (Allied Artists, 1957) 81 mins.; Joel McCrea, Virginia Mayo, Barry Kelley, Michael Ansara, Whit Bissell, James Dobson, George Neise, Adam Kennedy, Michael Pate, Leo Gordon, Ray Teal, Phillip Phillips, Robert Foulk, Jennifer Lea, George J. Lewis, Guy Prescott, Ralph Reed, Tom London, Pierce Lyden, William Haade, Mauritz Hugo; D: Thomas Carr; SP: Christopher Knopf; S: "Showdown Trail."

Guns of the Timberline (Warner Brothers, 1960) 91 mins.; Alan Ladd, Jeannie Crain, Gilbert Roland, Frankie Avalon, Lyle Bettger, Noah Beery, Jr., Verna Felton, Alana Ladd, Regis Toomey, Johnny Seven, George Selk, Paul E. Burns, George J. Lewis; D: Robert D. Webb; SP: Joseph Petracca; P: Aaron Spelling.

Heller in Pink Tights (Paramount, 1960) 106 mins.; Sophia Loren, Anthony Quinn, Steve Forrest, Eileen Heckart, Edmund Lowe, Margaret O'Brien, Ramon Novarro; D: George Cukor; SP: Dudley Nichols, Walter Berstein; S: *Heller with a Gun.*

Taggart (Universal, 1965) 85 mins.; Tony Young, Dan Duryea, Dick Foran, Elsa Cardenas, John Hale, Emile Meyer, David Carradine, Peter Duryea, Tom Reese, Ray Teal, Claudia Barrett, Stuart Randall, Harry Carey, Jr., Bill Henry, Sarah Selby, George Murdock, Arthur Space, Bob Steele; D: R. G. Springsteen; SP: Robert Creighton Williams; P: Gordon Kay.

Kid Rodelo (Paramount, 1966) 91 mins.; Don Murray, Janet Leigh, Broderick Crawford, Richard Carlson, Julio Pena, Miguel Del Castils, Jose Nieto, Jose Villa Sante, Alfonso San Felix, Emilio Rodriguez, Fernando Hilbeck, Roberto Rubenstein, Bill Christnos, Jual Olaguibel, Alvard de Luna; D: Richard Carlson; SP: Jack Netteford, Eduardo Brochero; P: Jack O. Lamont, James Storrow, Jr.

Hondo and the Apaches (MGM, 1967) 85 mins.; Ralph Taeger, Michael Rennie, John Smith, Gary Clark, Buddy Foster, Victor Lundin, Steve Mario, William Bryant, Kathie Browne, Gary Merrill, Noah Beery, Jr., Randy Boone, Michael Pate, Jim Davis, John Pickard; D: Lee H. Katzin; SP: Andrew J. Fenady from the screenplay for *Hondo* by James E. Grant; S: "The Gift of Cochise"; P: Andrew J. Fenady.

Shalako (Kingston Films-Palomar Pictures, 1968) 113 mins.; Sean Connery, Brigitte Bardot, Stephen Boyd, Jack Hawkins, Peter Van Eyck, Honor Blackman, Woody Strode, Eric Sykes, Alexander Knox, Valerie French, Julian Mateos, Donald Barry, Rodd Redwing, Walter Brown, Bob Hall, Charles Stalnaker; D: Edward Dmytryk; SP: J. J. Griffith, Hal Hopper, Scot Finch; P: Evan Lloyd.

Catlow (MGM, 1971) 101 mins.; Yul Brynner, Richard Crenna, Leonard Nimoy, Jeff Corey, Jo Ann Pflug, David Ladd, Bessie Love, Michael Delano, Julian Mateos, Daliah Lavi; D: Sam Wanamaker; P: Evan Lloyd.

The Man Called Noon (Frontier Films, 1973) 94 mins.; Richard Crenna, Stephen Boyd, Rossana Schiaffino, Farley Granger, Patty Shephard, Aldo Sambrell, Charley Bravo; D: Peter Collison; P: Evan Lloyd.

Elmore Leonard

Elmore Leonard has only four writing credits that this author has found, but these four are great stories that brought substantial profits to the film producers.

Films Based on Elmore Leonard's Writings

3:10 to Yuma (Columbia, 1957) 92 mins.; Glenn Ford, Van Heflin, Felicia Farr, Leora Dana, Henry Jones, Richard Jaeckel, Robert Emhardt, Ford Rainey, George Mitchell; D: Delmer Daves; SP: Hairsten Wells; P: David Heilwell.

The Tall T (Columbia, 1957) 78 mins.; Randolph Scott, Richard Boone, Maureen O'Sullivan, Arthur Hunnicut, Skip Homire, Henry Silva, John Hubbars; D: Budd Boetticher; SP: Burt Kennedy; P: Harry Joe Brown, Randolph Scott.

Hombre (20th Century–Fox, 1967)

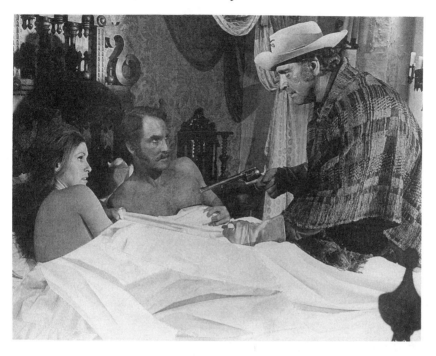

Burt Lancaster and Susan Clark in *Valdez Is Coming.*

110 mins.; Paul Newman, Fredric March, Richard Boone, Diana Cilento, Cameron Mitchell, Barbara Rush, Peter Lazer, Margret Blye, Martin Balsam, Skip Ward, Frank Silveria, David Canary, Val Avery, Larry Ward; D: Martin Ritt; SP: Irving Ravetch, Harriet Frank, Jr.; P: Martin Ritt, Irving Ravetch.

Valdez Is Coming (United Artists, 1971) 90 mins.; Burt Lancaster, Susan Clark, Jon Cypher, Barton Heyman, Richard Jordan, Lex Manson, Frank Silvera, Phil Brown, Juanita Penaoza; D: Edward Sherin; SP: Roland Kibbee; P: Roland Kibbee, Donald Rayfiel.

Alan LeMay

Alan LeMay wrote *The Searchers* (1956), one of the best westerns ever brought to the screen. He also wrote *Along Came Jones* (1943), but is best remembered for his screenplays for a number of fine westerns.

Films Based on Alan LeMay's Writings

Northwest Mounted Police (Paramount, 1940) 125 mins.; Gary Cooper, Madeleine Carroll, Paulette Goddard,

Preston Foster, Robert Preston, George Bancroft, Lynne Overman, Akim Tamiroff, Walter Hampden, Lon

Chaney, Jr., Montague Love, Francis J. McDonald, George E. Stone, Willard Robertson, Regis Toomey, Richard Denning, Douglas Kennedy, Robert Ryan, Lane Chandler, Ralph Byrd, Rod Cameron, Monte Blue, Chief Thunder Cloud, John Hart, Nestor Paiva, Soledad Jiminez, Phillip Terry, Eva Puig, Julia Faye, Clara Blandick, Mala Davidson Clark, Kermit Maynard, Franklyn Farnum, James Flavin; D/P: Cecil B. DeMille; SP: Alan LeMay, Jesse Lasky, Jr., C. Gardner Sullivan; S: R. G. Fetherstonhaugh.

The Story of Dr. Wassell (Paramount, 1944) 140 mins.; Gary Cooper, Laraine Day, Signe Hasso, Dennis O'Keefe, Carol Thurston, Carl Esmond, Paul Kelly, Elliott Reid, Stanley Ridges, Renny McEvoy, Philip Ahn, Barbara Britton, James Millican, Doodles Weaver, Richard Loo, Minor Watson, Harvey Stephens, Edward Fielding, Victor Varconi, Frank Puglia, Irving Bacon, Hugh Beaumont, Ann Doran, Julia Faye, Yvonne DeCarlo, Greta Granstedt, Elmo Lincoln; D: Cecil B. DeMille; SP: Alan LeMay, Charles Bennett; S: James Hilton.

Along Came Jones (RKO-Radio, 1945) 90 mins.; Gary Cooper, Loretta Young, Dan Duryea, William Demarest, Frank Sully, Russell Simpson, Arthur Loft, Willard Robertson, Don Costello, Ray Teal, Lane Chandler, Walter Sande, John Merton, Paul Sutton, Erville Alderson, Chris-Pin Martin, Hank Bell, Bob Kortman, Ernie Adams, Paul E. Burns, Ralph Dunn, Lou Davis, Erville Alderson, Geoffrey Ingram, Tom Herbert, Lee Phelps, Tony Roux; D: Stuart Heisler; SP: Nunnally Johnson; S: Alan LeMay; P: Gary Cooper.

San Antonio (Warner Brothers, 1945) 111 mins.; Errol Flynn, Alexis Smith, S. Z. Sakall, Victor Francen, Florence Bates, John Litel, Paul Kelly, Robert Shayne, John Alvin, Monte Blue, Robert Barrat, Pedro De Cordoba, Tom Tyler, Chris-Pin Martin, Charles

Stevens, Poodles Hanneford, Doodles Weaver, Dan White, Ray Spikes, Chalky Williams, Harry Cording, Lane Chandler, Wally Wales (Hal Taliaferro), James Flavin, Eddy Waller, Hap Winters, Howard Hill, Arnold Kent, Bill Steele; Allen Smith; D: David Butler; SP: Alan LeMay, W. R. Burnett; P: Robert Buckner.

Cheyenne (Warner Brothers, 1947) 100 mins.; Dennis Morgan, Jane Wyman, Janis Paige, Bruce Bennett, Alan Hale, Arthur Kennedy, Barton MacLane, Tom Tyler, Bob Steele, John Compton, John Alvin, Monte Blue, Tom Fadden, Britt Wood, Lee Lasses White, Robert Filmer, Snub Pollard, Ethan Laidlaw; D: Raoul Walsh; SP: Alan LeMay, Thomas Williamson; S: Paul I. Wellman; P: Robert Bruckner.

The Gunfighters (Columbia, 1947) 87 mins.; Randolph Scott, Barbara Britton, Dorothy Hart, Bruce Cabot, Charley Grapewin, Steven Geray, Forrest Tucker, Charles Kemper, Grant Withers, John Miles, Griff Barnett, Charles Middleton; D: George Waggner; SP: Alan LeMay; S: Zane Grey; P: Harry Joe Brown.

Tap Roots (Universal, August 1948) Van Heflin, Susan Hayward, Boris Karloff, Julie London, Whitfield Connor, Richard Long, Arthur Shields, Ruby Dandridge, Russell Simpson, Ward Bond, Hank Worden, Griff Barnett, Sandra Rodgers, Gregg Barton, Arthur Space, Jonathan Hale, Kay Medford, William Haade, Harry Cording, George J. Lewis, Helen Mowery, John James, Keith Richards, William Challee; D: George Marshall; S: James Street; SP: Alan LeMay; P: Walter Wanger.

The Walking Hills (Columbia, 1949) 78 mins.; Randolph Scott, Ella Raines, William Bishop, Edgar Buchanan, Arthur Kennedy, John Ireland, Jerome Courtland, Josh White, Russell Collins, Charles Stevens, Houseley Stevenson, Reed Howes; D: John Sturges; SP/S: Alan LeMay; P: Harry Joe Brown.

Trailin' West (Warner Brothers, 1949) 20 mins.; Chill Wills, Elaine Riley, Earle Hodgins, Jack Elam, John Spelvin; D: George Templeton; SP/S/P: Alan LeMay.

The Sundowners (Eagle-Lion, 1950) 83 mins.; Robert Preston, John Barrymore, Jr., Robert Sterling, Chill Wills, Cathy Downs, John Litel, Jack Elam, Don Haggerty, Stanley Price, Dave Kashner; D: George Templeton; SP: Alan LeMay; P: Alan LeMay, George Templeton.

High Lonesome (Warner Brothers, 1950) 81 mins.; John Barrymore, Jr., Chill Wills, Lois Butler, Kristine Miller, Basil Ruysdael, Jack Elam, John Archer; D/SP/S: Alan LeMay; P: George Templeton.

Rocky Mountain (Warner Brothers, 1950) 83 mins.; Errol Flynn, Patrice Wymore, Scott Forbes, Guinn (Big Boy) Williams, Dick Jones, Howard Petrie, Slim Pickens, Chubby Johnson, Buzz Henry, Sheb Wooley, Peter Coe, Rush Williams, Steve Dunhill, Alex Sharpe, Yakima Canutt, Nakai Snez; D: William Keighley; S: Alan LeMay; SP: Winston Miller, Alan LeMay.

The Vanishing American (Republic, 1955) 90 mins.; Scott Brady, Audrey Totter, Forrest Tucker, Gene Lockhart, Jim Davis, John Dierkes, Gloria Castillo, Julian Rivero, Lee Van Cleef, George Keymas, Charles Stevens, Jay Silverheels, James Millican, Glenn Strange; D: Joseph Kane; SP: Alan LeMay; S: Zane Grey; P: Herbert J. Yates.

The Searchers (Warner Brothers, 1956) 119 mins.; John Wayne, Jeffrey Hunter, Vera Miles, Ward Bond, Natalie Wood, John Qualen, Olive Carey, Henry Brandon, Ken Curtis, Harry Carey, Jr., Antonio Moreno, Hank Worden, Lane Wood, Pat Wayne, Jack Pennick, Nacho Galindo, Beulah Archuletta, Pippa Scott, Dorothy Jordan, Walter Coy, Chuck Roberson, Cliff Lyons, Away Luna, Smile White Sheep, Feather Hat, Jr., Frank McGrath, Harry Black Horse, Fred Kennedy, Chuck Howard, Terry Wilson, Percy Shooting Star, Pete Grey Eyes; D: John Ford; SP: Frank S. Nugent; S: Alan LeMay; P: Merian C. Cooper, C. V. Whitney.

The Unforgiven (United Artists, 1960) 125 mins.; Burt Lancaster, Audrey Hepburn, Audie Murphy, John Saxon, Charles Bickford, Lillian Gish, Albert Salmi, Joseph Wiseman, Kipp Hamilton, Arnold Merritt, Carlos Riva, Doug McClure; D: John Huston; SP: Ben Maddow; S: Alan LeMay; P: James Hill.

Johnston McCulley

Johnston McCulley was born February 2, 1883, in Ottawa, Illinois, and died November 23, 1958. He is known principally for creating the character Zorro, a swashbuckling Robin Hood of old California. He also wrote many stories that were made into B movies. However, *The Mark of Zorro* (1920) was a first-class action movie starring Douglas Fairbanks, and 20 years later Tyrone Power starred in a remake that was also an A production. The character Zorro has mainly been used in Republic serials.

The Zorro series contained about 30 novels. From 1957 to 1959 McCulley wrote scripts for the Zorro television series.

As a crime writer, McCulley published nearly 20 mystery novels, using such pseudonyms as Raley Brien, George Drayne, Fredric Phelps, Rowena

Rafey, and Harrington Strong. In addition, he worked as a special correspondent, both in the United States and abroad, as well as writing over 100 short stories for western magazines.

Films Based on Johnston McCulley's Writings

Unclaimed Goods (Paramount, 1918) 5 reels; Vivian Martin, Harrison Ford, Casson Ferguson, George McDaniel, Carmen Phillips, Dick La Reno, George Kunkel; D: Rollin S. Sturgeon; SP: C. Gardner Hunting;.

A White Man's Chance (Hodkinson, 1919); J. Warren Kerrigan, Lillian Walker, Joseph J. Dowling, Howard Davies, Andrew Arbuckle, Joseph Hazelton, George Field, Joseph Ray, Richard La Reno; D: Ernest C. Warde.

The Brute Breaker (Universal, 1919) 6 reels; Frank Mayo, Harry Northrup, Kathryn Adams, Jack Curtis, Burwell Hamrick, Bert Sprotte, Frank Brownlee, Charles Le Moyne; D: Lynn F. Reynolds; SP: Dorothy Barrett, Lynn F. Reynolds.

The Mark of Zorro (United Artists, 1920) 8 reels; Douglas Fairbanks, Marguerite De La Motte, Noah Beery, Sr., Robert McKim, Charles Hill Mailes, Claire McDowell, Albert McQuarrie, Charles Stevens, George Periolat, Walt Whitman, Tote Du Crow, John Winn, Charles Belcher, Sidney De Grey, Noah Beery, Jr., Gilbert Clayton; D: Fred Niblo; SP: Elton Thomas (Douglas Fairbanks); S: "The Curse of Capistrano."

Ruth of the Rockies (Pathe, 1920) 15 chapters; Ruth Roland, Herbert Heyes, Thomas Lingham, Jack Rollens, Fred Burns, William Gillis, Gilbert (Pee Wee) Holmes, Al Hoxie, Madeline Fairchild, Norma Nichols, Harry Maynard, Captain S. J. Bingham; D: George Marshall; SP: Frances Guihan; S: "Broadway Bab."

The Kiss (Universal, 1921) 5 reels; George Periolat, William E. Lawrence, J. P. Lockney, Carmel Myers, J. J. Lanoe, Harvey Clarke, Jean Acker, Ed Brady; D: Jack Conway; SP: A. P. Younger; S: "Little Erolinda."

Captain Fly-By-Night (FBO, 1922) 5 reels; Johnny Walker, Francis McDonald, Shannon Day, Edward Gribbon, Victory Bateman, James McElhern, Charles Stevens, Bert Wheeler, Fred Kelsey; D: William K. Howard.

Ride for Your Life (Universal, 1924) 6 reels; Hoot Gibson, Laura LaPlante, Harry Todd, Robert McKim, Howard Truesdell, Fred Humes, Clark Comstock, William Daly, Mrs. George Hernandez; D: Edward Sedgwick; SP: Raymond L. Schrock, E. Richard Schayer.

The Ice Flood (Universal, 1926) 6 reels; Kenneth Harlan, Viola Dane, Frank Hagney, Fred Kohler, DeWitt Jennings, Kitty Barlow, James Gordon; D: George B. Seitz; SP: George B. Seitz, Gladys Lehman, James D. Spearing; S: "The Brute Breaker."

Black Jack (Fox, 1927) 5 reels; Buck Jones, Barbara Bennett, Theodore Lorch, Harry Cording, George Berrell, William Caress, Buck Moulton, Murdock MacQuarrie, Frank Lanning, Mark Hamilton, Sam Allen; D: Orville O. Dull; SP: Harold Shumate; S: "The Broken Dollar."

Saddle Mates (Pathe, 1928) 5 reels; Wally Wales, Hank Bell, J. Gordon Russell, Peggy Montgomery, Charles Whitaker, Lafe McKee, Edward Cecil, Lillian Allen; D: Richard Thorpe; SP: Frank L. Inghram; S: Harrington Strong (Johnston McCulley).

The Outlaw Deputy (Puritan, 1935) 59 mins.; Tim McCoy, Nora Lane, Bud Osborne, George Offerman, Jr., Si Jenks, Jack Montgomery, George Holtz, Hank Bell, Tex Cooper, Jim Corey,

Edward Gribbon, Joseph Girard, Hooper Atchley, Dick Botiller, Charles Brinley, Bud Pope, Tom Smith, Ray Jones, Buck Morgan, Bob Card; D: Otto Brower; SP: Ford Beebe, Dell Andrews; S: "King of Cactusville"; P: Nat Ross.

The Bold Caballero (Republic, 1936) 69 mins.; Robert Livingston, Heather Angel, Sig Rumann, Ian Wolfe, Robert Warwick, Emily Fitzroy, Charles Stevens, Walter Long, Ferdinand Munier, King Martin (Chris-Pin Martin), Carlos De Valdez, John Merton, Jack Kirk, Slim Whitaker, Vinegar Roan, George Plues, Henry Morris, Chief Thunder Cloud, Pascale Perry, Jack Roberts, William Emile, Gurdial Singh; D/SP: Wells Root; P: Nate Levine.

The Trusted Outlaw (Republic, 1937) 57 mins.; Bob Steele, Lois January, Joan Barclay, Earl Dwire, Charles King, Dick Cramer, Hal Price, Budd Buster, Frank Ball, Oscar Gahan, George Morrell, Chick Hannon, Sherry Tansey, Clyde McClary, Jack Rockwell, Wally West, Ray Henderson, Jack C. Smith, Fred Parker; D: Robert N. Bradbury; SP: George H. Plympton, Fred Myton; P: A. W. Hackel.

Zorro Rides Again (Republic, 1937) 12 chapters; John Carroll, Helen Christian, Reed Howes, Duncan Renaldo, Noah Beery, Sr., Richard Alexander, Robert Kortman, Paul Lopcz, Jack Ingram, Tom London, Yakima Canutt, Chris-Pin Martin, Edmund Cobb, Murdock McQuarrie, Jack Kirk, Mona Rico, Jerry Frank, Rosa Turich; D: William Witney, John English; SP: Barry Shipman, John Rathmell, Franklyn Adreon, Ronald Davidson, Morgan B. Cox.

Rose of the Rio Grande (Monogram, 1938) 60 mins.; John Carroll, Movita, Antonio Moreno, Don Alvarado, Lina Basquette, George Cleveland, Duncan Renaldo, Gino Corrado, Martin Garralaga, Rose Turich; D: William Nigh; SP: Ralph Bettinson; P: George E. Kann.

Zorro's Fighting Legion (Republic, 1939) 12 chapters; Reed Hadley, Sheila Darcy, William Corson, Leander De Cordova, Edmund Cobb, John Merton, C. Montague Shaw, Billy Bletcher, Budd Buster, Carleton Young, Guy D'Ennery, Charles King, Jason Robards, Sr., Theodore Lorch, Jack O'Shea, Cactus Mack, Curley Dresden, Al Taylor, Joe De LaCruz, Bud Geary; D: William Witney, John English; SP: Ronald Davidson, Franklyn Adreon, Morgan Cox, Sol Shor, Barney A. Sarecky.

The Mark of Zorro (20th Century–Fox, 1940) 93 mins.; Tyrone Power, Linda Darnell, Basil Rathbone, Gale Sondergaard, Eugene Pallette, J. Edward Bromberg, Montagu Love, Janet Beecher, Robert Lowery, Chris-Pin Martin, George Regas, Belle Mitchell, John Bleifer, Frank Puglia, Eugene Borden, Pedro De Cordoba, Guy D'Ennery, Ralph Byrd, Stanley Andrews, Hector Sarno; D: Rouben Mamoulian; SP: Garret Ford, Bess Meredith; S: "The Curse of Capistrano": P: Raymond Griffith.

Doomed Caravan (Paramount, 1941) 62 mins.; William Boyd, Russell Hayden, Andy Clyde, Minna Gombell, Morris Ankrum, Georgia Hawkins, Trevor Bardette, Ray Bennett, Edward Cassidy, Bill Nestill, George Sounds, Pat J. O'Brien, Jose Luis Tortosa, Fred Burns, Martin Garralaga, Charles Murphy, Elias Gamboa, Art Dillard, Ray Brent, Cliff Parkinson, John Beach, Henry Wills, Tex Palmer; D: Lesley Selander; SP/S; Johnston McCulley, J. Benton Chaney; P: Harry Sherman.

Overland Mail (Universal, 1942) 15 chapters; Lon Chaney, Jr., Helen Parrish, Don Terry, Noah Beery, Jr., Bob Baker, Noah Beery, Sr., Tom Chatterton, Charles Stevens, Robert Barron, Harry Cording, Marguerite De La Motte, Ben Taggart, Jack Rockwell, Roy Harris (Riley Hill), Carleton Young, Ethan Laidlaw, Jack Clifford, Chief Thunder Cloud, Chief Many Treaties,

Henry Hall, William Gould, Forrest Taylor, Edmund Cobb, Curley Dresden, Tom Steele; D: Ford Beebe, John Rawlins; SP: Paul Huston; P: Henry MacRae.

Outlaws of Stampede Pass (Monogram, 1943) 58 mins.; Johnny Mack Brown, Raymond Hatton, Ellen Hall, Harry Woods, Milburn Morante, Edmund Cobb, Sam Flint, Jon Dawson, Charles King, Mauritz Hugo, Art Mix, Cactus Mack, Artie Ortego, Eddie Burns, Bill Wolfe, Hal Price, Dan White, Kansas Moehring, Tex Cooper; D: Wallace Fox; SP: Jess Bowers (Adele Buffington); P: Scott R. Dunlap.

Raiders of the Border (Monogram, 1944) 58 mins.; Johnny Mack Brown, Raymond Hatton, Ellen Hall, Craig Woods, Stanley Price, Ray Bennett, Edmund Cobb, Lynton Brent, Dick Alexander, Kermit Maynard, Ernie Adams; D: John P. McCarthy; SP: Jess Bowers (Adele Buffington); P: Scott R. Dunlap.

Zorro's Black Whip (Republic, 1944) 12 chapters; George J. Lewis, Linda Stirling, Lucien Littlefield, Francis McDonald, Hal Taliaferro (Wally Wales), John Merton, John Hamilton, Tom Chatterton, Tom London, Jack Kirk, Forrest Taylor, Jay Kirby, Si Jenks, Stanley Price, Tom Steele, Duke Green, Dale Van Sickel, Cliff Lyons, Roy Brent, Marshall Reed; D: Spencer G. Bennet, Wallace Grissell; SP: Basil Dickey, Jesse Duffey, Grant Nelson, Joseph Poland.

South of the Rio Grande (Monogram, 1945) 62 mins.; Duncan Renaldo, Martin Garralaga, Armida, George J. Lewis, Lillian Molieri, Francis McDonald, Charles Stevens, Pedro Regas,

Soledad Jiminez, Tito Renaldo, the Guadalajara Trio, Dennis Billy; D: Lambert Hillyer; SP: Victor Hammond, Ralph Bettinson; P: Philip N. Krasne.

Don Ricardo Returns (PRC, 1946) 63 mins.; Fred Colby, Isabelita (Lita Baron), Martin Garralaga, Paul Newton, Claire DuBrey, David Leonard, Anthony Warde, Michael Visaroff; D: Terry O. Morse; SP: Jack DeWitt, Duncan Renaldo; P: James S. Burkett.

Mark of the Renegade (Universal-International, 1951) 81 mins.; Ricardo Montalban, Cyd Charisse, J. Carroll Naish, Gilbert Roland, Andrea King, Antonio Moreno, George Backus, Robert Warwick, Armando Silvestre, Bridget Carr, Alberto Morin, Dave Wolfe; D: Hugo Fregonese; SP: Louis Solomon, Robert Hardy Andrews; P: Jack Cross.

The Sign of Zorro (Buena Vista, 1960) 91 mins.; Guy Williams, Henry Calvin, Gene Sheldon, Romney Brent, Britt Lomond, George J. Lewis, Tony Russo, Jan Arvan, Than Wyenn, Lisa Gaye, John Dehner; D: Norman Foster, Lewis R. Foster; SP: Norman Foster, Bob Wehling, Lowell S. Hawley, John Meredyth Lucas; P: William H. Anderson. Note. This film was assembled from episodes 1–13 of the TV series.

The Mark of Zorro (20th Century–Fox, 1974) 90 mins.; Frank Langella, Ricardo Montalban, Gilbert Roland, Yvonne DeCarlo, Louise Sobel, Robert Middleton, Anne Archer, Tom Lacy, George Cervera, Inez Perez, John Rose; D: Don McDougall; TP: Brian Taggert; S: "The Curse of Capistrano"; P: Robert C. Thompson, Rodrick Paul.

Larry McMurtry

Larry McMurtry has been placed in the forefront of present-day western writers as a result of *Lonesome Dove,* a lengthy story of a cattle drive from Texas to Montana in the 1880s. However, *Hud, The Last Picture Show* (which won an academy award for Ben Johnson), and *Lovin' Molly* are also good films that did well at the box office.

As a novelist McMurtry has made his reputation with novels designed to shatter myths of the heroic West.

McMurtry was born in Wichita Falls, Texas, on June 3, 1936. He received a B.A. degree from North Texas State College and an M.A. degree from Rice University. He has taught at several universities as a visiting lecturer and was an instructor of English and creative writing at Rice University 1963–69. In 1970 he became coowner of a bookstore in Washington, D.C. He received an Oscar from the Academy of Motion Picture Arts and Sciences for his screenplay for *The Last Picture Show*, and a Pulitzer Prize for fiction in 1986 for *Lonesome Dove*.

His principal writings are as follows: *Horseman, Pass By*, 1961; *Leaving Cheyenne*, 1963; *The Last Picture Show*, 1966; *In a Narrow Grave: Essays on Texas*, 1968; *Moving On*, 1970; *All My Friends Are Going to Be Strangers*, 1972; *Terms of Endearment*, 1975; *Somebody's Darling*, 1978; *Cadillac Jack*, 1982; *The Desert Rose*, 1983, and *Lonesome Dove*, 1985.

Films Based on Larry McMurtry's Writings

Hud (Paramount, 1963) 112 mins.; Paul Newman, Melvyn Douglas, Patricia Neal, Brandon De Wilde, John Ashley, Whit Bissell, Crahan Denton, Val Avery, Shelton Allman, Pitt Herbert, Peter Brooks, Curt Conway, Yvette Vickers, George Petrie, David Kent, Frank Killmond; D: Martin Ritt; SP: Irving Ravetch, Harriet Frank, Jr.; S: *Horseman, Pass By*; P: Martin Ritt, Irving Ravetch.

The Last Picture Show (Columbia, 1971) 118 mins.; Ben Johnson, Timothy Bottoms, Jeff Bridges, Cybill Shepherd, Cloris Leachman, Ellen Burstyn, Eileen Brennan, Clu Gulager, Sam Bottoms, Sharon Taggart, Randy Quaid, Joe Heathcock, Bill Thurman, John Hillerman; D: Peter Bogdanovich; SP: Peter Bogdanovich, Larry McMurtry; S: Larry McMurtry.

Lovin' Molly (Columbia, 1974) 98 mins.; Anthony Perkins, Beau Bridges, Blythe Danner, Edward Binns, Susan Sarandon, Conrad Fowkes, Claude Transverse, John Henry Faulk; D: Sidney Lumet; SP/P: Stephen Friedman; S: *Leaving Cheyenne*.

Lonesome Dove (Motown Productions/Pangaea/Quintex Entertainment, 1989) 4 episodes, 120 mins. each; Robert Duvall, Tommy Lee Jones, Diane Lane, Anjelica Huston, Robert Ulrich, Danny Glover, Ricky Shroeder, Frederick Forrest, D. B. Sweeney, Chris Cooper, Tim Scott, Glenne Headly, Barry Corbin, Barry Tubb, William Sanderson, Bradley Gregg, Travis Swords, Helena Humann, Leon Singer, David Carpenter, Lanny Flaherty, Nina Siemaszko, Jorge Martinez de Hoyos, Gavin O'Herlihy, Frederick Coffin, Kevin O'Morrison, Ron Weyward, Dan Kamin, Steve Buscemi, John Bark, Michael Berlin, Jerry Biggs, Kenny Call, Missy Crider; D: Simon Wincer; TP: Bill Wittliff.

Terms of Endearment (Paramount, 1983) 132 mins.; Shirley Maclaine, Jack Nicholson, Debra Winger, Danny DeVito, Jeff Daniels, John Lithgow; D/SP: James L. Brooks; S: Larry McMurtry.

William Colt MacDonald

William Colt MacDonald's claim to fame is primarily his creation of the Three Mesquiteers, who first appeared in the book *Law of the Forty Fives* in 1933. The book was adapted to the screen in 1935 under the same title. Also that same year the *Three Mesquiteers* made an appearance in *Powdersmoke Range* with an all-star cast headed by Harry Carey, Hoot Gibson, Bob Steele, Big Boy Williams, and Tom Tyler. Republic began its long-running Three Mesquiteers series in 1936. A few of the stories were written by MacDonald, but the majority of the films were written by Republic scriptwriters. Mac-Donald, in the early 1930s, worked at Columbia writing scripts for Tim McCoy westerns.

Films Based on William Colt MacDonald's Writings

Texas Cyclone (Columbia, 1932) 58 mins.; Tim McCoy, Shirley Grey, Wheeler Oakman, John Wayne, Wallace MacDonald, Harry Cording, Vernon Dent, Walter Brennan, Mary Gordon, James Farley; D: D. Ross Lederman; P: Randall Faye.

The Riding Tornado (Columbia, 1932) 64 mins.; Tim McCoy, Shirley Grey, Wallace MacDonald, Russell Simpson, Art Mix, Montague Love, Wheeler Oakman, Vernon Dent, Lafe McKee, Bud Osborne, Hank Bell, Art Mix (George Kesterson), Silver Tip Baker, Tex Palmer, Artie Ortego; D: D. Ross Lederman; SP: Burt Kempler.

Daring Danger (Columbia, 1932) 57 mins.; Tim McCoy, Alberta Vaughn, Wallace MacDonald, Robert Ellis, Edward J. LeSaint, Bobby Nelson, Max Davidson, Dick Alexander, Vernon Dent, Murdock McQuarrie, Edmund Cobb, Art Mix; D: D. Ross Lederman; SP/S: William Colt MacDonald, Michael Trevelyan.

The Western Code (Columbia, 1932) 61 mins.; Tim McCoy, Nora Lane, Mischa Auer, Wheeler Oakman, Gordon DeMain, Mathew Betz, Dwight Frye, Bud Osborne, Cactus Mack, Emilio Fernandez, Chuck Baldra; D: J. P. McCarthy; SP: Milton Krims.

Two-Fisted Law (Columbia, 1932) 64 mins.; Tim McCoy, Alice Day, Wheeler Oakman, Tully Marshall, Wallace MacDonald, John Wayne, Walter Brennan, Dick Alexander; D: D. Ross Lederman; SP: Burt Kempler.

Man of Action (Columbia, 1933) 57 mins.; Tim McCoy, Caryl Lincoln, Wheeler Oakman, Walter Brennan, Stanley Blystone, Charles K. French, Julian Rivero; D: George Melford; SP: Robert Quigley.

Powdersmoke Range (RKO-Radio, 1935) 6 reels; Harry Carey, Hoot Gibson, Bob Steele, Tom Tyler, Guinn (Big Boy) Williams, Boots Mallory, Wally Wales (Hal Taliaferro), Sam Hardy, Adrian Morris, Buzz Barton, Art Mix (George Kesterson), Frank Rice, Buddy Roosevelt, Buffalo Bill, Jr. (Jay Wilsey), Franklyn Farnum, William Desmond, William Farnum, Ethan Laidlaw, Eddie Dunn, Ray Meyer, Barney Furey, Bob McKenzie, James Mason, Irving Bacon, Henry Rocquemore, Phil Dunham, Silver Tip Baker, Nelson McDowell, Frank Ellis; D: Wallace Fox; SP: Adele Buffington; P: Cliff Reid.

Law of the 45s (First Division, 1935) 57 mins.; Guinn (Big Boy) Williams, Molly O'Day, Al St. John, Ted Adams, Lafe McKee, Fred Burns, Curly

Baldwin, Martin Garralaga, Broderick O'Farrell, Sherry Tansey, Glenn Strange, Bill Patton, Jack Kirk, Francis Walker, Jack Evans, Tex Palmer, Merrill McCormack, George Morrell, William McCall, Herman Hack, Ace Cain, Buck Morgan; D: John P. McCarthy; SP: Robert Tansey; S: *Law of the Forty-Fives*; P: Arthur Alexander.

Too Much Beef (Colony, 1936) 60 mins.; Rex Bell, Connie Bergen, Horace Murphy, Forrest Taylor, Lloyd Ingraham, Peggy O'Connell, Vincent Dennis, George Ball, Jimmy Aubrey, Jack Cowell, Fred Burns, Steve Clark, Jack Kirk, Dennis Meadows (Dennis Moore), Frank Ellis; D: Robert Hill; SP: Rock Hawley (Robert Hill); P: Max and Arthur Alexander.

The Three Mesquiteers (Republic, 1936) 61 mins.; Robert Livingston, Ray Corrigan, Syd Saylor, Kay Hughes, J. P. McGowan, Frank Yaconelli, Al Bridge, Stanley Blystone, John Merton, Jean Marvey, Milburn Stone, Duke Yorke, Allen Connor, Wally West, George Plues, Rose Plummer; D: Ray Taylor; SP: Jack Natteford; P: Nat Levine.

Riders of the Whistling Skull (Republic, 1937) 55 mins.; Robert Livingstone, Ray Corrigan, Max 'Terhune, Mary Russell, Yakima Canutt, Roger Williams, Fern Emmett, C. Montague Shaw, John Ward, George Godfrey, Frank Ellis, Earle Ross, Chief Thunder Cloud, John Van Pelt, Edward Piel, Jack Kirk, Iron Eyes Cody, Tom Steele, Wally West, Tracy Layne, Eddie Bowland, Ken Cooper, Elenor Stewart; D: Mack V. Wright; SP: Oliver Drake, John Rathmell, Bernard McConville; P: Nat Levine.

Two-Fisted Sheriff (Columbia, 1937) 60 mins.; Charles Starrett, Barbara Weeks, Bruce Lane, Ed Piel, Alan Sears, Walter Downing, Ernie Adams, Claire McDowell, Frank Ellis, Robert Walker, George Chesebro, Art Mix, Al Bridge, Dick Botiller, George Morell, Merrill McCormack, Edmund Cobb, Tex Cooper, Dick Cramer, Dick Alexander, Maston Williams, Ethan Laidlaw, Steve Clark, Wally West, Fred Burns, Al Haskell, Ray Jones, Blackjack Ward, Hank Bell, Charles Brinley, Jack Evans, Blackie Whiteford, Art Dillard, Fred Parker; D: Leon Barsha; SP: Paul Perez.

One Man Justice (Columbia, 1937) 59 mins.; Charles Starrett, Barbara Weeks, Hal Taliaferro (Wally Wales), Jack Clifford, Al Bridge, Walter Downing, Mary Gordon, Jack Lipson, Edmund Cobb, Dick Curtis, Maston Williams, Harry Fleischman, Art Mix, Hank Bell, Steve Clark, Frank Ellis, Ethan Laidlaw, Eddie Laughton, Ted Mapes, Lew Meehan, Merrill McCormack; D: Leon Barsha; SP: Paul Perez; S: William Colt MacDonald (credited to Peter B. Kyne).

Along the Navajo Trail (Republic, 1945) 66 mins.; Roy Rogers, George F. Hayes, Dale Evans, Estelita Rodriguez, Douglas Fowley, Nestor Paiva, Sam Flint, Emmett Vogan, Roy Barcroft, David Cota, Bob Nolan, Pat Brady, Edward Cassidy, Poppy Del Vando, Rosemond James, Tex Terry, Budd Buster, Sons of the Pioneers, Kit Guard, Hank Bell, Marin Sais, Eddie Kane, Frank O'Connor, George Morrell, Frank Stephens, Trigger (a horse); D: Frank McDonald; SP: Gerald Geraghty; AP: Eddy White.

E. B. Mann

There was not anything particularly outstanding about E. B. Mann's books, but they were enjoyable formula reading. Six of them made it to the screen as B westerns.

Films Based on E. B. Mann's Writings

Desert Phantom (Supreme/William Steiner, 1936) 64 mins.; Johnny Mack Brown, Sheila Mannors, Ted Adams, Karl Hackett, Hal Price, Nelson McDowell, Charles King, Forrest Taylor, Frank Ball, Fred Parker, George Morrell, Art Dillard, Roger Williams; D: S. Roy Luby; SP: Earle Snell; P: A. W. Hackel.

Boss Rider of Gun Creek (Universal, 1936) 65 mins.; Buck Jones, Muriel Evans, Harvey Clark, Lee Phelps, Tom Chatterton, Joseph Swickard, Ernest Hillard, Mahlon Hamilton, Alphonse Ethier, Alan Sears, William Lawrence, Edward Hearn, Silver (a horse); D: Lesley Selander; SP: Frances Guihan; S: *The Boss of Lazy 9*; P: Buck Jones.

Stormy Trails (Colony, 1936) 58 mins.; Rex Bell, Bob Hodges, Lois Wilde, Lane Chandler, Earl Dwire, Karl Hackett, Earl Ross, Lloyd Ingraham, Murdock McQuarrie, Jimmy Aubrey, Roger Williams, Chuck Morrison, George Morrell; D: Sam Newfield; S: *Stampede*; P: Arthur and Max Alexander.

Lightnin' Crandall (Republic, 1937) 60 mins.; Bob Steele, Lois January, Dave O'Brien, Horace Murphy, Charles King, Ernie Adams, Earl Dwire, Frank LaRue, Lloyd Ingraham, Lew Meehan, Dick Cramer, Jack C. Smith, Sherry Tansey, Tex Palmer, Edward Carey, Art Felix; D: Sam Newfield; SP: Charles Francis Royal; P: A. W. Hackel.

Guns in the Dark (Republic, 1937) 56 mins.; Johnny Mack Brown, Claire Rochelle, Dick Curtis, Julian Madison, Ted Adams, Sherry Tansey, Slim Whitaker, Lew Meehan, Tex Palmer, Francis Walker, Frank Ellis, Budd Buster, Oscar Gahan, Merrill McCormack, Dick Cramer, Steve Clark, Syd Saylor, Jack C. Smith, Roger Williams, Jim Corey, Chick Hannon; D: Sam Newfield; SP: Charles Francis Royal; P: A. W. Hackel.

Ridin' the Lone Trail (Republic, 1937) 56 mins.; Bob Steele, Claire Rochelle, Charles King, Ernie Adams, Lew Meehan, Julian Rivero, Steve Clark, Hal Price, Frank Ball, Jack Kirk, Horace Murphy, Jack Evans, Bob Roper; D: Sam Newfield; SP: Charles Francis Royal; P: A. W. Hackel.

Clarence E. Mulford

Clarence E. Mulford was born on February 3, 1883, in Streator, Illinois. He was educated there and in Utica, New York. Fresh out of school, he went to work for the *Municipal Journal and Engineer* of New York. Later he joined the civil service, but was also writing. He maintained a card file of western data that exceeded 17,000 items.

Mulford went to Brooklyn, New York, in 1899, and in 1926 moved to

Fryeburg, Maine. His intention was to have an easy life, but he found he could not stop writing. He died in 1956.

Mulford's first western story was published in *Metropolitan Magazine*. He followed with a series of stories for *Outing* magazine. *Hopalong Cassidy* appeared in 1910 and other Cassidy books followed. One silent film was based on Mulford's novel *The Orphan*. The film was *The Deadwood Coach* starring Tom Mix. In 1935 Mulford entered into an agreement with producer Harry Sherman whereby Sherman could make films based on Mulford's Bar 20 characters. *Hop-a-Long Cassidy* was released that same year. Over 60 films followed, a few based on Mulford's books but most of them written by scriptwriters.

The Bar 20/Cassidy stories have entranced large audiences. The stories have little to recommend them according to book critics, but the western reader savored them, just as western moviegoers did the Hoppy films. Mulford was a formula writer: a user of convention rather than a literary innovator.

The principal works of Clarence Mulford are as follows: *Bar 20* (short stories), 1907; *The Orphan*, 1908; *Hopalong Cassidy*, 1910; *Bar 20 Days*, 1911; *Buck Peters, Ranchman*, 1912; *The Coming of Cassidy*, 1913; *The Man from Bar 20*, 1918; *Johnny Nelson*, 1920; *The Bar 20 Three*, 1921; *Tex*, 1922; *Bring Me His Ears*, 1923; *Black Buttes*, 1923; *Rustlers' Valley*, 1924; *Hopalong Cassidy Returns*, 1924; *Cottonwood Gulch*, 1925; *Hopalong Cassidy's Protege*, 1926; *The Bar 20 Rides Again*, 1926; *Carson of the J.C.*, 1927; *Mesquite Jenkins*, 1928; *Me an' Shorty*, 1929; *The Deputy Sheriff*, 1930; *Hopalong Cassidy and the Eagle's Brood*, 1931; *Mesquite Jenkins, Tumbleweed*, 1932; *The Roundup*, 1933; *Trail Dust*, 1934; *On the Trail of the Tumbling T*, 1934; *Hopalong Cassidy Takes Cards*, 1937; and *Hopalong Cassidy Serves a Writ*, 1941.

Films Based on Clarence F. Mulford's Writings

The Deadwood Coach (Fox, 1924) 7 reels; Tom Mix, George Bancroft, DeWitt Jennings, Doris May, Buster Gardner, Lucien Littlefield, Norma Willis, Sid Jordan, Nora Cecil; D/SP: Lynn F. Reynolds; S: *The Orphan*.

Hop-A-Long Cassidy (Paramont, 1935) 63 mins.; William Boyd, Jimmy Ellison, Paula Stone, Robert Warwick, Charles Middleton, Frank McGlynn, Jr., Kenneth Thompson, George Hayes, James Mason, Frank Campeau, Ted Adams, Willie Fung, Franklyn Farnum, John Merton, Wally West; D: Howard Bretherton; SP: Doris Schroeder; P: Harry Sherman.

The Eagle's Brood (Paramount, 1935) 59 mins.; William Boyd, Jimmy Ellison, William Farnum, George F. Hayes, Addison Richards, Joan Woodbury, Frank Shannon, Dorothy Revier, Paul Fix, Al Lydell, John Merton, Juan Torena, Henry Sylvester; D: Howard Bretherton; SP: Doris Schroeder, Harrison Jacobs; P: Harry Sherman.

Bar 20 Rides Again (Paramount, 1935) 65 mins.; William Boyd, Jimmy Ellison, Jean Rouveral, George F. Hayes,

Frank McGlynn, Jr., Howard Lang, Harry Worth, Ethel Wales, Paul Fix, J. P. McGowan, Joe Rickson, Al St. John, John Merton, Frank Layton, Chill Wills and the Avalon Boys, Jack Kirk; D: Howard Bretherton; SP: Gerald Geraghty, Doris Schroeder; P: Harry Sherman.

Call of the Prairie (Paramount, 1936) 65 mins.; William Boyd, Jimmy Ellison, Muriel Evans, George F. Hayes, Al Bridge, Chester Conklin, Hank Mann, Willie Fung, Al Hill, John Merton, James Mason, Chill Wills and the Avalon Boys; D: Howard Bretherton; SP: Doris Schroeder, Vernon Smith; S: *Hopalong Cassidy's Protege*; P: Harry Sherman.

Hopalong Cassidy Returns (Paramount, 1936) 71 mins.; William Boyd, George F. Hayes, Gail Sheridan, Evelyn Brent, Stephen Morris (Morris Ankrum), William Janney, Irving Bacon, Grant Richards, John Beck, Ernie Adams, Joe Rickson, Claude Smith, Ray Whitley, Fred Burns, Frank Ellis, Robert Burns, Lew Meehan; D: Nate Watt; SP: Harrison Jacobs; P: Harry Sherman.

Trail Dust (Paramount, 1936) 77 mins.; William Boyd, Jimmy Ellison, George F. Hayes, Gwynne Shipman, Stephen Morris (Morris Ankrum), Britt Wood, Dick Dickinson, Earl Askam, Al Bridge, John Beach, Ted Adams, Tom Halligan, Dan Wolheim, Al St. John, Harold Daniels, Kenneth Harlan, John Elliott, George Chesebro, Emmett Day, Robert Drew; D: Nate Watt; SP: Al Martin; P: Harry Sherman.

Borderland (Paramount, 1937) 82 mins.; William Boyd, Jimmy Ellison, George F. Hayes, Stephen Morris (Morris Ankrum), John Beach, George Chesebro, Nora Lane, Charlene Wyatt, Trevor Bardette, Earle Hodgins, Al Bridge, John St. Polis, Edward Cassidy, Slim Whitaker, Cliff Parkinson, Karl Hackett, Robert Walker, Frank Ellis; D: Nate Watt; SP: Harrison Jacobs; S: *Bring Me His Ears*; P: Harry Sherman.

Hills of Old Wyoming (Paramount, 1937) 75 mins.; William Boyd, Russell Hayden, George F. Hayes, Stephen Morris (Morris Ankrum), Gail Sheridan, Clara Kimball Young, John Beach, Earle Hodgins, George Chesebro, Steve Clemente, Paul Gustine, Leo McMahon, John Powers, James Mason, Chief Big Tree; D: Nate Watt; SP: Maurice Geraghty; S: *The Roundup*; P: Harry Sherman.

North of the Rio Grande (Paramount, 1937) 70 mins.; William Boyd, George F. Hayes, Stephen Morris (Morris Ankrum), Russell Hayden, John Beach, Bernadine Hayes, John Rutherford, Walter Long, Lee J. Cobb, Lorraine Randall, Al Ferguson, Lafe McKee, Leo McMahon, Bill O'Brien, Hank Bell, Ted Billings, Cliff Lyons, Bill Nestall, Fred Burns, Lee Brooks, Dick Cramer, Harry Bernard, Buck Morgan, Herman Hack, Horace B. Carpenter, Carl Mathews, George Morrell, Charles Murphy, Cliff Parkinson, Al Haskell; D: Nate Watt; SP: Joseph O'Donnell; S: *Cottonwood Gulch*.

Rustler's Valley (Paramount, 1937) 60 mins.; William Boyd, George F. Hayes, Russell Hayden, Stephen Morris (Morris Ankrum), Muriel Evans, John Beach, Lee J. Cobb, Oscar Apfel, Ted Adams, Bernadine Hayes, John St. Polis, Horace B. Carpenter, John Powers, Al Ferguson; D: Nate Watt; SP: Harry O. Hoyt; P: Harry Sherman.

Hopalong Rides Again (Paramount, 1937) 65 mins.; William Boyd, George F. Hayes, Russell Hayden, Harry Worth, Nora Lane, William Duncan, Lois Wilde, Billy King, John Rutherford, Ernie Adams, Frank Ellis, Artie Ortego, Ben Corbett, John Beach, Blackjack Ward; D: Les Selander; SP: Norman Houston; S: *Black Buttes*; P: Harry Sherman.

Texas Trail (Paramount, 1937) 60 mins.; William Boyd, George F. Hayes, Russell Hayden, Judith Allen, Alexander Cross, Robert Kortman, Billy King, Karl

Hackett, Jack Rockwell, John Beach, Rafael Bennett, Philo McCullough, Earle Hodgins, Ben Corbett, John Judd, Clyde Kinney, Leo McMahon, John Powers, Jim Corey, Cliff Parkinson, Cliff Lyons; D: David Selman; SP: Joseph O'Donnell; S: *Tex*; P: Harry Sherman.

Partners of the Plains (Paramount, 1938) 68 mins.; William Boyd, Russell Hayden, Harvey Clark, Gwen Gage, Hilda Plowright, John Warburton, Al Bridge, Al Hill, Earle Hodgins, John Beach, Jim Corey, Herman Hack, Bud McClure; D: Lesley Selander; SP: Harrison Jacobs; S: *Bar 20 Days*; P: Harry Sherman.

Cassidy of the Bar 20 (Paramount, 1938) 56 mins.; William Boyd, Russell Hayden, Nora Lane, Frank Darien, John Elliott, Robert Fiske, Margaret Marquis, Gertrude Hoffman, Carleton Young, Gordon Hart, Edward Cassidy, Jim Toney; D: Lesley Selander; SP: Norman Houston; S: *Me and Shorty*; P: Harry Sherman.

Bar 20 Justice (Paramount, 1938) 70 mins.; William Boyd, Russell Hayden, George F. Hayes, Paul Sutton, Gwen Gaze, Pat O'Brien, Joseph DeStefani, William Duncan, Walter Long, John Beach, Bruce Mitchell, Frosty Royce, Jim Toney; D: Lesley Selander; SP: Arnold Belgard, Harrison Jacobs; P: Harry Sherman.

Pride of the West (Paramount, 1938) 56 mins.; William Boyd, George F. Hayes, Russell Hayden, Charlotte Field, Earle Hodgins, Billy King, Kenneth Harlan, Glenn Strange, James Craig, Bruce Mitchell, Willie Fung, George Morrell, Earl Askam, Jim Toney, Horace B. Carpenter, Henro Otho, John Powers, Leo McMahon, Bob Woodward; D: Lesley Selander; SP: Nate Watt; P: Harry Sherman.

In Old Mexico (Paramount, 1938) 62 mins.; William Boyd, George F. Hayes, Russell Hayden, Betty Amann, Jane Clayton, Al Garcia, Glenn Strange, Trevor Bardette, Anna Demetrio, Tony Roux, Fred Burns, Cliff Parkinson, Paul Sutton; D: Edward D. Venturini; SP: Harrison Jacobs; P: Harry Sherman.

The Frontiersman (Paramount, 1938) 74 mins.; William Boyd, George F. Hayes, Russell Hayden, Evelyn Venable, William Duncan, Clara Kimball Young, Charles (Tony) Hughes, Dickie Jones, Roy Barcroft, Emily Fitzroy, John Beach, Blackjack Ward, George Morrell, Jim Corey, St. Brenden Boys Choir; D: Lesley Selander; SP: Norman Houston, Harrison Jacobs.

Sunset Trail (Paramount, 1939) 60 mins.; William Boyd, George F. Hayes, Russell Hayden, Charlotte Wynters, Jane Clayton, Robert Fiske, Glenn Strange, Kenneth Harlan, Anthony Nace, Kathryn Sheldon, Maurice Cass, Alphonse Ethier, Claudia Smith, Jack Rockwell, Tom London, Jim Toney, Fred Burns, Jerry Jerome, Jim Corey, Frank Ellis, Horace B. Carpenter; D: Lesley Selander; P: Harry Sherman.

Three Men from Texas (Paramount, 1940) 70 mins.; William Boyd, Russell Hayden, Andy Clyde, Esther Estrella, Morris Ankrum, Morgan Wallace, Thornton Edwards, Davidson Clark, Dick Curtis, Glenn Strange, Nayle Marx, Robert Burns, Jim Corey, George Morrell, George Lollier, Frank McCarroll, Lucio Villegas, Carlos De Valdez, Fred Burns, Ethan Laidlaw, Roy Bucko, Frank Ellis, Bill Nestell, John Miller, Roy Butler, Charles Murphy; D: Lesley Selander; SP: Norman Houston; S: *The Bar 20 Three*; P: Harry Sherman.

Hoppy Serves a Writ (United Artists, 1943) 62 mins.; William Boyd, Andy Clyde, Jay Kirby, Victor Jory, George Reeves, Jan Christy, Forbes Murray, Robert Mitchum, Earl Hodgins, Hal Taliaferro (Wally Wales), Roy Barcroft, Byron Foulger, Ben Corbett, Art Mix; D: George Archainbaud; SP: Gerald Geraghty; S: *Hopalong Cassidy Serves a Writ*; P: Harry Sherman.

Bar 20 (United Artists, 1943) 54 mins.; William Boyd, Andy Clyde, Victor Jory, Douglas Fowley, Dustin Farnum, George Reeves, Betty Blythe, Earle Hodgins, Robert Mitchum, Fran- cis McDonald, Buck Bucko; D: Lesley Selander; SP: Morton Grant, Norman Houston, Michael Wilson; P: Harry Sherman.

William MacLeod Raine

William MacLeod Raine was one of the best western writers of the 1920s, 1930s, and 1940s. He developed a formula and structure for his articles and books. Gene Gressley states that Raine's formula western contained standard parts: setting, heroes, villains, and action.[5] The hero personified similar if not identical traits in story after story. He was not only noble, brave, and true, but also a man of leisure who held disdain for worldly accomplishment. He was his own man; his values were the author's values, and his perceptions were the reader's perceptions. Heroes were destined to do their jobs, and the villain was the complete opposite of the hero. Both played their parts usually — though not inevitably — through violent action. The formula demanded the resolution (in favor of the hero) of the conflict, but frequently not until the reader was exhausted and the characters erased.

Raine's books have sold at least 20 million copies and at least 23 stories have been filmed as B movies. By age 83 Raine had written enough pages to fill 80 novels and more than 200 magazines or newspaper stories.

Among writers who contributed to the evolution of the popular western novel, Raine ranked with Zane Grey, Max Brand, W. C. Tuttle, and Luke Short in giving the adventure novel its twentieth-century focus.

Raine was born in London, England on June 22, 1871. At the age of ten he was brought to the United States, where the family settled in Arkansas, and pursued cattle raising and fruit growing as their livelihood. He received his elementary and high school education in Arkansas public schools, and his college education at Sarcey College (Arkansas) and Oberlin College, from which he received a B.A. degree. After college he drifted west, worked on a ranch, was a high school principal in Seattle, and tried to enlist in the Spanish-American War but was turned down because of weak lungs. He finally was obliged to move to Denver to try to regain his health. There he worked as a newspaper reporter and editorial writer on the *Republican*, the *Post*, and the *Rocky Mountain News*. He began to write short stories and ultimately was able to write full time. He finally found his niche with the novel. At first he wrote romantic historical novels with an English background, but soon turned his full attention to the West. It has been estimated that he wrote upward of 7 million words during his writing career. He usually turned out 2 books a year.

Raine's writing turned out to be very rewarding. Income from articles,

houn, Alan Hale, Charlotte Merriam, Otis Harlan, Kitty Bradbury, Joseph Rickson; D: David Smith; SP: Jay Pilcher.

Chain Lightning (Fox, 1927) Buck Jones, Dione Ellis, Ted McNamara, Jack Baston, William Welch, Marte Faust, William Caress, Silver (a horse); D/SP: Lambert Hillyer; S: *The Brass Commandments*.

Silver Spurs (Universal, 1936) 60 mins.; Buck Jones, Muriel Evans, J. P. McGowan, George F. Hayes, Dennis Moore, Robert Frazer, Bruce Lane, William Lawrence, Earl Askam, Charles K. French, Beth Marion, Kernan Cripps, Eddy Waller, Helen MacKellar, Silver (a horse); D: Ray Taylor; SP: Joseph Poland; P: Buck Jones.

Luke Short

Writing under the pseudonym of Luke Short, Frederick Dilley Glidden has authored over 15 works in the western genre. His stories have been serialized in the *Saturday Evening Post, Colliers*, and *Adventure* magazines. With sales over 30 million volumes, he joins Louis L'Amour in being the best-selling western author. Paperback racks generally offer a selection of his books, testifying to his continued popularity. In addition to his experiences as a newspaperman, homesteader, and novelist, Short spent two years as a trapper in the subarctic region of Canada and helped to establish a thorium corporation in Colorado.

Short was born Frederick Dilley Glidden in Kewanee, Illinois, in 1908. In 1930 he received a degree in journalism from the University of Missouri and subsequently went to work as a journalist on various newspapers. In 1936 he became a freelance writer of western fiction. He was a prolific writer and continued to turn out western novels until his death in 1975. The year before (1974) he received the Western Heritage Award from the National Cowboy Hall of Fame and Western Heritage Center in Oklahoma City.

His principal works are as follows: *The Feud at Single Shot*, 1936; *Man on the Blue*, 1937; *King Colt*, 1937; *Guns of the Double Diamond*, 1937; *Marauder's Moon*, 1937; *Bull-Foot Ambush*, 1938; *Misery Lode*, 1938; *The Branded Man*, 1938; *Weary Range*, 1939; *Six Guns of San Jon*, 1939; *Gold Rustlers*, 1939; *Raiders of the Rimrock*, 1939; *Flood Water*, 1939; *Bounty Guns*, 1940; *Brand of Empire*, 1940; *War on Cimmaron*, 1940; *Bought with a Gun*, 1940; *Dead Freight for Piute*, 1940; *Gunman's Chance*, 1941; *Ride the Man Down*, 1942; *Hardcase*, 1942; *Sunset Graze*, 1942; *Ramrod*, 1943; *Gauntlet of Fire*, 1944; *And the Wind Blows Free*, 1945; *Coroner Creek*, 1946; *Fiddlefoot*, 1946; *Station West*, 1946; *High Vermillion*, 1948; *Ambush*, 1949; *Play a Lone Hand*, 1950; *Vengeance Valley*, 1950; *Barren Land Murders*, 1951; *The Whip*, 1951; *Saddle by Starlight*, 1952; *Silver Rock*, 1953; *Rimrock*, 1955; *Riders West*, 1956, editor; *Colt's Law*, 1958, editor; *Rawhide and Bobwire*, 1958; *First Claim*, 1961; *Last Hunt*, 1963; *Desert Crossing*, 1963; *The Some-Day Country*, 1964; *First Campaign*, 1964; *Trigger Country*, 1965; *Paper Sheriff*, 1966; *Savage Range*, 1966; *Primrose Try*,

1967; *Guns of Hanging Lake*, 1968; *Donovan's Gun*, 1968; *The Outrider*, 1972; *The Stalkers*, 1973; *The Man from Two Rivers*, 1974; *Savage Range*, 1974; *Barren Land Showdown*, 1974; *The Man with a Summer Name*, 1974; *The Deserters*, 1975; *Bold Rider*, 1975; *Trouble Country*, 1976; and *Sunset Gaze*, 1976.

Films Based on Luke Short's Writings

Hurry, Charlie, Hurry (RKO-Radio, 1941) 65 mins.; Leon Errol, Mildred Coles, Kenneth Howell, Cecil Cunningham, George Watts, Eddie Conrad, Noble Johnson, Douglas Walton, Georgia Caine, Lalo Encinas; D: Charles E. Roberts; SP: Paul Gerard Smith; P: Howard Benedict.

Ramrod (United Artists, 1947) 94 mins.; Joel McCrea, Veronica Lake, Ian McDonald, Charlie Ruggles, Preston Foster, Arleen Whelan, Lloyd Bridges, Donald Crisp, Rose Higgens, Chic York, Sarah Padden, Don DeFore, Nestor Paiva, Cliff Parkinson, Trevor Bardette, John Powers, Ward Wood, Hal Taliaferro (Wally Wales), Wally Cassell, Ray Teal; D: Andre de Toth; SPZ: Jack Moffitt, Graham Baker, Cecile Kramer; P: Harry Sherman.

Albuquerque (Paramount, 1948) 90 mins.; Randolph Scott, Barbara Britton, George F. Hayes, Russell Hayden, Lon Chaney, Jr., Catherine Craig, George Cleveland, Irving Bacon, Bernard Nedell, Karolyn Grimes, Russell Simpson, Jody Gilbert, Dan White, Walter Baldwin, John Halloran; D: Ray Enright; SP: Gene Lewis, Clarence Upson Young.

Coroner Creek (Columbia, 1948) 90 mins.; Randolph Scott, Marguerite Chapman, George Macready, Sally Eilers, Edgar Buchanan, Barbara Reed, Wallace Ford, Forrest Tucker, William Bishop, Joe Sawyer, Russell Simpson, Douglas Fowley, Lee Bennett, Forrest Taylor, Phil Shumaker, Warren Jackson; D: Ray Enright; SP: Kenneth Gamet; P: Harry Joe Brown.

Station West (RKO-Radio, 1948) 92 mins.; Dick Powell, Jane Greer, Agnes Moorehead, Burl Ives, Tom Powers, Gordon Oliver, Steve Brodie, Guinn (Big Boy) Williams, Raymond Burr, Regis Toomey, Michael Steele, Olin Howlin, John Berkes, Dan White, John Kellogg, Charles Middleton, John Doucette, Suzi Crandall, Bud Osborne, Ethan Laidlaw, Leo McMahon, Al Hill, Bill Phipps, Monte Montague, Stanley Blystone, Marie Thomas, Robert Gates, Robert Jefferson; D: Sidney Lanfield; SP: Frank Fenton, Winston Miller.

Blood on the Moon (RKO-Radio, 1948) 88 mins.; Robert Mitchum, Barbara Bel Geddes, Robert Preston, Walter Brennan, Phyllis Thaxter, Frank Faylen, Tom Tully, Charles McGraw, Tom Tyler, Richard Powers (Tom Keene), Clifton Young, Geroge Cooper, Bud Osborne, Zon Murray, Robert Bray, Ben Corbett, Harry Carey, Jr., Chris-Pin Martin, Al Ferguson, Iron Eyes Cody, Ruth Brennan, Erville Alderson, Joe Devlin, Al Murphy, Robert Malcolm; D: Robert Wise; SP: Harold Shumate, Luke Short; S: Luke Short; P: Sid Rogell.

Ambush (MGM, 1950) 88 mins.; Robert Taylor, John Hodiak, Arlene Dahl, Don Taylor, Jean Hagen, John McIntire, Bruce Cowling, Leon Ames, Pat Moriarity, Charles Stevens, Chief Thundercloud, Ray Teal, Robin Short, Richard Bailey; D: Sam Wood; SP: Marguerite Roberts; P: Armand Deutsch.

Vengeance Valley (MGM, 1951) 83 mins.; Burt Lancaster, Robert Walker, Joanne Dru, Sally Forrest, John Ireland, Ted De Corsia, Carleton Carpenter, Ray Collins, Hugh O'Brian, Will Wright, Grace Mills, James Hayward, James

Harrison, Stanley Andrews, Glenn Strange, Bob Wilke, Al Ferguson, Monte Montague, Dan White, Paul E. Burns, John R. McKee, Tom Fadden, Roy Butler, Margaret Bert, Norman Leavitt, Harvey Dunn; D: Richard Thorpe; SP: Irving Ravetch; P: Nicholas Nayfack.

Silver City (Paramount, 1951) 90 mins.; Edmond O'Brien, Yvonne De Carlo, Richard Arlen, Barry Fitzgerald, Gladys George, Laura Elliott, Edgar Buchanan, Michael Moore, John Dierkes, Frank Fenton, Cliff Clark, Howard Negler, Leo McMahon, Myron Healey, Paul E. Burns, Harvey Parry, Slim Gaut, Don Dunning, Frank Cordell; D: Byron Haskins; SP: Frank Gruber; P: Nat Holt.

Ride the Man Down (Republic, 1953) 90 mins; Brian Donlevy, Rod Cameron, Ella Raines, Forrest Tucker, Barbara Britton, Chill Wills, J. Carroll Naish, Jim Davis, Taylor Holmes, James Bell, Paul Fix, Al Caudebec, Roydon Clark, Roy Barcroft, Douglas Kennedy, Chris-Pin Martin, Jack LaRue, Claire Carleton; D/AP: Joseph Kane; SP: Mary McCall, Jr.

Hell's Outpost (Republic, 1954) 80 mins.; Rod Cameron, Joan Leslie, John Russell, Chill Wills, Jim Davis, Kristine Miller, Ben Cooper, Taylor Holmes, Barton MacLane, Ruth Lee, Arthur Q. Bryan, Oliver Blake, Harry Woods, John Dierkes; D/AP: Joseph Kane; SP: Kenneth Gamet; S: *Silver Rock*.

The Hangman (Paramount, 1959) 86 mins.; Robert Taylor, Fess Parker, Tina Louise, Jack Lord, Shirley Harmer, Mickey Shaughnessey, Gene Evans, James Westerfield, Mabel Albertson, Lucille Curtis; D: Michael Curtiz; SP: Dudley Nichols; P: Frank Freeman, Jr.

Frank Hamilton Spearman

Frank Hamilton Spearman is best known as the creator of the character Whispering Smith, the hero of several books and at least six movies. His best-known fiction was written around railroad themes.

Films Based on Frank Hamilton Spearman's Writings

The Girl and the Game (Signal/Mutual, 1915) 15 chapters; Helen Holmes, Leo D. Maloney, J. P. McGowan, George McDaniel, J. H. Farley, William Brunton, Edward Sutherland; D: J. P. McGowan; SP: J. P. McGowan, Helen Holmes.

Whispering Smith (Signal/Mutual, 1916) 5 reels; Helen Holmes, Belle Hutchinson, J. P. McGowan, Paul C. Hurst, Leo D. Maloney, F. M. Van Norman, Samuel Appel, Walter Rogers, Thomas G. Lingham, William Behrens, C. V. Wells, J. E. Perkins, N. E. Wood, G. H. Wisschussen, Chance Ward, William Brunton, Hugh Adams, Slim Roe; D: J. P. McGowan.

Medicine Bend (Signal/Mutual, 1916) 5 reels; Helen Holmes, J. P. McGowan, Paul Hurst, Thomas Lingham, Leo Maloney, William Brunton, F. Van Norman, N. Z. Woods, Chance Ward, Belle Hutchinson; D: J. P. McGowan.

Nan of Music Mountain (Paramount, 1916) 5 reels; Wallace Reid, Ann Little, Theodore Roberts, James Cruze, Charles Ogle, Raymond Hatton, Hart (Jack) Hoxie, Guy Oliver, James P. Mason, Henry Woodward, Ernest Joy, Horace B. Carpenter, Alice Marc; D: George H. Melford.

Money Madness (Universal, 1917) 5

reels; Charles H. Mailes, Don Bailey, M. Everett, Alfred Vosburg, Mary MacLaren, Rex de Roselli, Eddie Polo; D: Henry McRae; SP: William Parker; S: *Whispering Smith.*

The Love Special (Paramount, 1921) 5 reels; Wallace Reid, Agnes Ayres, Theodore Roberts, Lloyd Whitlock, Sylvia Ashton, William Gaden, Clarence Burton, Snitz Edwards, Ernest Butterworth, Zelma Maja; D: Frank Urson; SP: Eugene B. Lewis; S: *The Daughter of a Magnate.*

Whispering Smith (PDC, 1926) 7 reels; H. B. Warner, Lillian Rich, John Bowers, Lilyan Tashman, Eugene Pallette, Richard Neill, James Mason, Warren Rodgers, Nelson McDowell, Robert Edeson; D: George Melford; SP: Elliott J. Clawson, Will M. Ritchey.

The Runaway Express (Universal, 1926) 6 reels; Jack Daugherty, Blanche Mehaffey, Tom O'Brien, Charles K. French, William A. Steele, Harry Todd, Madge Hunt, Sid Taylor; D: Edward Sedgwick; SP: Curtis Benton; S: *The Nerve of Foley.*

Whispering Smith Rides (Universal, 1927) 10 chapters; Wallace MacDonald, Rose Blossom, J. P. McGowan, Clark Comstock, Henry Herbert, W. M. McCormick, Harry Todd, Willie Fung, Frank Ellis; D: Ray Taylor; SP: Arthur Henry Gooden; S: *Whispering Smith.*

The Night Flyer (Pathe, 1928) 7 reels; William Boyd, Jobyna Ralston, Philo McCullough, Ann Schaeffer, De Witt Jennings, John Milerta, Robert Dudley; D: Walter Lang; SP: Walter Woods; S: *Held for Orders; Being Stories of Railroad Life.*

Whispering Smith Speaks (20th Century-Fox, 1936) 7 reels; George O'Brien, Irene Ware, Kenneth Thompson, Maude Allen, Spencer Charters; D: David Howard; SP: Don Swift, Dan Jarrett, Gilbert Wright, Rex Taylor.

Whispering Smith (Paramount, 1949) 88 mins.; Alan Ladd, Robert Preston, Donald Crisp, Brenda Marshall, William Demarest, Fay Holden, Murvyn Vye, Frank Faylen, John Eldredge, Robert Wood, J. Farrell MacDonald, Will Wright, Don Barclay, Eddy Waller, Ashley Cowan, Jimmy Dundee, Ray Teal, Bob Kortman; D: Leslie Fenton; SP: Frank Butler, Karl Kamb.

Whispering Smith vs. Scotland Yard (RKO-Radio, 1952) 82 mins.; Richard Carlson, Greta Gynt, Rona Anderson, Herbert Lorn, Alan Wheatley, Reginald Beckwith, Dora Bryan, Daniel Wherry, Michael Ward, Danny Green, James Raglan; D: Francis Searle; SP: John Gilling, Steve Fisher.

Whispering Smith (NBC-TV, 1961) 26 episodes; Audie Murphy, Guy Mitchell, Sam Buffington.

W. C. Tuttle

Wilbur Coleman Tuttle was born November 11, 1883, in Glendive, Montana. He had only a grade school education. Career wise, he worked as a sheep herder, cowpuncher, salesman, railroader, forest ranger, baseball player, and baseball manager, finally becoming a freelance writer of fiction, mainly westerns. He published under the pseudonyms Wilbur C. Coleman and W. C. Coleman, as well as the more familiar W. C. Tuttle. He authored many books and contributed over 1,000 stories in magazines. He even found time to serve as president of the Pacific Coast Baseball League, 1935–43.

America, 1939; *Angel with Spurs*, 1942; *Bowl of Brass*, 1944; *The Walls of Jericho*, 1947; *Death on Horseback* (a combination of *Death on the Prairie* and *Death in the Desert*), 1947; *The Chain*, 1949; *The Iron Mistress*, 1951; *The Comancheros*, 1952; *The Female: A Novel of Another Time*, 1953; *Glory, God and Gold*, 1954; *Portage Bay*, 1957; *Jericho's Daughters*, 1957; *Gold in California*, 1958; *Ride the Red Earth*, 1958; *The Fiery Flower*, 1959; *Stuart Symington*, 1960; *Indian Wars and Warriors: East*, 1959; *Indian Wars and Warriors: West*, 1959; *Race to the Golden Spike*, 1961; *The Blazing Southwest: The Pioneer Story of the American Southwest*, 1961; *A Dynasty of Western Outlaws*, 1961; *Magnificant Destiny: A Novel about the Great Secret Adventure of Andrew Jackson and Sam Houston*, 1962; *Spawn of Evil: The Invisible Empire of Soulless Men Which for a Generation Held the Nation in a Spell of Terror*, 1964; *The Devil's Disciples: The Most Dreadful of all Historic Conspiracies, Brewed and Finally Foiled in the Dark Forests of America*, 1965; *The House Divides: The Age of Jackson and Lincoln, from the War of 1812 to the Civil War*, 1965; and *The Buckstones*, 1967.

Wellman served in the U.S. Army Signal Corps as a sergeant in 1918. For seven years he was a partner in a cattle ranch in Oregon. He died from cancer on September 17, 1966, in Los Angeles.

Films Based on Paul Wellman's Writings

Cheyenne (Warner Brothers, 1947) 100 mins.; Dennis Morgan, Jane Wyman, Arthur Kennedy, Janis Paige, Bruce Bennett, Bob Steele, Tom Tyler, Monte Blue, Britt Wood, Alan Hale, Barton MacLane, John Compton, John Alvin, Tom Fadden, Lee Lasses White, Robert Filmer, Snub Pollard, Ethan Laidlaw; D: Raoul Walsh; SP: Alan Lemay, Thomas Williamson; P: Robert Bruckner.

The Comancheros (20th Century–Fox, 1961) 107 mins.; John Wayne, Stuart Whitman, Ina Balin, Nehemiah Persoff, Lee Marvin, Michael Ansara, Pat Wayne, Bruce Cabot, Joan O'Brien, Jack Elam, Edgar Buchanan, Henry Daniell, Richard Devon, Steve Baylor, John Dierkes, Roger Mobley, Bob Steele, Luisa Triana, Aissa Wayne, George J. Lewis, Greg Palmer, Don Brodie, Jon Lormer, Phil Arnold, Alan Carney, Dennis Cole; D: Michael Curtiz; SP: James Edward Grant, Clair Huffaker.

The Iron Mistress (Warner Broth-

ers, 1952) 110 mins.; Alan Ladd, Virginia Mayo, Joseph Calleia, Phyllis Kirk, Douglas Dick, Anthony Caruso, Don Beddoe, Alf Ejellin, Robert Emhardt, Richard Carle, Jay Novello, Daris Massey; D: Gordon Douglas; SP: James M. Webb; P: Henry Blanke.

Jubal (Columbia, 1956) 101 mins.; Glenn Ford, Ernest Borgnine, Rod Steiger, Valerie French, Felicia Farr, Noah Beery, Jr., John Dierkes, Jack Elam, Robert Burton, Robert Knapp, Guy Wilkerson, Russell (Buzzy) Henry, Larry Hudson, Mike Lawrence; D: Delmer Daves; SP: Russell S. Hughes, Delmer Daves; S: *Jubal Troop*.

Apache (United Artists, 1959) 91 mins.; Burt Lancaster, Jean Peters, John McIntire, Charles Bronson, John Dehner, Paul Guilfoyle, Ian MacDonald, Walter Sande, Morris Ankrum, Monte Blue; D: Robert Aldrich; SP: James R. Webb; P: Harold Hecht.

Stewart Edward White

An important writer in his time, Stewart Edward White wrote several early novels, the first of which was *The Westerners* (1901). Originally serialized in *Munsey's* magazine, this work had a character called the Kid and indirectly involved Custer and Little Big Horn, although it is essentially a story of wagon trains and mining camps. It became the first of the large-scale westerns when it reached the screen in 1919. White himself participated in writing the scenario, and the story, improbable as it is, moves along at a fast pace. Other silent films adapted from White's work included *The Call of the North* (Paramount, 1921, based on *Conjuror's Horse: The Killer* (Pathe, 1920), later remade as *Mystery Ranch* (Fox, 1932); *The Gray Dawn* (Hodkinson, 1922); and *Arizona Nights* (FBO, 1927), based on a collection of short stories loosely strung together as a novel.[6]

White was born in Grand Rapids, Michigan, on March 12, 1873. Until he was about 9 he lived in a small mill town in Michigan, but from the age of 11 until he was 15 or 16 he lived on a ranch in California and spent much of his time in the saddle. He was 16 before his formal education began, but he made rapid progress, graduating from Grand Rapids High School at age 18. He earned both a bachelor's degree and a master's degree from the University of Michigan. Fresh out of school, he took a year to prospect for gold in the Black Hills and to work in a Chicago packing house. As much time as he could muster was spent cruising the Great Lakes in a 28-foot cutter sloop.

The year 1896–97 found White enrolled in law school at Columbia University. It was here that he started writing short stories. His first important work was *The Westerners*, first serialized in *Munsey's* and then printed in book form in 1901. He spent a winter in the Hudson Bay country where he wrote *The Blazed Trail*, which established his reputation as a writer. Other books followed, with *The Riverman* (1908) becoming a bestseller. He married in 1906 and he and his wife spent a lot of time in California, Arizona, and Wyoming. Out of their experiences came *The Pass* (1910). *The Cabin* followed in short order, while *Gold* (1913), *Gray Dawn*, and *Rose Dawn* had their settings in California. These stories were collected in a 1927 omnibus edition titled *The Story of California*.

White was a major in the 144th Field Artillery in World War I. When his wife died he turned to writing a series of religious books, beginning with *The Betty Book* (1937), based on his belief in psychics and his wife's existence in another world.

The following is a list of his principal works: *The Westerners*, 1901; *The Claim Jumpers*, 1901; *The Blazed Trail*, 1902; *The Forest*, 1903; *Conjuror's House*, 1903; *The Silent Places*, 1904; *The Pass*, 1906; *The Mystery* (coauthor), 1907; *Camp and Trail*, 1907; *The Riverman*, 1908; *The Rules of the Game*, 1909; *The Cabin*, 1910; *The Adventures of Bobby Orde*, 1911; *The Sign at Six*, 1912; *African*

Camp Fires, 1913; *Gold*, 1913; *Gray Dawn*, 1915; *The Rediscovered Country*, 1915; *The Leopard Woman*, 1916; *The Forty-Niners*, 1918; *Rose Dawn*, 1920; *On Tiptoe*, 1922; *Daniel Boone*, 1922; *The Glory Hole*, 1924; *Skookum Chuck*, 1925; *Secret Harbour*, 1925; *Credo*, 1925; *Lions in the Path*, 1926; *Back of Beyond*, 1927; *Why Be a Mud Turtle?* 1928; *Dog Days*, 1930; *The Shepper-Newfounder*, 1931; *The Long Rifle*, 1932; *Ranchero*, 1933; *Folded Hills*, 1934; *Pole Star* (coauthor), 1934; *The Betty Book*, 1937; *Across the Unknown* (coauthor), 1939; *The Unobstructed Universe*, 1940; *The Road I Know*, 1942; and *Stampede*, 1942.

Films Based on Stewart Edward White's Writings

The Call of the North (Jesse L. Lasky Feature Play Company, 1914) 5 reels; Robert Edeson, Theodore Roberts, Winifred Kingston, Horace B. Carpenter, Florence Dagmar, Milton Brown, Vera McGarry, J. Mullally, Sydney Deane, Fred Montague; D: Oscar Apfel, Cecil B. DeMille; SP: George Broadhurst; S: *Conjuror's House.*

The Westerners (Hodkinson/Pathe, 1919) 7 reels; Roy Stewart, Robert McKim, Wilfred Lucas, Mildred Manning, Mary Jane Irving, Graham Pettie, Frankie Lee, Clark Comstock, Dorothy Hagar; D: Edward Sloman; SP: E. Richard Schayer.

The Leopard Woman (Associated Producers, 1920) 7 reels; Louise Glaum, House Peters, Noble Johnson; D: Wesley Ruggles; SP: H. Tipton Steck, Stanley C. Morse.

The Killer (Pathe, 1921) 6 reels; Claire Adams, Jack Conway, Frankie Lee, Frank Campeau, Tod Sloan, Edward Peil, Frank Hayes, Will Walling, Milton Ross, Tom Ricketts, Zack Williams; D: Howard Hickman; SP: E. Richard Schayer.

The Call of the North (Paramount, 1921) 5 reels; Jack Holt, Madge Bellamy, Noah Beery, Francis McDonald, Edward Martindel, Helen Ferguson, Jack Herbert; D: Joseph Henabery; SP: Jack Cunningham; S; *Conjuror's House.*

The Gray Dawn (Hodkinson, 1922) 6 reels; Carl Gantvoort, Claire Adams, Robert McKim, George Hackathorne,

Snitz Edwards, Stanton Heck, Omar Whitehead, Claire McDowell, Maude Wayne, J. Gunnis Davis, Zack Williams, Grace Marvin, Charles Arling, Harvey Clark, Charles Thurston, Marc Robbins, Charles B. Murphy; D: Benjamin B. Hampton, Jean Hersholt, and others; SP: E. Richard Schayer, Marie Jenny Howe.

Arizona Nights (FBO, 1927) 7 reels; Fred Thomson, Nora Lane, J. P. McGowan, William Courtright, Lottie Williams, William McCormick, Dan Peterson, Silver King (a horse); D: Lloyd Ingraham; SP: Hal Conklin.

Under a Texas Moon (Warner Brothers, 1930) 8 reels; Frank Fay, Raquel Torres, Myrna Loy, Armida, Noah Beery, Georgia Stone, George Cooper, Fred Kohler, Betty Boyd, Charles Sellon, Jack Curtis, Tully Marshall, Sam Apfel, Mona Maris, Edythe Kramera, Inez Gomez; D: Michael Curtiz; SP: Gordon Rigby; S: *Two-Gun Man.*

Part Time Wife (Fox, 1930) 6–7 reels; Edmund Lowe, Leila Hyams, Tom Clifford, Walter McGrail, Louis Payne, Sam Lufkin, Bodil Rosing, George Corcoran; D: Leo McCarey, SP: Raymond L. Schrock, Leo McCarey, Howard Green; S: *The Shepper-Newfounder.*

Wild Geese Calling (20th Century–Fox, 1941) 78 mins.; Joan Bennett, Henry Fonda, Warren William, Ona Munson, Barton MacLane, Russell Simpson, Iris Adrian; D: John Brahm; SP: Horace McCoy.

Owen Wister

When Owen Wister published *The Virginian* in 1902, he set off a major detonation, the reverberations from which are still being heard. From the start the book was immensely popular, and within three months it had reached the top of the bestseller list, where it remained for six months.[7]

Sales continued to rise and by 1993 well over 2 million copies had been sold.

Wister is credited with creating the archetypical western novel and establishing the folk myth of the cowboy as a chivalrous hero. *The Virginian* originated many of the patterns of western fiction, most notably that of the cowboy as a brave and honorable gentleman who upheld democratic values.

The following comment on the 1946 version starring Joel McCrea, is from *Variety* (January 30, 1946):

> *The Virginian* stands up pretty well over the years. First filmed in 1914 for the silents, then in 1929 by Paramount, the present version of the Owen Wister novel is still a pleasant, flavorsome western, with much of the old charm of a daguerreotype. Filmed for first time in Technicolor, pic's gaudy setting, as well as cast and story, will round 'em up again at the b.o.
>
> Although story is a little dated as well as a mite slow, the yarn is still a satisfactory romance, with enough shooting and suspense to offset the plodding pace. Yarn hasn't been changed much, still being the story of the little schoolmarm from Vermont and the cowboy from Virginia, who meet in Montana and wed after the hero has disposed of a few troublesome cow rustlers.

Andy Adams wrote concerning *The Virginian*: "the story might have been more convincing to some readers if the author had given one glimpse of his hero in connection with his occupation. Had he been shown in the thick of a roundup, cutting out a trainload of beeves for his employer, his identification would have been complete. A cowboy without cattle is comperable to a lord without lands or a master without slaves."[8]

Wister was born in Philadelphia on July 14, 1860. His father was a wealthy physician and Owen received the best education possible. He attended St. Paul's School in Concord and also attended schools in Switzerland and England. He graduated from Harvard in 1882 with highest honors in music, and two more years in Paris advanced his musical education. He returned to the United States in 1884, worked for a while as a clerk for the Union Safe Deposit Vaults in New York, spent some time on a Wyoming ranch recuperating from a nervous breakdown, and attended Harvard Law School from 1885 to 1888. He was made a member of the Philadelphia bar after graduation and practiced law for a number of years.

In 10 years he made 15 visits to the West. His love of the area encouraged him to try writing. "Hank's Woman" and "How Lin McLean Went

West" were short stories that he wrote and these were published in *Harper's*. This success gave him the necessary enthusiasm to continue writing until his talent achieved full flowering with the highly successful *The Virginian*. The University of Pennsylvania conferred on him an honorary Doctor of Law degree in 1907, and other honors followed over the years. He died on July 21, 1938.

Wister's principal works are as follows: *The Dragon of Wantley*, 1892; *Red Men and White*, 1895; *Lin McLean*, 1898; *The Jimmyjohn Boss*, 1900; *The Virginian*, 1902; *Philosophy 4*, 1903; *Lady Baltimore*, 1906; *How Doth the Simple Spelling Bee*, 1907; *The Seven Ages of Washington*, 1907; *Members of the Family*, 1911; *The Pentecost of Calamity*, 1915; *A Straight Deal: Or the Ancient Grudge*, 1920; *Neighbors Henceforth*, 1922; *Watch Your Thirst*, 1923; *When West Was West*, 1928; and *Roosevelt: The Story of a Friendship*, 1930.

Films Based on Owen Wister's Writings

A Western Romance (Edison, 1910) 1 reel; J. Barney Sherry; D/SP: Edwin S. Porter.

A Woman's Fool (Universal, 1918) 5 reels; Harry Carey, Mollie Malone, Betty Schade, Roy Clarke, Vester Pegg, M. K. Wilson, William A. Carroll; D: John Ford; SP: George Hively; S: *Lin McLean*.

The Virginian (Preferred, 1923) 8 reels; Kenneth Harlan, Florence Vidor, Russell Simpson, Pat O'Malley, Raymond Hatton, Milton Ross, Sam Allen, Bert Hadley, Fred Gambold; D: Tom Forman; SP: Hope Loring, Louis D. Lighton; S: Owen Wister, Kirk La Shelle.

The Virginian (Paramount, 1929) 95 mins.; Gary Cooper, Walter Huston, Richard Arlen, Chester Conklin, Mary Brian, Eugene Pallette, E. H. Calvert, Helen Ware, Victor Potel, Tex Young, Charles Stevens; D: Victor Fleming; SP: Howard Estabrook.

The Virginian (Paramount, 1946) 90 mins.; Joel McCrea, Brian Donlevy, Sonny Tufts, Barbara Britton, Fay Bainter, Tom Tully, Henry O'Neill, Bill Edwards, William Frawley, Paul Guilfoyle, Marc Lawrence, Vince Barnett, Al Bridge, Martin Garralaga, Nana Bryant, Hank Bell, Bob Kortman, Stanley Andrews, Paul Hurst, Dick Curtis; D: Stuart Gilmore; SP: Frances Goodrich, Albert Hackett, Edward E. Paramore, Jr.; P: Paul Jones.

Harold Bell Wright

Harold Bell Wright was born May 4, 1872, in Rome, New York. As a lad he worked on the farm and attended a country school. When he was grown he had aspirations of attending college so he entered the preparatory department of Hiram College. Illness forced his withdrawal from school and he wound up in Missouri where he hoped to regain his health. With no formal seminary training he began preaching and served as a pastor of several churches during the next ten years. His health forced him to give up his church work, and it was then that he went into the Ozark Mountains to recuperate. There he wrote *The Shepherd of the Hills*, one of the bestselling books of all time. He died in 1944.

Shepherd of the Hills (1919) was a faithful adaptation of the book written by Wright because the author himself produced, directed, and wrote the screenplay. A second silent version (1928) also followed the basic plot of the Wright novel. The most famous version (1941) starred Harry Carey and John Wayne but deviated considerably from the original story. A 1964 film starring Richard Arlen was a closer adaptation but failed to achieve the popularity of the 1941 film. A total of 13 films have been based on Wright novels. In addition to *The Shepherd of the Hills*, *The Mine with the Iron Door* (1936) and *The Winning of Barbara Worth* (1926) were popular films.

The principal works of Wright are as follows: *That Printer of Udell's*, 1903; *The Shepherd of the Hills*, 1907; *The Calling of Dan Matthews*, 1909; *The Uncrowned King*, 1910; *The Winning of Barbara Worth*, 1911; *Their Yesterdays*, 1912; *The Eyes of the World*, 1914; *When a Man's a Man*, 1916; *The Re-Creation of Brian Kent*, 1919; *Helen of the Old House*, 1921; *The Mine with the Iron Door*, 1923; *A Son of His Father*, 1925; *God and the Groceryman*, 1927; *Long Ago Told*, 1929; *Exit*, 1930; *Ma Cinderella*, 1932; *The Man Who Went Away*, 1942; and *To My Sons*, 1944.

Films Based on Harold Bell Wright's Writings

Shepherd of the Hills (Harold Bell Wright Story Pictures, 1919) 10 reels; Harry G. Lonsdale, Cathrine Curtis, George McDaniel, Don Bailey, Elizabeth Rhodes, Lon Poff, C. Edward Raynor, Bert Sprotte, George Hackathorne, Louis Darclay, E. K. Kendall, Ardita Mellonino, William P. Du Vaull, J. Edwin Brown; D: Harold Bell Wright, L. F. Gottschalk; S/SP: Harold Bell Wright.

When a Man's a Man (Principal/ Associated First National, 1924) 7 reels; John Bowers, Marguerite De La Motte, Robert Frazer, June Marlowe, Forrest Robinson, Elizabeth Rhodes, Fred Stanton, George Hackathorne, Edward Hearn, John Fox, Jr., Arthur Hoyt, Ray Thompson, Charles Mailes; D: Edward F. Cline; SP: Walter Anthony, Harry Carr; P: Sol Lesser.

The Mine with the Iron Door (Principal, 1924) 8 reels; Pat O'Malley,

Dorothy Mackaill, Raymond Hatton, Charlie Murray, Bert Woodruff, Mitchell Lewis, Creighton Hale, Mary Carr, William Collier, Jr., Robert Frazer, Clarence Burton; D: Sam Wood; SP: Arthur Statter, Mary Alice Scully, Hope Loring.

The Re-Creation of Brian Kent (Principal, 1925) 7 reels; Helene Chadwick, Kenneth Harlan, Mary Carr, ZaSu Pitts, Rosemary Theby, T. Roy Barnes, Ralph Lewis, Russell Simpson, DeWitt Jennings, Russell Powell; D: Sam Wood; SP: Arthur Statter, Mary Alice Scully; P: Sol Lesser.

A Son of His Father (Paramount, 1925) 7 reels; Bessie Love, Warner Baxter, Raymond Hatton, Walter McGrail, Carl Stockdale, Billy Eugene, James Farley, Charles Stevens, Valentina Zimina, George Kuwa; D: Victor Fleming; SP: Anthony Coldeway.

The Winning of Barbara Worth (United Artists, 1926) 9 reels; Ronald Colman, Vilma Banky, Charles Love, Gary Cooper, Paul McAllister, E. J. Ratcliffe, Clyde Cook, Erwin Connelly, Sam Blum; D: Henry King; SP: Frances Marion.

The Shepherd of the Hills (First National, 1928) 9 reels; Alec B. Francis, Molly O'Day, John Boles, Matthew Betz, Romaine Fielding, Maurice Murphy, Edythe Chapman, Carl Stockdale, Marion Douglas (Ena Gregory), John Westwood; D: Albert Rogell; SP: Marion Jackson.

The Eyes of the World (United Artists, 1930) Una Merkel, Nance O'Neil, Brandon Hurst, William Jeffrey, John Holland, Fern Andra, Hugh Huntley, Frederic Bunt, Eulalie Jensen, Myra Hubert; D: Henry King; SP: N. Brewster Morse; P: Sol Lesser.

The Mine with the Iron Door (Columbia, 1936) 66 mins.; Richard Arlen, Cecilia Parker, Henry B. Walthall, Horace Murphy, Stanley Fields, Spencer Charters, Charles Wilson, Barbara Bedford; D: David Howard; SP: Howard Swift, Dan Jarrett; P: Sol Lesser.

Secret Valley (Principal/20th Century–Fox, 1937) 60 mins.; Richard Arlen, Virginia Grey, Jack Mulhall, Norman Willis, Syd Saylor, Russell Hicks, Willie Fung, Maude Allen, Tom London; D: Howard Bretherton; SP: Paul Franklin, Dan Jarrett, Earle Snell; P: Sol Lesser.

Western Gold (Principal/20th Century–Fox, 1937) 56 mins.; Smith Ballew, Heather Angel, LeRoy Mason, Ben Alexander, Otis Harlan, Vic Potel, Frank McGlynn, Horace Murphy, Tom London, Bud Osborne, Steve Clark, Howard Hickman, Al Bridge, Paul Fix, Art Lasky; D: Howard Bretherton; SP: Forrest Barnes; P: Sol Lesser.

Shepherd of the Hills (Paramount, 1941) 98 mins.; Harry Carey, John Wayne, Betty Field, Beulah Bondi, James Barton, Samuel S. Hinds, Marjorie Main, Ward Bond, Marc Lawrence, John Qualen, Fuzzy Knight, Tom Fadden, Hank Bell, Dorothy Adams, Fern Emmett, Vivita Campbell, Robert Kortman, Henry Brandon, Jim Corey, Selmer Jackson; D: Henry Hathaway; SP: Grover Jones, Stuart Anthony.

The Shepherd of the Hills (Howco International, 1964) 110 mins.; Richard Arlen, James W. Middleton, Sherry Lynn, James Collie, Lloyd Durre, Hal Meadows, James Bradford, Jay N. Houck, Jr., Gilbert Elmore, George Jackson, Delores James, Danny Spurlock, Reubin Egan, Tom Pope, Roy Idom, Jim Teague, Roger Nash, Jim Greene; D/SP: Ben Parker; P: Jim McCullough.

PART III

Cinematic Trails of the Snow Country

Chapter 4

James Oliver Curwood

James Oliver Curwood was to the Northwest what Zane Grey was to the West, only perhaps more so. Whereas Grey's works have been translated to the screen 110 times, a minimum of 156 films have been based on the writings of Curwood. This could well be the record for any literary figure. And also like Grey, Curwood received little praise from literary critics. They thought his characters unbelievable, his stories melodramatic, and his literary style tiring. He and Grey shared much of the same criticism by critics, but also much of the same praise by the public.

No author has ever equaled Curwood in popularity with the masses as a writer about God's country—his term for the great Northwest. He dealt with a type of life exactly suited at his precise moment in time with the vague imaginings of the rank-and-file citizen, and he instinctively availed himself of the conventional literary devices that made for popularity. Even in France he was raised to a pinnacle in popular favor formerly reserved for Upton Sinclair and Jack London. While he carefully fashioned his heroes to stand for everything that was strong and upright, there was also emphasis in his stories on the wholesomeness of the virgin land that served as a backdrop.

By 1927 he was being paid more per word for his stories than any other contemporary writer, including England's Poet Laureate, Rudyard Kipling, and Sir Arthur Conan Doyle. His 27 novels, published in 12 languages, had sold 4 million hardcover copies in the United States alone.

Curwood was born June 12, 1878, in Owosso, Michigan, and is said to have begun writing long adventure stories at the tender age of eight. His mischievous nature led to him being expelled from school, and for a while he bicycled his way through the South, working at whatever he could find to do. But always he wrote, and wrote, and wrote. At an age when other boys were playing baseball or "cowboys" or maybe starting to take an interest in girls, Curwood would write for hours each day whenever possible. Eventually, he wound up as a journalist for the *Detroit News-Tribune* before entering the University of Michigan for a couple of years. He returned to the newspaper as a reporter in 1900 and worked there until 1906, climbing to the editor's job. Subsequently, for two or three years he was a writer for the Canadian government. In 1909 he made his first visit to the wilds of the great Northwest. Having made the decision to devote all his time to writing, Curwood spent nearly half of each year for the next 18 years exploring Canada, getting to know the ways of Canadians, and acquiring story material. During these years he sometimes lived among the Eskimos and made many trips into unexplored regions. Before writing *The River's End*, he traveled 3,000 miles up and down the Saskatchewan. He became intimately familiar with the Athabaska, the Slave, and the Mackenzie rivers before writing *The Valley of Silent Men*, which sold 105,000 copies even before publication. The basis for *The Grizzly King* was his personal relationship with the wild animals while living in a cabin hundreds of miles from civilization. It was here, too, that *God's Country and the Woman* and *Kazan* flowed from the writer's fertile brain and pen.

Curwood eventually established his home in Owosso, Michigan, where he had constructed a replica of a French chateau on the Shiawassee River. Known as Curwood's Castle, it was in the turret commanding a good view of the river that he had his desk at which he spent hundreds of hours grinding out stories of the far North and fighting for the advancement of conservation, a cause dear to his heart. He once wrote, "It is the great law of existence that life must destroy in order to live; but to let live, when it is not necessary to destroy, is a beautiful thing to consider."

In the latter years of his life he threw himself into the nationwide crusade for conservation measures, and he was responsible for much favorable legislation designed to stop the destruction and pollution of Michigan's lakes, streams, and forests.

Curwood's portrayal of life as a titanic struggle between good and evil prompted author John Hepler to comment thus: "In this good-evil conflict, still popular today in the movies, fiction, and on TV, Curwood idealized the age-old dream of Good Triumphant. His epics treat of faith, courage, purity, and the will to win. Millions of Americans believed these were the virtues of our past, told and retold in the stories of our nation's development. The idealized people and morals were always the same, only locale changed. That was the major appeal of Curwood's fiction."

Curwood died in 1927, at age 49, as the result of a poisonous insect bite that went unattended too long.

Hollywood took notice of Curwood's writing very early and saw the monetary potential of bringing to the screen his adventures and romantic stories of the North country. *Looking Forward* (1910) is the first Curwood story of record to reach the screen and was filmed by Thanhauser. But in 1913 both Vitagraph and Selig commenced production on long series' of Curwood-based films. In 1914 and 1915 no less than 56 of these films based on the author's stories were released: a record unsurpassed by any other writer. Other

Kermit Maynard, Wheeler Oakman, and unidentified actor in *Code of the Mounted* (Ambassador, 1935).

companies, too, soon capitalized on the popularity of Curwood and his writings. However, since 1950 only 11 films have utilized stories by Curwood, a reflection of his lost popularity with both the reading and viewing public. In this respect he was not alone, for Zane Grey, Jack London, Rex Beach, Max Brand, Peter B. Kyne, and other writers popular with the public prior to the second World War all suffered the same fate. Perhaps it is time for audiences to rediscover the great adventure writers of the past.

The number of Curwood-based films released each year is as follows:

Year	Films	Year	Films	Year	Films	Year	Films
1910	1	1920	3	1930	1	1949	3
1913	14	1921	3	1934	2	1950	2
1914	28	1922	4	1935	10	1951	2
1915	28	1924	1	1936	7	1952	1
1916	10	1925	4	1938	1	1953	3
1917	6	1926	4	1940	1	1954	1
1918	3	1927	1	1942	1	1961	1
1919	4	1928	2	1946	3	1988	1

threatens the man, Paul Wescott, and goes to prison for it. Hilda obtains a divorce and marries Wescott. Upon his release, John, bent on revenge, goes to Paul's home intent on killing him. However, Lola and Peter Hyde, a friend of John's, prevent him from doing so. Shortly thereafter Paul is killed by lightning that also permanently blinds Hilda. John realizes his love for Lola, and she makes known her love for him.

Such a Little Pirate (Famous Players–Lasky, October 13, 1918) 5 reels; Lila Lee (Patricia Wolf), Theodore Roberts (Obadiah Wolf), Harrison Ford (Rory O'Malley), Guy Oliver ("Bad-Eye"), Forrest Seabury (Ellory Glendenning), J. Parks Jones (Harold Glendenning), Adele Farrington (Mrs. Glendenning), Sinbad, the orangutan (Himself); D: George Melford; SP: Monte Katterjohn; S: *Peggy the Pirate*. Synopsis: The old salt Obadiah Wolf makes his last payment on his schooner *The Laughing Lass* to Ellory Glendenning, who hopes to take over the schooner by any unlawful means possible so that he can sell it to the government at a sizable profit. Obadiah plans to sail his vessel to the South Seas to seek a treasure, the location of which is tatooed on his chest. A pirate called Bad-Eye forces Obadiah to accompany him to the treasure island. Meanwhile, Glendenning and his draft-dodging son, Harold, seize the schooner and force Obediah's granddaughter, Patricia and her boyfriend, Rory O'Malley, to sail it to the South Seas so that Harold will escape the draft. During a storm Patricia and Rory are able to take over the vessel and land on the island where Obediah and Bad-Eye have landed. Obadiah is rescued, leaving Bad-Eye on the island, and the party returns to the United States. Glendenning is forced to give the ship back to Obadiah and his son has to go into the army.

Some Liar (American Film Company, April 1919) 5 reels; William Russell (Robert Winchester McTabb), Eileen Percy (Celie Sterling), Haywood Mack (Sheldon Lewis Kellard), Gordon Russell (High Spade McQueen), John Gaugh (Loco Ike/Octagenarian Suitor); D: Henry King; SP: Stephen Fox (Jules Furthman). Synopsis: Robert Winchester McTabb is a traveling salesman with a line of cradles and coffins, and when he comes to the mining town of Yellow Jacket, Arizona, he is something of an accomplished liar and his yarns are such whoppers that the miners and a certain pretty girl are considerably impressed. Celie Sterling, as she is called, offers to invest in a coffin if Bob will get rid of an obnoxious individual by the name of Sheldon Lewis Kellard. As the salesman has told her of his murdering exploits, he has to live up to them, even though he is scared.

High Spade McQueen, the proprietor of the gambling hall, also has a score to settle against Kellard, and so Bob sells him a coffin. As the gambler attempts to get familiar with Celie, the young Ananias knocks him down, though he is warned to order a coffin for himself. While lunching with Celie soon after his fracas with McQueen, he happens to see Kellard and is scared stiff. The latter warns him that he has nothing to fear as long as he is with the girl. It is just one lie after another until Bob finds himself on the point of being lynched for supposed horse-stealing. When his innocence is proven in this case he still has Kellard and McQueen to deal with. The former has some compromising letters of Celie's in his possession and Bob recovers them after a severe tussle that involves not only these two men but also McQueen. When everything is straightened out and Celie has discovered what an enormous liar the salesman is, he squares himself by uttering the first truth he has ever told: "I love you."

Review:

The idea behind it, while reasonably true, seems somewhat forced in execution, if one may take into account a lot of repetitious detail. It being extremely weak, the picture runs its course early and the spectator is only kept at attention through Mr. Russell's enthusiasm for his work.... The picture departs from its farcical flourish in much of the action, and the melodramatic scenes substituted do not suffice to give it weight, although the principals work mighty hard to put it over. A few thrilling fights interspersed with the hero's lies and it is all over.

Motion Picture News (September 7, 1919)

Two Women (Vitagraph, April 28, 1919) 5 reels; Anita Stewart (Enid Arden), Earle Williams (John Leighton), Harry Northrup (W. G. Griggs); D: Ralph W. Ince. **Synopsis:** John Leighton, a geological expert, is sent away from home by his boss, W. G. Griggs, while the latter has an affair with John's wife. In the mountains during his survey, John meets Enid Arden, a beautiful, naive girl who falls in love with him. When John finds out about his wife's infidelity he fights with Griggs. Griggs and Emily go off to Europe together where Emily files for divorce. Griggs sees other women behind Emily's back and they fight. However, it is a jealous boyfriend of one of his female conquests that kills him. Emily returns to the United States and tracks John to the mountains, to which he had returned in his grief, and where he has found peace and romance with Enid. Emily is killed in a train wreck, leaving the path clear for a wedding between John and Enid.

Note:

This film was a reedited version of a three-reel film released 5 Jan 1915 which opened at the Vitagraph Theatre in New York on 2 Nov 1914. It was a Broadway Star Feature, released by General Film Company through their feature department. The names of the characters differ from the 1919 version; in the 1915 release, Anita Stewart played Anita, of the Woodland, Earle Williams played John Emerson, Julia Swayne Gordon played Cleo Emerson and Harry Northrup played Robert Lawler. The story also varies from that of the 1919 version; John, gone only part of a day, finds that his wife and his boss have been joyriding. After he divorces her, she marries the boss and they go to Europe. John then meets Anita in the mountains for the first time. At the end, John's first wife returns after the death of her husband and tracks John to his mountain cabin. Although he is blinded by her beauty at first, when Anita enters, he sends his divorced wife away and embraces Anita. The wife returns to the city. There is no train wreck.

American Film Institute, Feature Films, 1919–1920, p. 961

Beauty-Proof (Vitagraph, June 23, 1919) 5 reels; Harry T. Morey (Corporal Steele), Betty Blythe (Carol Thorpe), George Majeroni (Hodge/Garson), Denton Vane (Young Thorpe), Robert Gaillard (Inspector McGregor), Tenny Wright (A Half-Breed). **Synopsis:** Corporal Steele is considered to be beauty-proof, as he has apparently never shown any interest in women. For that reason he is assigned the job of arresting the brother of a young, beautiful woman who is determined to prevent him from doing his job. Carol's men jump the corporal and tie him up. He is placed in a box in Hodge's cabin, where he overhears Carol tell Hodge that her brother attempted to kill him because of his advances to her. Hodge again attempts to rape her but Steele gets loose and kills Hodge, having discovered that he is the same man who stole his own wife much earlier. He also discovers that he is in love with Carol.

Nomads of the North (Associated First National, October 11, 1920) 6 reels; Betty Blythe (Nanette Roland), Lon Chaney (Raoul Challoner), Lewis S. Stone (Corporal O'Connor), Francis

MacDonald (Buck McDougall), Melbourne MacDowell (Duncan McDougall), Spottiswoode Aitkin (Old Roland); D: David M. Hartford. Synopsis: Nanette Roland is engaged to Raoul Challoner, who is missing. Buck McDougall wants to marry her and fakes evidence of Raoul's death. Nanette then yields to his marriage demands, but at the wedding Raoul shows up. A fight ensues in which Raoul accidentally kills a man and is arrested. Nanette helps him escape and they disappear into the Northern wilderness. Corporal O'Connor is put on their trail but it is three years before he discovers their cabin in the wilds with the help of Buck. Nanette and Raoul now have a baby. When a forest fire breaks out, Corporal O'Connor is injured by a falling tree and rescued by Raoul, while Buck dies in the fire. Out of gratitude O'Connor agrees to testify that Raoul is dead, thus freeing forever the fears of Raoul and Nanette.

Back to God's Country (First National, September 28, 1919) 6 reels; Nell Shipman (Dolores Le Beau), Wapi (Wapi, the Killer), Wheeler Oakman (Peter Burke), Wellington Playter (Captain Rydell), Ralph Laidlow (Baptiste Le Beau), Charles Arling (Blake), Great Dane (Himself); S: *Wapi, the Walrus*. Synopsis: In the Northern wilds of Canada lives Dolores and her father. She has grown up among the semi-savage beasts of the field and woods and has made pets of them. She meets Peter, a government investigator, and they fall in love. After her father's death at the hands of a desperado—a renegade vessel captain who had temporarily journeyed inland to hide from the officers— she marries Peter, and they set sail for the far North on his government mission of investigating the Eskimo.

Rydell, the renegade sea captain, is master of the vessel and after wounding her husband he tries to force his attentions upon Dolores but is successfully repulsed. The villain's partner in the far North has a savage dog that he constantly beats and keeps chained. It is called Wapi, the Killer.

When the young wife pleads for a dog team to take her husband overland to a surgeon she is refused. Her love for wild animals stands her in good stead when she wins over the Great Dane. For when she is eventually given a dog team for herself and another for her husband she suspects foul play is contemplated and so escapes with her husband on one sled. In the mad chase with the villain after her the Great Dane breaks loose from his chain and harrasses the pursuer so successfully that Dolores is able to make her way with her sick husband to civilization.

Review:

An out of the ordinary film production occupying a field all its own. It is a unique novelty and while presenting a dramatic story realistically it also possesses great value scenically and is naturally entertaining because of the great array of animals used: lions, bears, deers, porcupine, wildcats and, last, but not least, the Great Dane, a dog of marvelous intelligence.

The cast is well balanced and the continuity is favored with the suspensive element, but easy to follow. Direction and photography are very good and there are many thrills augmented by several tense periods. Locale is generally amid Alaskan snows and ice with a sympathetic love element in the story which will register generally.

Motion Picture News (October 11, 1919)

The Courage of Marge O'Doone (Vitagraph, May 1920) 7 reels; Pauline Starke (Marge O'Doone), Niles Welch (David Raine), George Stanley (Michael O'Doone), Jack Curtiss (Brokaw, the Brute), William Dyer (Hauck), Boris Karloff (Tavish), Billie Bennett (Margaret O'Doone), James O'Neill (Mukoki, the Faithful), Tarra (The Grizzly

Bear), Baree (The Outlaw Dog); D: David Smith; SP: Robert N. Bradbury. **Synopsis:** Michael and Margaret O'Doone live up in the big snows. Michael is a friend of all and when an Indian comes to him because his wife is sick, he makes a long trip to see if he can help. Because he stays away overnight Margaret goes momentarily insane and believes that a licentious trapper is her husband. The viewer is led to believe that the trapper takes advantage of Margaret. It causes the separation of the O'Doones and throws their baby, Marge, into the hands of rough characters. Years pass and Michael has become doctor of souls and bodies of the whole North. He meets David Raine, a youth from the East, disillusioned in love. David has found a picture of Marge left in the railway carriage seat by Margaret and decides to go north to find her because it says on the photograph that "she is alone."

The rest of the picture is taken up with David's finding Marge and his fights to keep her from falling into the hands of the brute. After a bear fight has been rung in and a man and dog fight is related in the subtitles the happy ending is brought in with David and Marge together and Michael and Margaret reunited. It seems after all that the trapper didn't take advantage of Margaret. **Reviews:**

They haven't been altogether successful in communicating the atmosphere of "bigness" to *The Courage of Marge O'Doone*. This is an atmostphere that James Oliver Curwood always strives for in his stories of the northern snows and was doubtless part of this one in its printed form. The producers, however, haven't quite succeeded in catching this element. Perhaps the chief fault is that they left the job for the subtitles to undertake. But Curwood's descriptive color should have been injected into the action itself to make it convincing.

Wid's Daily (June 6, 1920)

Comes a Western (call it a Northwestern) to the screen which for its picturesque quality hasn't been excelled in many a day. The scenic grandeur, the vast reaches of snow and mountains, the rugged character of the landscapes prove a rich background for one of James Oliver Curwood's stories of the Northwest. While there is no marked originality of theme or treatment, the director, David Smith, has so embellished it with surefire touches and scenic effects that its familiarity never becomes noticeable. It is a simple story—this one of Curwood's. Carrying for its theme the pluck and courage of a lonely girl who is oppressed by primitive brutes, the plot accumulates in interest, sending out during its progression a fine flavor of dramatic conflict, a spiritual note, an element of pathos and some redblooded action.

Motion Picture News (June 12, 1920)

Isobel, or the Trail's End (Davis-Carewe Productions, December 1920) 6 reels; House Peters (Sergeant William MacVegh), Jane Novak (Isobel Dean), Edward Pell (Scottie Dean), Tom Wilson (Corporal Bucky Smith), Bob Walker (Private Thomas Pelliter), Pearlie Norton (Little Mystery), Dick LaReno (Jim Blake), Horin Konishe (Chief Bye-Bye); D: Edwin Carewe; SP: Finis Fox; SP: *Isobel, a Romance of the Northern Trails*. **Synopsis:** Scotti Dean throws Jim Blake overboard from a Northbound steamer when Blake attempts to dishonor Dean's wife. Dean is naturally labeled a murderer and for four years is hounded by Sergeant William MacVegh of the Royal Northwest Mounted Police. McVegh eventually catches up to his man, only to find Mrs. Dean drawing a box on a sled in which she claims is the body of her dead husband.

The officer puts her up for the night but the next morning the box is empty— the two have fled. An enemy of the officer, believing MacVegh has forfeited his oath, vows to get Dean himself. But the officer reaches the couple first. Sometime later Dean appears at MacVegh's cabin begging help for his wife who is ill in a distant hut. After learning that Blake isn't dead, Dean dies and MacVegh, who had previously acknowledged his love for Mrs. Dean, goes to her but she condemns him for hounding her husband.

Mrs. Dean is ill and after she recovers, MacVegh goes away. A couple of years later he receives a letter which indicates that the woman is dead. he goes to Montreal, where he finds Isobel very much alive. Then comes the clinch.

Reviews:

Some gaps in continuity present themselves during the run of the picture and whether the cutter or the director is to blame isn't evident. At any rate, and to be specific, one scene shows an officer of the R.N.W.M.P. conversing in his cabin and the next, with no title between scenes, shows him coming in from out-of-doors with his coat on, and carrying flowers. Inasmuch as the exteriors show snow a couple of feet deep, the wonder is whence cometh the blossoms. And just where the little girl arrived from is difficult to understand. It isn't explained.

The photography is a feature of the production and some effective color bits add to its artistic side.

Wid's Daily (December 5, 1920)

The picture is remarkably lifelike, Mr. Carewe seeing to it that full emphasis is given to the vital touches. Some of the shots are punctuated with Prizma coloring which enhances their beauty. All are rich in picturesque photography. The types are splendid. The picture carries every element which spells entertainment. It has bold, vivid strokes. It is not only Carewe's best picture—it is the best snow picture that any director ever made.

Motion Picture World (December 4, 1920)

The Golden Snare (Associated First National, July 1921) 6 reels; Lewis S. Stone (Sergeant Philip Rainey), Wallace Beery (Bram Johnson), Ruth Renick (Celie), Melbourne MacDowell (Douglas Johnson), Little Esther Scott (The Baby), Wellington Playter (Black Dawson), DeWitt Jennings (Fighting Fitzgerald), Francis McDonald (Pierre Thoreau); D: David M. Hartford; SP: James Oliver Curwood. **Synopsis:** Bram Johnson, who for many years has evaded the law since the death of his father which he avenged by killing 12 men, is the object of a government search headed by Sergeant Philip Rainey. While searching, Rainey comes upon a sick Northlander who takes him to his cottage to give him a dying message. He begs him to take care of the tiny infant in the next room, and gives him what is known as "the golden snare"—a rabbit snare made of a girl's hair, which belongs to Bram Johnson.

Rainey starts off with the baby and meets Celie, a mysterious young lady who falls in love with the baby at once. She takes both strangers home with her. Her home proves to be that of Johnson, who has befriended her since babyhood and who is immediately recognized by Rainey. Rainey, however, does not reveal his mission. A gang of marauders led by Black Dawson, infatuated with Celie, has threatened Bram unless he consents to give her up. This he has refused and while Rainey is present they make a second attack. They succeed in capturing the two and carry them off on their dog sleds as prisoners. At the critical moment, however, Bram, whose mind has been slightly affected for some time, becomes himself and, in a terrific fight, defeats the gang, and is fatally wounded. Before his death, however, he tells Rainey the story of his own life and how he found Celie when, as a mere infant, she had been abandoned on board, a marauded ship. Celie and Rainey then plan to make life happy for the baby.

Review:

Typical of the sharp contrasts and quick changes in emotional play are the exquisite photographic and scenic effects in *The Golden Snare*. An Arctic romance — the beauty of the settings and the projection of atmosphere have been made the salient feature. White-spirited scenes at dimly lighted dusk, and again at brilliant noon, soft shading of fir trees, wide wastes tracked by proud sleigh dogs and their hardy masters all reveal a splendor of imagination and a fine technical skill. There are picturesque flashes changing the trend of human feeling, such as a shift from a fearful duel to a close-up of one of the most winsome babies ever photographed, or from a wild chase for mercy to a remote white grave. It is touches such as these that afford for the spectator that comfortable alternation of thrills and calm that make for true artistic balance.

Motion Picture World (July 23, 1921)

Kazan (Export and Import Film Company, October 28, 1921) 6 reels; Jane Novak (Joan Radisson), Benjamin Haggerty (Frank Radisson), Edwin Wallock ("Black" McCready), Kazan (Himself); D: Bertram Bracken; P: William N. Selig. **Synopsis:** When Kazan's master is killed, the dog goes back to the wild, where he has an opportunity to save the life of Joan Radisson, who has come north with her younger brother to visit her father and older brother, a mountie. Kazan joins a pack of wolves, becoming

their leader, but becomes docile when he is around Joan. When her mountie brother is murdered and her younger brother turns out to be a worthless sort, she sets out for a remote cabin where her father is reported dying. She is forced to trust a stranger to accompany her. On the way Kazan's pack of wolves is about to attach when Kazan recognizes Joan, and he makes the pack back off.

At the cabin they find the elder Radisson dead, murdered by the same unknown person who killer her brother. The killer has destroyed evidence linking him to the crime and tries to pin the murder on the man who has accompanied Joan. However, her father has left a note inside his watch identifying his killer, and when it is discovered the killer attacks Joan but is repelled and killed by Kazan.

Flower of the North (Vitagraph, December 4, 1921) 7 reels; Henry B. Walthall (Philip Whittemore), Pauline Starke (Jeanne D'Arcambal), Harry Northrup (Thorpe), Joe Rickson (Pierre), Jack Curtis (Blake), Emmett King (D'Arcambal), Walter Rodgers (MacDougal), William McCall (Cassidy), Vincent Howard (Sachigo); D: David Smith; SP: Bradley J. Smollen. **Synopsis:** American Philip Whittemore establishes the Northern Fish and Development Company in the Canadian wilds, where MacDougal lives with his daughter Jeanne, "the Flower of the North." Whittemore is backed by Brokaw, a New York financier, who sends his associate Thorpe to delay the work of the company so that he might take control. There is a charming love story shrouded in an atmosphere of struggle, mystery, and foul play. Sinister and powerful forces are surrounding Whittemore and retarding his work. The situation is complicated when he falls in love with Jeanne, whom he rescues from drowning. She in turn rescues him with the aid of Indian friends when Thorpe attacks Whittemore's camp with his hooligans. In the end the couple find happiness together.

Review:

When you see a picture which carries a charming romance balanced by conflicts engendered by primitive hates and jealousies, and told against a background of impressive scenes which take in mountains, turbulent torrents, forests and other vistas of the big outdoors — when you see such a picture which relies upon spectacular thrills, battles, colorful incident, you are certain to vote it a good entertainment. *Flower of the North*, a Vitagraph special, is a typical Curwood story. It contains the qualities which one look upon as synonymous with the author's name. Action, conflict, thrills and romance — these are ever dominant here. Anyone in search of good adventure need look no further than this picturesque photoplay.

Motion Picture News (January 28, 1922)

Jan of the Big Snows (American Releasing Corporation, March 1922) 5 reels; Warner Richmond (Jan Allaire), Louise Prussing (Nancy Cummings), William Peavey (Frederick Cummings), Baby Eastman Haywood (Freddie), Frank Robbins (Mukee), Richard R. Neill (Blanding); D/P: Charles M. Seay; SP: Frederick Gaye; S: *Honor of the Big Snows*. **Synopsis:** Nancy Cummings is worshipped by the 17 inhabitants of the trading post on the Hudson Bay where her husband has brought her. Jan Allaire in particular idolizes her. An unscrupulous representative of a fur company comes to the post and forces his attentions on the young bride while her husband is off on a trapping mission. The code of the post is that any man who takes what belongs to another shall not live, and the inhabitants swear to protect the girl against Blanding, the intruder. When Jan discovers Cummings's frozen body, he attempts to keep the news from Nancy for a while. When she is imposed upon by Blanding, the men of the camp

drive him away. Ultimately, Nancy's husband's fate is revealed to her and she departs with her young child for the United States, with Jan hoping all the while that some day she may return to the post, as he is in love with her.

Review:

Icebergs, snow and love may not harmonize in sound, but the simple uniqueness with which the story of *Jan of the Big Snows* has been handled might lead one to believe that the frozen North is a mecca for true lovers. Aside from a few minor phases of the production, which depict the characteristic life of seventeen hardy trappers of the North, the plot is composed chiefly of a love story.... The moral code of the traders of an isolated northern village carries a genuine appeal that will score heavily with any audience. It is the violation of this moral code that forms the main network of the theme.... It's work to make a picture such as this one, and the most unsophisticated member of an audience cannot help but realize it. It is among James Oliver Curwood's best.

Motion Picture News (1922)

Hell's River (aka *The Man from Hell's River*) (Western Pictures Exploitation Company, May 1922) 5 reels; Irving Cummings (Pierre of the R.N.W.M.P.), Wallace Beery (Gaspard, the Wolf), Robert Klein (Lopente), Frank Whitson (Sergeant McKenna), Eva Novak (Maballa), Rin Tin Tin (Himself), William Herford (The Padre). **Synopsis:** A pretty girl in the little French-Canadian post is looked upon with covetous eyes by a trader of wolfish character. Having knowledge that her "father" (the girl is an orphan) is a fugitive from justice, he threatens the man to give him the girl in marriage or suffer the penalty of the law. But she has looked with romantic eyes upon Pierre, the redcoat officer, and he has mushed back to camp eager to share her company. The pathos of the situation is caught when he discovers her to be the wife of this scoundrel; but she cannot tell him why for it means her father's arrest.

The trader, suspicious of the officer, goes to kill him. The padre informs the mountie and the pursuit is on — over the trackless wastes. The redcoat catches up with the trapper and a pitched battle takes place on the edge of a mountainous cliff. Suddenly, with a tigerish spring the huskie of the mountie goes to the rescue and pushes his master's enemy over the precipice.

Review:

The spectator is greeted to some awe-inspiring backgrounds which have been collected from the Yosemite National Park during the winter season. Thus it offers exteriors which have never been used before. The interest is evenly divided between these locations and the drama of the elemental inhabitants.... The picture is vital with action, builds evenly and in a progressive fashion straight to its big punch. It is well provided with atmosphere and local color and always suggestive of the country in which it is laid. Irving Cummings enacts the part of the Mountie in acceptable romantic fashion, acting always with restraint and poise. Wallace Beery as usual contributes a cameo performance as the picturesque Gaspard. His villainy is superb. Eva Novak makes a charming heroine of the girl.

Motion Picture News (1922)

I Am the Law (Affiliated Distributors, June 1922) 7 reels; Alice Lake (Joan Cameron), Kenneth Harlan (Robert Fitzgerald), Rosemary Theby (Mrs. Georges Mardeaux), Gaston Glass (Tom Fitzgerald), Noah Beery (Sergeant Georges Mardeaux), Wallace Beery (Fu Chang); D: Edwin Carewe; SP: Raymond L. Schrock; S: *The Poetic Justice of Uko San*. **Synopsis:** Joan Cameron is saved from the evil clutches of dancehall owner Fu Chang by Mountie Robert Fitzgerald, who is enamored by her. However, she falls in love with his brother, Tom, who is carrying on an affair with another man's wife. Discovered by the husband, Tom apparently kills him. Robert, knowing that Joan loves Tom and believing himself to be dying, takes the blame. Later Tom arrests Robert and a lynch mob is about to hang Robert when Joan forces a confession from the widow of the slain man. Tom kills himself, and Joan realizes that she is very much in love with Robert.

The Valley of Silent Men (Cosmopolitan/Paramount, September 10, 1922) 7 reels; Alma Rubens (Marette Radison), Lew Cody (Corporal James Kent), Joseph King ("Buck" O'Connor), Mario Majeroni (Pierre Radison), George Nash (Inspector Kedsty), J. W. Johnston (Jacques Radison); D: Frank Borzage; SP: John Lynch. **Synopsis:** Corporal Kent, seriously wounded, assumes the guilt for murders apparently committed by his friend, Jacques Radison. He miraculously recovers and with his recovery Marette Radison, Jacques's sister, effects his escape from jail. Two mounties pursue Kent and Marette into the Valley of Silent Men. Reaching her home in the valley, they are overtaken by the mounties who are about to take them back to headquarters when the girl's father makes a dying confession that he committed the triple crime out of revenge for his wife's death.

Review:

The pictorial appeal of *The Valley of Silent Men* is everything here. It actually dwarfs the story which concerns a couple of Mounties chasing a Mountie and the girl of his choice.... Curwood seldom varies his plots. Consequently the steady follower of his stories can anticipate the end far in advance. But hats off to Borzage and his settings. And Alma Rubens makes an attractive heroine. Lew Cody is the hero and you'd never know that once he scoffed at true love when portraying male vamp parts, so easily and naturally does he play his role here.

With Hearst newspaper publicity, a popular author, a fine cast and a tried and true theme, what more can the exhibitor ask for?

Motion Picture News (September 9, 1922)

The Alaskan (Paramount, September 1924) 7 reels; Thomas Meighan (Alan Holt), Estelle Taylor (Mary Standish), John Sainpolis (Rossland), Frank Campeau (Stampede Smith), Anna May Wong (Keok), Alphonse Ethier (John Graham), Maurice Cannon (Tautuk), Charles Ogle (The Lawyer); D: Herbert Brenon; SP: Willis Goldbeck. **Synopsis:** Alaskan Alan Holt has a ranch wanted by a big syndicate, a group, who were responsible for his father's death. The wife of the syndicate head is coveted by Alan. Holt succeeds in destroying the power of the syndicate and rescuing Mary Standish from her villain husband, who is eventually killed when he falls off a cliff.

Review:

The cameraman, James Howe, is really the star of this production, judging from its scenic display. Aside from its marvelously picturesque backgrounds and atmosphere, it hasn't much to recommend it. Its scenes are truly magnificent — and they have been caught from all angles.

Its plot offers very little compensation, being devoid of story interest, carrying little novelty and practically no suspense — and its action being extended through far too much footage. The result is the director pads the scenes and

is compelled to rely upon the backgrounds. He prolongs unimportant sequences for the sake of providing the necessary footage. And the players are consequently guilty of too much emotional display in view of the lack of sustaining points of drama.

It's a picture lacking imagination in its story and direction. The director plants his scenes and detail too obviously.

Motion Picture News (September 27, 1924)

The Hunted Woman (Fox, March 22, 1925) 5 reels; Seena Owen (Joanne Gray), Earl Schenck (John Aldous), Diana Miller (Marie), Cyril Chadwick (Culver Rann), Francis McDonald (Joe De Bar), Edward Piel (Charlie), Victor MacLaglen (Quade); D: Jack Conway; SP: Robert N. Lee, Dorothy Yost. **Synopsis:** John Aldous grubstakes two miners who discover a rich gold mine. He meets Joanne Gray — who has arrived in the mining camp searching for her husband — when he intercedes on her behalf after she is insulted by the local dancehall proprietor, Quade. Later, Quade overhears one of the miners tell his girlfriend of the gold strike and so he tortures the miner into revealing the mine's location. Quade dynamites a shack, trapping John and Joanne inside. While trapped they confess their love for one another. Joanne's husband turns out to be Rann, Quade's partner in crime. Quade turns on his partner after kidnapping Joanne and kills him but is himself killed by De Bar, one of the miners grubstaked by Aldous. Thus John and Joanne are free to enjoy life together.

Review:

Typically western in its plot and atmosphere (why not with James Oliver Curwood as the author?) this Fox production suffices in being a first rate action picture — one which quickens the pulse — if it doesn't stimulate the imagination — with its assortment of thrills and its quality of suspense. It tells a tale of the quest for gold with men brave and fearless, men mean and cowardly — with a good woman, and one not so good as its characters. Curwood is in his element with this type of story — and he has written a melodramatic yarn — which told with logically developed scenes against appropriate backgrounds, offers an entertaining outdoor drama.

Motion Picture News (April 4, 1925)

My Neighbor's Wife (Elfelt/David Distributing Division, May 21, 1925) 6 reels; E. K. Lincoln (Jack Newberry), Helen Ferguson (Florence Keaton), Edwards Davis (Mr. Keaton), Herbert Rawlinson (Allen Allwright), William Russell (Eric von Greed), William Bailey (Green's Assistant), Chester Conklin (Camera Operator), Tom Santschi (Inventor), Mildred Harris (Inventor's Wife), Douglas Gerard (Bertie), Margaret Loomis (Kathlyn Jordan), Ralph Faulkner (William Jordan); D: Clarence Geldert; S: *The Other Man's Wife*. Synopsis: Jack Newberry, having grown up as the pampered son of a millionaire, determines to make it on his own in the business world. After exhausting his own funds, he borrows $40,000 from his girl's father to finance a motion picture. He hires a foreign director, Eric von Greed, who, to just about everyone's surprise, brings in a winner. Having proven himself as a businessman, Jack marries his girl.

Steele of the Royal Mounted (Vitagraph, June 1925) 6 reels; Bert Lytell (Phillip Steele), Stuart Holmes (Bucky Nome), Charlotte Merriam (Isobel Becker), Mabel Julienne Scott (Mrs. Thorpe), Sydney DeGrey (Colonel Becker), John Toughey (Colonel MacGregor); D: David Smith; SP: Jay Pilcher. Synopsis: With the idea of arousing the jealousy of Phillip Steele, whose interest she has aroused, Isobel

Becker, visiting a California resort, persuades her father to permit himself to be introduced as her husband. The scheme does not work, for Steele, bitterly disappointed, tries to forget her in the Canadian wilds and is attracted to the service of the mounted police. Isobel follows him with her father, who is interested in the fur business in northern Canada. Steele wins a promotion and is sent on the trail of Bucky Nome, who has escaped from jail in the uniform of a mounted policeman. Bucky and his companions wreck a treasure train and capture Isobel, but she is rescued by Steele, who resigns from the force to resume his place in the social world.

Review:

When it comes to making a better class of western picture which does not depend upon long hard rides and trick shooting, we know of no director who can achieve more certain results than David Smith, and with a story by James Oliver Curwood to work with he has done exceptionally well.

In the opening scene the story falters a little because the "mystery" of Isobel Becker is too heavily stressed. Those unfamiliar with the story are all set for some deep mystery when the director switches and then slips into the real story. Some of these mystery leaders could be suppressed with excellent results. But once the story swings into action (and that is very quickly) he offers a nicely timed story of adventure and romance, straightly told in a direct sequence and both well directed and well played.

Moving Picture World (June 27, 1925)

The Ancient Highway (Paramount, November 1925) 60 mins.; Jack Holt (Cliff Brant), Billie Dove (Antoinette St. Ives), Montagu Love (Ivan Hurd), Stanley Taylor (Gaspard St. Ives), Lloyd

Whitlock (John Denis), William A. Carroll (Ambrose), Marjorie Bonner (Angel Fanchon), Christian J. Frank (George Bolden); D: Irvin Willat; SP: Shelly Hamilton, Eve Unsell. **Synopsis:** Ivan Hurd has the Canadian lumber situation in his lap. So much so that the inherited forest tracts of Antoinette St. Ives are almost lost to her with Hurd's price to cease his oppression before marriage. Cliff Brant disrupts a conference between the girl and Hurd in the latter's office by a call that terminates in Brant administering a terrific beating to the lumber monarch. This is in retaliation for Hurd having ruined young Brant's father and causing his death. Antoinette is in the next room while the hand-to-hand warfare is going on but gets a glimpse of Brant as he departs.

A sprained ankle of the heroine's brother paves the way for the entrance of Brant into the St. Ives home where the girl's cousin, managing her interests, hails Brant as his overseas captain who was believed dead. Brant joins forces with the St. Ives family.

Changing to the tree country, the spring drive is ready when the dirty work commences. Brant starts the logs downstream but Hurd's men blast out a side of a hill to halt the flow. Brant and the cousin make a frantic trip in a canoe to reply by exploding the resultant jam. They light the fuse but the cousin becomes imprisoned among the logs, and to complicate matters Antoinette selects this moment to become remorseful over her previous attitude toward Brant and rushes out to seek her lover's forgiveness. The fuse finally reaches its destination and the trio are hurled into the mad rush of water and timber. A rescue is finally effected with the usual clinch finish.

Review:

A program feature consuming but around 60 minutes is an oddity these days, and that this release has been so cut as to curtail the running time is much in its favor.

This film could easily have become a screen bore if permitted to run at large due to its much used plot, a fact which someone evidently realized.

William Carroll gets comedy into the sequence although some of the bits designed for him are out-and-out hoke. Holt convinces as the very masculine hero while Love is obligingly and sufficiently underhanded to become appropriately disliked. Miss Dove's appearance is a pleasing study regarding her previous appearance in comedies.

Nothing great about this release but suitable program fare, helped by the cast names, and as the houses grow smaller its entertaining capabilities will increase.

Variety (November 11, 1925)

The Country Beyond (Fox, October 1926) 58 mins.; Olive Borden (Valencia), Ralph Graves (Roger McKay), Gertrude Astor (Mrs. Andrews), J. Farrell MacDonald (Sergeant Cassidy), Evelyn Selbie (Martha Leseur), Fred Kohler (Joe Leseur), Lawford Davidson (Henry Harland), Alfred Fisher (Father John), Lottie Williams (Valencia's Maid); D/SP: Irving Cummings. **Synopsis:** Valencia is the wild rose of the Northwest forests, an orphan, left with the Hawkinses, rude backwood people. Roger McKay meets her as he passes, hunted by the police for some prank. They fall in love, but Valencia's guardian wants to sell the girl to one of his friends.

At the nearby fashionable camp is Harland, producer of Broadway shows. He sees the girl dancing in a leafy clearing. He also falls in love with her, offering to make her a fortune on the Broadway stage.

Harland provides Cassidy, the mounted constable, information about McKay's whereabouts and the Sergeant has to take the fugitive into custody, much as he dislikes the task. Valencia's guardian is killed by his wife, driven to a frenzy by his persecutions, and McKay, returning to find the body, supposes the girl has done the deed and takes the crime upon his own shoulders as he goes off to Vancouver.

Nothing is left for the girl but to take Harland's offer. Next she is seen as a reigning queen of the stage. Cassidy comes to Broadway seeking her out. There is a fight between the soldier and the theatrical manager and the rugged trooper of the Royal Canadian Mounted Police carries the stage beauty back to her native woods for a romantic reunion with her old lover, now cleared of the crime. They meet in their canoes out on the lake in a pretty idyllic series of views for the usual happy ending. Instead of the lover's clinch, however, the finale has Cassidy riding off into the landscape whistling his satisfaction at the happy ending of his plottings.

Review:

A mechanical bit of magazine fiction made into a highly interesting picture by the very beauty of its scenic features and the lavish scale upon which the production has been made. Curwood grinds out enormous quantities of fiction of the kind magazine readers consume as fast as it is served. Probably this is as good a test as anything for material suitable for the screen.

The picture is a good example of concentrated interest, for there isn't a foot of superfluous footage. The picture is the opposite of padding. Besides these outstanding merits, it has a first rate twist in the character of Cassidy, constable of the Northwest police, played to the queen's taste by J. Farrell MacDonald, veteran character man of the Fox forces.

Variety (November 24, 1926)

Prisoners of the Storm (Universal,

November 1926) 66 mins.; House Peters, Sr. (Bucky Malone), Peggy Montgomery (Joan Le Grande), Walter McGrail (Sergeant McClellan), Harry Todd (Pete Le Grande), Fred De Silva (Dr. Chambers), Clark Comstock (Angus McLynn), Evelyn Selbie (Lillian Nicholson); D: Lynn F. Reynolds; SP: Charles A. Logue; S: *The Quest of Joan.* Synopsis: Two prospectors have hit a vein and intend to follow each other to the trading post one day apart. The older man, Le Grande, is anxious to see his daughter Joan, so is the first to leave and is murdered en route by the post doctor, who has overheard Mountie McClellan tell Joan that her father is coming in with gold.

Le Grande's failing to show up starts McClellan on a search and he runs into Malone, who is following his partner into town. The officer is convinced Malone has murdered his partner and in a scuffle hurts his leg. Malone drags him to a cabin and when the sergeant falls ill goes for the post doctor. There he meets Le Grande's daughter. Joan and the doctor follow Malone to the cabin. Dr. Chambers tries to turn Joan against Malone, accusing him of killing her father. The cabin is buried by an avalanche of snow. In their efforts to escape, Chambers is killed by an explosion and exposed as the murderer. Malone and Joan reach for each other at the finish inasmuch as they have fallen in love.

Review:

It's average double feature day material minus any particular kick, despite a snow avalanche that hems in the principal parties. It doesn't rate the 66 minutes consumed and probably an entire reel could have come out and no harm would have been done. Pretty slow in parts.

Obvious scenario minus a twist or outstanding punch. Peters does well enough as the handcuffed hero, with Miss Montgomery a passable heroine. McGrail seemed to get more out of his role of the Mountie than anyone else, with Harry Todd taking care of the comedy early in the running before [being] bumped off. De Silva was rather a white-haired villain, the dirty deed being done by sub-title.

Minor screen material bound to play that class of theatre.

Variety (November 24, 1926)

The Flaming Forest (Cosmopolitan/ MGM, November 1926) 70 mins.; Antonio Moreno (Sergeant David Carrigan), Renée Adorée (Jeanne-Marie), Gardner James (Roger Audemard), William Austin (Alfred Wimbledon), Tom O'Brien (Mike), Emile Chautard (Andre Audemard), Oscar Bereg (Jules Lararre), Clarence Geldert (Major Charles McVane), Frank Leigh (Lupin), Charles S. Ogle (Donald McTavish), Roy Coulson (Francois), D'Arcy McCoy (Bobbie), Claire McDowell (Mrs. McTavish), Bert Roach (Sloppy), Mary Jane Irving (Ruth McTavish); D: Reginald Barker; SP: Waldemar Young. Synopsis: Lagarre, a half breed, is pushing the Indians into a rebellious mood to establish himself as a monarch of the Northwest when the Canadian mounties arrive. This holds up his plans a bit, but not before he has persecuted the pioneers and evicted them from their homes.

It's at this point that the mounties appear, so the pioneers reverse course and replace the furniture. Jeanne-Marie's mother and dad have been killed at the instigation of Lagarre. When further goaded by a couple of the latter's hirelings, Roger, the brother, sneaks out and shoots his tormentors. This leads to complications, for Sergeant Carrigan is in love with the sister and must arrest the boy.

The commander of the mounties leads a detachment away from the post, whereupon the Indians light the well-known beacon on the hilltop, and the battle is on. Carrigan eventually breaks through the Indian lines to bring back the departed force.

Review:

Add another glorified western to the list, for this is it. Not such a much either, although it's been nicely handled, and some of it is in natural color, if that helps.

An Indian attack on a fort and a forest fire, with the rescue brigade riding through double photography and the flames to save the home folks, consummate the film's punch. Meanwhile, Miss Adorée and Mr. Moreno uphold the love interest on a lightweight scenario thread which about serves the purpose and that's all.

The Northwest Mounted uniforms help the color bit, are the main substance of it, and no denying it dresses the release up a bit. It needs it, too, for the story isn't so strong.... Just average program footage at best, needing the "break" it will get from those who dote on their westerns.

Variety (November 24, 1926)

A Captain's Courage (Rayart, November 30, 1926) 6 reels; Richard Holt, Eddie Earl, Jack Henderson, Al Ferguson, Lafe McKee, Dorothy Dwan; D: Louis Chaudet; SP: George Pyper. Synopsis: The story is set in the mid–1850s around Lake Michigan, where two factions fight for possession of an island.

Back to God's Country (Universal, September 1927) 68 mins.; Renée Adorée (Renee Debois), Robert Frazer (Bob Stanton), Walter Long (Captain Blake), Mitchell Lewis (Jean Debois), Adolph Milar (Frenchie Leblanc), James Mason (Jacques Corbeau), Walter Ackerman (Clerk), Flying Eagle (Indian); D: Irvin Willet; SP: Charles Logue. Synopsis: The action takes place in a trading post, apparently on the coast where a trading schooner, with its dissolute captain and raggamuffin crew, calls twice a year or so. The captain's roving eye falls upon the daughter of a backwoods trapper at the post to sell his winter's catch of pelts.

The trapper kills a crook in self-defense and the captain tries to force the girl to marry him on threat of turning the woodsman over to the authorities for murder.

It is here than an American engineer comes to the rescue, because he has fallen in love with the girl. Thus the story becomes a contest between engineer and sailor. It all gets down to a dog sled race through a blizzard, a device well worked in its scenic features and storm effects, building up to a capital climax, when a fierce dog—which the girl has treated kindly and which the heavy has beaten—returns the scales in favor of the fugitives. Battle between dog and man is fought out with a good deal of realism, ending when the dog drives the snow-blinded villain over a cliff.

Review:

Curwood is something of a cult among magazine readers of the "Cosmopolitan" class and his work commands an enormous popular interest. Renée Adorée, of course, has the huge prestige of the "Parade." These two elements are more than sufficient to insure the draw of any picture.

The feature makes good on the screen. It has several good stunt bits, a clean cut romantic story and much pictorial beauty in its snow scenes, some of which may be manufactured, but all of which are thoroughly convincing.

Variety (October 26, 1927)

The Old Code (Anchor, November 1928) 6 reels; Walter McGrail (Pierre Belleu), Lillian Rich (Marie d'Arcy), Cliff Lyons (Jacques de Long), Melbourne MacDowell (Steve MacGregor), J. P. McGowan (Raoul de Valle), Neva Gerber (Lola), Ervin Renard (Henri Langlois), Mary Gordon (Mary Mac-Gregor), Rhody Hathaway (Father Le Fane), John Rainbow; D: Ben Wilson, SP: E. C. Maxwell. **Synopsis:** The story revolves around Pierre, a trapper, Marie d'Arcy, an orphan, Lola, an Indian girl, and a villain, Raoul de Valle, who makes life miserable for all concerned until killed by Pierre in a duel on a deserted island.

Hearts of Men (Anchor, February 15, 1928) 6 reels; Mildred Harris (Alice Weston), Thelma Hill (Doris Weston), Cornelius Keefe (John Gaunt), Warner Richmond (William Starke), Julia Swayne Gordon (Mrs. Robert Weston), Harry McCoy (Tippy Ainsworth); D: James P. Hogan; SP: E. C. Maxwell; P: Morris R. Schank. Note: No information on the story. *Variety* (June 6, 1928) simply says; "The poor lad thwarts his rich competitor, knocking over barriers of a killing and a burglary, to win the girl."

The River's End (Warner Brothers, November 1930) 74 mins.; Charles Bickford (John Keith; Sergeant Conniston), Evalyn Knapp (Miriam), J. Farrell MacDonald (O'Toole), David Torrence (Colonel McDowell), ZaSu Pitts (Louise), Junior Coghlan (Mickey), Walter McGrail (Martin), Tom Santschi (Martin); D: Michael Curtiz; SP: Charles Kenyon. **Synopsis:** A sergeant and a supposed murderer, John Keith, resemble one another. The latter forsakes a getaway to save the sergeant and his guide from a blizzard. When the mountie dies the guide conceives the idea of Keith doubling for the mountie, which he does. Back at the post Keith falls for the post commander's daughter and his rival digs up official data showing the sergeant has a wife in England. Keith confides his real identity to Miriam but does not reveal the true story to the mounties and consequently is flogged. But when he leaves the post Miriam runs to the boat to make it a double departure. Meanwhile, news comes that the real murderer has confessed.

Review:

Yarn is, perhaps, the best known of the Curwood stories. It was made back in '20 as a silent by First National with Lewis Stone. New version is delineation of an adventure script which will satisfy small theatre audiences, principally due to the performance of Charles Bickford and J. Farrell MacDonald plus Evalyn Knapp's appearance. She looks pretty well here. To help it along a bit ZaSu Pitts in a few feet as the village tale-bearer.

Technically the dialog stands out because it has steered clear of over-emphasis and registers as reasonable. Curtiz hasn't uncovered anything special in direction but there's a smooth double photography sequence for Bickford in his dual role. Not a high cost picture, outside of the not too convincing snow stuff. Not a release to cause any excitement and aimed at the middle class houses where it will gain modest financial rating.

Variety (March 11, 1931)

The Trail Beyond (Lonestar/Monogram, October 22, 1934) 55 mins.; John Wayne (Rod Drew), Verna Hillie (Felice Newsome), Noah Beery, Sr. (George Newsome), Noah Beery, Jr. (Wabi), Iris Lancaster (Marie LeFleur), Robert Frazer (Jules LaRocque), Earl Dwire (Benoit), Eddie Parker (Constable Ryan), Artie Ortego (Towanga), James Marcus (Mr. Ball), Yakima Canutt (Stunts), Reed Howes (Badman); D: Robert N. Bradbury; SP: Lindsley Parsons; S: *The Wolf Hunters*; P: Paul Malvern. **Synopsis:** Sent into the trackless wastes of the North on a quest for a missing girl, Rod Drew meets a college chum, Wabi, a half-breed Indian, on the train. When Wabi becomes involved in a shooting scrape with a group of gamblers, Rod rescues him, and the two of them jump off the moving train.

In a cabin the pair discover the first clue to Rod's quest — a map for hidden gold on the Ombibaki River — and they determine to find it after a visit to George Newsome, factor of Wabinosh House, and his daughter, Felice. The quest is deferred, however, by the kidnapping of Felice, when Jules LaRocque learns of the map. In a thrilling encounter with the heavies, Rod and Wabi rescue Felice, and after Rod's quest and his growing romance with Felice have been complicated by the advent of Marie LeFleur, an accomplice of LaRocque's, the two youths start on the canoe trip up the river. Captured by LaRocque, the two rescue a mounted policeman and continue the trip while LaRocque is sent on a false quest. On their return with the gold, they are attacked in the river by LaRocque and his man, Benoit, but escape to Wabinosh House, although Ryan, the mounted policeman, is wounded.

Rounding up his henchmen, LaRocque determines to attack Wabinosh, but Rod learns of his plans, and brings a mounted police detachment from a nearby post in time to capture the gang. Felice turns out to be the missing niece of Mr. Ball that Rod came north to find.

Review:

There is plenty of action in this one and some thrilling spills, though the tale is somewhat lacking in suspense.

Film Daily, September 15, 1934).

The Fighting Trooper (Ambassador, November 1, 1934) 61 mins.; Kermit Maynard (Burke), Barbara Worth (Diane), LeRoy Mason (La Farge), Charles Delaney (Blackie), Robert Frazer (Hatfield), Walter Miller (Sergeant Leyton), Joseph W. Girard (Inspector O'Keefe), George Regas, Charles Delaney, George Chesebro, Charles King, Artie Ortego, Lafe McKee, Milburn Morante, Gordon DeMain, Nelson McDowell, George Morrell, Merrill

McCormack; D: Ray Taylor; SP: Forrest Sheldon; S: *Footprints*; P: Maurice Conn. **Synopsis:** A tenderfoot mountie volunteers to avenge the murder of a fellow mountie. Accompanied by a pal he masquarades as a trapper and finds the supposed murderer, who just happens to have a beautiful sister. The presumed culprit is found to be innocent of the crime, which makes possible a serious romance between the mountie and the girl.
Review:

Horse opera about the Northwest Mounted. Fairly effective drama with usual gun shooting and galloping steeds. Second feature material. Outdoor stuff well photographed and performers meet expected standards. Dialog is simple and won't annoy.

Variety (date unknown)

Northern Frontier (Ambassador, February 1, 1935) 60 mins.; Kermit Maynard (MacKenzie), Eleanor Hunt (Beth Braden), Russell Hopton (Duke Milford), J. Farrell MacDonald (Inspector Stevens), Ben Hendricks, Jr. (Same Keene), Gertrude Astor (Mae), Charles King, Nelson MacDowell, Walter Brennan, Dick Curtis, Kernan Cripps, Jack Chisholm, Lloyd Ingraham, Lafe McKee, Tyrone Power, Jr., Artie Ortego, Rocky (a horse); D: Sam Newfield; SP: Barry Barringer; S: *Four Minutes Late*; P: Maurice Conn.
Review:

An old James Oliver Curwood story suggested *Northern Frontier*. Producers have freshened up the material by bringing in a gang of post-prohibition racketeers with their raw tactics and machine guns. Against this background the Northwest Mounties have an associate in the form of a Federal agent. *Northern Frontier* is average entertainment of its kind in spite of its flaws and liberties. If a tie-in is possible with a current radio commercial series on the Mounties over at NBC, it might help the picture.

Cast is among the picture's weaknesses except for the heavy, Russell Hopton, and some minor characters such as J. Farrell MacDonald. Kermit Maynard is too much the cowboy rather than the Mountie. He is forever doing gymnastic stunts on his horse. Opposite him Eleanor Hunt makes little impression. She's continually in a riding habit that would look more at home on a bridle path.

Somewhat illogical that the Mountie could so easily become a member of a counterfeiting gang without being detected. His actions are too free and the suspicion of his gang associates too absent to make the story very convincing. Considerable suspense, however, and much fighting, narrow escapes and hard riding.

Variety (February 27, 1935)

Wilderness Mail (Ambassador, March 9, 1935) 65 mins.; Kermit Maynard (Rance Raine; Keith Raine), Fred Kohler (Lobo McBain), Paul Hurst (Jules), Doris Brook (Lila), Syd Saylor (Oora), Dick Curtis (Jacques), Nelson McDowell (Mailman), Kernan Cripps (Inspector); D: Forrest Sheldon; SP: Bennett Cohen, Robert Dillon; P: Maurice Conn. **Synopsis:** Trapper Rance prepares a welcome for his Northwest mounted police corporal brother, Keith, at a snowbound trading post. Keith, on the way, comes upon Lobo, who has killed and robbed a pair of trappers of their furs. Though wounded, the officer is taking Lobo in when he falls exhausted. Devilish Lobo conceives the idea of tying him to a tree and letting wolves finish the job of exterminating him. Found by his brother, Rance, he dies in Lobo's cabin before he can name his assailant.

Though the Northwest police undertake the job of running down the killer, Rance takes a hand in the chase. Much that is melodramatic ensues, while romance crops up between Lila, Lobo's step-daughter, and Rance. Finally forcing a confession from one of the gang that Lobo is the killer, Rance sets out to get him. In the meantime, Lobo has robbed gold prospectors and, seeking to make his escape he is aided by Rance, who via a dog team takes him to the place where his brother had been tied to the tree, so that the fate he planned for the mountie may be his. Officers, however, come and prevent Rance from committing murder.

With Lobo out of the way, the path is cleared for romance between Rance and Lila.

Review:

This is an action melodrama of the north woods. As thrills, excitement and movement are sought for and attained, romantic love interest is merely a secondary feature, as is formula comedy contrast. The story, presented against a beautiful outdoor snow-woods background, retains much of the silent technique wherein motion, rather than dialogue, interprets the plot. Through this, and other popular appeal values, dramatic suspense fulfills a function that quickly creates and continually holds mass interest.

Motion Picture Herald (March 16, 1935).

The Red Blood of Courage (Ambassador, June 1, 1935) 55 mins.; Kermit Maynard (Jim Sullivan), Ann Sheridan (Beth Henry), Reginald Barlow (Mark Henry), Ben Hendricks, Jr. (Bart Slager), George Regas (Frenchy), Nat Carr (Meyer), Charles King (Joe), Rocky (a horse) (Himself), Carl Matthews, Milburn Morante, Art Dillard. **Synopsis:** Jim Sullivan is a heroic mountie who saves Beth Henry and her uncle, Mark Henry, from a gang of

hijackers who have discovered that the uncle's land is rich in oil.

Trails of the Wild (Ambassador, August 1, 1935) 60 mins.; Kermit Maynard (McKenna), Billie Seward (Jane), Fuzzy Knight (Windy), Monte Blue (Doyle), Theodore von Eltz (Kincaid), Matthew Betz (Hunt), Robert Frazer (Stacey), Wheeler Oakman (Hardy), Charles Delaney (Brent), John Elliott (Mason), Frank Rice (Missouri), Roger Williams (Hammond), Dick Curtis (Roper); D: Sam Newfield; SP: Joseph O'Donnell; S: *Caryl of the Mountains*; P: Maurice Conn, Sigmund Neufeld. **Synopsis:** Through the death of a pal, McKenna is ushered into the Canuck bloodhound brigade to avenge the killing. He and Windy are assigned to clean up Ghost Mountain, a deserted mining area. While so doing McKenna bags the long-sought killer, rescues a kidnapped miner, snares the heart of the latter's daughter, and gives a good fist and six-gun account of himself.

Review:

Author Curwood's tag combined with the westernly famous Maynard name should help drag 'em in for this celluloid glorification of the Canadian mounties. Presence of Maynard tag and shooting irons is sufficient attraction despite the fact that Kermit is slightly less personable than his circus-minded brother Ken and, consequently, must render more mugging. Won't beat trails but should do well enough in the western grooves.

Variety (December 1936).

His Fighting Blood (Ambassador, October 15, 1935) 60 mins.; Kermit Maynard (Tom Elliott), Polly Ann Young (Doris), Ted Adams (Marsden), Paul Fix (Phil Elliott), Joseph Girard (RCMP Commander), Ben Hendricks, Jr. (Mac), Frank O'Connor (Dave), Charles King (Black), Frank LaRue (Al

Gordon), Theodore Lorch (Leslie), Jack Kirk, Chuck Baldra, Glenn Strange (The Singing Constables), Rocky (a horse) (Himself); D: John English; SP: Joseph O'Donnell; P: Maurice Conn, Sigmund Neufeld. **Synopsis:** Tom Elliott's brother, Phil, gets involved in a robbery. Tom has always looked after him and takes the blame. He goes to jail figuring that his sacrifice will straighten out his brother. While Tom is in jail Phil lines up with a gang, one of whose members is killed. Before dying, he confesses that he was the stickup man on the job for which Tom is serving time. Tom's ambition was to join the mounties and on his release from prison he is able to make the grade. While hunting a gang, the leader of the outfit is found dead. Guilt points toward Tom's brother. To cover up Phil is ready to kill Tom but he can't do it. Instead, he reveals the identity of the murderer and in so doing is shot. The fadeout shows Tom forgiving his brother, who is dying. Note: Kermit Maynard plays a more dramatic part than usual in this story of brotherly love. The scenery is pleasant and Kermit gives a fine exhibition of trick riding. There is more drama and less fighting than in the regular westerns, but there is enough action to keep things interesting throughout. Two well-placed song numbers are included.

Timber War (Ambassador, November 1, 1935) 60 mins.; Kermit Maynard (Jim Dolan), Lucille Lund (Sally Martin), Lawrence Gray (Larry Keene), Robert Warwick (Ferguson), Wheeler Oakman (Murdock), Lloyd Ingraham (O'Leary), Roger Williams (Bowman), Rocky (a horse) (Himself), George Morrell, James Pierce; D: Patricia Royal, Sam Newfield; SP: Joseph O'Donnell; P: Maurice Conn, Sigmund Neufeld. **Synopsis:** Jim Dolan, by accident, is compelled to impersonate Larry Keene, a wastrel heir to large timberlands that opposition forces are conspiring to destroy. His efforts are energized by the presence of beautiful Sally Martin.

Review:

James Oliver Curwood Story, reduced here to its rough-and-tumble angles, is an action film and the Curwood name should help. It has one good attribute, changes pace every so often by falling away from the common chatter of the characters and fist fights to show off scenery of the timberlands and lumberjack activity. Whether or not the shots are library they're interesting just the same.

Variety (March 4, 1936)

Trail's End (Beaumont, 1935) 61 mins.; Conway Tearle, Claudia Dell, Baby Charlene Barry, Fred Kohler, Ernie Adams, Pat Harmon, Victor Potel, Gaylord Pendleton, Stanley Blystone, Jack Duffy, Black King (a horse); D: Al Herman; SP: Jack Jevne; P: Mitchell Leichter. **Review:**

This one has a little of everything in the plot, adapted from the James Oliver Curwood story of the same name. Conway Tearle is framed and sent to prison, and on coming out he evens the score with the man who sent him there. He eventually lands in a town that is being overrun by a tough gang from a nearby ranch, and when he bests one of these men in an argument, the town makes him sheriff. There is a lot of side interest with an attractive young widow and her little girl, the latter taking a great liking to the new sheriff. Meanwhile the old gang that the ex-convict used to pal around with are after him to help lift the mine payroll that the girl is minding in the safe in her home. The plot works out satisfactorily in the end as Tearle succeeds in saving the payroll after the gang have overpowered him and taken the key to the vault.

Film Daily (August 22, 1935)

Skull and Crown (Reliable/William Steiner, December 1935) 56 mins.; Rin Tin Tin, Jr. (Rin), Regis Toomey (Bob Franklin), Molly O'Day (Ann Orton), Jack Mulhall (Zorro), James Murray (Matt Brent), Lois January (Barbara Franklin), Tom London (Jennings), John Elliott (John Norton), Robert Walker (Saunders); D: Elmer Clifton; SP: Bennett Cohen, Carl Krusada; P: Bernard B. Ray. **Synopsis:** Bob Franklin, a member of the U.S. Customs Patrol on the Mexican border, is joyously preparing for the homecoming of his sister Barbara from a fashionable school. The little cottage is being gaily decorated by Bob with Rin gathering the flowers in anticipation of her arrival. Ed, a brother officer, arrives to tell Bob that Zorro, a notorious smuggler, has just crossed the line with a contraband cargo.

Leaving Rin at the station at the wheel of his car with a note explaining his regrets, Bob hastens with Ed on the trail of Zorro. The contraband truck and its driver, Matt, are captured, but Zorro escapes afoot.

Meanwhile, Barbara has arrived, is met by Rin, and they proceed to Bob's cottage to await his arrival. Zorro, passing the cottage, sees the car, and bent on obtaining the keys from Barbara, enters the house. While furtively seeking means to obtain them, they hear the approach of riders. Barbara is ruthlessly killed by Zorro, although valiantly defended by Rin who is stunned by Zorro's gun. The latter makes his escape with the car as the station master arrives with a wire for Bob and comes upon the tragic scene, followed shortly afterward by Bob.

Incensed at the apparent disloyalty of Rin whom he had charged with the safekeeping of his sister, Bob turns him out in contempt and anger, unaware that Rin had been subdued by Zorro. Overcome with grief, and determined to capture the slayer, Bob resigns from the service. Masquerading as a smuggler and a friend of the captured Matt, he obtains admission to "Skull and Crown," a fashionable resort owned by John Norton, who, together with his daughter, Ann, are held prisoners there by Zorro and his cohorts who have commandeered the lodge. Rin, who will not renounce his worship and devotion to Bob, has followed his master at a safe distance, and also gains entrance but is captured.

Zorro's lieutenant, knowing that Rin would go to his master, lines up all the gang, including Bob, with instructions to one of his henchmen to shoot down the first man that Rin recognizes.

Rin's intuition warns him, and the coup fails. Matt, who had been purposely released by the patrol as a decoy to find the hideout, arrives and denounces Bob as an impostor, revealing his true identity. Bob is imprisoned to await the arrival of Zorro. Meanwhile, Rin, escaping from his bonds, finds his way to Bob and releases his master as Zorro enters the room. There is a terrific fight, climaxed with the capture of the master smuggler and his gang. Rin and Bob are reunited.

Review:

This is a comedy, unintentional, but still a comedy. There's no portion of the screen audience left which will take it legit as it's played. Technique, cutting, photographic speed and action is of the school at least 20 years down the road behind us.

Maybe it's because it's a Rin-Tin-Tinner, the dog taking most of the story, which concerns itself with the breakup of a smuggling ring by the border patrol. Regis Toomey becomes extremely laughable in his early scenes with the pooch, and the remainder of the cast, especially Jack Mower, the villain, are equally amusing.... Sound recording is atrocious and the film spotted and streaked. A print better unplayed.

Variety (March 2, 1938)

Kermit Maynard, Wheeler Oakman, Fuzzy Knight, Andrea Leeds, George F. Hayes, Horace Murphy, and Lee Shumway in *Song of the Trail* (Ambassador, 1936).

Song of the Trail (Ambassador, March 15, 1936) 59 mins.; Kermit Maynard (Jim Carter), Evelyn Brent (Myra), Fuzzy Knight (Pudge), George F. Hayes (Hobson), Antoinette (Andrea) Leeds (Betty), Wheeler Oakman (Arnold), Lee Shumway (Stone), Roger Williams (Miller), Ray Gallagher (Blore), Charles McMurphy (Curtis), Horace Murphy (Sheriff), Lynette London (Marie), Rocky (a horse) (Himself), Bob McKenzie, Frank McCarroll, Artie Ortego; D: Russell Hopton; SP: George Sayre, Barry Barrington; S: *Playing with Fire*; P: Maurice Conn; **Synopsis:** Young Jim Carter, rodeo and pistol crack shot, in love with Betty Hobson, soon discovers that he must, single-handedly combat the combined crookedness of Bob Arnold and his gang of cutthroats, who are intent on separating the elder Hobson from his valuable mine property.

Meeting his sweetheart at the annual rodeo, Carter, at Betty's promptings, attempts to save her father, when he discovers him in a poker game with Arnold and his henchmen. Calmly watching the game, he does not speak his mind until he witnesses Hobson lose control of the mine in a card game in which five aces appear.

Carter and Hobson leave, though Hobson threatens to get even. Later at the pistol matches, two of Arnold's men, onlookers at the match, suddenly crumple to the ground, drilled through. Hobson is immediately suspected and the posse sets out to capture him. Jim, however, takes matters into his own hands and hides the old man away long enough to give Arnold and his gang ample opportunity to quarrel among themselves over the spoils.

Hobson is discovered in his hideaway by Arnold and left for dead, but Jim, finding that the old man has just been wounded, plots to assemble Arnold and his gang at the ranch house and, with the sheriff and his men present, confront him with the information that Hobson saw his assailant before he was shot.

While they wait for Hobson to regain consciousness, Arnold slips out of the house and rushes to the saloon where he gathers together his spoils and makes ready to skedaddle. His men come upon him as he is cleaning out the safe and he kills them rather than split the money. He rides away with Jim in close pursuit.

Arnold is finally subdued, some of his men inform the sheriff that it was he who killed Curtis and Stone on the pistol range, and Hobson recovers the deed to the mine, which he presents to Jim and Betty.

Review:

Evelyn Brent and Kermit Maynard share the billing in this formula western but that's about all they share, for there's no glory to split. Never for a moment diverges from the standard track. Title won't help any and is just another example of non-inventiveness of labelers. Kids will revel in the yarn's opening shots of preparation and practice for a rodeo and the rodeo roper which, once again, serves as Maynard's excuse to exhibit his cowhand past.

Variety (December 23, 1936).

Caryl of the Mounties (Reliable/ William Steiner, March 27, 1936) 68 mins.; Francis X. Bushman, Jr. (Brad Sheridan), Rin Tin Tin, Jr., (Rin Tin Tin, Jr.), Lois Wild (Caryl Foray), Earl Dwyer (Inspector Bradshaw), Robert Walker (Enos Calvin), Steve Clark (Captain Edwards), Jack Hendricks (Captain Gary), George Chesebro (Constable O'Brien), Josef Swickard (Doray); D: Bernard B. Ray; SP: Tom Gibson; P: Bernard B. Ray.

Review:

One of James Oliver Curwood's mounted police stories pulled out of shape to provide a starring vehicle for Rin Tin Tin, Jr. As it stands it's too much dog and too little story, and strictly for the lesser dual bills.

Scenario job is perfunctory with far too much time taken up in riding to and from cabins. Nothing much happens during these approaches and departures and they grow very tiresome. Script is labored and indifferent. Direction helps little and the sound recording is poor. Voices come through fairly well but much paper is handled and the sound is not toned down.

Francis X. Bushman, Jr., like Rinty, is not the man his father was, but gets by with the chief assignment. Lois Wild is pretty, reads her lines fairly well but lacks warmth of personality. Robert Walker does little with the heavy and Swickard is over-directed in his brief bit. Others are unimportant.

Variety (date unknown).

The Country Beyond (20th Century–Fox, April 24, 1936) 73 mins.; Rochelle Hudson (Jean Alison), Paul Kelly (Sergeant Cassidy), Robert Kent (Corporal King), Alan Hale (Jim Alison), Alan Dinehart (Ray Jennings), Andrew Tombes (Senator Rawlings), Claudia Coleman (Mrs. Rawlings), Matt McHugh (Constable Weller), Paul McVey (Fred Donaldson), Holmes Herbert (Inspector Reed), Buck (Buck), Wolf (Prince); D: Eugene Forde; SP: Lamar Trotti, Adele Commandini; P: Sol Wurtzel.

Review:

The script is built up first for laughs, with a tedious sequence at the railroad station and later in barracks. Later on, with the progression into the plot (in the third reel) there is a time out for playful spats between Miss Hudson and Robert Kent and even a couple of rough and tumble fights between the pair that reduces her to the level of a rough soubrette and detracts from appeal. The story does work up to some smash toward the close, but it is too late to make them forget what has gone before.... Productionally there are some good natural backgrounds in the snow country, and a snow slide that is almost impressive had it not followed so closely on the heels of some of the comedy.

Variety (May 6, 1936)

Wildcat Trooper (Ambassador, July 1, 1936) 60 mins.; Kermit Maynard (Gale), Lois Wilde (Ruth), Hobart Bosworth (Doctor Martin), Fuzzy Knight (Pat), Yakima Canutt (The Ravan), Jim Thorpe (Indian), Eddie Phillips (Reynolds), John Merton (McClain), Frank Hagney (Foster), Roger Williams (Slim), Richard Curtis (Henri), Ted Lorch (Rogers), Hal Price (Buyer). **Synopsis:** Northwest mountie Gale and his partner Pat investigate a murder and find themselves in the middle of a feud between rival fur-trapping companies.

Phantom Patrol (Ambassador, September 30, 1936) 60 mins.; Kermit Maynard, Joan Barclay, Dick Curtis, Harry Worth, George Cleveland, Paul Fix, Julian Rivero, Eddie Phillips, Roger Williams, Lester Lorr, Rocky (a horse); D: Charles Hutchison; S: *Fatal Note*; P: Maurice Conn.

Vengeance of Rannah (Reliable, 1936) 5 reels; Bob Custer (Ted Sanders), John Elliott (Doc Adams), Victoria Vinton (Mary Warner), Roger Williams (Norcross), Oscar Gahan (Nolan), Eddie Phillips (Macklin), Edward Cassidy (Barlow), Wally West (Stranger), Rin Tin Tin, Jr. (Rannah), George Chese-

bro, Jimmy Aubrey; D: Franklin Shamray (Bernard B. Ray); SP: George Stevenson; P: Bernard B. Ray; AP: Harry S. Webb. **Synopsis:** The Cloverdale Stage, its driver, and a large payroll has disappeared, no trace being found by a posse from the little mountain town. Pop Warner, the driver, known to be in financial difficulties, is suspected, but his pretty daughter, Mary, believes in his innocence. Insurance detective Ted Sanders investigates. At the bottom of a ravine he discovers Rannah, a dog, watching over the dead body of his master, Pop Warner. Ted finds the burned remains of the stage, but no trace of the missing money.

While Ted is conferring with Norcross — the banker who sent out the payroll — an attempt is made to shoot Rannah through the window. Mary takes Rannah to her ranch. That night Ted captures a mysterious stranger outside his cabin. The man reveals himself as a deputy from the county seat, and they agree to work together. Mary phones to say there are prowlers around her ranch. The deputy overhears the message and slips away. Ted rides to Mary.

The deputy arrives first and joins the men there. They ambush Ted and tie him up, then enter the house to kill the dog. The dog escapes, finds Ted and gnaws off his bonds. Ted secures a rifle and drives the invaders away. Following, Ted and Rannah discover a wounded man. Rannah tries to attack him, but Ted takes him to the town doctor. The man says he is the real deputy, shot by the outlaws, his clothes taken and others substituted. He believes Rannah attacked him because he was wearing the real assassin's clothes.

Ted goes after Mary and Rannah. Returning, they find the man gone and the doctor knocked out. Ted and Rannah discover the body of the stranger, and Ted is now convinced he is the real deputy. Ted asks the doctor to order an inquest and gives him the names of the witnesses he wants present; Norcross, the fake deputy, and two men he believes to be members of the gang.

It is announced that the inquest will be delayed, pending the arrival of the sheriff from the county seat. The phoney deputy shows signs of panic on hearing this. He is about to confess, when he is killed by one of his confederates. The latter makes a getaway from Norcross, the real gang leader. Ted rides in pursuit and captures them.

Wild Horse Round-Up (Ambassador, December 1936) 5 reels; Kermit Maynard (Jack Benson), Betty Lloyd (Beth Marion) (Ruth Williams), Dickie Jones (Dickie Williams), Budd Buster (Mopey), John Merton (Charlie Doan), Frank Hagney (Steve), Roger Williams (Pete), Dick Curtis (Bill), Jack Ingram (Outlaw); D: Alan James; SP: Joseph O'Donnell; P: Maurice Conn. Synopsis: The Standard Railroad Company contemplates running its road through White Horse Valley. This is known by Charlie Doan, who seeks to buy up all of the land possible in the valley, in order to reap huge returns by reselling to the railroad. Ranchers are forced to sell through fear of the "Night Riders," a group of henchmen brought together by Doan to terrorize the ranchers. Doan is making the valley a tough place in which to live.

Ruth Williams is the owner of the Running M Ranch. She lives there with her kid brother, seven years of age. Doan has tried repeatedly to buy the Running M Ranch, as this is the key property to the valley. Ruth refuses to sell at any price. Doan orders his henchman, Steve, to make it difficult for Ruth, but under no circumstances harm her.

Jack Benton, with his pals, Harry, Bill, and Chuck, ride by the Running M. Ranch. They are held up by Dick, Ruth's kid brother, and, at the point of a gun, forced to make tracks for the ranch house. Dick's boyish ambition is to round up the Night Riders. Jack and his pals take all of this in fun and exaggerate great fear. Ruth sees the humor in the situation and Jack learns from her all about the Night Riders and of Doan's efforts to buy the ranch. Being short of help for the round-up, Jack and his pals agree to be extra hands for her.

Doan learns that Jack, having bought an option on Jimmie Green's ranch, used this to turn Ruth against Jack and she orders him from the ranch and never to set foot upon her property again, under the penalty of being shot. Her kid brother, loyal to Jack, wants to go with him, but Jack insists upon him staying at the ranch to protect Ruth.

Doan moves to force Jack to leave the country and, in the showdown, Jack reveals that he is the special investigator for the railroad, and is empowered to make purchases of property for the right of way in his own name. Jack links up with Doan in the deal to get the property, apparently double-crossing his employers. The first move is to force Ruth to sell and then have Doan's gang drive off all of her stock, but they are outwitted by Jack and his pals and Jack regains Ruth's faith and her hand, to little Dick's great delight.

Valley of Terror (Ambassador, January 1937) Kermit Maynard, Harlene Wood, John Merton, Jack Ingram, Roger Williams, Dick Curtis, Frank McCarroll, Hank Bell, Hal Price, Slim Whitaker, Jack Casey, George Morrell, Blackie Whiteford; D: Al Herman; SP: Joseph O'Donnell; S: *Game of Life*; P: Maurice Conn.

God's Country and the Woman (Warner Brothers, January 1937) 85 mins.; George Brent (Steve Russett), Beverly Roberts (Jo Barton), Barton MacLane (Bullhead), Robert Barrat (Jefferson Russett), Alan Hale (Bjorn Skalka), Joseph King (Red Munro), El Brendel (Ole Oleson), Joseph Crehan (Jordan), Addison Richards (Gaskett), Roscoe Ates (Gander Hopkins), Billy Bevan (Plug Hat), Bert Roach (Kewpie), Vic Potel (Turpentine), Mary Treen (Miss Flint), Herbert Rawlinson (Doyle),

Harry Hayden (Barnes), Pat Moriarity (Tim O'Toole), Max Wagner (Gus), Susan Fleming (Grace Moran); D: William Keighley; SP: Norman Reilly Raine, Peter Milne, Charles Belden. Synopsis: Beautiful Jo Barton is managing a lumber camp, while Jefferson Russett, a dastardly sort, operates a camp in competition with her and does everything possible to put her out of business. However, his brother, Steve Russett, likes Jo and sides with her against her brother. The result is that good wins out over bad and romance blossoms in the end.

Review:

Hackneyed and incredible story, of the type once known as "the great outdoors," count against this one. Fact that it was made in technicolor adds little to its b. o. chances and likelihood is for tough sledding.

James Oliver Curwood's type of wide-eyed incredible Americana seems now washed up, under present standards. There's still room for cowboy stories and westerns — but even the kids aren't as credulous these days as they used to be.

William Keighley has tried to pound some action into the yarn but can't completely get away with it. Story is of such an automatic melodramatic character as to make most of the actors exaggerate somewhat, and Keighley doesn't seem to have tried to stop them. Perhaps he figured that the yarn would be even tougher to take if played straight. El Brendel and Barton MacLane are best in support.

Photography is good and the color job A1 but one wishes there was a bit better reason for it.

Variety (January 13, 1937)

The Silver Trail (Reliable, February 27, 1937) 58 mins.; Rex Lease (Bob Crandall), Mary Russell (Molly Welburn), Edward Cassidy (Sheridan),

Roger Williams (Dunn), Steve Clark (Tom), Slim Whitaker (Slug), Oscar Gahan (Curt), Sherri Tansey (Tex), Tom London (Looney), Rin Tin Tin, Jr. (Rinty); D: Raymond Samuels; SP: Bennett Cohen, Forest Sheldon; P: Bernard B. Ray. Synopsis: Molly Wellburn, in male disguise, holds up a wagon carrying ore from the silver mines. Bob Crandall intervenes, and pursues Molly. He overtakes her but, in response to her plea, hides her from the pursuing guards, whom he puts on a wrong scent. Molly disappears and Bob continues on his way to the town of Bonanza. He is in search of a pal, Larry Moore, who had a mining claim near Bonanza. Sheridan, head of a land development company, has been secretly gaining possession of most of the claims, and adding them to the Triangle Mines which he controls. Owners who refused to sell had been murdered by Sheridan's henchmen. Dunn, the town recorder, is in Sheridan's power. When Bob calls at the recording office, he is told there is no trace of Larry as a mine owner.

In a restaurant Bob has a run-in with three of Sheridan's thugs when he interferes to prevent them ill-using Rinty, a dog, who turns out to have been Larry's property. Bob bests the trio, and is thenceforth marked by Sheridan as a man to get rid of. Molly Wellburn, under an alias, works in Sheridan's office. She is trying to find out who killed her father, and later, when she meets, Bob, tells him her attempted stage holdup was the result of her belief that the bullion was part of the silver taken from her dead father's mines, of which he had been robbed. The two join forces. Bob visits the site of Larry's claim, finds traces of him, is ambushed by Sheridan's men, but shoots his way out. Incidentally, he is aided by one Looney, supposed to be a crazed prospector, but who is really a U.S. marshal investigating the recent murders.

Bob turns over Rinty to Molly's care. He enters the recorder's office by a window at night and is looking over the record book when the Sheridan gunmen, Slug, Curt, and Tex, attack him. He escapes but is wounded slightly. Dunn, the recorder, is shot and killed by Slug, and Sheridan lays the blame on Bob. Meanwhile, Sheridan discovers Molly's identity, admits to the girl that he killed her father, but boasts that she is helpless. This is overheard by Looney, who now has the evidence he wanted.

Sheridan holds Molly captive and takes her to the mine. Looney saves Bob from walking into an ambush and the two follow Sheridan's trail. They, in turn, are followed by Slug, Curt, and Tex. Bob dismounts, climbs a tree, and as the three gunmen pass, he ropes the trio, hurls them from their saddles, and Looney ties them up. Sheridan makes a getaway with Molly in a buckboard. Bob gallops in pursuit and overhauls him. Bob leaps into the wagon and knocks out Sheridan. In the end Molly and Bob consolidate their future fortunes.

Whistling Bullets (Ambassador, May 3, 1937) 57 mins.; Kermit Maynard (Larry Graham), Harlene Wood (Anita Saunders), Jack Ingram (Tim Raymond), Maston Williams (Ace Beldon), Bruce Mitchell (Captain Saunders), Karl Hackett (Dave Stone), Sherry Tansey (Sam), Cliff Parkinson (Bart), Cherokee Alcorn (Karl), Herman Hack, Bill McCall, Buck Moulton, Rocky (a horse); D: John English; SP: Joseph O'Donnell; S: *The Fifth Man*; P: Maurice Conn. **Synopsis:** Texas Ranger Larry Graham is assigned by his commanding officer, Captain Saunders, to uncover the whereabouts of $200,000 in missing bonds. Ace Beldon has been convicted of the robbery, so it is decided to send Graham to prison and hope he can gain Beldon's confidence. Aided by Ranger Tim Raymond, Graham and Beldon make a prison break, and Beldon leads them to the ranch of Dave Stone, who, with his henchmen, Sam, Bart, and Karl, were parties to the crime. Graham eventually recovers the loot and apprehends the

whole gang, but not before his ranger sidekick is killed when the crooks learn of their true identities.

Review:

Whistling Bullets is noteworthy in proving what an indie producer, having a limited budget, can accomplish with a story about Texas Rangers when film-making staff works intelligently. Instead of a meandering cactus fable, film is nearly a full hour of tingling excitement, action galore and nicely pitched suspense. It should rate high on twinners where they relish western fare.

For once, the scripter followed closely the general idea of the original author, James Oliver Curwood.... Story is kept moving at an even tempo by director Jack English, who has cashed in on several suspenseful moments effectively. Joseph O'Donnell has done commendable scripting, with the producers wisely making the smooth dialog incidental to the action. Jack Greenhalgh's photography, except for a few lapses, is unusually good.

Variety (October 6, 1937)

The Fighting Texan (Ambassador, June 1937) 59 mins.; Kermit Maynard (Glenn), Elaine Shepard (Judy), Frank LaRue (Walton), Budd Buster (Old Timer), Edward Cassidy (Hadley), Bruce Mitchell (Sheriff), Murdock McQuarrie (Slim), Art Miles (Carter), Merrill McCormack (Bart), Wally West (Henchman), Blackie Whiteford (Bartender), Bob Woodward (Henchman), John Merton (Henchman), Rocky (a horse) (Himself); D: Charles Abbott; SP: Joseph O'Donnell; P: Maurice Conn. **Synopsis:** Glenn buys a half interest in the Bar W Ranch, owned by his old friend of long standing, Slim. He believes the place to be a peaceful spot where a ranchman may carry on his business without interference of rustlers and other enemies of the cattlemen.

The illusion is soon dispelled, for, upon his arrival, he finds himself enmeshed in a host of situations that resulted in the murder of his partner. Suspicion immediately points to Walton, owner of the Bar V Ranch and his lovely daughter, Judy, when it is discovered that for some time stock had been missing from Walton's ranch, only to be discovered on the Bar W Ranch with the "V" brand changed into a "W."

Before his murder, Slim had disclaimed any knowledge of the rustling and believed it to be the work of someone anxious to bring about animosity between himself and Walton.

Determined to get to the bottom of the mystery, after the sheriff's inquest brings forth a verdict of murder committed by "person or persons unknown," Glenn goes to the Bar V Ranch and accuses Judy and her father of complicity in the crime; his assertions being grounded on the fact that it was her father's gun that had fired the bullet, which on the day of the murder was being carried by her.

Subsequently, Judy convinces Glenn that her father is innocent and aids Glenn when he is suspected by the sheriff of being the murderer. Following a series of exciting events culminating in a mountaintop confrontation between the sheriff and his posse, Glenn, Judy, Walton, Hadley, owner of the Lazy B Ranch, and "Old Timer"—a secret government agent—and gang members, it is revealed that Hadley is the guilty party. Hadley grabs Judy, whirls her in front of him and, thus shielded, starts to back down the hill.

Glenn manages to fool Hadley into thinking someone is behind him. With Hadley momentarily off his guard, a bullet from Glenn's gun brings him to the ground. With the prisoner handed over to the sheriff, Glenn and Judy ride off together thinking of more pleasant things.

Galloping Dynamite (Ambassador, July 1937) 58 mins.; Kermit Maynard (Jim Dillion), Ariane Allen (Jane Foster), John Merton (Reed), John Ward (Wilkes), David Sharpe (Bob Dillion), Stanley Blystone (Jenkins), Francis Walker (Dalton), Tracy Layne (Mosby), Robert Burns (Sheriff), Allen Greer (Deputy), Earl Dwire (Pop), Budd Buster (Barber), Rocky (a horse) (Himself); D: Harry Fraser; SP: Sherman Lowe, Charles Condon; S: *Mystery of Dead Man's Isle*; P: Maurice Conn. Synopsis: Gold has been discovered by Bob Dillion in a mountain stream that runs through the ranch property of Jane Foster and her father, but Reed, a murderer at heart, Wilkes, a greedy miser, and Jenkins, a coward, plot amongst themselves to keep news of the discovery from the owners of the property in order that they might profit themselves, although they have no legal right. Their plan is to purchase the ranch ridiculously cheap, as the Fosters are virtually poverty-stricken. Dillion, a poor, but honest chap, refuses to become a partner in the plot and threatens to carry the good news of the discovery to the Fosters. The dishonest schemers apparently acquiesce, but as Bob rides away they shoot and kill him. Reed reconciles his partners in crime by impressing on them that this was the only way out in order to keep the secret for themselves. The three, however, fear retribution from the murdered man's brother, Jim Dillion, a Texas ranger, and one of the West's toughest characters.

A year passes and Jim Dillion arrives in the village in which his brother had been working, only to hear that he had been murdered by rustlers. He meets Jane and learns of the plot executed by the three villains, whereby they purchased the property shortly after his brother's death and discovered gold soon afterward. The entire situation appears illogical to him and he determines to investigate, despite the expressed fears of Jane, who warns him of the three dangerous characters. He outlines his plan of attack, explaining that their own fear and cowardice will bring them to justice, without the use of guns.

The first of the three villains is dispensed with when his plot to kill Jim goes awry and he is shot by his own pals. Jim then plays on the greedy instincts of the other two to also bring about their downfall.

With the outlaws out of the way, Dillion clears his name of all blame for the crimes of which he was accused and succeeds in having the property restored to Jane and her father, after which he settles down as a member of the family.

Rough Riding Rhythm (Ambassador, August 15, 1937) 57 mins.; Kermit Maynard (Jim Langley), Beryl Wallace (Helen Holbert), Ralph Peters (Scrubby), Olin Francis (Jake Horne), Betty Mack (Ethyl Horne), Curley Dresden (Soapy Phillips), Cliff Parkinson (Hank), Dave O'Brien (Detective Walters), Newt Kirby (Detective Thomas), J. P. McGowan (Pete Hobart), Rocky (a horse) (Himself); D: J. P. McGowan; SP: Arthur Everett; S: *Getting a Start in Life*; P: Maurice Conn. Synopsis: While driving their herd of cattle from Texas to a new range, Jim Langley and his old pal, Scrubby, stop off in Cottonwood to visit Scrubby's sister, Ethyl Horne. Her husband, Jake Horne, is a cattle rustler whom Jim once saved from jail because of his friendship for Scrubby and Ethyl. Jake has gone back to his old ways and has formed a gang of cattle rustlers and stagecoach robbers, headed by Soapy and Hank. Because of their child, Ethyl has stuck with him but decides to leave when she learns he killed a sheriff in a recent holdup. The angered Jake hits her on the temple and she dies.

Jim and Scrubby find her dead on the floor, Jake gone, and the baby crying in the next room. Jim rides off to get some milk for the baby and is discovered milking a cow at a nearby ranch by the owner's daughter, Helen Hobart, who thinks he is a rustler. Jim disarms her and takes her back to look after the baby.

Two detectives arrive and arrest Jim and Scrubby as the stagecoach robbers. The two escape and capture Jake, Soapy, and Hank when they come back after the loot.

Roaring Six Guns (Ambassador, September 1, 1937) 57 mins.; Kermit Maynard (Buck Sinclair), Mary Hayes (Beth Ringold), Sam Flint (Ringold), Budd Buster (Wildcat), Robert Fiske (Harmon), Edward Cassidy (Commissioner), John Merton (Mileaway), Curley Dresden (Slug), Dick Morehead (Bill), Slim Whitaker (Skeeter), Earle Hodgins (Sundown), Rene Stone (Rene), Rocky (a horse) (Himself), J. P. McGowan, Oscar Gahan, Bob Woodward; D: J. P. McGowan; SP: Arthur Everett; P: Maurice Conn. Synopsis: Although Buck Sinclair, a young rancher, is in love with Beth Ringold, her father is one of his most bitter enemies. Ringold is bent on Beth marrying his conniving partner, Mileaway, despite the fact that the girl is in love with Buck.

Buck leases from the government some very valuable grazing land, control of which Ringold and Mileaway are anxious to obtain, since their own land is barren. When Buck's lease expires, Ringold instructs the local bank (of which he is the largest stockholder) not to underwrite Buck's bid, since the Ringold ranch will bid against him.

But Wildcat, another ranch owner, comes to Buck's aid. Realizing that should the Ringold crowd gain control of the land the other ranchers would be frozen out. Wildcat backs Buck and aids him to renew his lease, although the bidding reaches three times the actual value of the property.

Having failed legally to gain control of the coveted property, Ringold and Mileaway then decide to resort to force. In the ensuing difficulties, Wildcat is killed and Buck swears to avenge his death.

Sundown, a professional gunman of the area, is hired to dispose of Buck, but the rancher is too good for him and gives

Sundown a flesh wound before any harm comes to himself.

En route to complete negotiations for the lease of the land — which is revokable unless taken care of within a certain length of time — Ringold and his gang try to hold him for the attempted murder of Sundown. Buck, however, contrives to elude them and gets to the government bureau in time to complete his lease.

He returns to the ranch, bringing with him proof that Mileaway has killed Wildcat. This brings about the thrilling climax in which Mileaway is killed, and Ringold realizes his underhanded methods are wrong, withdraws his objections to Buck marrying Beth, and all ends happily with the end of the range war.

Review:

A little slow for a western, which should above all things have action. *Roaring Six Guns* will find most of the fans accepting it on a run-of-mill basis. Fact that those who attend western pic showings seldom show much qualms about quality is biggest thing in its favor.

Kermit Maynard, by a fine line, is usually a better performer than the more illustrious Ken, but he's still no rafter-shaking thespian by any means.

Variety (October 13, 1937)

Call of the Yukon (Republic, April 18, 1938) 70 mins.; Richard Arlen (Gaston), Beverly Roberts (Jean), Lyle Talbot (Hugo), Mala (Olee John), Carry Owen (Connor), Ivan Miller (O'Malley), James Lono (Topek), Emory Parnell (Swede Trapper), Billy Dooley (Watchman), Al St. John (Joe), Anthony Hughes (Hill), Nina Campana (Knudka); D: B. Reeves Eason; SP: Gertrude Orr, William Bartlett; S: *Swift Lightning*; AP: Armand Schaefer. **Synopsis:** Gaston persuades writer Jean to leave a deserted Eskimo village. En route to civilization they encounter numerous obstacles, falling in love in the course of overcoming them.

River's End (Warner Brothers, August 10, 1940) 69 mins.; Dennis Morgan (John Keith; Sergeant Conniston), Elizabeth Earl (Linda), Victory Jory (Talbot), James Stephenson (McDowell), George Tobias (Andy), Steffi Duna (Cheeta), John Ridgely (Jeffers), Frank Wilcox (Kentish), Edward Pawley (Crandall); D: Ray English; SP: Barry Trivers, Bertram Milhauser; AP: William Jacobs. **Synopsis:** In this third film version of Curwood's novel Dennis Morgan plays a dual role. John Keith is convicted of a murder he did not commit and seeks to lose himself in the Canadian wilderness. Sergeant Conniston pursues and catches him but dies as the result of an accident. Keith discovers that he and Conniston are lookalikes and assumes the mountie's identity. Through a series of circumstances that are a little hard to believe, he succeeds in clearing himself.

Review:

According to the record it was about time *River's End* was made again; that is, if 10 years between each time is the way to do it. The old James Oliver Curwood story of the Canadian woods country and mounties was made by First National in 1920 and again by Warners in 1931. The creaky old adventure story, in its third version, is still a tiresome story, plotted out very obviously, but it has one strong redeeming feature. That is the performance of George Tobias.

Playing a French Canadian whose source of livelihood is never explained, Tobias not only turns in a fine characterization but loads the picture with plenty of good laughs.... Romantic interest is suitably spotted into the story with Elizabeth Earl opposite Morgan on that assignment. Victor Jory does the heavy, while

James Stephenson plays a police inspector. The rest are minor. Exteriors are good; most of the film carries a brownish sepia rather than being sharp black-and-white.

Variety (August, 28, 1940)

Law of the Timber (PRC, December 19, 1941) 68 mins.; Marjorie Reynolds ("Perry" Lorimer), Monte Blue (Hodge Mason), J. Farrell MacDonald (Adams), Hal Brazeal (John Gordon), Jack Holmes, George Humbert, Sven-Hugo Borg, Earle Ebe, Milburn Morante, Betty Roadman, Eddie Phillips, Zero (a dog); D: Bernard B. Ray; SP: Jack Natteford; S: *A Speck on the Wall*; P: Bernard B. Ray. Synopsis: "Perry" Lorimer falls heir to the lumber business when her father perishes in the forest fire, touched off by Hodge Mason and his dastardly associates. "Perry" is engaged in filling a national defense order, and Mason is determined to sabotage the endeavor. Mason puts on a couple of slugfests with the handsome stranger, who poses as a lumberjack but is really half owner of the business, just out of college, and ready to give his all for right and justice. In the happy ending, the boy finds a horse conveniently saddled in the wildwoods, gallops along the railroad, leaps aboard the engine, and goes into a clinch with the girl, who had suspected him as a culprit. Review:

Action and ever more action make *Law of the Timber* a fast-moving, exciting little melodrama in which the skullduggery and the heroics start where the usual meller of this type leaves off, while skillful of the story's episodes with stock shots of logging in the timberlands has given it good production value.

The story does not pretend to offer any great novelty, but combines its elements strictly for the purpose of making things happen. On the whole, the cast is good.

Marjorie Reynolds is attractive and effective as the girl lumber queen, with Monte Blue as a potent heavy and J. Farrell MacDonald capable as always.

Hollywood Reporter (December 22, 1941)

Dawn on the Great Divide (Monogram, December 18, 1942) 67 mins.; Buck Jones (Buck Roberts), Mona Barrie (Sadie Rand), Raymond Hatton (Sandy Hopkins), Robert Lowery (Terry), Rex Bell (Jack Carson), Harry Woods (Jim Corkle), Christine McIntyre (Mary), Betty Blythe (Elmire Corkle), Robert Frazer (Judge Corkle), Tris Coffin (Rand), Jan Wiley (Martha), Dennis Moore (Tony Corkle), Roy Barcroft (Loder), Silver (a horse) (Himself), Steve Clark, Reed Howes, Bud Osborne, George Morrell, Ray James, Lee Shumway, Herman Hack, Merrill McCormick, Maude Eburne, Al Haskell, Denver Dixon, Chief Yowlatchie, Kansas Moehring, Spade Cooley, Horace Carpenter; D: Howard Bretherton; SP: Jess Bowers (Adele Buffington); S: *Wheels of Fate*; P: Scott R. Dunlap. Synopsis: Buck Roberts, Jack Carson, and Sandy Hopkins, U.S. marshals, are entrusted with the delivery of a wagon train of railroad supplies to the town of Beaver Lake. Formerly, every such wagon train has been attacked, robbed, and every member killed, supposedly by Indians, before it has reached the town. Carson discovers from his Indian friends that they have had nothing to do with the attacks, and rides into Beaver Lake seeking further information. Buck and Sandy are in charge of the wagon train, in which are Judge Corkle, going to the town to visit his brother Jim, the crooked boss who really runs the settlement; Jack and Sadie Rand, who plan to set up a gambling house in Beaver Lake; and Martha, an expectant mother who dies when her baby is born during the trip. The Rands learn that she was the secret wife of Tony Corkle, son of Jim.

That night the train is attacked by

white men disguised as Indians and several of the party, including Rand, are killed, though most of the supplies are saved. Meeting the caravan when it arrives at Beaver Lake, Carson befriends Mrs. Rand and so fully wins her confidence that she invites him to join her in the establishment of the gambling house. To force Jim Corkle to grant them the gambling privilege, Carson and Mrs. Rand threaten to publicize the son's relationship with the dead Martha and her desertion by Tony. Jim, actually the leader of the desperado gang, leads his men in another attack on the caravan just after it leaves to proceed beyond Beaver Lake, and the band is repulsed. The Corkles and their henchmen are arrested when it transpires that they, ruling the town in a lawless manner, have been fighting against the entrance of the railroad and its accompanying law and order.

Review:

Here is a western of the old old school, set in the days of the covered wagon and Indians. It is just the sort of western that the late Buck Jones liked. So it is fitting that its release follows closely on his untimely death in the Cocoanut Grove fire in Boston. He would have liked his legion of fans to remember him in the kind of role he himself preferred.

Motion Picture Herald (December 1942).

Dawn on the Great Divide really is the "special" production Monogram has been touting. The Scott R. Dunlap production has more elaborate values than ordinary and a stronger cast. It is fitting that Buck Jones rides to the last round-up under the most advantageous circumstances in the final picture he made.

Hollywood Reporter (December 11, 1942).

Northwest Trail (Acton/Lippert, November 30, 1945) 66 mins.; Bob Steele (Matt O'Brien), Joan Woodbury (Katherine Owens), John Litel (Inspector Means), Madge Bellamy (Mrs. Yeager), George Meeker (Yeager), Raymond Hatton (Morgan), Ian Keith (Inspector McGrath), Poodles Hanneford (Poodles Hanneford), John Hamilton (Owens), Charles Middleton (Pierre), Grace Hanneford (Jim Hanneford), Bill Hammond (Lacey), Bud Osborne (Dutch), Al Ferguson (Sandy), Bob Duncan (Ollie), John Carpenter (Knuckles); D: Derwin Abrahams; SP: Harvey H. Gates, L. J. Swabacher; P: William B. David, Max M. King. **Synopsis:** Mountie Matt O'Brien investigates the claim of an old settler that the stream that runs through his property periodically dries up, and he is shot at when he goes to investigate. O'Brien's investigation leads him to Morgan's Post, where he eventually proves that Owens, under the guise of buying timber land, is head of a gang taking gold from an old placer mine. The gang had diverted the stream to wash out the dust and was robbing the Canadian government by flying the gold across the border. O'Brien also proves that Inspector Means is an imposter, having replaced the real inspector who was murdered.

Review:

Producers Max King and William B. Boyd (*sic*) have gone all out for quality in every department. The cast is composed almost entirely of names that draw the western fans. The screenplay is carefully, if not brilliantly, written, and the background and introduction of color in this field does all that's necessary to place the film on a stratum above its fellows.

The Cinecolor process is without the full color range of Technicolor, but much of the limitation apparent here is unquestionably due to bad make-up and choice of camera values.... A criticism of the direction is difficult, because the action requires little but speed. Marcel Picard's camera work is fair, with his lack of experience in color apparent only to the trained eye. The editing is tight.

Variety (November 16, 1945)

God's Country (Action/Screen Guild, April 15, 1946) 64 mins.; Robert Lowery, Helen Gilbert, William Farnum, Buster Keaton, Stanley Andrews, Trevor Bardette, Si Jenks, Estelle Zarco, Juan Reyes, Al Ferguson, Ace (a dog); D: Robert Tansey; SP: Robert Tansey; P: William B. David. Synopsis: A shady lumber company destroys hundreds of little trees for every two or three big ones taken out of the northwoods. Lowery, on the lam from a manslaughter rap, makes friends with the traders and trappers whose livelihood is being hurt by the lumber robbers, and the latter make use of him to carry out their dirty work. Virtue triumphs, however, when Lowery, redeemed of the false accusation, and his police dog, Powder, rout the rascals.

Review:

Action Pictures have put everything but a stagecoach holdup into this galloper, which purports to be a western but which drags into its washed-out cinecolor haze diverse shots of logging operations, wild life, a hand-to-hand fray a la *The Spoilers*, a hero falsely accused of manslaughter, bad guys who shoot innocent animals, dog-and-man fight, dog-and-wolf-pack fight, and a scene in which Buster Keaton, a crow and a racoon collaborate in mixing up recipes for chili con carne and nut cake. It'll do okay with fans who thrive on saddle fodder, but needs plenty of exploitation.

Robert E. Tansey's direction makes for a meandering plot. Photography is okay insofar as composition goes, but the pre-dominantly orange-and-green, hard-on-the-eyes color results in an overall impression of a postcard that has been out in the sun too long. Sound job isn't too smart, either, with Lowery's lips lagging way behind the sound track in "Trees" at the tee-off.

Variety (October 11, 1946)

'Neath Canadian Skies (Golden Gate/Screen Guild, October 15, 1946) 40 mins.; Russell Hayden (Tim Ranson), Inez Cooper (Linda Elliott), Douglas Fowley (Ned Thompson), Cliff Nazarro (Wilbur Higgins), I. Stanford Jolley (Hale), Kermit Maynard (Stoney Carter), Jack Mulhall (Captain Sharon), Dick Alexander (Pete), Pat Hurst (Harding), Gil Patrick (Kinney), Boyd Stockman (Joe Reed), Jimmie Martin (Lewis); D: B. Reeves Eason; SP: Arthur V. Jones; P: William B. David. Synopsis: Mountie Tim Ranson is sent to investigate the murder of a prospector and a gang of claim jumpers. In the guise of an outlaw, he works a gold mine and finds a strain that the gang intended to acquire for themselves. After a spirited battle the mounties arrive in time to save Tim and Linda.

Review:

Golden Gate Pictures — a name most likely inspired by the San Francisco exhibitor background of Screen Guild's guiding light, Robert Lippert — though the shortened running time for these pictures would help the bookings in the double feature situations. From here it looks like a good idea — tho' Hal Roach used the same approach on a couple of mid–40's comedy series and flopped — but our town's Lyric used to play them as a single feature. Thirty years later, we're still mad about the twelve cents we blew on a 40-minute picture. Count us among the early victims of the post-war rip-offs.

Yesterday's Saturdays (no 11, February 1977) Note: Advertising for this film read "James Oliver Curwood's great action novel comes to life," but it is a challenge to determine what novel it was based on.

North of the Border (Golden Gate/ Screen Guild, November 15, 1946) 40 mins.; Russell Hayden (Robert "Utah" Neyes), Inez Cooper (Ruth Wilson), Lyle Talbot (Sergeant Jack Craig), Douglas Fowley (Nails Nelson), Anthony Warde (Jean Gaspee), Guy Beach (George Laramie), I. Stanford Jolley (Ivy Jenkins), Jack Mulhall (Captain Swanson), Dick Alexander (Tiny Muller); D: B. Reeves Eason; SP: Arthur V. Jones; P: William B. David. **Synopsis:** Cowboy Utah Neyes crosses the border into Canada to meet his partner, only to find that the latter has been murdered by a gang led by Nails Nelson. Utah, with the aid of mountie Jack Craig and trapper Ivy Jenkins, manages to clear his own name of suspicion and breaks up Nelson's fur stealing and smuggling racket. Utah returns to his ranch with Ruth as his wife. Note: There is no indication as to what Curwood story this film is based on.

Trail of the Yukon (Monogram, July 31, 1949) 69 mins.; Kirby Grant (Bob McDonald), Suzanne Dalbart (Marie), Bill Edwards (Jim Blaine), Dan Seymour (Duval), William Forrest (Dawson), Anthony Warde (Muskes), Maynard Holmes (Buck), Jay Silverheels (Poleon), Iris Adrian (Paula), Guy Beach (Matt Blaine), Stanley Andrews (Rogers), Dick Elliott (Sullivan), Bill Kennedy (Constable), Harrison Hearne (Bank Teller), Peter Manakos (Rand), Chinook (Himself); D: William X. Crowley; SP: Oliver Drake; S: *The Gold Hunters*; P: Lindsley Parsons. **Synopsis:** Dawson arranges the theft of his bank by henchmen Muskes, Buck, and Rand. The trio, at Dawson's command, talk Matt Blaine and his son Jim into participating in the robbery. Because of injustices Dawson has caused Blaine, he and his son Jim agree to help in the robbery.

Dawson's plan is to pin the robbery on the pair. Following the robbery, the trio of bandits try to double-cross the Blaines but are outwitted. Matt Blaine, however, is killed and Jim Blaine is saved by Bob McDonald, the mountie.

After an overdrawn tug-of-war, Muskes, Buck, and Rand are shown the strong arm of justice along with Dawson. Jim Blaine, because of his help in the fight against the knaves, gets off lightly for his part in the bank holdup.

Review:

Trail of the Yukon has taken the stereotyped chase western plot and moved it before a Canadian backdrop. Replacing the cowpoke hero is the Northwest mounted policeman. Dialog and action fall far below pace set usual run of low budget westerns. However, Chinook, the canine, takes top honors in thespian field.

Kirby and Edwards manage their respective roles well considering the poor dialog and badly staged fights under which they labored. Producer William F. Broidy did little to help film's stature. William X. Crowley's direction is weak, showing off some uninspired thespian chores and bad pacing. Lensing by William Sickner is stock.

Variety (July 28, 1949)

The Wolf Hunters (Monogram, October 30, 1949) 70 mins.; Kirby Grant (Red), Jan Clayton (Greta), Chinook (Himself), Edward Norris (Henri), Helen Parrish (Marcia), Charles Lang (McTavish), Ted Hecht (Muskoka), Luther Crockett (Cameron), Elizabeth Root (Minnetaki); D: Oscar (Budd) Boetticher; SP: W. Scott Darling; P: Lindsley Parsons. **Synopsis:** A Northwest mountie (Kirby Grant), with the help of a fur trapper (Edward Norris) and a dog (Chinook) tracks down the man responsible for a series of murders and fur robberies in a remote Canadian village.

Kazan (Columbia, 1949) 65 mins.; Stephen Dunne (Thomas Weyman), Lois Maxwell (Louise Maitlin), Joe Sawyer (Sandy Jepson), Roman Bohnen (Maitlin), George Cleveland (Trapper), John Dehner (Henri Le Clerc), Kazan (a dog) (Himself), Ray Teal (McCready); D: William Jason; SP: Arthur A. Ross; P: Robert Cohn. **Synopsis:** Thomas Weyman comes to a government settlement in the far North on government business, to find Sandy Jepson selling tickets to a pit battle between a great dane and what he claims to be a white wolf. Weyman knows the dog is a sled dog and tries to buy it, but Jepson won't sell. With the old prospector, Weyman pieces together the dog's story. Zero, lead dog of a team, is left alone in the wilds when his owner is killed by an avalanche, lives like a wild animal, takes a wolf for his mate, but she and the pups are killed by a cougar. Zero kills the cougar. Louise Maitlin, on the trail with her father who is going to open a store in the settlement, finds Zero and adopts him. Her father orders the guide to kill him, but the man only drives him away. Weyman is with a trapper when Zero is caught in one of his traps and saves the dog's life. Sawyer captures Zero and the sadistic storekeeper puts on a pit battle with Zero and a savage great dane. However, the dogs refuse to fight. The disappointed spectators maul Jepson. Weyman jumps into the ring and rescues Zero, who gets away peacefully with him and Louise.
Review:

Kazan, based on James Oliver Curwood's famous dog story of the far north, comes to the screen with the beautifully-trained great white dog, Zero, in the title role and filmgoers have not seen better by a canine star.... Robert Cohn's production supplies effective and authentic backgrounds and many fine snow scenes and the beautiful photography. Henry Freulich does a great job to make the film colorful and outstanding. Direc-

tor William Jason makes the most of a capable cast and a mob of male extras and he handles the dogs, animals, wolves, and cougars very skillfully. Paul Palmentola does an excellent job of art direction and Mischa Balaleinikoff's music builds up and sustains the drama and suspense of the story. The editing by Richard Fantl is clean cut. The picture will do well in supporting position.

Source unknown.

Timber Fury (Eagle Lion, June 1950) 65 mins.; David Bruce (Jim), Laura Lee (Phyllis), Nicole De Bruno (Yvonne), Sam Flint (Henry Wilson), George Slocum (McCabe), Lee Phelps (Sheriff), Gilbert Frye (Pete), Paul Huffman (Spike), Spencer Chan (Chung), Zoro (a dog) (Himself); D: Bernard B. Ray; SP: Sam Neuman, Nat Tanchuck, Michael Hansen; S: *Retribution*; P: Bernard B. Ray. **Synopsis:** *Timber Fury* deals with attempts of a logging superintendent to prevent delivery of a timber shipment so the owner's rival can get the order. Conflict enters the scene when the owner brings in a young engineer to solve problems down river on time. A timberman is murdered and his death is blamed on the engineer by the superintendent, who actually committed the crime. The remainder of the action has to do with the engineer clearing himself.
Review:

Timber Fury is a routine logging meller with little to offer in way of novelty. Blowing up of a logjam is highlight scene, but this is brief and balance of action is pretty static. Suitable for small situations only.

Source unknown.

Snow Dog (Monogram, July 16, 1950) 63 mins.; Kirby Grant (Rod), Elena Verdugo (Andree), Rick Vallin (Louis), Milburn Stone (Doctor McKen-

zie), Richard Karlin (Biroff), Jane Adams (Red Feather), Hal Gerard (Antoine), Richard Avonde (Phillippe), Duke York (Duprez), Guy Zanette (Baptiste); D: Frank McDonald; SP: William Raynor; S: *Tentacles of the North*; P: Lindsley Parsons. **Synopsis:** Rod, a Northwest mountie, seeks a killer wolf that is keeping trappers out of a certain section of the woods.

Call of the Klondike (Monogram, December 17, 1950) 67 mins.; Kirby Grant (Rod), Chinook (a dog) (Himself), Anne Gwynne (Nancy), Lynne Roberts (Emily), Tom Neal (Mallory), Russell Simpson (McKay), Marc Krah (Mancheck), Paul Bryar (Fred Foley), Pat Gleason (Billy), Duke York (Luke); D: Frank McDonald; SP: Charles Long; P: Lindsley Parsons. **Synopsis:** Rod, a Northwest mountie, and his dog Chinook go to a remote trading post to investigate some murders and to locate Nancy's father, who has disappeared after discovering a lost gold mine. Rod and Chinook discover that Emily and her brother Mallory are responsible for the killings and are stealing gold through a secret tunnel from a rich mine to their worthless one.

Northwest Territory (Monogram, December 9, 1951) 61 mins.; Kirby Grant (Rod Webb), Chinook (a dog) (Himself), Gloria Saunders (Ann DeMere), Pat Mitchell (Billy Kellogg), John Crawford (LeBeau), Duke York (Dawson), Warren Douglas (Morgan), Tristram Coffin (Kincaid), Don Harvey (Barton), Sam Flint (Kellogg); D: Frank McDonald; SP: William Raynor; P: Lindsley Parsons. **Synopsis:** An old prospector who has a map showing the location of oil deposits is killed just before Rod Webb, a Canadian mountie, arrives at Fort MacKenzie with the prospector's orphaned grandson. Determined to track down the killers, Webb sheds his uniform and in the guise of a novice prospector sets about to find the killers. He eventually exposes the killers and restores the claim to the grandson.

Review:

For a product obviously aimed at the action market, pic is woefully lacking in the ingredient…. Considering the screenplay, Grant does an okay job as the Mountie. Gloria Saunders, only femme in the cast, is a looker with sex appeal and deserves being brought out of the northwest woods. John Crawford, as one of the killers, speaks his lines without conviction, while Duke York, Warren Douglas, and Tristram Coffin make acceptable heavies. Sam Flint, as the old prospector, and Pat Mitchell, as his grandson, turn in standard performances. Lensing and other technical credits are adequate.

Variety (February 13, 1952)

Yukon Manhunt (Monogram, December 9, 1951) 61 mins.; Kirby Grant, Gail Davis, Chinook (a dog), Margaret Field, Rand Brooks, Nelson Leigh, John Doucette, Paul McGuire; D: Frank McDonald; SP: William Raynor; P: Lindsley Parsons. **Synopsis:** The mystery concerns what's happening to the Kenmore mine payrolls. Sent to clear up the case is Canadian mountie Kirby Grant and his faithful canine companion Chinook. The mountie follows through in the "always get their men" tradition, only in this instance it is several persons — the Kenmore mine owner himself, his niece, and several accomplices.

Review:

Monogram's *Yukon Manhunt* presents mystery and adventure amidst picturesque surroundings. For lower level dual bracketing, pic will satisfy in that category and should especially please followers of Kirby Grant and Chinook, for the latest is a bit above average for the series…. Lindsley Parsons, assisted by William F. Broidy, has again rounded up the regular series stars, picked an interest-holding yarn and used

Kirby Grant and Mary Ellen Kay in *Yukon Vengence* (Allied Artists, 1954).

fine backgrounds to enhance the overall effect. Frank McDonald's direction keeps an air of mystery around the action so as to sustain interest, and technical credits shape up as stock for a lower-budgeter.

Variety (August 2, 1951)

Yukon Gold (Monogram, August 31, 1952) 62 mins.; Kirby Grant, Martha Hyer, Harry Lauter, Philip Van Zandt, Frances Charles, Mauritz Hugo, James Parnell, Sam Flint, I. Stanford Jolley, Chinook (a dog); D: Frank McDonald; SP: Bill Raynor; P: William F. Broidy. **Synopsis:** A mountie, Rod Webb, is on the trail of a murderer in a lawless mining settlement. With the help of his faithful dog Chinook and a pretty girl he is able to bring the murderer to justice and law and order to the settlement.

Fangs of the Arctic (Allied Artists,

January 18, 1953) 62 mins.; Kirby Grant (Rod Webb), Lorna Hansen (Sandra Dubois), Warren Douglas (Matt Oliver), Leonard Penn (Morgan), Richard Avonde (Cheval), Robert Sherman (Mike Kelly), John Close (Howell), Phil Tead (MacGregor), Roy Gordon (Briggs), Kit Carson (Andrew), Chinook (a dog) (Himself); D: Rex Bailey; SP: Bill Raynor, Warren Douglas; P: Lindsley Parsons. **Synopsis:** Corporal Rod Webb and Constable Mike Kelly of the Canadian Mounties, with Rod's dog Chinook, are sent to the Blackfoot Crossing country to find the murderer of Antoine Dubois, a trapper, and also to investigate reports of illegal deals in beaver pelts. Mike, a rookie, is elated by the assignment, because it takes him to his home, where he again sees Sandra Dubois, a childhood sweetheart. In Sandra's cabin they meet Matt Oliver, introduced as a mining engineer, who shows jealousy when Mike receives a warm welcome from the girl. Rod and Mike, posing as trappers, soon get on the trail of Morgan, Cheval, and Howell, the illegal beaver trappers. While searching for evidence in the trading post of MacGregor, Mike is surprised by Morgan and Cheval and is killed. As the trail closes in Oliver is revealed as the leader of the gang. In a final fight, Chinook disables Oliver, and Rod arrests Morgan and the others for their crimes, which include the murder of Sandra's father.

Northern Patrol (Allied Artists, July 12, 1953) 67 mins.; Kirby Grant (Rod Webb), Chinook (a dog) (Himself), Marion Carr (Quebec Kid), Bill Phipps (Frank Stevens), Claudia Drake (Oweena), Dale Van Sickel (Jason), Gloria Talbot (Meg Stevens), Richard Walsh (Ralph Gregg), Emmett Lynn (Old Timer), Frank Lackteen (Dancing Horse), Frank Sully (Bartender); D: Rex Bailey; SP: Warren Douglas; P: Lindsley Parsons. **Synopsis:** Corporal Rod Webb and his dog Chinook discover the body of a young trapper, apparently a suicide. The mountie knows better, however, and by the time he is through with his investigation he has uncovered a plot by the Quebec Kid (a female gunslinger in leather pants), Frank Stevens, and Jason to steal what is believed to be treasure accumulated over the years in an Indian burial ground, known as the Valley of Death.
  Review:

  This is a mild story in Allied Artists' program action series dealing with the adventures of a mountie and his dog. It will serve as bill-filler.
  It's a hackneyed concoction in all departments. Rex Bailey's direction is no better than the poor script by Warren Douglas, and the casting is on the same level, although Miss Carr tries to bolster her role. Two other femmes also come off better than the males. They are Claudia Drake,

an Indian girl, and Gloria Talbot, as Phipps' sister.

Variety (July 15, 1953)

  Back to God's Country (Universal, September 1953) 78 mins.; Rock Hudson (Peter Keith), Marcia Henderson (Dolores Keith), Steve Cochran (Paul Blake), Hugh O'Brien (Frank Hudson), Chubby Johnson (Billy Shorter), Tudor Owen (Fitzsimmons), John Clift (Joe), Bill Radovich (Lagi), Arthur Space (Carstairs), Pat Hogan (Uppy), Ivan Triesault (Reinhardt), Charles Horvath (Nelson); D: Joseph Pevney; SP: Tom Reed; P: Howard Christie. **Synopsis:** A ship's captain, Peter Keith, and his wife Delores are detained in a remote Canadian harbor by Paul Blake, who covets Delores and plans to do away with Peter.

  Yukon Vengeance (Allied Artists, January 17, 1954) 68 mins.; Kirby Grant, Monte Hale, Mary Ellen Kay, Henry Kulky, Carol Thurston, Park MacGregor, Fred Gauborie, Billy Wilkerson, Marshall Bradford; D: William Beaudine; SP: Bill Raynor; P: William F. Broidy.

  Nikki, Wild Dog of the North (Buena Vista, July 12, 1961) 74 mins.; Jean Coutu (Andre Dupas), Emile Genest (Jacques Lebeau), Uriel Luft (Makoki), Robert Rivard (Durante), Nikki (dog) (The Malamute), Neewa (bear) (The Bear), Taao (Dog) (Fighting Dog), The Nomads (Singers), Jacques Fauteux (Narrator); D: Jack Couffer, Don Haldane; SP: Ralph Wright, Winston Hibler; S: *Nomads of the North*; P: Winston Hibler. **Synopsis:** Andre Dupas, his dog Nikki, and an adopted bear cub, Neewa, are traveling on a boat that capsizes in rough waters. Andre makes it to shore but the animals are carried a considerable distance downstream before they are able to crawl ashore, still tied together by a leash. They fight with one another but are forced to hunt together for food and eventually become friends, even after the leash binding them together is broken. When winter comes Neewa hibernates, while Nikki wonders off alone, stealing bait from traps set by villainous trapper Lebeau and his Indian companion Makoki. Eventually, the full-grown dog is captured by Lebeau, who trains him as a killer fighting dog.

Andre, the new factor in the area, learns that Lebeau is illegally promoting dog fights and challenges him. During a confrontation Lebeau pushes Andre into the dog pit with Nikki, the brutalized killer dog. However, Nikki recognizes his old master and aids him against Lebeau, who is accidentally killed with his own knife. Later in the woods Nikki sees Neewa, who remains in the forest while Nikki returns to be with his master Andre.

The Bear (Tri-Star, 1988) 91 mins.; Ka Douce (bear; Youk), Bart (bear; Kaar), Doc (bear), Griz (bear), Blanca (bear), Check-Up (puma), Teheky Karyo (hunter), Jack Wallace (hunter), Andre Lacombe (hunter); D: Jean-Jacques Annaud; SP: Gerard Brach; S: *The Grizzly King*; P: Pierre Grunstein. **Synopsis:** This film follows the adventures of a bear cub who loses his mother in a landslide and falls into the company of a no-nonsense adult grizzly bear. They have little time for bear hugs because a couple of determined hunters are literally after Kaar's hide. A series of pursuits and encounters follow, climaxing in a terrifying face-to-face between Kaar and one of the pursuers.

Cornering the human, Kaar scares the living daylights out of him, but mysteriously and anticlimactically spares him. The hunter, transformed, returns the favor by not shooting the retreating beast and by freeing the cub that he had captured. Reviews.

> *The Bear* is a remarkable achievement only on its own terms, which happen to be extremely limited and peculiar. No less amazing than the material Mr. Annaud has captured on the screen is the fact that he has gone to such crazily elaborate lengths to capture it all.

New York Times (October 25, 1988)

> Jean-Jacques Annaud's $20,000,000 shaggy bear saga is good family fare whose principal weakness is that it's a lot less fascinating than its long preproduction and production history.
>
> Annaud and screenwriter Gerard Brach, freely adapting a backwoods literary yarn by James Oliver Curwood, bank on the familiar schemas of physical danger and survival, cuddly sentiment and ecological sentimentality ("live and let live"). Annaud has sufficient taste and control to avoid most excesses, though he and Brach are presumptuous enough to offer us some ursine dream sequences that are a rip in the film's texture.

Variety (October 26, 1988)

Chapter 5

Jack London

The cards were stacked against Jack London from his birth as the illegitimate son of W. H. Chaney, an itinerant Irish astrologer, and Flora Wellman, the black sheep of a wealthy family in Ohio. She left home at age 25 and never looked back. In Seattle she met Chaney and lived with him for a year (1874–75) in San Francisco, during which time Jack was conceived.

In 1876 Flora, shortly after an attempted suicide, married John London, a widower with two daughters. The Londons lived at the poverty level, working at one thing and another. Jack had little childhood compared with other boys his age. Delivering newspapers, working on ice wagons and in bowling alleys, and laboring in canneries and jute mills — at ten cents an hour for a ten-hour day — gave Jack an intimate sympathy with working-class life and a permanent distaste for its drudgery.

At an early age Jack developed an insatiable appetite for reading and he spent many an hour devouring books borrowed from the Oakland Public Library.

At age 16 Jack was an oyster pirate and longshoreman in the San Francisco area, and at 17 was a seaman on a sealing vessel. When gold was discovered in Alaska in 1876 Jack went to the Klondike hoping to find gold so that he might help his mother and stepfather financially. He found no gold and returned home penniless but with experiences that enabled him to write the classic *The Call of the Wild* (1903), which initially sold 1.5 million copies. London received $750 for the story. It was first filmed in 1908, followed by later versions in 1935, 1973, 1976, and 1993. Other books or short stories were written based on his experiences in the North country. He helped to establish virtually an automonous subdivision of the western genre, and with stirring tales made himself the Bret Harte of the Alaskan gold fields.

Recognition of London both in the United States and Europe followed closely upon the start of his writing career; and the continued appeal of his stories nourished a rapid growth of reader interest. Both *The Call of the Wild* and *The Sea Wolf* became bestsellers. To date *The Sea Wolf* has been filmed eight times.

Charles Bickford, Alan Bridge and Marc Lawrence in *Romance of the Redwoods* (Columbia, 1939).

By 1913 London was credited as the highest-paid, best known, and most popular writer in the world. Of London's 51 titles, all but four have been translated into at least one and usually many of 58 different languages. The most widely translated title is *The Call of the Wild*, followed by *White Fang, Martin Eden, The Sea Wolf, The Iron Heel, Smoke Ballew, Before Adam, Burning Daylight*, and *John Barleycorn*.

London was especially popular in Russia because of his socialistic convictions.

Overwork, financial difficulties, and heavy drinking caused his literary output to deteriorate in the last year or two of his life, and London committed suicide on November 20, 1916. To date, 65 films have been made based on London stories, and there is renewed interest in his books.

Jack London's most successful books are *The Son of the Wolf*, 1900; *The God of His Fathers*, 1901; *Children of the Frost*, 1902; *The Call of the Wild*, 1903; *The Kempton-Wace Letters*, 1903; *The People of the Abyss*, 1903; *The Sea Wolf*, 1904; *War of the Classes*, 1905; *The Game*, 1905; *White Fang*, 1906; *Before Adam*, 1906; *The Road*, 1907; *The Iron Heel*, 1908; *Martin Eden*, 1909; *Burning Daylight*, 1910; *The Cruise of the Snark*, 1911; *Smoke Bellew*, 1912; *John Barleycorn*,

1913; *The Night-Born*, 1913; *The Valley of the Moon*, 1913; *Mutiny of the Elsinore*, 1914; and *The Star Rover*, 1915.

Other London works include *A Daughter of the Snows* 1902; *The Faith of Men, and Other Stories*, 1904; *Moon-Face, and Other Stories*, 1906; *Love of Life, and Other Stories*, 1906; *Lost Face*, 1910; *When God Laughs, and Other Stories*, 1911; *Adventure*, 1911; *South Sea Tales*, 1911; *The Strength of the Strong*, 1911; *The House of Pride, and Other Stories*, 1912; *The Abysmal Brute*, 1913; *The Little Lady of the Big House*, 1916; *The Human Drift*, 1917; *The Red One*, 1918; *On the Makaloa Mat*, 1919; *Hearts of Three*, 1920; *Dutch Courage, and Other Stories*, 1922; and *The Assassination Bureau Ltd.* (completed by Robert Fish), 1963.

Films Based on the Writings of Jack London

For Love of Gold (Biograph, August 1908) 1/2 reel; Harry Salter, Charles Gorman, Charles Inslee; D/SP: D. W. Griffith; S: "Just Meat."

Call of the Wild (Biograph, October 1908) 1 reel; Florence Lawrence, Charles Gorman, Mack Sennett, Charles Inslee; D/SP: D. W. Griffith. **Synopsis:** This is the first filming of London's classic about a man and the Saint Bernard dog that he befriends.

Jack London's Adventures in the South Sea Islands (1913) Approximately 120 mins.; Jack London. **Synopsis:** This is a documentary filmed on one of London's voyages. Martin Johnson was responsible for the photography. Locales included New Zealand and the Fiji Islands.

Two Men of the Desert (Biograph, August 1913) 1 reel; Harry Carey, Blanche Sweet, Henry B. Walthall, Walter Miller, Alfred Paget, Jennie Lee, Donald Crisp, Mae Marsh, Marshall Neilan, Charles Hill Mailes; D/SP: D. W. Griffith.

The Sea Wolf (Bosworth, December 1913) 2 reels; Hobart Bosworth (Wolf Larsen), Herbert Rawlinson (Humphrey Van Weyden), Viola Barry (Maude Brewster), J. Charles Haydon (Mudridge), Jack London (A Sailor), Gordon Sackville (Johnson), Joe Ray; D: Hobart

Bosworth. **Synopsis:** Humphrey Van Weyden is picked up by the crew of a schooner named *Ghost* after his ferry has collided with another vessel in the San Francisco Bay. Wolf Larsen is the captain of *Ghost* and Van Weyden finds him to be a very cruel captain. Nevertheless, the two hit it off fairly well and Larsen makes Van Weyden the first mate. Later, the ship rescues a number of shipwrecked passengers, among whom is Maude Brewster. Humphrey immediately forms an attachment to her. Wolf Larsen's intentions toward her are quite dishonorable. When he attacks Maude he is stricken with one of his bouts of blindness. Humphrey and Maude seize the opportunity to escape to a nearby island. Later, the crew abandons the ship, leaving Wolf on board alone. When his sight returns he finds Humphrey and engages in a fight with him. Humphrey is the victor and he and Maude sail for home, leaving a dead Larsen behind.

Review:

The film is not an unqualified success. Even such filmable stories as those of London cannot be allowed to go upon the screen undramatized.

The process of adaptation must be a process of elimination, too, and the tendency must be toward simplifying and strengthening the action. In this respect the film falls short. Five reels would have been better than seven. Bosworth, as the Sea Wolf, found his footing at the first great dramatic moment and never lost it afterwards. It was his acting which was chiefly responsible for the sharp revival of interest toward the end of the story just as the action was beginning to drag.

The motion picture art is in a fair way to profit by further screen adaptations of the London series. I predict that in his second venture Mr. Bosworth will touch perfection. He has the ability and he has the ambition which is justified and useful only as it is supported by ability. There is a lavish expenditure of money in the production, an item that accounts for much when the money is expended judiciously, as it was in the present case. Every friend of the good motion picture will hail the present and the future of Mr. Bosworth with sincere joy.

The support was fair. Viola Barry, the only woman in the story, is conscientious in her work. It would have been better if she had not emerged from the shipwreck with her makeup in a flourishing condition.

W. Stephen Bush, *The Moving Picture World* 18, no. 5 (November 1, 1913):480

John Barleycorn (Bosworth, July 1914) 6 reels; Elmer Clifton (Jack, 3rd period), Antrim Short (Jack, 2nd period), Matty Roubert (Jack, 1st period), Viola Barry (Haydee), Hobart Bosworth (Scratch Nelson), Joe Ray; D: Hobart Bosworth; SP: Hettie Gray Baker. **Synopsis:** Aboard his yacht *The Roamer,* author Jack London recounts his lifelong struggle with alcoholism. At age 5, as a California farmboy, Jack drinks some beer from an overflowing pail

intended for his father and falls down drunk. Several times during his youth he has encounters with drunkeness, while a San Francisco newsboy, an oyster pirate, an explorer, and a seal hunter. Eventually, Jack meets and marries Haydee, who helps him overcome his addiction.

The Valley of the Moon (Bosworth, June 22, 1914) 6 reels; Jack Conway (Billy Roberts), Myrtle Stedman (Saxon, His Wife), Ernest Garcia (Bart), Rhea Haines (Mary, His Wife), Joseph Ray (Teamster), Hobart Bosworth; D: Hobart Bosworth; SP: Hettie Gray Baker. **Synopsis:** Billy Robert, a boxer and teamster, meets Saxon, a laundress, at a picnic. They marry, but shortly afterward a strike occurs among the teamsters and strike breakers are brought in. During a riot Billy's best friend is killed, then Saxon has a miscarriage and Billy begins to drink. After further disappointments and failures, Billy and Saxon buy a farm in Sonora with Billy's winnings from a boxing match.

Martin Eden (Bosworth/W. W. Hodkinson, August 16, 1914) 6 reels; Lawrence Peyton (Martin Eden), Viola Barry (Ruth Morse), Herbert Rawlinson (Arthur Morse), Rhea Haines (Lizzie Connolly), Ann Ivers (Maria Silva), Ray Myers (Russ Brissenden), Elmer Clifton (Cub Reporter), Hobart Bosworth, Myrtle Stedman; D/SP: Hobart Bosworth. **Synopsis:** Martin Eden becomes tired of life in the South Seas and returns to Oakland, California. He saves Arthur Morse from a gang of ruffians and the two become friends. Eden falls in love with Arthur's sister. Embarrassed by his lack of education, he attempts to educate himself but runs out of money and returns to sea. He begins writing while at sea but publishers consistently turn down his manuscripts. Because of his friendship with an anarchist poet, he becomes a socialist. When Arthur hears of this, he convinces his sister to break with Martin. Martin eventually becomes successful but he avoids forming friendships and cares only for his widowed Italian landlady, whom he helps financially. He eventually becomes so despondent that he drowns himself.

Burning Daylight: The Adventures of "Burning Daylight" in Alaska (Bosworth/Paramount, September 14, 1914) 5 reels; Hobart Bosworth (Harnish/Burning Daylight), Rhea Haines (Nell), J. Charles Haydon (Elijah), Elmer Clifton (Charley Bates), Jack Conway (Joe Hines); D: Hobart Bosworth; SP: Hettie Gray Baker; S: *Burning Daylight*. Synopsis: Elam Harnish, called Burning Daylight, is a leader among the men of Circle City, Alaska, before the gold rush. Nell, a dance hall girl, loves Harnish but he has never demonstrated anything but friendship for her. When gold is found and the gold rush is on, Harnish stakes many claims and eventually accumulates $11 million. He leaves Alaska for San Francisco, not knowing that Nell has committed suicide because he has left.

Burning Daylight: The Adventures of "Burning Daylight" in Civilization (Bosworth/Paramount, October 3, 1914) 5 reels; Hobart Bosworth (Harnish/Burning Daylight), Myrtle Stedman (Dede Mason), Rhea Haines, J. Charles Haydon, Elmer Clifton, Jack Conway; D: Hobart Bosworth; SP: Hettie Gray Baker; S: *Burning Daylight*. Synopsis: Elam Harnish returns to San Francisco with the fortune he has made in Alaska. He nearly loses his money to crooked financiers but emerges from the experience a wiser man and a formidable competitor in the financial world. He becomes cruel and obsessed with pleasure. He falls in love with his secretary, Dede Mason. Ultimately, Harnish is forced to choose between his fortune and Dede. Dede wins out and Harnish returns to Alaska with her.

The Chechako (Bosworth/Paramount, 1914?) 5 reels; Jack Conway (Smoke Bellew), Myrtle Stedman (Joy Gastelf), Gordon Sackfield (Big Olaf), Joe Ray (Shorty); D: Hobart Bosworth; SP: Hettie Gray Baker; S: *Smoke Bellew*. Synopsis: Kit "Smoke" Bellew, a journalist, goes with his uncle to Alaska prospecting. There he toughens up and decides to remain in Alaska when his uncle departs for San Francisco. Bellew and his partner lose out on a gold stampede when Joy Gastelf steers them the wrong way in order to give the oldtimers a chance to stake their claims first. Later, Joy helps Bellew to obtain the rights to a $0.5 million claim. After many adventures Bellew is captured by Indians but escapes with the help of the chief's daughter, who dies during the escape. Bellew returns to Dawson and Joy, whom he loves. Note: According to the AFI *Catalog of Features* for the years 1911–20, it is doubtful if this film was ever released. Paramount pulled it from its release schedule at the last minute. This was at the end of 1914. Universal was approached about picking up the film but declined. Paramount may or may not have released it at some point.

An Odyssey of the North (Bosworth, 1914) Hobart Bosworth (Naass), Rhea Haines (Unga), Gordon Sackfield (Axel Gunderson); D: Hobart Bosworth; SP: Hettie Gray Baker. Synopsis: On the day of Naass's wedding to Unga, she is abducted by Axel Gunderson. Naass follows Gunderson's ship to the seal-hunting grounds, but there he is captured by Russians and sent to Siberia for several years of hard labor. When he is released, he resumes his search for Unga and Gunderson, only to find that they are happily married. Unga does not recognize her former lover. Angry, Naass plans a cruel revenge. Using a map of the Alaskan gold fields, Naass talks Axel and Unga into traveling with him into the interior of Alaska, where he steals their food and kills their dogs. He watches with pleasure as Gunderson starves to death and then he reveals himself to Unga. Unga refuses to leave the body of her husband and becomes very angry with Naass, who, downhearted, returns to civilization.

It's No Laughing Matter (Bosworth/Paramount, January 14, 1915) 5 reels; Maclyn Arbuckle (Hi Judd), Adele Farrington (Widow Wilkins), Myrtle Stedman (Bess Judd), Herbert Standing (Townsman), Charles Marriott (Jim Skinner), Frank Elliott (Sam), Cora Drew (Mrs. Judd); D/SP: Lois Weber. **Synopsis:** Hi Judd, postmaster and philosopher, is the sunshine of the village, a veritable doctor of happiness. His right arm is what the little world of the village leans on; the kind words he scatters reap their harvest of love for the old postmaster; and the verses he writes (sometimes when he should be working) proclaim him the wit of the village. But because of the verse writing, Mrs. Judd is often discouraged. Hi confesses to his daughter, Bess, that he often stands in awe of Mrs. Judd when she catches him writing, with the woodpile untouched and the chores not done. But Bess consoles him, and when Hi is not around she makes a collection of the verses and sends them to a great newspaper.

Theirs is a peaceful life that must have its dramatic climax and it descends upon them all at once. Jim Skinner, an unscrupulous, grasping old miser, holds the mortgage on the house and also has designs upon Hi's position as postmaster. Then the bank fails. The mortgage is due. Heartbroken, Hi and family are preparing to leave the little home when word comes from the newspaper: "Verses accepted, send them as fast as you can write them." Hi, with his $500 check from the newspaper pays off the mortgage, and other family problems resolve themselves.
Review:

There can never be an oversupply of such pictures as this. *It's No Laughing Matter* has an abundance of clean kindly humor and a wealth of wholesome pathos. It is refreshingly free from the conventional b'gosh melodrama.

The Moving Picture World, January 30, 1915).

Note: Though at least one source has credited this story to London, it is doubtful that he wrote it.

Creation Can Be Bought (Nye Dlya Deneg Radivshisya) (Neptune Studios/Antik Russia, April 1918) Vladimir Mayakovsky, David Burliuk, Vasili Kamensky, Margarito Kibalchich; S: *Martin Eden.*

The Iron Heel (Zhelaznaya Pyata) (Gos-Kino/VCKO, November 7, 1919); Leonid Leonidov, A. Shakhalov, N. Znamensky, Olga Preobrazhenskays; D: Vladimir Gardin.

Burning Daylight (Metro, May 1920) 6 reels; Mitchell Lewis (Burning Daylight), Helen Ferguson (Dora), William V. Mong (Necessity), Alfred Allen (Nathaniel Letton), Edward Jobson (Dowsett), Robert Bolder (Guggenhammer), Gertrude Astor (Lucille), Arthur E. Carew (Arthur Howison), Louis Morrison (Dan McDonald), Newton Hall (Jack), Aaron Edwards (Crandall); D: Edward Sloman; SP: Albert Shelby Le Vino. **Synopsis:** The central figure in *Burning Daylight* is a miner known to his associates by this name. He is the only living thing in the Alaskan mining town of Garaguk, according to the girls in the dance hall. One evening he comes to the Tivoli, a hotel kept by Dan MacDonald, with rare pickings of gold, which discloses the fact that he has struck it rich.

In the saloon that night is the agent of one of the biggest mining syndicates of New York, who tries to overhear what Daylight is telling his companions. For his trouble he is thrown outside, but not soon enough to prevent his carrying the story back to his employers. Immediately, the head of the syndicate takes the trail for Alaska. Daylight sells his claim and right of way for $6 million and accepts an invitation to visit New York, where later he opens an office, falls for the wiles of the schemers who bought out his Alaskan property, and loses all he has made. When he discovers the plot, he forces Letton to return the money at gunpoint. He then returns to Alaska with Dora, his friend Necessity's daughter whom he loves.

Note: Generally speaking, the production might have been developed in a more masterly fashion; for, while the story contains good situations, the screen version allows trivial details to interfere with a stronger appeal. Mitchell Lewis proves himself well suited to the role of Burning Daylight. His impersonation of the rugged character carries conviction.

The Sea Wolf (Famous Players–Lasky/Paramount, May 16, 1920) 7 reels; Noah Beery (Wolf Larsen (the Sea Wolf), James Gordon ("Death" Larsen), Raymond Hatton (Thomas Magridge), Eddie Sutherland (George Leach), Walter Long ("Black" Harris), Fred Huntley (Old Man Johnson), Mabel Juliene Scott (Maude Brewster), Tom Forman (Humphrey Van Weyden); D: George Medford; SP: Will M. Richey. **Synopsis:** Humphrey Van Weyden and Maude Brewster are rescued by the crew of the *Ghost* when their ferryboat collides with the larger ship. They ask the captain, Wolf Larsen, to put them ashore, but he refuses because he is short-handed and also because he is attracted to Maude. Humphrey is put to work as a cabin boy. Maude has refused to marry Humphrey because she considered him a weakling, whereas Wolf Larsen is just the opposite. As the *Ghost* nears its destination, Wolf attacks Maude with intentions of raping her. However, he is seized by a terrible headache, temporarily blinding him. Maude and Humphrey use the opportunity to escape in a small boat over to an island. Later, the *Ghost* drifts in apparently deserted. They go aboard and find only Wolf, who is still blind. With his last spark of life Wolf attempts to attack Humphrey but is seized by another headache and dies. Maude comes to realize that Humphrey is not a whimp and that she loves him.

The Mutiny of the Elsinore (Metro Pictures, September 10, 1920) 6 reels; Mitchell Lewis (John Pike), Helen Ferguson (Margaret West), Noah Beery (Andreas Mellaire), Casson Ferguson (Dick Somers), William V. Mong (Snoop Jenkins, the "Rat"), Norval MacGregor (Captain Nathaniel Somers), Sidney D'Albrook (Crimp Sherman), J. P. Lockney (Jason West), Patch (a dog) (Himself); D: Edward Sloman; SP: Albert Shelby Le Vino. **Synopsis:** When Captain Somers is killed by thugs, his friend, first mate Pike, promises to care for the captain's son Dick. Pike realizes that Dick is a wastrel who has squandered his life seeking pleasure. Pike manages to get Dick aboard the *Elsinore* and sets sail. Mellaire, one of the thugs who killed the captain, is aboard with his pal "the Rat." Margaret West is also on board and is loved by both John Pike and Dick Somers. When a storm comes up, Mellaire and the Rat lead the crew in a mutiny. At first Pike singlehandedly fights the crew, but Dick, who has become a man, jumps in to help him. Mellaire and the Rat are washed overboard. With their leaders gone, the crew give up the fight. Pike, severely wounded, gives command of the ship to Dick, who is in love with Margaret and she with him. Pike gives them his blessing.

The Star Rover (Metro, November 22, 1920) 6 reels; Courtenay Foote (Dr. Hugh Standing), Thelma Percy (Faith Levering), Doc Cannon (Inspector Burns), Dwight Crittenden (District Attorney), Jack Carlyle (Sergeant Andover), Chance Ward (Chance Ward), Marcelle Daley (Maizie), Walter Lewis, Irene Boyle, Eva Gordon; D: Edward Sloman; SP: Albert Shelby Le Vino. **Synopsis:** Dr. Hugh Standing is seated in his box at the theater when a shot rings out from behind the curtain behind him. Killed is political boss Tubbs, seated in the opposite box. Standing is arrested for the murder and taken to police headquarters. Inspector Burns begins to torture Standing in order to extract a confession from him. But instead of extracting the desired confession, the torture sends the soul of Standing, who believes in reincarnation, back over the ages, reliving his former existences. Upon learning of the torture, Faith Levering, Standing's fiancée appeals to the district attorney, who puts an end to the outrage. She then begs that the doctor be tortured once more in hopes that his wandering soul will disclose the murderer. Upon becoming unconscious again, Standing recounts the events of the evening, establishing that Maizie, a chorus girl wronged by Tubbs, was the murderer. The girl confesses, the brutality of Burns is punished, and Standing and Faith are free to live together in happiness.

The Mohican's Daughter (American Releasing, May 7, 1922) 5 reels; Nancy Deaver (Jees Uck), Hazel Washburn (Kitty Shannon), Sazon King (Neil Bonner), William Thompson (Amos Pentley), Jack Newton (Jack Hollis), Paul Panzer (Father La Cloise), Nick Thompson (Chatanna), Mortimer Snow (Nashinta), John Webb Dillon (Halfbreed), Rita Abrams (Inigo); D/SP: S. E. V. Taylor; S: "The Story of Jees Uck." **Synopsis:** Jees Uck, a half-breed maiden is desired by Chatanna, chief of the tribe with which she lives. She defies tribal law by getting medicine from the trading post for the sick child of her friend, Inigo. Nashinta, the medicine man, defends her against the chief. Chatanna kills Nashinta and puts the blame on Jees Uck, who flees into the arms of Neil Bonner, trading post manager, who loves her. Neil finds evidence against the chief, delivers him to the authorities, and marries Jees Uck.

The Son of the Wolf (R-C, June 11, 1922) 5 reels; Wheeler Oakman (Scruff Mackenzie), Edith Roberts (Chook-Ra), Sam Allen (Father Roubeau), Ashley Cooper (Ben Harrington), Fred Kohler (Malemate Kid), Thomas Jefferson (Chief Thing Tinner), Fred Stanton

(The Bear), Arthur Jasmine (The Fox), William Eagle Eye (Shannon); D: Norman Dawn; SP: William Haywood. **Synopsis:** Scruff Mackenzie decides to seek a wife. Later, he meets Father Roubeau and his Indian ward, Chook-Ra, whom Scruff comes to love. However, the priest forbids their marriage until her father, Chief Tinner, arrives. When Scruff goes to a nearby town to buy gifts for Chook-Ra he becomes infatuated with a dance hall girl. Chook-Ra determines to win him back. She takes some dancing lessons and surprises him at the local ball. Chief Tinner arrives and forces Chook-Ra to return to her own people. Scruff follows and after much bargaining wins Chook-Ra, but the chief decrees that he must first fight the Bear, who also is her suitor. The latter is killed when they fight and Scruff and Chook-Ra depart for civilization.

The Abysmal Brute (Universal-Jewel, April 15, 1923) 8 reels; Reginald Denny (Pat Glendon, Jr.), Mabel Juliene Scott (Maude Sangster), Charles French (Pat Glendon, Sr.), Hayden Stevenson (Sam Stubener), David Torrence (Mortimer Sangster), George Stewart (Wilfred Sangster), Buddy Messinger (Buddy Sangster), Crauford Kent (Deane Warner), Dorothea Wolbert (Mrs. McTavish), Julia Brown (Violet McTavish), Harry Mann (Abe Levinsky), Kid Wagner (Battling Levinsky), Jack Herrick (Rough House Ratigan), Ione Haisman (Gwendolyn), Nell Craig (Daisy Emerson), Will B. Walling (Farrell); D: Hobart Henley; SP: A. P. Younger. **Synopsis:** Reared in the California mountains by his father, an ex-prizefighter, Pat Glendon, Jr., shows great strength and skill but is terribly shy of women. When he finally enters competition in San Francisco he achieves success and the title "the Abysmal Brute." One day he rescues a man from drowning, meets socialite Maude Sangster as a result, and falls in love with her at first sight. He does not tell her about his profession. When Maude does learn that he is a fighter she repudiates him, but Pat is persistent and eventually wins her from his rival.

The Call of the Wild (Hal Roach/ Pathe, September 23, 1923) 7 reels; Jack Mulhall (John Thornton), Buck (a dog) (Himself), Walter Long (Hagin), Sidney D'Allbrook (Charles), Laura Roening (Mercedes), Frank Butler (Hal); D/SP: Fred Jackman. Synopsis: Buck, a young St. Bernard, is stolen from his home in England and shipped to Canada where he is used on a dogsled. He is treated badly until John Thornton, a prospector, befriends him. When Thornton's life is at stake Buck rescues him. Thereafter, he settles down to life with Thornton.

Adventure (Paramount, April 27, 1929) 9 reels; Tom Moore (David Shelton), Pauline Starke (Joan Lackland), Wallace Beery (Morgan), Raymond Hatton (Raff), Walter McGrail (Tudor), Duke Kahanamoka (Noah Noa), James Spencer (Adam), Noble Johnson (Goomony); D: Victor Fleming; SP: A. P. Younger, L. G. Rigby. Synopsis: David Shelton owns a plantation in the Solomon Islands. He comes down with blackwater fever, as do many of his field hands. Joan Lackland arrives in the islands by schooner and with her crew protects David from attack by natives under the leadership of Goomony. Joan nurses David back to health and goes into partnership with him, protecting his mortgaged property from two crooked moneylenders. The moneylenders incite the natives to revolt and David's plantation is set on fire. Joan is kidnapped and taken aboard the moneylenders' schooner. David saves her and the two realize they are in love with each other.

White Fang (R-C/FBO, May 24, 1925) 6 reels; Theodore von Eltz (Weedon Scott), Ruth Dwyer (Mollie Holland), Matthew Betz (Frank Wilde), Walter Perry (Joe Holland), Charles Murray (Judson Black), Tom O'Brien (Matt), Steve Murphy ("Beauty" Smith), John Burch (Bill Morry), Margaret McWade (Mrs. Black), Silver (a wolf) (Himself), Strongheart (a dog) (White Fang); D: Laurence Trimble; SP: Jane Murfin. Synopsis: Weedon Scott is saved from a pack of wolves by his friend Joe Holland. Frank Wilde, an executive engaged to Holland's daughter Mollie, buys White Fang, a vicious dog from an Indian and matches him with a bulldog in a pit fight. Scott saves White Fang and tames him. After Mollie marries Wilde, she discovers that he is robbing the mine of which Holland is superintendant. She tells Scott about it but Wilde escapes, killing Holland. Orphaned Mollie goes to the home of Judson Black, owner of the mine. Wilde attempts to kidnap her but is killed by White Fang. Scott and Mollie eventually find happiness together.

Morganson's Finish (Tiffany, May 1926) 7 reels; Anita Stewart (Barbara Wesley), Johnnie Walker (Dick Gilbert), Mahlon Hamilton (Dan Morganson), Victor Potel (Ole Jensen), Crauford Kent (G. T. Williams), Rose Topley (Doctor's Wife); D: Fred Windemere. Synopsis: Dick Gilbert and Barbara Wesley become engaged when Dick receives a job promotion. Morganson, a jealous rival, convinces the general manager that Dick should not receive the promotion, and in despair Dick resigns his position. At a party given by Morganson, Dick hears a discussion of the recent gold strike in Alaska and decides to go there. Morganson accompanies him to the gold country, and after they make a strike Morganson causes a snowslide to bury Dick. Escaping, Dick discovers an even larger gold deposit; and Ole, their hired man, tells him of Morganson's treachery. Dick and Morganson fight and Morganson is knocked off a cliff and dies. Dick marries Barbara, who has followed them to Alaska.

By the Law (First Studio of Goskino, Moscow, December 3, 1926) Alexandra Khoklova, Sergei Komoarov, Vladimir Fogel, Pyott Galadzhev, Porfifi

Podobed; D: Lev Kuleshov; S: "The Unexpected." Note: No other information is available on this film.

The Haunted Ship (Tiffany-Stahl, December 1, 1927) 5 reels; Dorothy Sebastian (Goldie Kane), Montagu Love (Captain Simon Gant), Tom Santschi (Glenister, First Mate), Ray Halor (Danny Gant), Pat Harmon (Mate), Alice Lake (Martha Gant), Bud Duncan (Dinty), Blue Washington (Mose), Sojin (Bombay Charlie), Andree Tourneur (Goldie's Companion), William Lowery; D: Forrest K. Sheldon; SP: Forrest K. Sheldon, Ben Ali Newman; S: "The White and the Yellow." Synopsis: Believing that his wife, Martha, has been unfaithful to him, Captain Gant puts her adrift in a small boat. He also believes their son Danny has been fathered by first mate Glenister. Danny is put adrift, along with his mother, and Glenister is put in chains. Captain Gant tortures him daily trying to extract a confession from him. Years later Gant shanghais Goldie Kane, a chorus girl, and a boy he thinks is Danny. He puts Danny in a cell with Glenister. Later, the ship's crew mutinies and the ship explodes. All except Gant and Glenister escape.

The Devil's Skipper (Tiffany-Stahl, February 1, 1928) 6 reels; Belle Bennett (The Devil's Skipper), Montagu Love (First Mate), Gino Corrado (Philip La Farge), Mary McAllister (Marie La Farge), Cullen Landis (John Dubray), G. Raymond Nye (Nick, the Greek), Pat Hartford (Captain McKenna), Adolph Milar (Mate Cornish), Caroline Snowden (Slave), Stepin Fetchit (Slave); D: John G. Adolfi; SP: John Francis Natteford; S: "Demetrious Contos." Synopsis: The female skipper of a slave ship finds out that the man who has inflicted suffering on her is La Farge, a Louisiana planter. She lures him on board with the pretext of selling him slaves. In her cabin she tells him the story of a woman whose husband shanghais her to a hell ship and has her child killed in her presence. She

tortures La Farge and turns over to her drunken crew the young girl he has brought on board with him. La Farge tells the Devil's Skipper that the girl is her daughter. Hearing this, she rescues the girl from a drunken Greek crewman, but is mortally wounded by him. The Devil's Skipper manages to have her daughter and husband put ashore safely and then dies in the arms of her loyal first mate, who vows to take revenge on Nick, the Greek.

Burning Daylight (First National, March 11, 1928) 7 reels; Milton Sills (Burning Daylight), Doris Keyon (The Virgin), Arthur Stone (French Louie), Big Boy Williams (English Harry), Lawford Davidson (Morton), Jane Winton (Martha Fairbee), Stuart Holmes (Blake), Edmund Breese (John Dossett), Howard Truesdale (Letton), Frank Hagner (Johnson), Harry Northrup (The Stranger); D: Charles J. Brabin; SP: Louis Stevens. Synopsis: Burning Daylight makes a fortune in Alaskan real estate. However, he loses it all to a group of crooked investment sharks. He forces them at gunpoint to return his millions, pays off all his debts, and returns to Alaska with the girl he loves.

Stormy Waters (Tiffany-Stahl, June 1, 1928) 6 reels; Eve Southern (Lola), Malcom McGregory (David Steele), Roy Stewart (Captain Angus Steele), Shirley Palmer (Mary), Olin Francis (Bos'n), Norbett Myles (First Mate), Bert Apling (Second Mate); D: Edgar Lewis; SP: Harry Dittmar; S: "The Yellow Handkerchief." Synopsis: Angus Steele is captain of a ship on which his younger brother is a crewman. David has a fiancée, but he falls for Lola, a barfly, while in Buenos Aires. Lola tells Angus that she and David are married, and he allows her to return to New York with the brothers. Lola becomes bored with housekeeping and plans to run away with a boxer, but Angus prevents it. He takes her and David back to Buenos Aires, sets Lola adrift in a small boat near the harbor, and brings David back to his fiancée in New York.

Prowlers of the Sea (Tiffany-Stahl, June 20, 1928) 6 reels; Carmel Myers (Mercedes), Ricardo Cortez (Carlos De Neve), George Faucett (General Hernandez), Gino Corrado (The Skipper), Frank Lackteen (Ramon Sanchez), Frank Leigh (Felipe), Shirley Palmer (Cuban Maid); D: John G. Adolfi; SP: John Francis Natteford; S: "The Siege of the *Lancashire Queen*." **Synopsis:** Cuban authorities appoint Carlos De Neve to captain the coastguard, believing that he may be able to stop the smuggling of guns to revolutionaries. Ramon Sanchez, knowing that De Neve will not accept a bribe, has Mercedes, a friend, utilize her charms to keep De Neve occupied on the night when guns are to be smuggled in. However, Mercedes falls in love with De Neve and he with her. The smugglers are caught and Carlos and Mercedes plan marriage.

Tropical Nights (Tiffany-Stahl, December 10, 1928) 6 reels; Patsy Ruth Miller (Mary Hale), Malcolm McGregor (Jim), Ray Hallor (Harvey), Wallace McDonald (Stavnow), Russell Simpson (Singapore Joe); D: Elmer Clifton; SP: Bennett Cohen; S: "A Raid on the Oyster Pirates." **Synopsis:** Harvey and his brother Jim operate a pearl-diving barge in partnership with Stavnow. Harvey makes a pass at Mary, a stranded opera singer working in a waterfront dive. She knocks him out and Stavnow, a witness to the event, steals Jim's pearls from his person before he regains consciousness, at which time Stavnow kills Harvey with a stone jar. Mary, who believes herself responsible, takes refuge with Jim, and they fall in love. Later Stavnow drowns when his foot is caught in a giant clam, but he manages to confess to the killing before he dies. In the end Jim and Mary are married.

Smoke Bellew (Big 4/First Division, January 25, 1929) 7 reels; Conway Tearle (Kit "Smoke" Bellew), Barbara Bedford (Joy Gastrell), Mark Hamilton (Shorty), Alphonse Ethier (Harry Sprague), William Scott (Stine), J. P. Lockney, Alaska Jack; D: Scott Dunlap; SP: Fred Myton. **Synopsis:** During the gold rush of 1897 there is great rivalry between the "Sourdoughs," who were oldtimers, and the "Chekakos," the newcomers. A girl and her father stake their claim through the aid of Smoke Bellew, who has come to the Klondike to forget his past. Romance enters his life when he meets the girl whose loyalty and heroism have brought her father and her through many hardships.

The Sea Wolf (20th Century–Fox, September 30, 1930) 90 mins.; Milton Sills (Wolf Larsen), Jane Keith (Lorna Marsh), Raymond Hackett (Allen Rank), Mitchell Harris (Death Larsen), Nat Pendleton (Smoke), John Rogers (Mugridge), Harold Kinney (Leach), Harry Tenbrook (Johnson), Sam Allen (Nelson); D: Alfred Santell; SP: Ralph Block. **Synopsis:** Wolf Larsen, captain of the hell ship *Ghost*, attempts to attract Lorna Marsh, a prostitute. At first she turns down the offer on Larsen's sealer, but she comes aboard when Allen Rand, with whom she is infatuated, is shanghaied along with two or three sailors taken from the crew of a steamer belonging to Wolf's brother, "Death." At sea Larsen promotes Rand to first mate for saving his life when the crew makes an attempt at mutiny.

After Wolf has made a particularly large catch of seals off the Aleutians, he tries to seduce Lorna forcibly. Rand tries to interfere but is knocked out by Wolf. Larsen is about to rape Lorna when "Death" overtakes his ship. Lorna and Rand escape in a sealing boat while Mugridge avenges a previous mutilation at the hands of Wolf by blinding him with a hot poker. After days adrift Lorna and Rand sight the *Ghost*, ravaged by "Death." The crew is gone but Wolf is still alive but knows he is dying, and so he gives the couple directions to the nearest land.

Call of the Wild (20th Century–Fox, April 30, 1935) 91 mins.; Clark Gable (Jack Thornton), Loretta Young (Clair Blake), Jack Oakie (Shorty Hoolihan), Frank Conroy (John Blake), Reginald Owen (Smith), Sidney Toler (Groggin), Katherine DeMille (Marie), Charles Stevens (Francois), Lalo Encinas (Kali), James Burke (Ole), John T. Murray, Bob Perry, Marie Wells, Sid Grauman, Herman Bing, Wade Boteler, John Ince, Syd Saylor, Joan Woodbury, Arthur Aylesworth, Buck (a dog), Duke Green; D: David Butler; SP: Gene Fowler, Lionard Praskins. **Synopsis:** Thornton and Hoolihan rescue Miss Blake, whose husband has apparently lost his way and perished; their finding of a goldmine; their encounter with the villainous Smith; the return of Miss Blake's husband, lending a bittersweet finish to the romance, are the highlights of the story's human element. The dog gets his share in the training scenes and a vicious fight with another member of the pack, as well as in the 1,000-pound haul and the mating sequences.
Review:

The lion-hearted dog that was Jack London's creation as the leading character of *Call of the Wild* emerges now as a stooge for a rather conventional pair of human lovebirds. Changes have made the canine classic hardly recognizable, but they have not done any damage for this *Call of the Wild* as rewritten and produced as a talker is strong entertainment. Both on merit and cast names it will do business.

Variety (August 21, 1935).

White Fang (20th Century–Fox, July 1936) 70 mins.; Michael Whalen (Weedon Scott), Jean Muir (Sylvia Burgess), Slim Summerville (Slats), Charles Winninger (Doc McFane), John Carradine (Beauty Smith), Jane Darwell (Maud Mahoney), Thomas Beck (Hal Burgess), Joseph Herrick (Kobi),

George Ducount (Francois), Marie Chorie (Nomi), Lightning (a dog) (White Fang); D: David Butler; SP: Gene Fowler, Hal Lang, S. G. Duncan. **Synopsis:** White Fang is bought from an Indian and matched with a bulldog in a fight to the finish. Weedon Scott saves White Fang and a strong bond grows between them.

Les Mutinerie De L'Elsineur (French production, 1936) D: Pierre Chenel; S: "The Mutiny of the *Elsinore.*" Note: No other information is available on this film.

The Mutiny of the Elsinore (English production, 1937) Paul Lucas; D: Roy Lockwood; S: Jack London. Note: No other information is available on this film.

Conflict (Universal, 1937) 60 mins.; John Wayne (Pat), Jean Rogers (Maude), Tommy Bupp (Tommy), Eddie Borden (Spider), Frank Sheridan (Sam), Ward Bond (Carrigan), Margaret Mann (Ma Blake), Harry Wood (Kelly), Bryant Washburn (City Editor), Frank Hagney (Nalone); D: David Howard; SP: Charles Logue, Walter Wrems; S: *The Abysmal Brute*; P: Trem Carr. **Synopsis:** Pat is a crooked pugilist who becomes a law-abiding citizen after meeting orphaned Carrigan. Maude is Pat's curvaceous trainer who exerts a good influence on him.

Romance of the Redwoods (Columbia, March 30, 1939) 61 mins.; Charles Bickford (Steve), Jean Parker (June), Alan Bridge (Whittaker), Gordon Oliver (Malone), Anne Shoemaker (Mother), Lloyd Hughes (Carter), Pat O'Malley (Yerkes), Marc Lawrence (Joe), Earl Gunn (Socko), Don Beddoe (Forbes), Erville Alderson (Jackson), Lee Prather (Judge Handley); D: Charles Vidor; SP: Michael L. Simmons. **Synopsis:** Steve is a hairy-chested lumberjack in love with June, who has grown up in the timberlands. Malone is a city gent who blows into camp and bowls her over with a few choice lines from Edgar Guest. Steve is one of the strong, silent types and just watches as Malone, the city smoothie, wins June. However, Malone is a gentleman, even if he wears store-made clothes. Malone, who works alone with Steve on the saw, is hurled to his death in the blade. It appears that Steve was responsible, having a motive of jealousy. This leads to a scandalous trial, and a forest fire climax.

Torture Ship (PRC, October 22, 1939) 62 mins.; Lyle Talbot (Lieutenant Bob Bennett), Irving Pichel (Dr. Herbert Stander), Jacqueline Wells/Julie Bishop (Joan Mariel), Sheila Bromley (Mary Slaviah), Russell Hopton (Harry), Anthony Averill (Dirk), Eddie Holden (Ole Olson), Wheeler Oakman (Ritter), Leander de Cordova (Ezra), Dmitri Alexis (Murano), Skelton Knaggs (Jesse), Adis Kuznetzoff (Krantz), Stanley Blystone (Briggs), William Chapman (Bill), Fred Walton (Fred); D: Victor Halperin; SP: George Wallace Sayre, Harvey Huntley; S: "A Thousand Deaths." **Synopsis:** Doctor Stander is convinced that glandular troubles are at the root of all criminality. Unable to experiment on land, he charters a yacht, fits it up with an operating room, helps eight killers to escape from jail, and takes them on a sea voyage. The assorted group of tough guys resent being made guinea pigs and the doctor is killed in one of the continuous scuffles to take over the ship, which is commanded by Bob Bennett. Joan Mariel is a suspected killer, but turns out to be innocent — which Bennett knew all the time — when the glandular operation makes her former boss, Mary Slavish, repent and tell all.
Review:

Quickie action thriller that misses fire all the way on its possibilities, *Torture Ship* will find screen space only at the foot of twin bills in two-gun palaces patronized by trade that's not too fussy about its fare as long as it

holds hope of a thrill. Couple of names are included in the cast, but they'll hardly mean much at the b.o. Lyle Talbot, who handles what love interest there is, gets top billing over Irving Pichel, although it is the latter who really holds the prime role. Jacqueline Wells is Talbot's heart interest. Actually, whatever selling is done on this — and it does offer possibilities — must be based on the name of Jack London, whose story, "A Thousand Deaths," suggested *Torture Ship*.

Source unknown.

Queen of the Yukon (Monogram, August 26, 1940) 74 mins.; Charles Bickford (Ace), Irene Rich (Sadie), Melvin Long (Thorne), George Cleveland (Grub), Guy Usher (Stake), June Carlson (Helen), Dave O'Brien (Bob), Tristram Coffin (Carson); D: Phil Rosen; SP: Joseph West. **Synopsis:** Sadie rules the Yukon and runs a riverboat, which eventually she has to sell in order to be reunited with her daughter Helen. Ace has an eye for Sadie and looks after her welfare.

Sign of the Wolf (Monogram, 1941) 68 mins.; Michalen Whalen (Rod Freeman), Grace Bradley (Judy), Darryl Hickman (Billy), Manton Moreland (Ben), Louise Beavers (Beulah), Wade Crosby (Gunning), Tony Paton (Red), Joseph Bernard (Hank), Ed Bradley (Jules), Eddie Kane (Martin), Brandon Hurst (Dr. Morton); D: Howard Bretherton; SP: Elizabeth Hopkins, Edmond Lelso. **Synopsis:** The story is about two rival Alsatian (German shepherd) dogs, one of which is used by silver fox thieves, while the other saves his master's life and is wrongly blamed for the fox killings.

The Sea Wolf (Warner Brothers, 1941) 100 mins.; Edward G. Robinson (Wolf Larsen), John Garfield (George Leach), Ida Lupino (Ruth Webster), Alexander Knox (Humphrey Van Weyden),

Gene Lockhart (Dr. Louis Prescott), Barry Fitzgerald (Cooky), Stanley Ridges (Johnson), Francis McDonald (Svenson), David Bruce (Young Sailor), Howard De Silva (Harrison), Louis Mason (Crewman); D: Michael Curtiz; SP: Robert Rossen. **Synopsis:** Wolf Larsen is the psychopathic captain of the *Ghost*, a veritable death ship for its crew, many of whom have been shanghaied. While the intellectual Humphrey Van Weyden attempts to understand Larsen, escaped convicts George Leach and Ruth Webster plot to escape his fascist domination.

Larsen's death ship is little more than a pirate schooner on which the captives suffer through beatings, a suicide, and finally a mutiny, during which the survivors attempt to escape. Finally Van Weyden, Leach, and Webster, who have escaped in an open boat but are adrift aimlessly in the fog, are pursued by Larsen on the *Ghost*. The malevolent captain suffers from severe headaches, however, and is overcome by a seizure accompanied by blindness. When the small boat finally comes alongside the *Ghost* in the fog, the three escapees stumble back aboard to find the captain alone and blind in his mutiny-ruined ship, evil to the end.

Note: This is undoubtedly the best film version of London's book. In his adaptation of the novel, Rossen made some important changes in the characters. London had narrated his story from the point of view of Humphrey Van Weyden, an effete intellectual who, although a weakling at the beginning, gradually becomes stronger, outwitting Larsen in the process. The film adopts an omniscient view, and the character of Van Weyden is eased from the center of the story. The primary result of this change is that Larsen looms as a much more dominant figure in the film than he was in the novel. In addition, one of the novel's minor characters, George Leach, who had drowned halfway through the book, is moved to a leading role in opposition to Larsen in the film version. It is

ultimately Van Weyden who drowns along with Larsen in order to save Leach. With this shift in the plot, the character of Van Weyden's romantic interest, Maude Brewster, is eliminated. In her place is substituted a new female character, Ruth Webster, who is the type of good-bad girl ideally suited to the character of Leach as portrayed by John Garfield. Although she serves a similar function to that of London's Maude, she is more directly pivotal to the conflict between Leach and Larsen.

The Adventures of Martin Eden (Columbia, February 26, 1942) 87 mins.; Glenn Ford (Martin Eden), Claire Trevor (Connie Dawson), Evelyn Keyes (Ruth Morley), Stuart Erwin (Joe Dawson), Dickie Moore (Johnny), Ian MacDonald (Butch Ragan), Frank Conroy (Carl Brissenden), Resina Wallace (Mrs. Morley), Rafaela Ottiano (Marie Sylva), Pierre Watkin (Mr. Morley), Robert J. McDonald (Judge); D: Sidney Salkow; SP: W. L. River. **Synopsis:** A sailor turned author, Martin Eden, writes a novel about his experiences aboard a ship with a very rough captain, Butch Ragan. There is always time for romance, however.

Jack London (United Artists, December 24, 1943) 92 mins.; Michael O'Shea (Jack London), Susan Hayward (Charmain), Osa Massen (Freda Maloof), Harry Davenport (Professor Hilliard), Frank Craven (Old Tom), Virginia Mayo (Mamie), Ralph Morgan (George Brett), Louise Beavers (Mammy Jenny), Jonathan Hale (Kerwin Maxwell), Leonard Strong (Captain Tanaka), Paul Hurst (Lucky Luke Lannigan), Regis Toomey (Scratch Nelson), Hobart Cavanaugh (Mike), John Kelly (Red John), Robert Homans (Captain Allen), Morgan Conway (Richard Harding Davis), Robert Katcher (Hiroshi), Olin Howlin (Mailman), Albert Van Antwerp (French Frank), Ernie Adams (Whiskey Bob), Edward Enrie (James Hare), Arthur Loft (Fred Palmer),

Lumsden Hare (English Correspondent), Brooks Benedict (American Correspondent), Mel Lee Foo (Geisha Dancer), Pierre Watkin (American Consul), Paul Fung (Japanese General), Charlie Lung (Interpreter), Bruce Wong (Japanese Official), Eddie Lee (Japanese Sergeant), John Fisher (Spider), Jack Roper (Victor), Sven Hugo Borg (Axel), Sid Dulbrook (Pete), Davison Clark (Commissioner), Harold Minjir (Literary Guest), Roy Cordon (Literary Guest), Torben Meyer (Literary Guest), Charlene Newman (Bit Child), Edmund Cobb (Bit Father), Wallis Clark (Theodore Roosevelt), Charles Miller (William Leob), Richard Lee (Japanese Ambassador), Dick Curtis (Cannery Foreman), Sarah Padden (Cannery Woman), Evelyn Finley (Indian Maid), Rose Plummer (Charmian's Secretary); D: Alfred Santell; SP: Ernest Pascal; S: *The Book of Jack London*. Synopsis: The story takes up London's career at the time he turned oyster pirate to escape the drudgery of a San Francisco sweat shop, and carries through the episodes reponsible for *The Sea Wolf* and *Call of the Wild*, the Boer War, and concludes with his adventuring as a correspondent in the Russo-Japanese War.
Review:

Michael O'Shea, physically resembling London, does a forthright job as the writer, hitting the peak in the final episode. Susan Hayward delivers with the customary excellence as Charmain London, a role quite different from her usual wayward characters. Osa Massen is seen all too briefly as the Dawson dance hall girl who shared London's northern adventuring. Harry Davenport lifts a bit as a college professor to one of the film's high spots. Virginia Mayo is good as London's partner during his oyster pirating days.

Variety (November 24, 1943)

Note: This film is not based on the works of Jack London; rather, it is a film about the life of London. It seems appropriate to include it in this list of films.

Alaska (Monogram, November 18, 1944) 76 mins.; Kent Taylor, Margaret Lindsay, John Carradine, Dean Jagger, Nils Asther, Iris Adrian, George Cleveland, Lee "Lasses'" White, Dewey Robinson, John Rogers, Jack Norton, John Maxwell, Warren Jackson, Dick Scott, Glenn Strange, Tex Cooper; D: George Archainbaud; SP: George Wallace Sayre, Malcolm Stuart Boylan, Harrison Orkow; S: "Flush of Gold." Synopsis: Taylor, a mining engineer, arrives in the teeming gold settlement Moose Creek. While in the bar run by Asther, he catches the interested eye of Miss Lindsey, an entertainer. Taylor drops the glance promptly when he learns she is married and morally loyal to Carradine, an actor and unfortunately inebriate. Moving on to his father's mine, Taylor is picked up for murder when he kills a couple of claim jumpers who have just killed his dad. Jagger, a U.S. marshal, brings him in. While waiting for the trail to Juneau to open, Jagger allows Taylor a little liberty in which to run down the organizers of the jumping ring.

Taylor finally traces the gang to Nils Asther, owner of the bar, and a noteworthy fight ensues. Asther is beaten and confesses he is not the head of the ring but only an underling. He is shot as he is about to name the boss, and Taylor finds Jagger facing him from behind a gun. He then realizes Jagger is head of the ring. Taylor manages to subdue Jagger and take him to justice.
Reviews.

The full rich juices Jack London stirred up in his best work are caught in Monogram's *Alaska*. A top-budget property for that lot which will certainly play to gratifying returns. Adapted from London's "Flush of Gold," the picture has the authentic air of the gold-fevered Klondike era, and atmospherically is a distinct achievement.

Into this background, producer Lindsley Parsons, with Trem Carr as executive director, has ushered five superbly-cast principals in Kent Taylor, Margaret Lindsay, John Carradine, Dean Jagger, and Nils Asther, backed by some unusually capable supporters, notably George Cleveland.

Hollywood Reporter (October 6, 1944)

Had Jack London been on hand to write his own screenplay for *Alaska*, an adaptation of his novel "Flush of Gold," it might not have missed so badly the action that typified the author. However, the screenplay was written by George Wallace Sayre, Harrison Orkow, and Malcolm Stuart Boylan and, while dialog is okay, it takes them too long to get into the story and it fails to move as it should when the plot finally begins to unravel.

Taylor, Carradine and Jagger give excellent performances, with the latter getting far too little footage. He is an exceedingly capable actor seen far too seldom. Margaret Lindsay, as the patient and loyal wife of a drunkard, fighting against her love for another man, is up to her usual good standards.

Variety (October 6, 1944)

White Fang (Voentekhfilm, USSR, 1947) Oleg Giakov; Nina Ismailova; D: Alexander Sguridi.

The Fighter (United Artists, 1952) 78 mins.; Richard Conte (Felipe), Vanessa Brown (Kathy), Lee J. Cobb (Durango), Frank Silvera (Pauline), Roberta Haynes (Nevis), Hugh Sanders (Roberts), Claire Carleton (Stella), Martin Garralaga (Luis), Argentina Brunetti (Maria), Rodolfo Hayes, Jr. (Alvarado),

Margaret Pedilla (Elba), Paul Fierro (José), Rico Alaniz (Carlos), Robert Wells (Rivas); D: Herbert Kline; SP: Aben Kandel, H. Kline; S: "The Mexican." Synopsis: A Mexican boxer, Felipe, uses his winnings to buy arms to help a group of patriots overthrow Diaz, whose soldiers murdered his family.

Tales of Adventure (Pathe, 1954) Lon Chaney, Don DeFore, Rita Moreno, Robert Hutton, Robert Lowery, Eve McVeagh, Coleen Gray, Frank Silvera; D: Herbert Kline; S: "Tales of Adventure" and "Flight from Adventure." Note: Issues only to TV and made up of three 1952 segments of the series "The Schlitz Playhouse of Stars."

Captain David Grief (Guild Films, 1956) Maxwell Reed (Captain David Grief); D: Harry Gerstad. Note: Guild Films picked up distribution rights for this cheapie filmed in Mexico. Stuck with a lemon, Guild resolved to make lemonade. The company piled up several sales by promoting the fact that the series' 26 episodes were shot in color, and emphasizing that "Captain David Grief" was the first TV series based on the works of Jack London. But few markets bothered to renew their contracts after the first year, even when Guild reissued the program as "Jack London Stories."

The Mexican: Meksikanets (Mosfilm/Artkino, 1957) 62 mins.; O. Striz henov (Felipe Rivera), A. Andreyev (Pauline Vera), D. Sagal (Arellano), N. Rumyantseva (May), V. Dorofeyev (Diego), T. Samoilova (Maria); D: V. Kaplunovsky; SP: E. Braginsky. Synopsis: Poor Mexican revolutionaries, living in Los Angeles, plan to overthrow their hometown government. To raise the needed money, Felipe wins a grueling 17-round professional fight.

Wolf Larsen (Allied Artists, 1958) 83 mins.; Barry Sullivan (Wolf Larsen), Peter Graves (Van Weyden), Gita Hall (Kristina), Thayer David (Mugridge), John Alderson (Johnson), Rico Alantz

(Louis), Robert Gist (Matthews), Jack Grinnage (Leach), Jack Orrison (Haskins), Henry Rowland (Henderson); D: Harmon Jones; SP: Jack DeWitt, Turnly Walker; SP: *The Sea Wolf*; P: Lindsley Parsons. **Synopsis:** This is yet another filming of the Jack London classic, and it stays closer to the book than some other films have. It is an excellent version of *The Sea Wolf*, and Barry Sullivan is very good as the tyrannical captain of the *Ghost*.

The Assassination Bureau (Paramount, 1969) 106 mins.; Oliver Reed (Ivan Dragomdoff), Diana Rigg (Sonya Winter), Telly Savalas (Lord Bostwick), Curt Jurgens (General von Pinck), Philippe Noiret (Lucoville), Warren Mitchell (Weiss), Beryl Reid (Madame Otero), Clive Revill (Cesare Sado), Kenneth Griffith (Popescu), Vernon Dobtcheff (Muntzov), Annabella Incontrera (Eleanora); D: Basil Dearden; SP: Michael Ralph; S: *The Assassination Bureau, Ltd.*; P: Michael Ralph, Basil Dearden. **Synopsis:** The film is a rather unusual comedy. The Assassination Bureau is an international organization of murderers for hire. A young reporter, Sonya Winter, investigates it with the backing of her publisher, Lord Bostwick.

The Cry of the Black Wolves/Der Schrei der Schwarzen Wolfe (Lisa Productions/Constantin, 1972) 110 mins.; Ron Ely (Robinson), Raimund Harmsdorf (Parker), Gila von Weltershausen, Heinrich Schweiger, Arthur Braus; D: Harold Reini; SP: Kurt Nachmann; S: *The Son of the Wolf*. **Synopsis:** Bill Robinson saves Jack Parker from being crushed by an avalanche and doesn't know that this professional head hunter is after his life for a price.
Review:

Advance word-of-mouth and pre-publicity sounded as though the adaptors of Jack London's novel, *The Son of the Wolf*, attempted to use the great yank storyteller in the hope of duplicating the b.o. bonanza they had reaped for years from the writings of the fake Western author, Karl May. As that implied reducing a lively and exciting adventure yarn to the stale artificiality of the "Old Shatterhand" flickers, the more discriminating cinema buffs anticipated a nuisance.

The outcome was better than that, although scriptor Karl Nachmann and director Harold Reini, the latter with already seven Karl May pix to his credit, by no means lost sight of their initial goal. They did inject Jack London with a good deal of May humbug clearcut division in saint-pure heroes and satanic heavies, endless gun sprees and fist fights and horseback chases, those "pioneer belles" in the snowbound wilderness whose superfine make-ups and hairdoes matched their superfine souls.

Fortunately, pieces of the original *Son of the Wolf* escaped falsification and came alive under their own power. The story unfolds forcefully and with speed and suspense.

Another asset is good acting, mainly by Ron Ely (Robinson) whom this film catapults from the "Tarzan" B-brackets into a "dashing young hero." Gila von Weltershausen, first time not in the nude, also shows thespian gifts. Raimund Harmsdorf (Parker) is stil a "type" who suits all parts which suit his bearlike looks.

Variety (October 1972)

Der Seewolf/The Sea Wolf (ZDF Television, 1973) Raimund Harmsdorf. Note: This is a 26-part German TV series; no additional information is available.

Call of the Wild (CCC Constantin, 1973) 100 mins. (U.S. release: Intercontinental Productions); Charlton Heston, Raimund Harmsdorf; Michele Mercier,

George Eastman (Luigi Mirafiore), Sancho Garcia, Rick Battaglia, Maria
Rohm; D: Ken Annakin; SP: Hubert
Frank, Tibor Reves. Synopsis: Its
another verion of the classic story. Two
fortune hunters in Alaska are saved from
their rivals time and time again by Buck,
their dog. Note: This is a West German/
Spanish/Italian/French coproduction
filmed in Norway.

Zanna Bianca/White Fang (Ocean-
ina Film Incine/Fox Europe, 1974) 101
mins. (U.S. release: American Cinema,
1975, as *White Fang*); Franco Nero,
Virna Lisi, Fernando Rey, Harry Carey,
Jr., Carole Andre, Rick Battaglia,
Daniele Dublino, John Steiner, Daniel
Martin; D: Lucia Fulci; SP: Peter Wel-
back. Note: No other information is
available on this film.

Il Ricaiamo del Lupo (Dunamis/
Estudios, 1975) 87 mins. (U.S. release:
The Great Adventure; Pacific Interna-
tional); Jack Palance, Joan Collins, Fred
Romer (Fernando Romero), Manuel de
Elas (Manolo de Blas), Elisabeth Virgili
(Elisabetta Virgili), Remo de Angelis;
D: Paul Elliotts (Gianfranco Bal-
danello); P: Elliott Geisinger, Joseph
Allegro. Note: No other information is
available on this film.

The Call of the Wild (Charles Fries
Productions, May 1976) 120 mins.; John
Beck, Bernard Fresson, John McLiam,
Donald Moffat, Michael Pataki, Pene-
lope Windust, Billy Green Bush, Johnny
Tillotson, Ray Guth; D: Jerry Burkley;
TP: James Dickey; P: Malcolm Stuart.

Wolf Larsen (U.S. release: 1978,
filmed in 1975 as *The Legend of the Sea
Wolf*) 92 mins.; Chuck Connors, Barbara
Bach, Giuseppe Pambieri; D: Joseph
Green (Giuseppi Vari); S: *The Sea Wolf*.

*Klondike Fever: Jack London's Klon-
dike Fever* (CFI Investments, 1980) 60
mins.; Jeff East (Jack London), Rod
Steiger (Soapy Smith), Angie Dickinson
(Belinda McNair), Lorne Green (Sam
Steele), Barry Morse (John Thornton),
Michael Hogan (Will Ryan), Merritt

Sloper (Robin Gammell), Lisa Langlois
(Gertie), Sherry Lewis (Louise); D: Peter
Carter; SP: Charles E. Israel, Martin
Lager; P: Gilbert W. Taylor. Synopsis:
London (a clinched-jawed hero of high
ideals and a stout heart) and his partner,
Robin Gammell, land in Skagway,
Alaska, on their way to hit the Klondike
trail. The young writer grits his teeth
even more as he encounters the baseness
of the gold-maddened men churning
around him. When he sees a cruel trainer
breaking dogs for the sleds, he rescues
one, Buck, a good deed that leads to a
string of troubles with Soapy Smith, a
renegade priest who runs the town.
Review:

Although he was known as a
novelist, American writer Jack
London was basically a yarn-spin-
ner. Peter Carter's "Klondike
Fever," based on London's own
exploits during the Klondike gold
rush, tries hard to be story book
cinema, but never succeeds in
establishing the fascination that
kept London's readers turning the
pages as rapidly as they could.

The film has the look of one
bound for television — and soon.
It also has a bit of the Disney
touch about it, but not enough of
the Disney genius to make the
stuff of solid G-fare.

The film is jerkily edited with
some jarring transitions. Director
Carter keeps losing track of the
dog, leaving him out entirely in an
unexciting scene in which London
and company shoot some angry
whitewater rapids.

Klondike Fever fails to capture
the spirit of adventure and excitement that drew London to the
area in the first place, or the brute
strength lionized in his own writings. As played by East the adven-
turer author looks as if he can
hardly wait to get back to Beverly
Hills.

Variety (February 13, 1980)

Note: This is a film about Jack London. It is not based on any specific work of London.

White Fang (Buena Vista, January 1, 1991) 104 mins.; Klaus Maria Brandauer (Alex), Ethan Hawks (Jack), Seymour Cassel (Skunker), Susan Hogan (Belinda), James Remar (Beauty), Bill Moseley (Duke), Clint B. Youngteen (Tinker), Pius Savage (Grey Beaver), Jed (a dog) (White Fang), Bart (a bear) (Himself); D: Randel Kleiser; SP: Jeanne Rosenberg, Nick Thiel, David Fallon. **Synopsis:** The essence of this story is familiar; boy meets wolf, boy loses wolf, and so on. When Jack first arrives in the Klondike, he catches sight of a "golden staircase," an endless line of miners climbing a snowy trail high up a mountain peak.

Soon after Jack arrives, he, Alex, and a grizzled fellow miner embark on a journey into the wilderness, taking with them sled dogs and the coffin of a friend. Before this man can be buried, the expedition becomes imperiled by a couple of gruesome but rivetingly staged mishaps.

Because the film's story has been molded out of separate episodes, it is held together chiefly by White Fang himself. First glimpsed as a puppy, he is later found in an Indian settlement working for Gray Beaver, who views him as a resource rather than a pet. When Jack finds White Fang living under these circumstances, he is saddened but helpless to woo the animal away. Only when White Fang is sold to the evil Beauty Smith, who means to train him as a fighter, does Jack have an opportunity to retrieve and rehabilitate his animal friend.

Reviews:

In *White Fang* London traces the domestication of a wild wolf-dog during the Klondike gold rush. White Fang must learn the ways of the man-animal if he is to survive. This film from Walt Disney Pictures, while pursuing the same theme, opts for a sentimental story of a boy and his dog. *White Fang* should please the audience to which it is pitched. It's certainly a sharp-looking production, filmed with great difficulty in Alaska last winter and spring.

Kirk Honeycutt, *Hollywood Reporter* (January 18, 1991)

White Fang, adapted from Jack London's tale of a wolf-dog hybrid and his encounters with civilized man, is a scenic and enveloping nature film about a young man and his beloved pet.

The screenplay has almost nothing to do with London's novel, which has only a slender human-related story and is presented from the wolf-dog's point of view. The screenwriters have invented a seasoned gold miner named Alex and a young man named Jack, who comes to Alaska to pick up his late father's prospecting claim.

Janet Maslin, *New York Times* (January 18, 1991)

Call of the Wild (Craft General Foods (CBS, 1993) Ricky Schroeder, Mia Sara, John Thornton, Duncan Fraser, Richard Newan. Note: This is a retelling of the familiar story, this time for television.

The Sea Wolf (Primedia Productions/Andrew J. Fenady Productions/ Bob Bonner Productions, 1993) 93 mins.; Charles Bronson, Christopher Reeve, Catherine Mary Stewart, Marc Singer, Len Cariou, Styon Barrett, Gavin Buhr, Garry Chalk, Bill Croft, John Destry, Andrew J. Fenady, Eli Gaboy, Peter Hayworth, Rachel Hayward, Dee Dee Jackson, Shane Kelly, Tom McBeath, John Novak, Russell J. Roberts, William Samples; D: Michael Anderson; TP: Andrew J. Fenady; P: Duke Fenady. Note: In this version of *The Sea Wolf* Charles Bronson plays the part of Wolf Larsen.

documents. Helen is unaware of what the papers are and has no inkling of what her uncle is up to. Roy Glennister's claim to the Midas Mine is disputed. Both Glennister and Cherry Malotte, owner of the local gambling saloon, are suspicious of McNamara, who is the gold commissioner for that area. Cherry is secretly in love with Glennister, but he appears to be more interested in Helen Chester. Meanwhile, the Broncho Kid, the faro-table dealer, has fallen in love with Cherry.

McNamara's scheme is almost accomplished until Glennister and his partner Dextry — with the aid of lawyer Bill Wheaton — bring about the arrest of the conspirators and the restoration of the miners' claims. The Broncho Kid is killed during the fighting between the miners and McNamara's men, but before he dies he tells Glennister of McNamara's plot. The Kid is revealed as Helen's long-lost brother. Glennister and McNamara engage in a bloody fist fight, which Glennister wins. Cherry Malotte discovers that Glennister was never in love with Helen, and the two are reunited.

Reviews:

To the rabid movie fan — the one who revels in action, excitement, and a panoramic succession of real life adventures — this picture hands him a wallop — *The Spoilers* is a red blooded, peppery story that will catch wideawake live Americans....*Variety* went on to applaud Beach, who had apparently kept a watchful eye on the production, particularly as far as the re-creation of the city of Nome.

William Farnum is the Glennister of the picture and a manly, strong, rugged, healthy character he made of it. He handled the strenuous role [of] the big miner so capably there was no fault to be found with his acting. Farnum has broad shoulders and a deep chest

and they stand him in good stead in the rougher climaxes of the picture. Thomas Santschi was McNamara and he made the villainous role loom up in the wicked manner in which Beach described him in the book. He appeared to be much slenderer than Farnum yet in the big fight scene he held his own well. Kathlyn Williams looked after the Cherry Malotte so effectively it is doubtful if any other actress could have improved upon the part. As for Bessie Eyton's interpretation of Helen Chester she is due for all the bouquets that will come her way. Frank Clark was superb as the "silverhaired old Texas pirate, Dextry." Wheeler Oakman was Broncho Kid and he did the role without exaggerating it from the book's standpoint. Marshall Farnum played Lawyer Wheaton but didn't have much to do, while E. MacGregor was a capable Judge Stillman.

Mark, *Variety* 34, no. 7 (April 17, 1914), p. 22

Note: *The Spoilers* had its premiere at Chicago's Orchestra Hall on March 25, 1914, before an audience of some 2,000 people. It was subsequently chosen as the opening night film for New York's new Strand Theater and became an immediate popular and critical success.

The photography has a perhaps unintentional harsh documentary quality. One is reminded of William S. Hart's *Hell's Hinges* (1916). What chiefly creates an impact are the sets. The buildings and muddy streets capture the harsh, unrelenting cruelty that must have been an integral part of the Alaskan pioneering spirit. Similarly, the characters look as though they might have stepped out of late nineteenth-century photographs of the Alaskan goldfields. The costumes are drab, the women are buxom and relatively plain, and the men

John Wayne, Harry Carey, George Cleveland and players in *The Spoilers* (Universal, 1942).

are shabbily dressed, with weather-beaten faces.

The Spoilers has been filmed five times, the most popular adaptation being the 1942 film starring John Wayne and Randolph Scott. However, the first filming has generally been claimed to be the most faithful to the original work. The film was one of the screen's first major feature-length productions, preceding by nine months *The Birth of a Nation*.

The British distributor was forced to cut the film down to four reels, since the public was not used to such a long film. However, in America it was not only accepted in the 9-reel version but in 1916 it was reissued in an expanded 12-reel version, which included footage of Beach at work in his study.

The Footsteps of Captain Kidd

(Grand Feature Film Company, March–April 1915) 6 reels; Rex Beach, Edward A. Salisbury, George Stone, Charles Dahl; D: Edward A. Salisbury. Note: This is a documentary film made up of different scenes shot by Edward Salisbury on an expedition to Central and South America. Rex Beach was a member of the expedition.

On the Spanish Main (Grand Feature Film Company, March–April 1915) 5 reels; Edward A. Salisbury, Rex Beach, George Stone, Charles Dahl, Mary Roberts Rhinehart. Note: This is a documentary film shot by Edward A. Salisbury on an expedition to Central and South America aboard the yacht *Wisdom*. This footage is different from that of *The Footsteps of Captain Kidd*.

Pirate Haunts (Grand Feature Film Company, March–April 1915) 5 reels;

Edward A. Salisbury, Rex Beach, George Stone, Charles Dahl; D: Edward A. Salisbury. Note: Additional documentary footage filmed on the Edward A. Salisbury expedition to Central and South America. Most of the footage was filmed in Costa Rica and the Canal Zone.

With Bridges Burned (Edison, April 1915) 3 reels; D/SP: Ashley Miller. Note: No additional information has been found on this film.

The Barrier (Rex Beach Pictures Company, February 1917) 10 reels; Mabel Juliene Scott (Necia/Merridy), Russell Simpson (John Gaylord/John Gale), Howard Hall (Dan Bennett/Ben Stark), Victor Sutherland (Lieutenant Meade Burrell), Mitchell Lewis (Poleon Doret), Edward Roseman (Runnion), W. J. Gross ("No Creek" Lee), Mary Kennevan Carr (Alluna); D: Edgar Lewis; SP: Adrian Gil-Spear; Supv: Rex Beach, Benjamin B. Hampton. Synopsis: The barrier standing between Lieutenant Meade Burrell and Necia, the daughter of Alaskan trader John Gale, has its origin in her Indian blood. Burrell has proposed to Necia but is released from his proposal of marriage when Necia realizes that there would be problems for Burrell if he married a half-breed. She eventually learns that she is not the daughter of John Gale and his Indian woman, Alluna, With the barrier removed the two lovers are reunited.

The Ne'er-Do-Well (Selig, December 28, 1915) 10 reels; Wheeler Oakman (Kirk Anthony), Kathlyn Williams (Mrs. Edith Courtlandt), Harry Lonsdale (Stephen Courtlandt), Frank Clark (Darwin K. Anthony), Norma Nichols (Chiquita Garavel), Will Machin (Weller [alias Locke]), Jack MacDonald (Alan Alan), Sidney Smith (Ramon Alfarez), Fred Huntley (Andres Garavel), Laram Johnston (Runnels), Harry De Vere (Detective Williams); D: Colin Campbell; SP: Lanier Bartlett. Synopsis: A spoiled son is shanghaied and taken to Panama at the request of his father, who was disgusted with his son's lifestyle. In Panama the son falls in love, becomes a successful railroad employee, and straightens out his life. In the end he returns to the United States with his recently acquired wife to ask forgiveness of his father.

Pardners (Mutual Film Corporation, January 29, 1917) 5 reels; Charlotte Walker (Olive), Richard Tucker (Justus Morrow), Leo Gordon (Alonza Struthers), Charles Sutton (John Graham), Redfield Clarke, Harry Limson, William Worth, Jessie Stevens; SP: Paul H. Sloane. Synopsis: Justus Morrow, a civil engineer working on a new railroad line, falls in love with and marries Olive, who teaches the children of the workmen. Alonza Struthers is hired by a competing railroad to prevent Morrow from finishing his job. At the same time he, too, falls in love with Olive and after blowing up the tracks that Morrow has laid, plots to take Olive from Morrow. Justus goes to Alaska to make his fortune, leaving Olive behind, and so Alonza goes to work. He doctors some photographs to make it appear Justus is cavorting with saloon girls. Olive files for divorce. However, the marriage is saved when Justus's partner shows up and forces Alonza at gunpoint to tell the truth.

The Auction Block (Rex Beach Film Corporation (Goldwyn Distributing Corporation, December 1917) 7 reels; Rabye De Remer (Lorelei Knight), Florence Deshon (Lilas Lynn), Dorothy Wheeler (Mrs. Peter Knight), Florence Johns (Adoree Demorest), Tom Powers (Bob Wharton), Walter Hitchcock (Jarvis Hammon), Ned Burton (Hannibal Wharton), Charles Graham (Max Melcher), George Cooper (Jimmy Knight), Alec B. Francis (John Merkle), Francis Joyner (Campbell Pope), Bernard Randall (Noble Bergman), Peter Lang (Peter Knight); D: Larry Trimble; SP: Gil Spear. Synopsis: Lorelei Knight gets a job as a show girl in New York but her good-for-nothing family soon comes to live off her earnings. When she loses her job, in desperation she marries the drunken son of a millionaire, but refuses to consummate the marriage until her husband reforms and quits his drinking. She becomes acquainted with Lilas Lynn, who is planning revenge on steel mill boss Jarvis Hammon, the man responsible for her father's death. Lilas shoots Jarvis and Lorelei becomes involved. Lorelei's brother and his gang blackmail her reformed husband for the crime. However, the gang is broken up and all ends well for the newlyweds.

Heart of the Sunset (Goldwyn, April 1918) 2 reels; Anna Q. Nilsson, Herbert Heyes, Robert Tabor, E. L. Fernandez, Jane Miller, William Frederick, Irene Boyle, Lule Warrenton; D: Frank Powell; SP: Frederic Chapin. Note: No further information is available on this film.

Laughing Bill Hyde (Rex Beach Pictures/Goldwyn, September 1918) 6 reels; Will Rogers (Laughing Bill Hyde), Anna Lehr (Ponotah), John M. Sainpolis (Black Jack Burg), Mabel Ballin (Alice), Clarence Oliver (Dr. Evan Thomas), Joseph Herbert (Joseph Wesley Slayforth), Robert Conville (Denny Slevin), Dan Mason (Danny Dorgan); D: Hobart Henley; SP: Willard Mack. **Synopsis:** Laughing Bill Hyde and his friend Danny Dorgan break out of prison, but Danny is mortally wounded. A local doctor to whom Bill takes Danny tries his very best to save Danny's life but to no avail. Later, Bill and the doctor meet in Alaska and become friends. When a dying man gives his mine to the doctor, Bill investigates and finds that it is worthless and sells it to a crook, Joseph Slayforth, for $50,000, money he turns over to the doctor. Slayforth attempts to cheat Ponotah, an Indian girl who owns another mine. Bill again investigates and finds that the superintendent is systematically stealing gold from the mine. Bill robs him of the gold and buries it near his cabin. Most of the gold he gives to Ponotah, who accepts his marriage proposal.

Too Fat to Fight (Rex Beach Pictures/Goldwyn, December 10, 1918) 6 reels; Frank McIntyre (Norman "Dimples" Dalrymple), Florence Dixon (Helen Brewster), Henrietta Floyd (Mrs. Brewster), Comtesse Floria de Martimprey (Belle Rainey), Harold Erstwistle (Major Brewster), Jack McLean (Freddie), Frank Badgley (British General); D: Hobart Henley; SP: Charles A. Logue. **Synopsis:** Norman Dalrymple wants to enlist in the army in World War I but is rejected because of his weight. Through the intercession of a wealthy friend he enrolls in the Goldberg, YMCA where he trims down. He says goodbye to his sweetheart Helen Brewster and goes to France, where he serves with the Allied soldiers as a "soup carrier." When he attempts to rescue Helen's wounded father from the battlefield, he is seriously hurt. By this time Helen has enrolled in the ambulance corps. She drives Norman to the hospital, where his leg has to be amputated. Helen's love and a decoration for heroism restore Norman's happiness.

The Brand (Rex Beach Pictures/Goldwyn, March 9, 1919) 7 reels; Kay Laurell (Alice Andrews), Russell Simpson (Dan McGill), Robert McKim (Bob Barclay), Robert Kunkel (Hopper), Mary Jane Irving (The Child), Gus Saville; D: Reginald Barker. **Synopsis:** To the town of Ophir, in Alaska, come stragglers from the United States, Bob Barclay, a vaudeville actor, who has heard of the gold rush, and Alice Andrews, his partner in more ways than one. Bob deserts Alice to go north in search of gold, and she, believing he will not return, marries Dan McGill, an old prospector, when he proposes. Dan treats her tenderly but all his love cannot compensate for the lonely hours she spends in the far North. When Bob returns she begs him to take her away. Dan discovers them in each other's arms and drives them from his home. They are unable to go far owing to the terrible storm that rages and Dan, believing the town too small for the three of them, sets out himself.

It is the general belief that Dan has perished but only a year or so later he is revealed as the mysterious owner of a new strike, the man who made the town of McDaniel, the same name he is known by. To this town come Alice and Bob, the latter now a professional gambler, the former a dance hall girl, due to Bob's tyranny. He tells her to see McDaniel, with the idea of bleeding him for his money and, despite the heavy beard, Alice recognizes him as her husband. She takes him to see her child — their child — and at the sight of the youngster, Dan works himself into a rage against Bob.

Going to the saloon he drags Bob from the card game, forces him back over the table and with the sight of his pistol brands a cross on his forehead. Bob is driven from the town by the supporters of Dan while he returns for his wife and child to take them to his home.

The Crimson Gardenia (Rex Beach Pictures/Goldwyn, May 5, 1919) 6 reels; Owen Moore (Roland Van Dam), Heddy Nova (Madelon Dorette), Hector V. Sarno (Emile Le Duc), Sydney Deane (Papa LaForge), Tully Marshall (Alfred Le Duc), Sydney Ainsworth (Francois "the Spider"), Edwin Stevens (Jean, "the Wolf"), Gertrude Clair (Mere Felice), Betty Schade (Eleanor Banniman), Alec B. Franxis (Mr. Banniman), Kate Lester (Mrs. Banniman); D: Reginald Barker; SP/S: Rex Beach. **Synopsis:** Roland Van Dam, a wealthy New Yorker, goes to New Orleans during the Mardi Gras seeking adventure. He is mistaken for Emile Le Duc, an escaped convict, by a cousin he has never met, Madelon Dorette, because Roland is wearing a red gardenia, which Emile was to wear. Emile's gang, thinking that he is going to betray them, kidnap Roland, but he escapes. When Emile dies, Madelon is made to believe that Roland is a secret service agent and that he has killed Emile. She entices Roland to the home of her uncle, the gang leader. There she discovers that Roland is innocent. Eventually, Roland and Madelon are saved because Roland was able to transmit a call to the police. In the end Roland marries Madelon.

The Vengeance of Durand (Vitagraph, November 24, 1919) 7 reels; Alice Joyce (Marion Durand), Gustar Von Seyffertitz (Henri Durand), Percy Marmont (Tom Franklin), William Bechtel (Armand La Farge), Eugene Strong (Captain St. Croix Trouvier), Herbert Pattee (Theophile), Mark Smith ("Tubby" Livingston); D: Tom Terriss; SP: Mr. and Mrs. George Randolph Chester. **Synopsis:** Marion Durand is driven to suicide by her extremely jealous husband, Henri Durand, who accuses her of having a love affair with her childhood friend, Tom Franklin. Twelve years later when Tom returns from a long expedition, Henry still wants revenge. Henri coaches his daughter, Beatrice, who resembles Marion, to court Tom. After Tom and Beatrice become engaged, Henri forces Beatrice to flirt with other men. Tom is overcome with jealousy and about to commit suicide when Beatrice admits her real love for him. Tom is pacified when he receives a confession from Mario's refused suitor that absolves Tom of any guilt. Durand then permits the marriage of Beatrice and Tom.

The Girl from Outside (Eminent Authors Pictures/Goldwyn, September 1, 1919) 7 reels; Clara Horton (June Campbell), Cullen Landis (The Curly Kid), Sydney Ainsworth (Spencer), Hallam Cooley (Harry Hope), Colin Kenny (The Magpie), Walter McNamara (Mike), Ernest Spencer (The Swede), Wilton Taylor (Jim Denton), Louis Cheung (Chow), Bert Sprotte (The Marshal), Billie Bennett (Mamie), Gus Saville; D: Reginald Barker; S: "The

Wag Lady"; P: Rex Beach. **Synopsis:** June Campbell is stranded in Nome, Alaska, after her father dies enroute from the United States. However, she is befriended by the Curly Kid and his four friends, the "Wags." They help her to open a hotel through dishonest means, but she is unaware that they are crooks. Harry Hope, the owner of the hotel property and manager of a trading company, falls in love with her as do the Wags and almost everyone else who meets her. Gambler Jim Denton, owner of the leading saloon, also desires June. He forges a codicil to an option on Harry's profitable gold mine. The Curly Kid, realizing his love for June is hopeless since she loves Harry, destroys the option but is killed by Denton. The Kid's Chinese cook Chow knifes Denton before the Wags arrive to take revenge. Through June's influence the Wags reform and June and Harry are married.

The Silver Horde (Eminent Authors Pictures/Goldwyn, May 1920) 6–7 reels; Myrtle Stedman (Cherry Malotte), Curtis Cookley (Boyd Emerson), Betty Blythe (Mildred Wayland), R. D. MacLean (Wayne Wayland), Robert McKim (Marsh), Hector Sarno (Constantine), Bull Durham (Swanson), M. B. Flynn (Thug), Neola Mae (Snowbird), E. J. Denecke (Thug), Frederick Stanton (Big George Bolt), Carl Gerard (Alton Clyde), Murdock MacQuarrie (Richard Jones); D: Frank Lloyd; SP: Lawrence Trimble, J. E. Nash. **Synopsis:** Boyd Emerson wants to marry the daughter of Wall Street financier Wayne Wayland. He goes to Alaska in the hope of winning his fortune and the girl he loves. In Alaska Boyd joins forces with Big George Bolt and Cherry Malotte, who are fighting the trust led by Marsh for their share of the salmon catch known as "the silver horde." As luck would have it, Wayne Wayland backs Marsh, who attempts to sabotage the efforts of the trio. Marsh and Wayland fabricate a story that Boyd has

fathered an illegitimate child, in the hopes of breaking up the romance between Boyd and Mildred Wayland. Boyd and his partners manage to corner the salmon market in spite of Marsh and Wayland, and Boyd discovers that he loves Cherry more than Mildred Wayland.

Going Some (Eminent Authors Pictures/Goldwyn, June 19, 1920) 6 reels; Cullen Landis (J. Wallingford Speed), Helen Ferguson (Jean Chapin), Lillian Hall (Helen Blake), Lillian Langdon (Miz Gallagher), Kenneth Harlan (Donald Keap), Ethel Grey Terry (Mrs. Roberta Keap), Willard Louis (Larry Glass), Walter Hiers (Berkeley Fresno), Frank Braidwood (Culver Covington), Nelson McDowell (Still Stover), Snitz Edwards (Willie), Hayward Mack (Laden), M. B. Flynn (Skinner); D: Harry Beaumont; SP: Laurence Trimble; S: Rex Beach and Paul Armstrong. **Synopsis:** J. Wallingford Speed decides to impress his girl Helen by posing as a runner. He, Helen, and other friends accompany Roberta Keap to her Western ranch while awaiting her divorce. Donald, her husband, takes up residence at the Gallagher ranch. A rivalry develops between the two ranches. Helen talks Speed into challenging the Keap homestead in a foot race. Roberta and Mrs. Gallagher bet all they have on the race. Miraculously, the intense competition spurs Speed to win both his match and Helen's love, while also bringing about the reconciliation of Donald and Roberta.

The North Wind's Malice (Eminent Authors Pictures/Goldwyn, August 7, 1920) 7 reels; Tom Santschi (Roger Folsom), Jane Thomas (Lois Folsom), Joe King (Henry Carter), Henry West (Jack Harkness), William H. Strauss (Abe Guth), Walter Abel (Tom Folsom), Vera Gordon (Rachel Guth), Edna Murphy (Dorothy Halstead), Dorothy Wheeler (Malice), Julia Stewart (Mrs. Carter); D: Carl Harbaugh and Paul Bern. **Synop-**

sis: Lois Folsom is constantly complaining about her husband's sloppy ways. One day he gets so tired of her nagging that he leaves her. Lois finds friendship and help from Henry Carter, a mutual friend of Lois and Roger Folsom. Roger's brother Tom, angry at Lois for interfering in his romance with Dorothy Halstead, tells Roger that Lois has kissed Carter. Roger is hurt by this news; he also joins with Jack Harkness in a gold mining expedition. Roger is unaware that Lois is pregnant and she accepts Carter's care. When the Guth's store is destroyed by fire, Tom helps the family by stealing food for them. His efforts land him in jail.

After Lois's baby is born, Carter ventures north to inform Roger. There is a confrontation at first, but Carter convinces Roger that he has acted only as a friend to Lois. Roger returns home to his wife and also manages to get Tom freed from jail. Tom confesses his deceit and wins Dorothy Halstead's heart.

Fair Lady (United Artists, March 19, 1922) 7 reels; Betty Blythe (Countess Marcherita), Thurston Hall (Caesar Maruffi), Robert Elliott (Norvin Blake), Gladys Hulette (Myra Nell Drew), Florence Auer (Lucrezia), Walter James (Gian Norcone), Macy Harlan (Count Modena), Henry Leone (Riccardo), Effington Pinto (Count Martinello), Arnold Lucy (Uncle Bernie Drew); D: Kenneth Webb; SP: Dorothy Farnum; S: "The Web"; P: Whitman Bennett. Synopsis: A Mafia leader in Sicily, Cardi, warns Countess Marcherita that she must not marry Count Martinello. Cardi's henchmen murder Count Martinello as he is enroute to the wedding. Norvin Blake, an American wounded during the killing of Martinello, breaks the news to the countess, who swears to avenge the death. Several years later Marcherita, posing as a nurse, meets Blake, who declares his love for her. Maruffi, a suitor of Marcherita, is discovered to be Cardi. During a fight between Blake and Cardi, the latter is stabbed by Marcherita's maid. Blake finally wins Marcherita.

The Ne'er-Do-Well (Paramount, April 29, 1923) 8 reels; Thomas Meighan (Kirk Anthony), Lila Lee (Chiquita), Gertrude Astor (Edith Cortlandt), John Miltern (Stephen Cortlandt), Gus Weinberg (Andres Garavel), Sid Smith (Ramon Alfarez), Jules Cowles (Allen Allan), George O'Brien (Clifford) Laurence Wheat (Runnels); D: Alfred E. Green; SP: Louis Stevens. Synopsis: Kirk Anthony's father becomes disgusted with his carefree, spendthrift son and arranges to have him shanghaied to Panama. There Kirk falls in love with Chiquita, the daughter of a Panamanian general. Deciding to make something of himself, he gets a railroad job through Stephen Cortlandt. Stephen's death is blamed on Kirk, but Edith Cortlandt, Stephen's sister, produces a suicide note which clears him. Kirk is successful in his job and returns to the United States with Chiquita to ask his father's forgiveness.

The Spoilers (Jesse D. Hampton Productions/Goldwyn, August 5, 1923) 8 reels; Milton Sills (Roy Glennister), Anna Q. Nilsson (Cherry Malotte), Barbara Bedford (Helen Chester), Robert Edeson (Joe Dextry), Ford Sterling (Slapjack Simms), Wallace MacDonald (Broncho Kid), Noah Beery (Alex McNamara), Mitchell Lewis (Marshal Voorhees), John Elliott (Bill Wheaton), Robert McKim (Struve), Tom McGuire (Captain Stevens), Kate Price (Landlady), Rockliffe Fellowes (Matthews), Gordon Russell (Burke), Louise Fazenda (Tilly Nelson), Sam De Grasse (Judge Stillman), Albert Roscoe (Mexico Mullins), Jack Curtis (Bill Nolan); D: Lambert Hillyer; SP: Fred Myton, Elliott Clawson, Hope Loring. Synopsis: Roy Glennister and his partner are victimized by a crooked political plot that involves the possession of gold mines in Alaska. Alex McNamara, the Nome political boss, and Judge Stillman

unite in robbing the owners by jumping their claims. Roy has befriended Helen Chester, Stillman's niece, but believes she is in cahoots with McNamara and Sullivan. He saves Stillman from hanging; however, Helen, now suspicious of her uncle, investigates. She is saved from a compromising situation by her brother, and McNamara gets his just desserts after a terrific beating at the hands of Glennister.
Review:

> After all, "Action" is the biggest thing the screen can have. When there is action with a capital A, such as *The Spoilers* possesses, and a full-blooded story that holds on its active as well as romantic side, along with such superb production and direction as Jesse D. Hampton has given to this picture, there isn't an exhibitor in the country who needs think twice.
>
> It's great work; it's intelligent work; and while it may be said the story is there, which it is, one cannot gainsay at the same moment that the worth of a story must be brought out in the celluloid. That's what Hampton has done. He has made that beach story stand and dance. It never lies down. That's why it's Action and that's why Action is the film's best seller.

Variety (August 9, 1923)

Big Brother (Paramount, December 23, 1923) 7 reels; Tom Moore (Jimmy Donovan), Edith Roberts (Kitty Costello), Raymond Hatton (Cokey Joe Miller), Joe King (Big Ben Murray), Mickey Bennett (Midge Murray), Charles Henderson ("Father Dan" Marron), Paul Panzer (Mike Navarro), Neil Kelley (Monk Manelli), William Black (Loman Duryea), Martin Faust (Spike Doyle), Milton Herman (Izzy), Florence Ashbrook (Mrs. Sheean), Yvonne Hughes (Navarro's Girl), Charles Hammond (Judge); D: Allan Dwan; SP: Paul

Sloane. **Synopsis:** Jimmy Donovan is made guardian of Midge, the 7-year-old brother of his friend Big Ben Murray. He decides to reform and rear Midge properly. He proves himself by recovering a payroll stolen by some of his former colleagues, thereby winning Midge and Kitty, his girl.

Flowing Gold (Associated First National, March 1, 1924) 8 reels; Anna Q. Nilsson (Allegheny Briskow), Milton Sills (Calvin Gray), Alice Calhoun (Barbara Parker), Crauford Kent (Henry Nelson), John Roche (Buddy Briskow), Cissy Fitzgerald (The Suicide Blonde), Josephine Crowell (Ma Briskow), Bert Woodruff (Pa Briskow), Charles Sellon (Tom Parker); D: Joseph DeGrasse; SP: Richard Walton Tully. **Synopsis:** The Briskows have wealth from the discovery of oil on their property. They engage Calvin Gray, a soldier of fortune, to manage their investments. He thwarts several attempts to swindle the Briskows and winds up marrying Allegheny Briskow.

The Recoil (Metro-Goldwyn, April 27, 1924) 7 reels; Mahlon Hamilton (Gordon Kent), Betty Blythe (Norma Selbee), Fred Paul (William Southern), Clive Brook (Marchmont), Ernest Hilliard (Jim Selbee); D: T. Hayes Hunter; SP: Gerald C. Duffy. **Synopsis:** Gordon Kent owns mines in South America, products from which he sells in Paris. While there he falls in love with penniless Norma Selbee and marries her. She soon runs off with an admirer, Marchmont. Kent hires a private detective and the two soon find out that Marchmont has a criminal record and also that Norma's first husband, Jim Selbee, is still alive. Kent condemns the Selbees to their mutual misery but relents when Norma saves him from a blackmail plot instigated by Selbee. Kent returns to Norma, who has repented of her actions.

A Sainted Devil (Paramount, November 17, 1924) 9 reels; Rudolph

Valentino (Don Alonza Castro), Nita Naldi (Carlotta), Helen D'Algy (Julietta), Dagmar Godowsky (Dona Florencia), Jean Del Val (Casimiro), Antonio D'Algy (Don Luis), George Siegmann (El Tigre), L. Rogers Lytton (Don Baltasar), Isabel West (Dona Encarnacion), Louise Lagrange (Carmelita), Rafael Bongini (Congo), Frank Montgomery (Indian Spy), William Betts (Priest), Edward Elkas (Notary), A. De Rosa (Jefe Politico), Ann Brody (Duenna), Evelyn Axzell (Guadulupe), Marie Diller (Irala); D: Joseph Henabey; SP: Forrest Halsey; S: "Rope's End." **Synopsis:** El Tigre is talked into robbing the Castro estate by Carlotta, former sweetheart of Don Alonza Castro, who is marrying Julietta. El Tigre not only robs the estate but kidnaps Julietta. Alonza goes to her rescue but sees a woman in Julietta's bridal veil making love, with El Tigre. Bent on revenge, Alonza confronts El Tigre in a cafe and they fight. El Tigre is winning but is killed by his enemy Don Luis. Dancer Carmelita tells Alonza that he mistook Carlotta for Julietta, who is safe in a convent.

Winds of Chance (First National, August 1925) 10 reels; Anna Q. Nilsson (Countess Courteau), Ben Lyon (Pierce Phillips), Viola Dana (Rouletta Kirby), Hobart Bosworth (Sam Kirby), Dorothy Sebastian (Laura), Larry Fisher (Frank McCaskey), Fred Kohler (Joe McCaskey), Claude Gillingwater (Tom Linton), Charles Crockett (Jerry), J. Gunnis Davis (Danny Royal), Fred Warren (Kid Bridges), Tom London (Sergeant Rock), William Conklin (Inspector), J. W. Johnston (Mountie), Victor McLaglen (Poleon Doret), Wade Boteler (Jack McCaskey), Barney Furey (Corporal), Philo McCullough (Count Courteau), Anne M. Wilson (Dancer), Fred Sullivan (Morris Best), John T. Murray (Lucky Broad), Charles Anderson (Fred Miller), James O'Malley (Mountie); D: Frank Lloyd; SP: J. G. Hawks. **Synopsis:** Pierce Phillips joins the Alaska gold rush but loses all his money in a shell game. He goes to work for Countess Courteau and a mutual love develops, but she tells him that she is already married to Count Courteau. Pierce returns to Dawson and gets a job as a gold weigher. He is framed for robbery by the jealous Count Courteau, who has found out about the love affair between the countess and Pierce. Countess Corteau manages to get evidence that clears Pierce, but then Pierce is blamed for the death of the count. However, the mounties find the real killer, leaving Pierce and the countess to renew their love for each other.

The Goose Woman (Universal, December 27, 1925) 8 reels; Louise Dresser (Mary Holmes/Marie de Nardi), Jack Pickford (Gerald Holmes), Constance Bennett (Hazel Woods), Spottiswoode Aitken (Jacob Riggs), Gary Cooper (Reporter), Gustav Von Seyffertitz (Mr. Vogel), George Nichols (Detective Lopez), Marc MacDermott (Amos Ethridge); D: Clarence Brown; SP: Melville Brown. **Synopsis:** Marie de Nardi is at the height of her career as an international known opera singer when she gives birth to an illegitimate son. As a result, she loses her following and becomes bitter, blaming her son for her downfall. She turns to drink and eventually goes to a small village where she lives as Mary Holmes in a ramshakle shack, tending sheep for her livelihood. She is the only possible witness to the murder of Amos Ethridge, a millionaire who was backing the local stock company. Gerald Holmes, Mary's illegitimate son, becomes engaged to Hazel Woods, a local actress. Out of spite, Mary tells her son of his illegitimacy.

A reporter covering the murder of Ethridge investigates and discovers that Mary was once a famous opera singer. She is cleaned up and questioned by the press. As she tells her fabricated stories, she unknowingly implicates her son Gerald in the murder. When she learns what she has done, she calls in the press and retracts her false stories. The doorman of the theater confesses that it was he who murdered Ethridge because Ethridge had seduced a number of young actresses, and he wanted to protect Hazel from his vile advances.

The Auction Block (MGM, February 1, 1926) 7 reels; Charles Ray (Bob Wharton), Elinor Boardman (Lorelei Knight), Sally O'Neil (Bernice Lane), Ernest Gillen (Carter Lane), Charles Clary (Homer Lane), David Torrence (Robert Wharton, Sr.), James Corrigan (Mr. Knight), Forest Seabury (Edward Blake), Ned Sparks (Nat Saluson); D: Hobart Henley; SP: Fanny Hatton; S: *The Auction Block*. Synopsis: Lorelei Knight wins a beauty contest and becomes the toast of New York. She meets Bob Wharton at a charity ball and marries him two days later. Bob's father tells her of Bob's poor character and she returns home to Palmdale, South Carolina, her home, and tells no one of her marriage. Bob follows and finds work in a shoestore and quickly becomes popular with the young ladies of the town. Bernice Lane purposely strands Bob on a country road all night. Her father attempts to make Bob marry her. When he finds out that Bob is already married, he goes gunning for him. Lorelei makes Bernice tell her father the truth that Bob is innocent of any wrongdoing. Lorelei and Bob are finally reunited. Note: This is a remake of the 1917 film, but the story is quite different.

The Barrier (MGM, March 8, 1926) 7 reels; Norman Kerry (Meade Burrell), Henry B. Walthall (Gale Gaylord), Lionel Barrymore (Stark Bennett), Marceline Day (Necia), George Cooper (Sergeant Murphy), Bert Woodruff (No Creek Lee), Mario Carillo (Poleon Doret), Pat Harman (First Mate), Shannon Day (Necia's Indian Mother), Princess Neola (Alluna); D: George Hill; SP: Harvey Gates; S: *The Barrier*. Synopsis: During a storm off the coast of Alaska, Stark Bennett, a cruel sea captain, forces his wife to assist the men.

She is fatally hurt in an accident. Seaman Gaylord agrees to take her child away from the influences of the father. Seventeen years later Gaylord is a storekeeper in Flanbeau, Alaska. He has reared the child, Necia, as his daughter in ignorance of her half-caste parentage. Necia falls in love with Lieutenant Meade Burrell. When Bennett's ship comes into the port, he reveals the truth about the girl's parentage. Necia leaves with her brutal father without seeing Meade again. When the ship is ice-jammed, the crew deserts. Burrell arrives over the ice and rescues Necia, leaving the unconscious Bennett, who is destroyed in an ice flow.

Padlocked (Paramount, August 1926) 7 reels; Lois Moran (Edith Gilbert), Noah Beery (Henry Gilbert), Louise Dresser (Mrs. Alcott), Helen Jerome Eddy (Belle Galloway), Allan Simpson (Norman Van Pelt), Florence Turner (Mrs. Gilbert), Richard Arlen ("Tubby" Clark), Charles Lane (Monte Hermann), Douglas Fairbanks, Jr. ("Sonny" Galloway), Charlot Bird (Blanche Galloway), Josephine Crowell (Mrs. Galloway), Andre Lanoy (Lorelli), Irma Kornelia (Pearl Gates); D: Allan Dwan; SP: James Shelly Hamilton; Adapt: Becky Gardiner. Synopsis: Edith Gilbert leaves home to seek her fortune in New York. She gets work as a café dancer and attracts two suitors — Monte Hermann, a man-about-town, and youthful Norman Van Pelt. Hermann leaves for Europe following an argument with Edith, while Edith's father, a bigoted and puritanical reformer, finds out that Edith is a café dancer and, through his influence, has her committed to a reformatory. Gilbert has married Belle Galloway only to find out that she is after his money. Therefore, Gilbert pays her off to leave him. He seeks out Edith to make amends for the past. In the end Edith and Norman are reunited.

The Michigan Kid (Universal, June 30, 1928) 6 reels; Renée Adorée (Rose

Morris), Fred Esmelton (Hiram Morris), Virginia Grey (Rose, as a Child), Conrad Nagel (Jimmy Cowan), Maurice Murphy (Jimmy Cowan as a Child), Adolph Milar (Shorty), LLoyd Whitlock (Frank Hayward), Donald House (Frank Howard as a Child); D: Irvin Willat; SP: Peter Milne; Adapt: G. Hawkes, Charles Logan, Irvin Willat. **Synopsis:** Jimmy Cowan goes to Alaska to seek his fortune so that he can marry his childhood sweetheart, Rose Morris. He becomes known as "The Michigan Kid," a lucky gambler and proprietor of a gambling hall. Hayward, Cowan's boyhood rival for Rose, also lives in Alaska. He sends for Rose so he can marry her. Before she arrives, however, he gets into trouble with the law and has to go into hiding. Jimmy meets the train carrying Rose, who soon decides that Hayward is not worthy of her. Instead, she marries Jimmy.

The Mating Call (Paramount, July 23, 1928) 7 reels; Thomas Meighan (Leslie Hatton), Evelyn Brent (Rose Henderson), Renée Adorée (Catherine), Alan Rosco (Lon Henderson), Gardner James (Marvin Swallow), Helen Foster (Jessie Peebles), Cyril Chadwick (Anderson), Luke Cosgrove (Judge Peebles), Will R. Walling; D: James Cruze; SP: Walter Woods; P: Howard Hughes. **Synopsis:** Leslie Hatton, a World War I veteran, returns home to discover that his wife, Rose, has had their marriage annulled in order to marry Lon Henderson. When Rose becomes disillusioned with Henderson she tries to go back to Hatton. However, he will have no part of it. Instead, he goes to Ellis Island, where he persuades Catherine, an aristocratic Russian immigrant, to marry him in return for a home in the United States.

Jesse Peebles, a local girl, has an affair with Henderson and drowns herself in a pond on Leslie's farm. Henderson is head of the Ku Klux Klan and tries to get Leslie convicted of drowning Jessie. Leslie is found innocent after

documents are produced linking Henderson with Jessie. Leslie and Catherine find that they actually love each other — that it is not merely a marriage of convenience.

Son of the Gods (First National, March 9, 1930) 90 mins.; Richard Barthelmess (Sam Lee), Constance Bennett (Allana), Mildred Van Dorn (Eileen), King Hoo Chang (Moy), Barbara Leonard (Mabel), Frank Albertson (Kicker), Geneva Mitchell (Connie), James Eagle (Spud), E. Alyn Warren (Lee Ying), Ivan Christie (Café Manager), Anders Randolph (Wagner), George Irving (Attorney), Claude King (Bathurst), Dickie Moore (Boy), Robert Homans (Dugan); D: Frank Lloyd, SP: Bradley King. **Synopsis:** Sam Lee, reared by a wealthy Chinese merchant in San Francisco's Chinatown, is accepted in college only because of his money. He determines to prove himself and goes to Europe where he meets Allana, who falls madly in love with him. But when she finds out that he is Chinese she drops him quickly. Sam returns to San Francisco to see his dying father. Through Eileen, his best friend, he learns that he is the orphaned son of white parents. When Allana learns of this she repents of her treatment of Sam and returns to the United States to marry him.

Review:

High class general program release. Story weaknesses are the stumbling block. Accepting for treatment the delicate subject of a Chinaman in love with a white girl, and vice versa, realism is sacrificed to an obvious narrative device in order to convert the Chinaman into a white man for the final clinch.

Fine performances by everyone from Barthelmess down, and the restrained direction of Frank Lloyd maintains despite the things the mind fastens on critically en route. Constance Bennett offers a performance of exceptional excellence. Few actresses of her youth and looks can match the authenticity of her acting. She has both imagination and artistic sincerity. Also worthy of special mention was a small part played by Geneva Mitchell, early in the picture, as a white girl who calculates the percentage and decides a handsome Chinaman who has millions is not to be snubbed. She plays the limited opportunity for a really distinguished result. Dickie Moore, in a few short feet had the audience ready to adopt him. He's a postage stamp-full of sex appeal, about two years old and utterly infectious.

Variety (date unknown)

Framed (RKO, March 16, 1930) 62 mins.; Evelyn Brent (Rose Manning), Regis Toomey (Jimmy McArthur), Maurice Block (Bing Murdock), William Holden (Inspector McArthur), Robert Emmett O'Connor (Sergeant Schultze), Eddie Kane (Head Waiter); D: George Archainbaud; SP: Paul Schofield. **Synopsis:** Rose Manning is angry at Inspector McArthur for what she considers the unjust slaying of her father. Five years later she is a nightclub hostess wooed by Chuck Gaines, a bootlegger. However, Rose is interested in Jimmy Carter, who is the son of Inspector McArthur. Chuck investigates a raid on the club by the inspector. Rose warns Jimmy but is shot by Chuck, who in turned is killed by Jimmy. Rose declares that Chuck was killed by Bing Murdock. Inspector McArthur realizes Rose and Jimmy are truly in love and gives them his blessing. **Review:**

> *Framed* owes the business it will do as a standard programmer to the punchiness of the situations, lack of padding and the able direction, plus some very good acting. Nothing to set the picture's plot aside from stereotyped for-

mula, but for racketeering mellers it has been handled with a freshness that gives it a fairly good entertainment rating.

> Concentration of action with the least amount of preliminary matter and excess dialog existent, turns *Framed* into a product that holds the attention admirably. Sustaining of the suspense, without disturbing the smoothness of the continuity, is another outstanding trait.

Variety (date unknown)

The Spoilers (Paramount, September 20, 1930) 85 mins.; Gary Cooper (Roy Glennister), Kay Johnson (Helen Chester), Betty Compson (Cherry Malotte), William Boyd (McNamara), Harry Green (Herman), Slim Summerville (Slapjack Simms), James Kirkwood (Joe Dextry), Lloyd Ingraham (Judge Stillman), Oscar Apfel (Struve), Jack N. Holmes (Voorhees), Knute Ericson (Captain Stevens), Edward Coxen (Lawyer), Jack Trent (Broncho Kid), Edward Hearn (Lieutenant), Hal David (Bill Wheaton), John Beck (Hansen); D: Edwin Carewe; SP: Bartlett Cormack. **Synopsis:** Roy Glennister, co-owner of the Midas mine, meets Helen Chester on a voyage from the United States to Nome. Upon arrival he finds that his partners, Slapjack Simms and Joe Dextry, are frustrated by the actions of Marshal Voorhees, Judge Stillman, and McNamara, a politician. They cloud the titles of the various mines and take them over in the name of McNamara. The Midas mine falls into their hands and the personal cache of Glennister, Simms, and Dextry is stolen. In retaliation, Glennister forms a vigilante group to take back the mines by force. McNamara calls for a detail of soldiers to protect "his property." Justice prevails in the end with Glennister and friends getting their mines back and Glennister beating McNamara in a fight to the finish. Not only does Glennister get back his mine but he gets Helen Chester to boot.

The Silver Horde (RKO, October 29, 1930) 8 reels; Evelyn Brent (Cherry Malotte), Raymond Hatton (Fraser), Louis Wolheim (George Balt), Blanche Sweet (Queenie), Jean Arthur (Mildred Wayland), Joel McCrea (Boyd Emerson), Gavin Gordon (Fred Marsh), Purnell Pratt (Wayne Wayland), William Davidson (Thomas Hillard), Ivan Linow (Svenson); D: George Archainbaud; SP: Wallace Smith. Synopsis: Boyd Emerson and his friend Fraser arrive in the fishing village of Kalvik with their dogsled to find that the village is dominated by Balt, a brute of a man. Almost immediately he and Boyd tangle, and Boyd gives him a good thrashing. Cherry Malotte, a dance hall girl, puts an end to the argument and offers them hospitality. She tells them about Marsh, a ruthless exploiter, who will permit no outsiders to settle there.

Cherry is developing a copper lode and takes Boyd into partnership with her, having fallen in love with him. She schemes to stake him through Tom Hillard, a Seattle banker, planning to refinance Balt's fishery and compete with Marsh. Boyd, Fraser, and Balt leave for Seattle, where Boyd calls on his sweetheart, Mildred Wayland. Boyd secures financial backing but Marsh stops the credit. Cherry comes to his aid, and with the salmon industry in full swing, Boyd comes into conflict with Marsh. Fishing fleets meet in hand-to-hand fighting, and Marsh is beaten. He seeks revenge by slandering Cherry, but Boyd counters with Queenie, a discarded old flame.

Balt takes revenge on Marsh, strangling him, and Boyd and Mildred are united in love.

White Shoulders (Radio Pictures, June 6, 1931) 80 mins.; Mary Astor (Norma Selbee), Jack Holt (Gordon Kent), Ricardo Cortez (Lawrence Marchmont), Sidney Toler (William Sothern), Kitty Kelly (Maria Fontaine), Robert Keith, Nicholas Soussanin; D: Melville Brown; SP: J. Walter Ruben. Synopsis: An adulterous wife of a rich man takes up with a gigolo and, as punishment, her rich husband forces the gigolo and his wayward wife to stay together. Ultimately, the man and his wife reconcile.

Young Donovan's Kid (Radio Pictures, May 1931) 76 mins.; Jackie Cooper (Midge Murray), Richard Dix (Jim Donovan), Marion Shilling (Kitty Costello), Frank Sheridan (Father Dan), Boris Karloff (Cokey Joe), Dick Rush (Burke), Fred Kelsey (Collins), Wilfred Lucas (Duryea); D: Fred Nible; SP: J. Walter Ruben; S: *Big Brother*. Synopsis: A six-year old orphan is adopted by a gunman. The boy is brought up by the gangster, who does nothing to shelter the child from his rough lifestyle. In the end the gangster is reformed by the presence of the young boy.

Review:

It will be difficult for certain b.o. spots to reconcile the incongruities of this picture. That will be mostly in the small town. For the bigger spots this film looks a moderate success. It's about a kid adopted by a gunman. As a result the man reforms out of love for the boy. A slight romance on the side between a virtuous maid and the gunman is mild.

What buoys the picture's chances is the presence of Jackie Cooper. This kid actor fresh from *Skippy* makes a lovable character as *Young Donovan's Kid*, although a bit too precocious and somewhat ritzy with dialog.

Cooper plays a six-year old and the picture's pathos is all on his end, while the sentiment is with the gunman. That throws the entertainment recipe off balance but nevertheless attracts to a degree. How much will depend on type of audience.

Variety (May 27, 1931)

The Past of Mary Holmes (RKO-Radio, January 20, 1933) 70 mins.;

Helen MacKellar (Mary Holmes), Eric Linden (Geoffrey Holmes), Jean Arthur (Joan Hoyt), Skeets Gallagher (Pratt), Ivan Simpson (Jacob Riggs), Clay Clement (Etheridge), Franklin Parker (Brooks), Eddie Nugent (Flannigan), Roscoe Ates (Klondike), J. Carroll Naish (Kent), John Sheehan (Kinkaid); D: Harlan Thompson and Slavko Vorkapich; SP: Edward Marion Dix and Edward Doherty; S: *The Goose Woman.* Synopsis: A former opera star loses her voice and takes it out on guzzling gin, living in a sty and making her son miserable. A man is killed and the boy condemned by his mother's fake story to the court — a fake story brought about by a desire to see her name in the papers. The guilty man eventually confesses.

Review:

As *The Goose Woman* this film made quite an impression as a silent. The story is there, good writers and good actors handled it, but it now evolves as a lifeless, unbelievable piece of screen fare. For the small houses.

Louise Dresser was *The Goose Woman* in the silent. Helen MacKellar does it here. Miss MacKellar might have been able to handle the part were there somewhere around the studio a gently restraining hand. So she goes beserk with a vengeance. And Eric Linden, not to be outdone, goes Hamlet 100%.

The motivation is not made entirely clear, and it's tough enough to find some sympathy for the mother at best, without having her painted in quite such dark strokes. About the best performance comes from "Skeets" Gallagher as a newspaperman again. Jean Arthur and Ivan Simpson are suitable support.

Variety (date unknown)

The Barrier (Paramount, November 12, 1937) 90 mins.; Leo Carrillo (Poleon Doret), Jean Parker (Necia), James Ellison (Lieutenant Burrell), Robert Barrat (John Gale), Otto Kruger (Stark), Andy Clyde (No Creek Lee), Addison Richards (Runnion), Sara Haden (Alluna), J. M. Kerrigan (Sergeant Thomas), Sally Martin (Molly), Fernando Alvarado (Johnny), Alan Davis (Sergeant Tobin); D: Leslie Selander; P: Harry Sherman; SP: Bernard Schubert, Harrison Jacobs, Mordaunt Shairp. Synopsis: This is the third movie version of the story of a man named John Gale who kidnaps the daughter of a woman he once loved, then rears her to believe she is a half-breed Indian.

Review:

New version, which was made by Harry Sherman for Paramount, contains extraordinary scenic vestiture, the result of an enthusiastic pilgrimage into the wilds of M. Baker National Park, Washington. Here, on a river bank, was reconstructed a replica of the Alaskan village of Flambeau as it existed in the 90's when the Klondike gold rush started. Action spreads from valleys to pinnacles. The sheer beauty of the photography, captured by George Barnes, is impressive and a distinct factor in such satisfaction as the film provides.

A more concise screen script from which extraneous subplots and superfluous characterizations had been eliminated or condensed would have helped the picture. In completed form, the over-length will militate against its suitability as a strong secondary dualer. In spots where westerns and action pictures are popular, it rates the leadoff.

Robert Barrat plays the conscious-stricken John Gale, and his confession of his old time crime is tensely spoken. Jean Parker is attractive as Necia, the white child whose supposed mixed racial parentage is the barrier to marriage with the army lieutenant. James Ellison has the manly bearing for the hero. Otto Kruger is the menace, which his looks do not portray, and Andy Clyde is an amusing prospector.

Variety (November 3, 1937)

Flowing Gold (Warner Brothers, August 1940) 80 mins.; John Garfield (Johnny Blake), Frances Farmer (Linda Chalmers), Pat O'Brien (Hap O'Connor), Raymond Walburn (Wildcat Chalmers), Cliff Edwards (Hot Rocks), Tom Kennedy (Petunia), Granville Bates (Charles Hammond), Jody Gilbert (Tille), Edward Pawley (Collins), Frank Mayo (Mike Brannigan), William Marshal (Joe), Sol Gorss (Luke), Virginia Sale (Nurse), John Alexander (Sheriff); D: Alfred Green; SP: Kenneth Gamet. **Synopsis:** Johnny Blake is on the run, showing up in an oil town for a job while a fugitive from a murder charge. Hap O'Connor is the head driller of the outfit in love with the boss's daughter. Blake, O'Connor, and Linda Chalmers become friends, while the former takes the reverse technique of romance in winning the girl's hand. While this unfolds, there's the rush of getting a well drilled before the lease expires, with Blake driving the crew after Hap O'Connor sustains a broken leg. The general heroics are unfolded until the well comes in, and Blake returns to face the murder charge with the girl at his side.
Review:

Retaining nothing more than the title and booming oil fields' background of Rex Beach's story (which was originally turned out for First National in 1924 with Milton Sills and Anna Q. Nilsson) *Flowing Gold* is an action meller of obvious pattern. Aided by the combo of John Garfield, Frances Farmer, and Pat O'Brien for marquee dressing, picture will get by as a standard programmer for the adventurous inclined.

Picture looks like it rushed to catch first followup of oil industry dramas indicated by release of *Boom Town*. In fact, the similar situation of stories, displaying the conflict between two men for the love of a girl stands out prominently. Although *Flowing Gold* has its share of lusty and two-fisted action, script fails to generate high spots, too frequently relying on obvious situations to carry it along.

Variety (August 28, 1940)

The Spoilers (Universal, April 10, 1942) Marlene Dietrich (Cherry Malotte), Randolph Scott (Alex McNamara), John Wayne (Roy Glennister), Margaret Lindsay (Helen Chester), Harry Carey (Dextry), Richard Barthelmess (Broncho Kid), George Cleveland (Banty), Samuel S. Hinds (Judge Stillman), Russell Simpson (Flapjack), William Farnum (Wheaton), Marietta Canty (Idabelle), Jack Norton (Mr. Skinner), Charles Halton (Strove), Bud Osborne (Marshal), Drew Demarest (Galloway), Robert W. Service (The Poet), Ray Bennett, Forrest Taylor, Art Miles, Charles McMurphy; D: Ray Enright; SP: Lawrence Hazard and Tom Reed. **Synopsis:** The story tells of Alex McNamara — as the crooked gold commissioner — an equally unscrupulous judge, and their legal confiscation of the miners' claims. Roy Glennister, a prospector, loses the mine he jointly owns with Dextry through the crooked court. Cherry Malotte is the operator of a gin and gambling emporium. Dovetailed to this is the tempestuous romance between Glennister and Malotte, with McNamara as the bad third.
Review:

Since these are uncertain days for both producer and exhibitor, there can be no fault-finding with Hollywood's return to an unoriginal, though occasionally successful, formula for boxoffice effectiveness. The pattern in this case is that by-now classic of pictures, *The Spoilers*. Here and there are suggestions of mustiness that bespeak the approximately 40 years since *Spoilers* was first written by Rex Beach, but a first-rate production cast, direction and plenty of action assure sock b.o. returns wherever played.

Though the screen treatment has been apparently Haysed over the original novel and subsequent film versions, *The Spoilers* in its present form is still a teeming, raw saga of Alaska in the '98 gold rush days.

Of course, the big scene is the fight originally made one of the classic brawls of filmdom by Tom Santschi and William Farnum. The slugging match in the final reel between Glennister and McNamara is something that apparently was staged profitably at Madison Square Garden. It is that spectacular, starting from Cherry Malotte's boudoir, cascading through a balcony to the floor of the ginnery, out to the street and finally winding up in the wagon-churned mud of the road.

Performances are all uniformly good, with the stellar trio, of course, showing up best because of their prominent parts. Miss Dietrich is excellent in a role suggesting it was designed for her. Scott and Wayne are typical of the great outdoors men for which the parts call.

Variety (April 15, 1942)

Michigan Kid (Universal, March 1947) 69 mins.; Jon Hall (Michigan Kid), Victor McLagen (Curley), Rita Johnson (Sue), Andy Devine (Buster), Byron Fougler (Mr. Porter), Stanley Andrews (Sheriff), Milburn Stone (Lanny), William Brooks (Steve), Joan Fulton (Soubrette), Leonard East (Dave), Ray Teal (Sergeant), Eddy Waller (Post Office Clerk), Karl Hackett (Sam), Tom Quinn (Hank), Bert Le Baron (Rifleman), Edmund Cobb (Joe), Guy Wilkerson (Shotgun Messenger); D: Ray Taylor; SP: Roy Chanslor. Synopsis: *Michigan Kid* is an action-packed western in which a former U.S. marshal (Jon Hall) goes to Arizona where he thwarts a road gang's plot to claim money belonging to a pretty heiress (Rita Johnson).

The Avengers (Republic, March 1950) 92 mins.; John Carroll (Don Carless/Francisco Suarez), Adele Mara (Maria Moreno), Mona Maris (Yvonne), Roberto Airaldi (Colonel Luis Corral), Jorge Villoldo (Don Rafael Moreno), Vincente Padula (El Mocho/Hernandez), Vivian Ray (Carmencita), Cecile Lezard (Pamela), Juan Olaguivel (Sancho), Eduardo Gardere (Fencing Double), Angel M. Gordordo Palacios (Fencing Double); D: John H. Auer; SP: Lawrence Kimble, Aeneas MacKenzie; S: *Don Careless*. Synopsis: Marie Moreno, the colonial governor's beautiful daughter, is about to marry a man set on overthrowing the government, when she falls for Don Careless/Francisco Suarez, who rescues her and the colony.

The World in His Arms (Universal, 1952) 104 mins.; Gregory Peck (Jonathan Clark), Ann Blyth (Countess Marina), Anthony Quinn (Portugee), John McIntire (Deacon Greathouse), Carl Esmond (Prince Semyon), Andrea King (Mamie), Eugenie Leontovich (Madame Selanova), Hans Conried (Eustace), Rhys Williams (Eben Cleggett), Sig Ruman (General Vorashilov), Gregory Gay (Paul Shushaldin), Bill Radovich (Ogeechuk), Bryan Forbes (William Cleggett), Henry Kulky (Peter); D: Raoul Walsh; SP: Borden Chase, Horace McCoy. Synopsis: A sea captain, Jonathan Clark, falls in love with a Russian countess, Marina, who is fleeing a prearranged marriage to Prince Semyon.

The Spoilers (Universal, December 1955) 84 mins.; Anne Baxter (Cherry Malotte), Jeff Chandler (Roy Glennister), Rory Calhoun (Alex McNamara), Ray Danton (Blackie), Barbara Britton (Helen Chester), John McIntire (Dextry), Wallace Ford (Flapjack Simms), Forrest Lewis (Banty Jones), Carl Benton Reid (Judge Stillman), Raymond Walburn (Mr. Skinner), Ruth Donnelly (Duchess), Dayton Lummis (Wheaton), William Bouchey (Jonathan Struve), Roy Barcroft (Marshal), Byron Foulger (Montrose), Robert Foulk (Bartender), Arthur Space (Bank Manager), Harry Seymour (Piano Player), Bob Steele (Miner), Edwin Parker (Barry), Lee Roberts (Deputy), John Close (Deputy), John Harmon (Kelly), Paul McGuire (Thompson), Frank Sully (Miner), Lane Bradford (Sourdough), Terry Frost (Deputy); D: Jesse Hibbs; SP: Oscar Brodney, Charles Hoffman. **Synopsis:** The story deals with organized claim-jumping in Alaskan gold mines around Nome at the turn of the century. Alex McNamara is the organizer, posing as a gold commissioner, who has designs on the richest of the mines, co-owned by Roy Glennister and Dextry. With a phony judge, the latter's attractive so-called niece, and a crooked attorney, McNamara is doing fine until a hero who doesn't give up easily uncovers evidence of the illegal takeover. The epic fistfight (a label first handed out to the brawl between William Farnum and Tom Santschi in the 1914 Selig Polyscope version) sprawls from Cherry Malotte's plush apartment above the saloon, through the northern bistro, out of the window, and winds up in the mud of the Nome streets.

Review:

The outdoor action penned in early 1900's by Rex Beach in his *The Spoilers* novel has paid off big for Hollywood — either in the story itself or in its infinite variations. This is the fifth time around for the original and Universal's second version. There's still b.o. coin to be panned although not any longer in gold-rush quantity. This 1955 entry is a general market, frozen north actioner that should find the prospecting satisfactory.

Anne Baxter, Jeff Chandler, and Rory Calhoun are the principals, lending familiar marquee names to the Ross Hunter production. The trio bring off the show in suitable fashion for those who like their action spelled in a-b-c terms. Jesse Hibbs' direction of the script by Oscar Brodney and Charles Hoffman is breezy most of the way, but action fully rugged such as in the climaxing fisticuffs, between hero and heavy, when the plot demands roughness.

Variety (date unknown)

COWBOYS
UNDER THE BIG TOP

Chapter 7

Cinema Cowboys
Hit the Sawdust Trail

The Circus! What is it? For generations it has been that gaudy, glittering, glamorous institution that weaves so stout a thread through the fabric of happy memories. The very word conjures up the brazen voice of the calliope screaming out *The Thunderer* or *The Battle of the Bird* as the brightly painted wagon that carried it was drawn along Main Street by a team of majestic white horses. And older adults remember the goose pimples that grew when the great 20-piece circus bands struck up *Floto's Triumph, Robbins Brothers' Triumphal, Robinson's Grand Entry*, or *Barnum and Bailey's Favorite*, as a fantasy world burst into life under the big top.

The circus meant spangles and glitter; the spine-tingling roar of the big cats; the enchanting smell of sawdust, popcorn, cotton candy, and wild animals; the brave flutter of flags above the awesome big top; the marvelous, irresistible aura of the lithographs inviting one and all into a fairyland world; funny looking clowns; splendorous ladies; and, invariably, the stupendous wild west aftershows — or concerts, as they were usually called — when, for a quarter, everyone got a seat in the reserved section to watch a congress of cowboy rough riders perform. Often such concerts were headlined by western movie stars.

Circus exhibition in the United States had its beginning in 1785, but was not presented under canvas until 1826, and the combination of performance and wild animal menagerie did not enter the picture until 1851. When the Ringling Brothers put out their first real circus from Baraboo, Wisconsin, they owned 11 wagons, 20 horses, and a wild animal menagerie consisting of 1 lonesome hyena. That was in 1884.[1]

In the preceding year Buffalo Bill's Wild West was launched on the climb to circus popularity. Actually, his staging of an Old Glory Blow Out on July 4, 1882, in North Platte, Nebraska, marked the beginning of both the wild west show and the rodeo.

Now we ought to distinguish between wild west and circus. A circus included an assortment of acts, nonwestern related, and a wild animal menagerie. The wild west show was an exhibition illustrating scenes and events supposedly characteristic of the American West. In later years many circuses presented a wild west show as an aftershow, and many wild west shows presented acts normally associated with the circus. Thus, they gradually blended in the mind of the public. By the late 1920s both types of shows were referred to as "circus" by the average layman. But it should be noted that the circus, per se preceded the wild west show as a form of outdoor entertainment, and that the wild west show developed into the sport and exhibition of rodeo, with their beginnings intertwined.

The cinema cowboy's experience on the sawdust trail is an interesting part of cowboy history that first needs discovery, and then preservation. Much of that history now appears lost forever, as most of the western performers have passed on, with little having been recorded from their wild west show days. My own research was at best sadly insufficient. So what follows is only a beginning; and if any reader can add to this rather pleasant and entertaining phase of cowboy history I would appreciate their information. While some cinema cowboys are inseparably bound to the wild west show, other personalities have no doubt been overlooked in writing this story. This is especially true of the legion of supporting players who found their way into the movies in the early days of flickers and the golden age of the circus; many of them surely came from the rodeo or wild west show.

Both the circus and the wild west show provided a kaleidoscopic panorama of glittering pagentry in which a number of cinema cowboys found a niche — either on the road to success during their moviemaking days, or on the downhill ride to oblivion. This, then, is their story. It is not a potpourri of reminiscences about wild west shows and the cowboys and cowgirls who rode to fame or obscurity in them. Rather, it is a chronicle of a few special movie cowboys who came from the circus tent to the movie screen then returned to the circus, or who worked both arena and set, or the very few who made it big in movies and then went to the big top.

Everyone knows that Will Rogers was a humorist, actor, journalist, and philosopher. Not everybody knows that he was a real cowboy, born in Oologah, Indian Territory (now Oklahoma), in 1879. Fewer still know of his wild west show background. As a youth Will had the wonderlust, and he drifted from one ranch to another, working for $30–40 a month and his keep. His father gave him a small herd of cattle and he worked for a while on the Rogers's ranch along the Verdigris River.

Will spent a lot of time on the Miller Brothers' 101 Ranch in the late 1800s and early 1900s. He liked to prowl the Salt Fork range, and he would put up with the 101 outfit for a time doing more cow work in a week than some riders would do in a month, yet never taking one cent for it. Then he might drift over to the Mulhall range (also a famous show outfit), or pitch in with some other cow outfit for a time.[2]

Always restless — to the chagrin of his father — Will refused to stay home and tend his own or his father's cattle, preferring instead to go with a friend to Argentina, where he worked for a time punching cattle for $4 a month.[3] The year was 1902. Homesick and destitute, Will took a job on a cattle boat headed for South Africa that fall. There he worked as a cowboy on a cattle drive to Ladysmith, then worked on various ranches and trained horses for the British army.[4]

It was in South America that Will found himself, so to speak. There he discovered to his immense delight that he could earn a livelihood doing the thing he enjoyed most — twirling a lasso. Texas Jack's Wild West Circus was showing in Ladysmith, and Will went to see the showman. Texas Jack performed a rope trick called the Big Crinoline, in which all of a long rope was let out in a huge, twirling loop. Jack remarked that he was the only person in Africa who could do it. Will easily duplicated the feat and then went on to dance in and out of a big vertical rope spin. He was immediately hired at $20 a week as a circus headliner. At his own suggestion he was billed as "The Cherokee Kid — The Man Who Can Lasso the Tail Off a Blowfly."[5]

There were 35 or 40 people and 30 horses in the show, and the usual schedule was to stay in a town for two or three days. Texas Jack hired Will as a trick roper, but he also rode a bucking horse and performed in blood-curdling dramatizations of life in Western America, sometimes taking the part of an Indian, at other times that of a Negro. He often did the cakewalk and sang "coon songs," as the genre frequently sung by black-faced comedians was called.[6]

Will stayed nearly a year in South Africa, learning much about show business from Texas Jack. But a yearning for home and the Oklahoma range prompted him to leave the show and work his way by ship to Australia. There — and penniless — he took a job in the Wirth Brothers's Circus as a roper and trick rider with great success.[7]

Will finally worked his way home, and settled down briefly on the old Dog Iron Ranch in Oklahoma. But showbusiness was in his blood, and he was soon at work for the Cummings and Mulhall Wild West Show at the St. Louis World's Fair in 1904.[8]

In the spring of 1905 Will shipped Teddy, his trick pony and Comanche, his old roping horse, to New York where he made his debut in Madison Square Garden as a featured performer in Colonel Zack Mulhall's Wild West Show on April 27. During one performance a wild steer went on a rampage, jumped a guard rail, and ran amuck in the grandstand. Will grabbed his lasso, dashed up the steps and coolly, quickly roped the animal and pulled him back into the arena. The audience arose in loud applause, and the next day Will Rogers's name was on the front pages of the New York City newspapers.[9]

Rogers went on to become a stage performer, first strictly as a horse and roping act, then with his famous chatter and chewing gum routine. He played in England for two years. Over time he phased out the horse act and developed the comedy routine.[10] In the summer of 1915 Florenz Ziegfeld was convinced that Rogers would add needed humor to his productions, and for the following four years Will was at the Ziegfeld's Follies with his midnight frolic on the Amsterdam roof. During Will's first year with Ziegfeld he earned $125 a week; by his fourth year, he was making $600.[11]

In 1919 he abandoned the stage and made a series of silent films for Hal Roach, some of them westerns. But in 1922 he returned to the Follies and stayed on Broadway until 1929, when the advent of sound pictures brought him back to the screen in *They Had to See Paris*, a Fox production. That launched him on his great screen career.[12]

Tom Mix, the most successful and most famous of all screen cowpokes (born in 1880), was serving drinks across the mahogany in an Oklahoma City bar when Colonel Joe Miller blew into town for a cowman's convention in 1905. They got into a conversation, and Tom, a 22-year-old unruly veteran who had deserted during his second stint in the army, expressed his desire to work outdoors. Colonal Joe hired Tom as a full-time cowboy for $15 a month plus room and board to work for the Miller Brothers' 101 Real Wild West Ranch and Real Wild West Show.[13]

The 101 was on the lookout for some handsome, easy-talking men to wrangle tenderfeet on the 101 dude ranch. Tom just about filled the bill. His potential was unquestioned. A mixture of French-Canadian and Italian blood had given him a fine, tall figure and good looks; he wasn't shy around a stranger. All he needed was to learn to ride and rope a little.[14] That he certainly did.

Tom worked his first season for the 101 Real Wild West Ranch in 1906. His first job for the ranch was to act as host for vacationing Eastern "dude" cowboys and cowgirls. Colonel Zack Miller did not think much of Tom as a cowboy, but Mix proved to be an excellent host for the ranch. One oldtimer said, "Tom's duties at the ranch consisted mostly of just hanging around and looking pretty. He was not much of a cowboy as such when he came to work for the 101. People used to say that Tom could get lost in an 800-acre pasture.[15]

Tom Mix stayed with the 101 Ranch and Wild West Show during the seasons of 1907 and 1908. Vester Pegg, who would also find his way into the movies, worked with Tom during this time, and Tom and Will Rogers became fast friends through their mutual activities at the 101 Ranch and other wild west and rodeo programs.

Early in 1909 Tom and his third wife, Olive Stokes, joined the Wilderman Wild West Show, and Tom's roping act proved to be one of the top attractions. Later in the year the Mixes left to form their own wild west show, catering to the crowds attending the Alaska-Yukon-Pacific Exposition in Seattle. Tom had a troupe of 60 performers on his payroll and no previous managerial experience. Yet he somehow managed to realize a profit at the end of the exposition. Afterward, Tom and Olive joined Will A. Dickey's Circle D Wild West Show,[16] but Mix returned to the 101 Ranch show late in 1910, and remained for the season in 1911. He was also with the Kit Carson Buffalo Ranch and Vernon Seaver's Buffalo Ranch shows for short periods of time.[17]

Previously published stories about Mix state that he was a Texas ranger, sheriff in Oklahoma and Kansas, and deputy U.S. marshal from 1905 through 1910. Most of these stories are apparently highly exaggerated. Documentary evidence does show that he was a deputy sheriff and night marshal in Dewey, Oklahoma.[18]

Tom and Olive had a small spread in the Cherokee Territory, and it was because of this that he got into the movies. The Selig Company was looking for a ranch on which to shoot a picture and for someone who knew the surrounding country. Tom Mix volunteered his ranch and himself. The result was *Ranch Life in the Great Southwest*, released in 1910.[19] Tom was hired to handle stock and act as safety man, but he asked director Francis Boggs for a chance to be featured in the film. Boggs consented, and Tom was featured in a bronco-busting sequence.[20] Thus was launched Tom's bombastic career as a motion picture actor. In the summers of 1910 and 1911 he made motion pictures in Canon City, Colorado, often appearing in the films of William Duncan, famed serial king of the 1920s.

In 1912 Tom chose to go to Canada rather than make movies for Selig, and it was there that he headlined the Weadick Wild West Show. But in 1913 he was back making movies for Selig and quickly rose to stardom.[21]

Jack Hoxie, the big, beefy, popular cowboy of the 1920s who rode to fame at Universal, was an authentic cowboy — and then some! Born on Kingfisher Creek in Oklahoma's Indian Territory in 1888, he had to work hard as a youth to help support a large family, as his father had died when Jack was but a small child.

After his mother's remarriage, when Jack was about 17, he struck out on his own to tour the West as a cowhand, working on various ranches and getting a cowboy education that would serve him very well in his future vocation. His skill and riding ability made him popular in many rodeos as a bronco buster and bulldogger. He won a bulldogging championship at Bakersfield, California, as well as many other awards during his early days.[22]

Jack wound up breaking horses on an Indian reservation in the Salmon River country of Idaho. A schoolteacher's wife had taught him to read and write — his only formal education. He is reputed to have traveled with a circus around 1908, appearing in a wild west act.[23] In 1909 he signed with the Dick Stanley Wild West Show as a bronco rider and bulldogger. Despite keen competition, Jack soon became its top attraction; and when the show's owner was killed during a tour of the West coast, Hoxie took over as manager to compete the scheduled appearances before closing the show. The end of this tour left him in California, and overnight, bronco-busting Jack Hoxie became Hartford Hoxie, fledgling motion picture actor.[24]

From 1911 until 1915 Jack alternated between rodeos, wild west performances, and motion pictures, gradually rising to more important movie roles.[25] Real stardom eluded him until 1919, when he was given the male lead in National's *Lightning Bryce*, costarring Ann Little. For an independent serial, it was well done, and Jack appeared the following year with Marin Sais (later his wife) in *Thunderbolt Jack*, another National serial. He was a star at last.[26]

In 1921–22 Hoxie starred in a number of features for Arrow, Aywon, and Standard Film companies, then joined Universal in 1923. With his fast cross draw and astride his trusty steed, he rode to fame along with such other Universal cowboys as Harry Carey, Neal Hart, Pete Morrison, Art Acord, and Hoot Gibson. Fans spoke his name in the same near-reverent tone reserved for such kings of the sagebrush as Buck Jones and Tom Mix.[27] His greatest fame as a wild west showman and circus performer would come in the years following his movie career.

Art Acord was a movie cowboy before the emergence of the star system. Practically forgotten today except by the serious western film devotees, Acord rose to the heights of western movie fame following the release of the Universal serial *The Moon Riders* in 1920, and remained a top draw for several years. With the addition of sound, he disappeared from the screen and died in Chihuahua, Mexico, in 1931, from alcohol poisoning following various run-ins with the law in the United States.[28]

Often spoken of as the first real cowboy star, Acord was thick-browed and somewhat flat-featured, his steely, gray-blue eyes warming or freezing to given situations. He never lost the slow, boyish drawl of his early frugal years on the plains of Indian Territory around Stillwater, Oklahoma, where handling cattle, horses, guns, and fists were part of every frontier youngster's upbringing. Like any hand in the corral gangs he took up with after running away from home, he delighted in fighting at the drop of a stetson. But when he eventually filled out to 6'1" and 185 pounds, this obstreperous cowboy was in spirit just a big-hearted, sensitive, country boy.[29]

The rowdy ways of rodeo life and winning the world's bronco-busting championship were Art's idea of living. Education for him, as with Hoxie, had come mostly through a closeness to the earth, cow-punchers, and animals — no school ever could have taught him the skills he attained as a trick roper, bronco buster and bulldogger. Art just naturally drifted into wild west show employment. He appeared with the Dick Stanley-Bud Atkinson Wild West from 1908 to 1912, and in 1910 he and his friend Hoot Gibson both managed to appear as stuntmen in a D. W. Griffith film, *Two Brothers*.

In 1912 Art was working with the Stanley-Atkinson show in New York when he met a man named Adam Kessel, who was organizing a new movie studio called the Bison Film Company. Kessel gave Acord a job as a stuntman and player in some of the company's earliest one-reelers.[30] Later Art decided to accept a better offer to perform with Buffalo Bill Cody's Wild West Show on a tour of America and Europe.

Between 1910 and 1916 Art gradually rose in stature as a movie cowboy, while making every rodeo possible and appearing in several different wild west shows for short periods. By 1911 he had ridden second at the Pendleton, Cheyenne, and Salt Lake rodeos. He took the first prize silver belt for bronco riding in Klamath Falls in 1912. That same year he threw three steers in a combined time of 24 seconds to win the title in that event. In 1916, the year his movie fame was assured with the Buck Parvin series, he won 7 of 8 events in Calgary's Stampede. And, while making a film, he was thrown from the saddle and dragged down an embankment, breaking a leg, several ribs, and assorted vertebrae. Such was the life of cinema cowboys in the days before stuntmen did everything but kiss the girl in the fadeout.

Hoot Gibson, a genuine cowboy, first came into the limelight when a howling mob of Westerners declared him the world's champion cowboy at the Pendleton, Oregon, Roundup and presented him with a diamond-studded belt. That was in 1912. Before that, from 1907–10, he had toured Australia and America with the Dick Stanley-Bud Atkinson Wild West Show as a bronco rider and bulldogger with his friend, Art Acord. Even earlier, in 1906, he had been a performer with the Miller Brothers' 101 Ranch. Hoot was a fine athlete, and he loved horses and showbusiness. It was only natural that he would gravitate to the infant film industry as a stuntman and extra. Hoot had worked for a number of cattle outfits in Nebraska and Wyoming, and spent his early years in the movies (1912–17) primarily as a wrangler, stunt double, and bit player. He began to be featured in the Harry Carey westerns and was ultimately awarded his own Universal series in 1920.

Buck Jones was undoubtedly the best-loved and most idolized of western stars after Tom Mix. He was for real: a real gentleman, a real cowboy, a real actor, and a real friend to all—most especially to the young who needed a hero to emulate. Buck loved children, and they naturally responded to him. And that he was one of the film colony's most respected, most liked personalities is an irrefutable fact.[31]

A laconic person, Buck was born in Vincennes, Indiana, in 1891, and it was here he spent his formative years, though pressbooks always claimed he grew up on a ranch in Red Rock, Oklahoma. Heeding the call to adventure, he left home at 16, became a mechanic and roustabout at the Indianapolis Speedway, and served two hitches in the army. He saw action in the Philippines, where he was wounded by the Moros. In 1914, after his discharge at Texas City, Buck immediately looked up Joe Miller, whose 101 Ranch Show was running in Galveston. Miller gave him a job, and he became the show's top bronco buster and eventually a trick rider and roper.[32]

Buck met equestrienne Odille Osborn while with the 101 Show, and the two worked together in the Julia Allen Wild West Show the next year. They were married on horseback in center ring during a performance of the show in Ohio. Subsequently, they appeared with Ringling Brothers' Circus. Winding up in Los Angeles in 1917, and with Odille pregnant, Buck decided to try for a job at the studios. Hired as a $5 a day bit player and stunt rider, he later worked in Tom Mix and Franklyn Farnum westerns, and rose to stardom alongside Mix at Fox Studios.[33]

Ken Maynard was one of the cinema's greatest cowboys. He not only crashed the movies via the wild west show, but all his life preferred the sawdust trail to the sound stage and back lot. Most western fans are reasonably knowledgeable about his long, successful movie career that began in 1923 and ended in 1944. With his famous mount, Tarzan, he electrified audiences in the golden age of movies.

At age 12 Ken ran away from home to join a traveling wild west show, only to be brought back home by his father. But Ken remained obsessed with the idea of becoming a circus performer. At 16 he received permission from his parents to join a touring carnival. His formal education ended there.[34]

In 1912 Ken joined the Buffalo Bill Wild West Show and traveled throughout the country until mid–1913. Ken himself remembered those days as follows:

> I was with old Buffalo Bill the day the creditors came in and attached everything in the show and broke him. You know, the old man broke down and cried. I remember it; it was my birthday, July 21, 1913. My mother always sent me a birthday cake, all cinnamon drops on the icing and there we were the both of us sitting on bales of hay and him, white beard and all, crying all over my birthday cake. It really broke his heart when he lost his show that way. There wasn't a more finer and honorable man than him and with a little more time he could have saved it.[35]

Ken continued his career as a wild west show performer, improving as a rider as he went along. In 1914, though only 19 years old, he was a major attraction with the Kit Carson Wild West Show. The following year he signed with the great Hagenbeck and Wallace Circus, touring with it until World War I. In 1918, following his discharge from the army, he again appeared with Hagenbeck and Wallace.

Pawnee Bill's Wild West Show signed Ken in 1920, the year he was persuaded to enter rodeo competition and won the World's Champion Cowboy title as well as $42,000 in prize money. He held the title until he retired undefeated in 1922. In 1921 Ringling Brothers' Barnum and Bailey Circus hired him as a star of their wild west concert, and he continued in that position until the show appeared in Los Angeles in 1922. Impressed with the movie success of his friend Buck Jones, and invited to do a screen test by Lynn Reynolds (a director of Tom Mix westerns), Ken made the plunge into moviedom. After a few minor roles — the most important being as Paul Revere in *Janice Meredith*— Ken was signed for a western series by Davis Corporation, subsequently achieving world recognition for his fine westerns at First National in the declining days of the silent films. His career continued uninterrupted by the transition from silent to sound movies, and he became Universal's top cowboy in the early 1930s. But the circus had not seen the last of Ken Maynard.

What was true for Maynard was also true for several other screen cowboys who came from the wild west shows or circus. Many of them returned to the sawdust trail during, and, or after their movie days. Considering the personalities of the people involved, apparently their decisions to return to the traveling show were based about equally on financial considerations and the pure enjoyment of circus life.

Tom Mix was the most successful of all the circus-cinema cowboys. During the 1920s he often made guest appearances with the 101 Ranch Show, even though he was being paid $20,000 a week as an actor. Zack Miller and Tom eventually had a falling out, and a series of court battles in the 1930s proved harmful to both men.

As the 1920s passed into history, the cinema was breaking into the future by finding its voice. Fox discontinued westerns after building the studio primarily on the profits from Mix's films. Tom made a silent series for Federal Booking Office in 1929, a series that did not do well at the box office. That same year he toured with the Sells-Floto Circus as its stellar attraction, believing that sound would end the type of pictures he made. When asked why he joined Sells-Floto, Tom replied, "I started out on the sawdust trail, and it does something to you. It gets into your blood, and now in these years the old longing has returned, and naturally, I returned to my first love. This I enjoy and this I can do better now that I've had a great deal of experience."[36]

Tom remained with Sells-Floto for three seasons, 1929–31, before trying a movie comeback at Universal. His nine talkies proved popular enough, but Tom was seriously injured during the filming of *Rustler's Roundup* and retired again from the movies at the end of 1932.

In 1933 Mix went on the road with a theater group called the Tom Mix Roundup. The show consisted of Tony, Jr. (his movie horse), two liberty horses, some rope tricks, the Ward Sisters' aerial act, and a six-piece band. Mable Ward became his fourth wife.[37] Tom's popularity at that time had diminished very little, if any at all, and his show played to packed houses throughout the Southwestern states.[38]

Mix signed with the Sam B. Dill Circus in 1934, and the show premiered in Hot Springs, Arkansas, on April 20. It was soon apparent that Mix's name was filling the tent, so by May 2 newspaper advertising was titling the show "Tom Mix and Tony Heading Sam B. Dill's Big 3-Ring Circus." The show did a terrific business during the summer, and by October was being billed as "Tom Mix Wild West and Sam B. Dill Circus Combined." By November the title was "Tom Mix Wild West and Circus Combined," indicating that Dill had sold out.[39] The show traveled 14,000 miles and made 222 stands in 1934. Tom acquired it at a cost of $400,000.[40] The retitled Tom Mix Wild Animal Circus was the fanciest, most elaborate motorized circus ever formed. For three years it was the most successful show ever to tour the country.[41]

The season of 1935 was a successful one for Mix despite heavy competition and a billing war with the Al G. Barnes Circus. Until the weather became extremely warm, the matinees equaled or bettered the night performances in date after date. With this circus, more than any other since Buffalo Bill's Wild West, the personality of the star performer was the great drawing card. It was not what Mix did in the arena that drew the crowds; it was what he had done before and the fact that he was in the arena.[42]

Tom took time to make his last movie in 1935, starring in Mascot's 15-chapter serial, *The Miracle Rider*. It was a popular, if not artistic film. At 55, however, Tom showed his age and had to be doubled by Cliff Lyons in some of the action scenes. He earned $10,000 a week for four weeks' work, and the current release of the serial helped to keep alive the Mix name.

In 1936 the Tom Mix Circus was financially successful, traveling over 12,000 miles and play 217 stands in 25 states. It was the last good season the show was to have.[43] Business was only fair in 1937, but at least it stayed in the black. However, the next year was a disaster for all circuses, the personality of Tom Mix notwithstanding. The Mix Circus lurched along doing indifferent business until August, by which time Tom had grown so disconsolate that he decided to quit. He left the show, putting it in his daughter Ruth's hands. It foundered in Pecos, Texas, on September 10.[44]

What might have been has no place in this chronicle. The show fell apart at the end; but for over four seasons it was a lusty, thriving entity and brought great circus to millions of people. Few shows survived the debacle of 1938, and this one outlived most of those that went down. People to whom Mix was a childhood hero, the Ralston straight-shooter of films and radio, might wish that the show had had a neater, less ignominious end, but that is the stuff of fiction, not history.[45] Tom Mix enjoyed successes in the final two years of his life by making personal appearances with his horse Tony, Jr., in Europe. He died in an automobile accident near Florence, Arizona, on October 12, 1940.

Buck Jones, like Tom Mix, hit the sawdust trail in 1929, following the termination of his contract with Fox. His last film, *The Big Hop*, independently produced by Buck, lost money and he was poorer by about $50,000. He envisioned himself making $1 million with the wild west show. As a result, the Buck Jones Wild West Show and Round Up Days was begun in North Hollywood in the spring of 1929, and opened in Ventura on May 16. Buck had a 15-car train show employing 102 performers, with a total staff of 267 people. The show arena had a seating capacity of 10,000 and measured 130 by 400 feet. Buck led the grand entry mounted on Silver, with his wife Dell astride her horse, Clown. Both did trick riding, and Buck also gave a trick roping and trained horse exhibition. Montie Montana and Iron Eyes Cody both appeared with the show — Montie as a roper and Iron Eyes as an Indian dancer.[46]

It was evident from the start that the show had financial difficulties. At Kansas City in June it was reorganized and Buck made a valiant effort to keep it on the road. However, it folded in Danville, Illinois, on July 19 after approximately 40 shows.[47]

Buck lost several thousand dollars in this ill-timed venture. On July 24, 1929, he joined the Robbins Brothers' Circus in Freemont, Nebraska, and finished out the season as their star attraction with the circus advertising changed to read "Robbins Brothers' Circus and Buck Jones' Wild West Combined." In 1930 Jones went back to work as a motion picture star and rapidly rose to the position of number one cowboy in popularity.

Ken Maynard decided to frame a large wild west show to open during the spring of 1937. Cognizant of the success of his friend Tom Mix in the business over the past few seasons, Ken failed to profit by the mistakes of another friend, Buck Jones. His original idea was for a 30- or 40-car show, although it never materialized. Building the show in the spring of 1936, Ken decided to set it up on his ranch and put on weekend performances. The original plan of going on the road in 1937 was not altered. The opening performance was May 2, 1936. Two or three other performances were given on the ranch and the show had a three-day stand at the San Diego World's Fair. The performance itself was given in the arena 234 by 260 feet, typical 101 Ranch–style wild west. Ken and his horse Tarzan led the grand entry, with Ken later giving a demonstration of marksmanship. The opening spectacular, "The Old Wild West in Review," included a 14-piece band, 2 covered wagons drawn by oxen, a stagecoach with a 4-horse hitch, 2 elephants, an ostrich-drawn sulky, and all-performing personnel, including a large number of Indians. Maynard's show was colorful, but it lasted only 6 or 7 performances before being pushed into bankruptcy and most of the equipment sold to satisfy creditors. Thus ended Ken Maynard's Diamond K Ranch Wild West Circus and Indian Congress.[48]

Ken, however, was not through as a circus entertainer. In 1937, 1938, and 1940 he headed up the aftershow of the Cole Brothers' Circus, proving to be a popular attraction with Tarzan. The circus tours were worked into his schedule along with filmmaking. After his film career ended in 1944, Ken made personal appearances with rodeos for a number of years. His last circus appearances were with Biller Brothers' and Arthur Brothers' circuses in 1945. His passion for the sawdust trail was never quite abated, however, and he continued to find release in rodeo appearances through the 1950s.

Jack Hoxie, next to Tom Mix and Tim McCoy, was a most successful cinema/circus star, apparently thriving on the day-to-day thrills of the circus. When sound descended on the film industry, most of the cowboys were thrown out of work as the studios retooled for talkies. Hoxie had been a major western star at Universal, but had no contract in 1927. He took the time to tour the country with the Charles Sparks Circus, thrilling crowds with his ability as a trick rider. When Sparks sold his show after the season of 1928, Jack joined the Miller Brothers' 101 Ranch Show in Oklahoma, having appeared with them previously as a guest performer.

Hoxie had a good, fast-moving act and was assisted by Dixie Starr, the female trick rider, his famous horse Scout, and his dog Bunkie Bean, as well as a few cowboys. With the possible exception of Reb Russell, Hoxie had the best act of the movie cowboys, at least from the standpoint of raw action. He did not just appear, he performed the daredevil stunts so characteristic of his movies. Author George Virgines states as follows:

> Jack recalled one amusing experience with the 101 Ranch Show brought about by Colonel Zack Miller's suggestion for a new entrance. Zack wanted Hoxie to come riding in, with a gun in each hand and the reins in his teeth. Jack wasn't too much in favor of this but just couldn't refuse the Colonel. So Jack made his grand entrance astride Scout. The horse raced across the arena and stopped just short of the fence, almost bucking Jack off. Then Scout whipped around and raced back with Jack barely holding on. By that time both of his guns had gone flying in opposite directions. As they passed Zack Miller, the good Colonel almost fell off a wagon tongue laughing. Jack was lying crossways on the saddle — not a very dignified way for a cowboy star to be riding.[49]

Hoxie is reputed to have headlined the Kit Carson Buffalo Ranch Wild West Show, but I have not been able to verify this, or determine the year he was supposed to have traveled with the show. In the early 1930s he made his last series of westerns, a cheap group of independents that did nothing to bolster his sagging popularity with the movie patrons who were turning to the new breed of cowboys such as George O'Brien, Rex Bell, Tim McCoy, Bob Steele, and Johnny Mack Brown. Jack, with practically no education, found it difficult to handle scripts and dialogue. He retired from the screen for good.

In 1933 and 1934 Hoxie headlined the Downie Brothers' Circus; in 1935 he switched to Harley Sadler's Circus; then he returned to the road with Downie Brothers' in 1936.

By 1937 Jack was on the trail with his own show, the Jack Hoxie Circus. He didn't make a lot of money, but at least he lasted out the season, which was something Buck Jones and Ken Maynard were unable to do, and which Tim McCoy and Tom Mix would fail to do the following year.

Jack could not stand retirement as a steady diet, however, and in 1939 he headed up the Lewis Brothers' Circus. About 1944 he joined Mills Brothers' Circus and traveled with them for five seasons. Over the years he traveled with other shows, culminating his circus activity with the Bill Tatum Circus in 1959. He died of leukemia at Elkhart, Kansas, on March 27, 1965, and was buried at Keyes, in the Oklahoma panhandle.[50]

Hoot Gibson was the final big-league cowpoke who followed the circus trail after entering the movies via the wild west show. Hoot didn't especially want to hit the sawdust trail again, but he had to have the money. After making and spending a fortune during his years as a superstar at Universal (1921–1931), Hoot's fortunes began to tumble. Bad investments and bad marriages hurt him financially. His popularity waned and it was possible for him to work only because of the smaller independent studios. To keep creditors from his door, he cashed in on his past glory by headlining Wallace Brothers' Circus, Hagenbeck-Wallace Circus, Robbins Brothers' Circus, and Russell Brothers' Circus between 1937 and 1939. The Hooter was still a draw and a good showman. In the 1940s he returned briefly to moviemaking for Monogram Pictures and often appeared in rodeos. Falling on hard times in later years, he died almost penniless on August 23, 1962, after suffering from cancer for several years.

Such secondary western film personalities as Iron Eyes Cody, Montie Montana, and Tex Cooper continued to appear with wild west shows during the 1930s. Cody was with the short-lived Buck Jones and the Ken Maynard circuses and spent the years 1933–34 in Australia with a wild west show. He was with Tim McCoy in many of his shows, including Ringling Brothers' and the Tim McCoy Wild West Show. He also was featured in the Buff Jones Show (no relation to Buck). Montie Montana has toured for 50 years, mostly with his own unique show. Cooper could be seen with the Tim McCoy Show in 1938, and numerous others dating back to the 101 Ranch days.

The movies did produce at least one major circus cowboy who had no wild west or circus background prior to movie stardom. That cowboy was Colonel Tim McCoy, a Wyoming cowboy and authentic colonel in the U.S. Army, who had served with General Hugh Scott and as adjutant general of Wyoming. A cowboy he was, having worked on various ranches until he could save enough to buy his own spread; but a wild west performer he had not been.

In 1922 Tim left the army to accept a job as technical adviser on *The Covered Wagon*, the super-western being filmed by Jessie Lasky for Paramount. The success of this picture is now film history. Tim was fascinated with the world of makebelieve, and he and a troupe of Indians appeared for over a year on the stage in the United States and in Europe with a prologue act to the film itself. Audiences were elated.[51] His historical spectacle, *The Winning of the West*, played to a packed house for six months at the Philadelphia sesquicentennial in 1926.[52] MGM quickly hired the sagacious cowboy.

War Paint, released late in 1926, was the first in a series of 16 MGM–Tim McCoy features that extended through 1928. His films had the added advantage of big budgets, strong casts, and MGM distribution. In 1929 he made two serials for Universal. The first, *The Indians Are Coming*, was the first serial ever to gross $1 million. Thereafter, he began his long association with Columbia Pictures, later working for Victory, Puritan, PRC, and finally Monogram in the popular Rough Riders series in which he costarred with Buck Jones.

Tim always liked the thrill of the circus and wild west show. Between picture assignments he managed to squeeze in tours with Sells-Floto Circus in 1935, and Ringling Brothers' Barnum and Bailey Circus in 1936 and 1937. These were the finest circuses on the road, and Tim was at the height of his career as a western star. The combination spelled success.

In capsule form, McCoy offered the circus public some of the flavor of the old-time wild west show as given in former years by Buffalo Bill Cody and the Miller Brothers' 101 Ranch Show. Success naturally brought the thought of owning his own show to him. Late in 1937, the thought began to crystallize as McCoy began assembling a large railroad wild west show for the next season.[53]

The McCoy show, with the finest physical equipment any wild west show ever had, opened in Chicago's Amphitheater on April 14, 1938. *Billboard* praised the performance. The program ran nearly two hours with a variety of acts typical of wild west shows, including days of the covered wagon, bronco-busting, the old Deadwood stage, and roundup days on the range. Few daredevil thrill acts were included, as McCoy preferred to emphasize pageantry and extravaganza over straight cowboy antics. Audience reaction in the early days of the season persuaded McCoy to include some comedy and more traditional western rodeo type numbers and to cut back on the Far East acts.[54]

For one month the McCoy show swung along through the Midwest and East playing to somewhat less than full houses. The show was in financial trouble from the beginning and folded in Washington, D.C. on May 14. Many circus people stoutly insisted that the McCoy show was the best that ever went on the road, and that it could have made money if only the daily expenses of around $50,000 could have been cut considerably. Colonel McCoy played through the last performance, watched laborers tear down and pack away his $100,000 investment and said: "Well, for the past fifteen years I've had this wild west show in my system and now I have had my chance." The show went into receivership.[55] McCoy lost a great deal.

Most other shows, too, went to the barn in 1938 — Hagenbeck and Wallace, the Tom Mix Circus, Robbins Brothers' Circus, Cole Brothers', Sells-Sterling, Harris Brothers', Al G. Barnes, Sells-Floto, even Ringling Brothers' Barnum and Bailey. Obviously, 1938 was a bad year for outdoor shows.[56]

It was almost 20 years before McCoy again ventured into the sawdust arena, but he would — time and time again. On April 28, 1957, at the age of 66, he opened the season with the Al G. Kelly and Miller Brothers' Circus on its home grounds in Hugo, Oklahoma. Billed as "Colonel Tim McCoy and Congress of Indians and Rough Riders," Tim traveled in a 37 foot air-conditioned trailer, especially built for him by the circus owners — who also provided him a chauffeur and maid service.[57] His act consisted of trick shooting, roping, and a bow-and-arrow demonstration, as well as a minimal amount of hard riding. The show had a terrific season with many turnaway crowds throughout its old, familiar Kansas and Nebraska territory.

McCoy switched to the Carson-Barnes' Circus in 1958, opening at Casa Grande, Arizona, in April, and playing the West coast extensively. The show moved across to Montana and the Dakotas, and wound up in the fall in Arkansas and Louisiana before returning to winter quarters in Hugo, Oklahoma, "Circus Town, U.S.A."

Tim was again Carson-Barnes's featured attraction in 1959, as the circus headed up into eastern Canada for five weeks in Ontario. It also spent a good deal of time in Michigan on this tour.[58]

The season of 1960 found the Carson-Barnes show in western Canada for the first time, playing through Manitoba, Saskatchewan, and Alberta in 13 weeks. McCoy still had the concert. In 1961, with 70-year-old Tim McCoy as the major draw, the show headed eastward through Louisiana, Mississippi, Tennessee, Kentucky, Indiana, and Michigan into Canada with 13 weeks of shows in Ontario and Quebec.[59]

That was McCoy's last season under the big top. In 1962 the seemingly immortal cowboy joined Tommy Scott's Country Caravan and Wild West Stage Show, also billed at various times as Tommy Scott's Family Funtime Stageshow, Country Caravan and Hollywood Hillbillies, and Colonel Tim McCoy-Tommy Scott Country Music Circus and Wild West Show. He remained with this organization for 13 years! Actually, the last of the old-time vaudeville shows, the Scott troupe traveled circus style with ten pieces of road equipment, and did a variety show with country music with western acts that could be performed on stage — sharpshooting, rope spinning, whips, and the fast draw. McCoy also told stories of the old West and his Hollywood days. In 1975 Tim retired at the age of 84, finally dissuaded by his family from following the sawdust trail along the backroads of America for yet another year.

Reb Russell was a cowboy in Kansas and Oklahoma long before he became a movie star, and he was one of the most talented of all circus cowboys. His act — no powder puff affair — was reminiscent of the explosive wild west of the Miller Brothers' 101 Ranch days. This forthright all-American football player from Northwestern University starred in a series of Willis Kent westerns in the mid-1930s. Admittedly, Reb's acting ability was a little short of that of Spencer Tracy or James Stewart, but as an athlete, his physical prowess was incomparable. And he had a winning personality: always interested in others while never taking himself too seriously. His candor and country charm were as refreshing on the Hollywood scene as a dip in the cool waters of the old swimming hole in mid–August.

It was in 1936 that Reb hit the sawdust trail with Russell Brothers' Circus (no relation to him). His was the only bullwhip act of the time that was performed from a running horse. And to see Reb atop his golden palomino Goldie, cracking two bullwhips in time with the circus band's version of *Yankee Doodle Dandy* was an unforgettable experience. Reb was also adept at stunt-riding, throwing his 218-pound frame around with the grace of a cowboy 60 pounds lighter.[60] Supporting him in the wild west concert was a troupe of 36 Indians.

Russell Brothers' Circus left its winter quarters in Raleigh, Missouri, in April, making its way up through Illinois, Iowa, Nebraska, and back into Kansas, Oklahoma, and Texas before winding up its season in November. Throughout its circuit, it stayed west of the Mississippi.

At the beginning of the wild west aftershow, commonly called the "concert," the band would give Reb a big musical buildup and he would come charging into the main tent on the white gelding Rebel, his famed movie horse, rearing him high in a holding position, then taking him to his knees in a bow. Subsequently, he would sidestep the magnificent horse around the track. True, a number of cowboys could have done this, but few could have performed Russell's other acts.

One of his thrill sequences was a pony express ride that demonstrated the speed at which riders changed mounts. Starting with Goldie, Reb charged three-quarters of the circle of the tent, changing to a bald-faced horse at that point. After a few days of this, the bald-faced nag became so wild that it took three men to hold him, and sometimes he would fall back on them, so great was his desire to be elsewhere. Russell, reaching the horse, would hit the ground, take a leap for the saddle horn and hopefully land in the saddle as the horse raced away. Sometimes he would only manage to grab the cropper holds and would be dragged the entire length of the tent before he could vault into the saddle. A few times the horse went down, and one time Reb was not able to propel himself loose before the horse rolled over him — all 1,200 pounds of the animal. The saddle horn cut a deep gash in Russell's abdomen. Periodically, his strenuous daily stunts bruised the injured spot until it finally became malignant. Luckily, surgery was successful, and there was no reccurence.[61] On another occasion the same horse kicked Reb a glancing blow that tore a $40 pair of pants off him. Once Reb had to use a substitute horse because of an injury to old bald face. When the circus horse got even with the center ring, he suddenly cut across the ring to the back door at full gallop, scaring both rider and circus personnel because of the many aerial wires and cables about. But Reb and horse made it without a scratch. Old bald face didn't look so bad after that.

A favorite of circus fans, and an act performed by no other western movie star, was the shoulder stand Reb did on Goldie while the horse ran the track. Russell would drop into a vault and go around the horn, a most difficult act for any performer, but especially so for one weighing over 200 pounds. And it was the constant bruising of the injured spot on his stomach during this act that finally produced the malignancy.[62]

One of Reb's easier stunts — the one that most excited the crowds — was done standing in the stirrups on his running horse and twirling ropes as Goldie raced around the tent. One night in New England the horse stepped in a hole that had been filled with sawdust and went down. Luckily, Reb accomplished the difficult feat of freeing himself from the stirrups and jumping away from Goldie before the horse hit the ground and could have possible mangled him.

At the end of 1936 Reb left Russell Brothers' Circus. Although he had been treated fairly and with the respect due to a star, Reb could not go along with some of the owner's policies on less important personnel. Always a defender of the underdog, he quit.

Russell signed on for the season of 1937 with the 80-truck Downie Brothers' Circus, which was approximately one-third larger than Russell Brothers' and equivalent in size to a 30-car railroad circus. The show was owned by Charlie Sparks, one of the most respected showmen in the history of the circus.

Downie Brothers' wintered in Macon, Georgia, leaving there in the spring and making its way up through the Carolinas and along the coast into New England, and finally on up into Maine, showing within eight miles of the Canadian border. Then, on its return trip, the circus played in Vermont, New Hampshire, and bordering states, winding up in Florida. Russell's concert remained basically the same. He still carried 30 or more Indians recruited from Oklahoma, and for whom he was father-confessor, banker, instructor, and anything else required to keep them in line. Sparks had the top cookhouse of any circus, thanks to the direct supervision of Mrs. Sparks, and somewhere he got the idea that Indians had to have lots of meat or they would deteriorate physically. Well, the Indians got so fat that all wardrobes had to be let out to the maximum, and Russell had his hands full not only in keeping alcohol away from them, but in keeping them away from the all too abundant food.[63]

Reb's whip act enjoyed continued popularity and included cutting cigarettes from a girl's mouth, striking matches, assorted paper cutting, and the lifting of a bandanna from the pocket of a clown, who would run down the track holding his rear until he found a bucket of water in which to plop down and cool it off. However, the act that left audiences in tears was the one he performed with Goldie. The ringmaster would announce that Reb would do a scene from one of his motion pictures, one in which Reb discovered rustlers and chased them. Goldie stepped into a prairie dog hole and broke a leg. Reb wanted to get his horse home. With appropriate mood music, Reb then led the horse into the tent. One of Goldie's legs was tied with wire hidden by a bandanna. Man and horse entered the center ring. Reb removed the horse's saddle.

The announcer then concluded: "Now, Reb, you can't get him back to the ranch. You're going to have to destroy him." All the while, the band plays sob stuff that fits the situation. Reb takes his gun out, shakes his head — he just can't shoot. "You've got to, Reb. You can't leave him here for the wolves," the announcer pleads. Reb tries again. He can't. Goldie turns around and looks him in the eye. The music is getting to the audience. The rustlers return and shoot Reb, who falls, yet manages to crawl to Goldie and mount him. Goldie carries him about 50 feet on three legs, but is unable to make it and lays down. Reb finally has to shoot him. The performance was especially effective at night when different spotlights would be used. Charlie Sparks was so proud of the act that he always remained on hand for the aftershow to see that the superintendent of tents did not start tearing down the equipment prematurely or otherwise disrupt the act.

Russell's daughter, Betty, traveled with him at times and helped in his whip act. But two years on the road was enough for Reb, and, tired of both the circus and the movies, he returned to Kansas to become a successful rancher both there and in Oklahoma.[64] A resurgence of interest in B westerns in the 1970s brought him out of the woodwork and back into the entertainment world through guest star appearances at western film festivals, where his storytelling ability and openheartedness made him an instant hit. A natural storyteller with a delightful sense of humor, Reb could hold the attention of an audience indefinitely. He liked to poke fun at his own acting ability and often said that his total repertoire of dramatic talent was contained in but two facial expressions — constipation and relief. A director merely had to say, "I want expression no. 1," or "give me expression no. 2." Reb's death on March 16, 1978, was a personal loss to the many film buffs who knew him.

A number of popular screen cowboys were able to sign on with circuses as stars of the wild west concert on the basis of their fame as celluloid cowpokes rather than their actual skill as rough-and-tough wild west show cowboys ready to ride the meanest critter or bulldog the devil himself.

Bill Cody's career as a western star began in 1924, when Independent Pictures Corporation starred him in a series for state-right distribution. Previously he had worked as a stuntman. Later working for Associated, Pathé, Universal, Monogram, and Spectrum, Bill continued to grind out low-budget westerns until the mid–1930s. In 1932 he was featured in the Walter L.

Main Circus as well as in Bostoch's Circus. In 1935 he was with the ever-popular Downie Brothers' Circus. Although it is thought he toured with circuses in other years, this has not been verified at the time of this writing.

Lee Powell, star of Republic's classic serials, *The Lone Ranger* (1938) and *The Fighting Devil Dogs* (1938), became a headliner for Barnett Brother's Circus in 1939, billed as "The Lone Ranger of Motion Picture Fame." The show also featured Norma Rogers, daughter of the owner, Ray W. Rogers. She became Mrs. Lee Powell in 1941. The show had a good season, and during the winter of 1939–40 Powell was featured with the Hamid-Morton Circus, an indoor show that played weeklong stands in buildings for the Shriners and other such organizations. It had no tents or other transportation equipment.[65]

Sometime during the early weeks of 1950 Rogers decided to use the Wallace Brothers' title for the upcoming season, putting on the shelf for good his first and most widely used title, Barnett Brothers'. Wallace Brothers' Circus opened that season on April 18 at York, South Carolina, with Powell again featured as The Lone Ranger. Norma Rogers had the elephant act. Texas Ted Lewis and his wild west troupe supported Powell in the concert. Wallace Brothers' and Russell Brothers' at this time were the largest "mud" shows (truck circuses) still on the road.[66]

Lee did not have a great circus act, but it was an exciting event, nevertheless, for boys and girls (and, I suspect, many adults as well) to see the Lone Ranger come charging around the circus tent on a white horse yelling "Hi-yo Silver, A-w-a-a-a-," with hoofbeats providing almost perfect percussion for the *William Tell Overture*. Many children were in a trance for days after having seen the Lone Ranger in the flesh.[67] Lee was himself a friendly, quiet young man whose personality endeared him to most of his coworkers.

In June the Hamid-Morton outfit leased Wallace Brothers'—lock, stock, and barrel—added Clyde Beatty and his wild animals along with 14 more acts, and took to the road playing mainly Shriner engagements through August 10. Both Beatty and Powell were highly advertised. After August 10 the shows split up again, and Powell continued on with the Wallace Brothers' while Beatty went with Hamid-Morton.

In 1939, The Lone Ranger, Inc., sued Powell and the circus for illegal use of the name "The Lone Ranger." The suit dragged on until November 1940, before it came to trial with a decision in favor of Powell and the circus. The Lone Ranger, Inc., filed an appeal with the U.S. Court of Appeals in August 1941, but Rogers and Powell believed that with the slow-moving court procedure, the season could be completed before any possible adverse ruling against Powell could be made. So in 1941 Powell was again with Wallace Brothers' and featured as the Lone Ranger, after having played several winter dates with the Hamid-Morton-Shriner Circus.[68]

At the end of the season in 1941 the Wallace show was sold, and Powell made a western series for PRC Studios before joining the marines and dying a hero's death in the South Pacific during the invasion of Tinian on July 20, 1944. Ironically, he only achieved a modicum of success by playing a marine onscreen, yet he died as a real marine hero with little recognition of his death at the time by the press or public.[69]

In 1938, after completing eight westerns for Victory Pictures, famed cowboy star Tom Tyler joined Wallace Brothers' Circus. His weightlifting (he was a world champion for 14 years), daring stunts on the horizontal bar, and wild west acts became the season's big draw under the big top.[70]

Kirby Grant is best remembered now for his syndicated television series "Sky King," which entertained the young fry for many a Saturday morning. Back in the mid–1940s he was Universal's answer to Gene Autry and Roy Rogers, but soon gave up the warbling when distributors howled at the thought of another guitar-strumming cowboy. He was more successful as a Northwest mountie in a series for Monogram Pictures in the late 1940s and early 1950s. In 1965 Carson-Barnes Circus hired him more or less as a replacement for Tim McCoy, who had departed from the show. Grant remained with Carson-Barnes for six seasons before finally quitting, supposedly after seeing his salary gradually decline to one-third of the original amount. However, his decision was immediately influenced by a request one day that he help shovel horse manure. That did it! He did not return for the 1971 season.

Certainly one reel cowboy who can hardly be overlooked — because of his size, if nothing else — is Sunset Carson, one of the four movie cowboys inducted into the Circus Hall of Fame (the others are Buck Jones, Tom Mix, and Tim McCoy). The 6'6" star of Republic Pictures in the mid–1940s began his riding career at the age of 2 and had competed in over 40 rodeos by the time he was 12. By age 15 he had won two all-around world championship rodeos in South America. He was signed on as a trick rider with the Tom Mix Circus in 1938. Since then he has probably shot several million shells while performing his own pistol and rifle trick shooting act all over the world.

Sunset was a headliner for the Clyde Beatty Circus in 1950–51 and 1956, with Wirth Circus in 1960, and Bullens Circus in 1961. There may have been others. He also traveled with the Tommy Scott Wild West Caravan, along with Tim McCoy, though the Scott show was neither a circus nor a wild west show.

Several other movie cowboys traded on their names to enter the big top in the twilight of their careers, including Harry Carey (Barnett Brothers' Circus, 1934); Bob Steele (Clyde Beatty Circus, 1950); Art Mix (Kay Brothers' Circus, 1938, 1941; Art Mix Buffalo Ranch Wild West Show, 1947); William Boyd (Cole Brothers' Circus, 1950); Duncan Renaldo and Leo Carrillo (Cole Brothers' Circus, 1953); William Desmond (Barnett Brothers' Circus, 1938); Lash LaRue (Dales Brothers' Circus, 1949); Buzz Barton (Walter L. Main Circus, 1933); Al Jennings and Tex Cooper (Tim McCoy's Real Wild West and Congress of Rough Riders, 1938); Betsy Ross (Joe B. Webb Circus, 1936; Seal Brothers' Circus, 1936); and Buck Owens (Robbins Brothers, 1930, 1931; Downie Brothers, 1932; Hunt Brothers, 1933; Lewis Brothers, 1935; Buck Owens Circus, 1946; Rogers Brothers' Circus, 1947). Doubtless there were others along the way. Most of these reel cowboys merely made appearances and talked, smiled, and waved. Few of them actually were skilled horsemen who could perform as had Reb Russell, Tom Mix, Ken Maynard, Buck Jones, Jack Hoxie, Art Acord, Will Rogers, or Hoot Gibson.

Unfortunately, memories of the American wild west show and circus have not endured like the cedars of Lebanon — straight, tall, and seemingly permanent. A more appropriate comparison would be with castles built shoddily on the shifting sands of a tempestuous sea of time — decaying and crumbling with the tides lapping tenaciously at their foundations. The traditional wild west show is almost in a category with the pterodactyl, the flying reptile that ruled the skies during the Mesozoic era. It commanded the attention of all creatures over which it cast its huge shadow. Yet the pterodactyl slowly vanished from the earth, after a struggle for survival which was, in the end, futile. It could not adapt sufficiently to a changing environment. The American circus, too, is fighting for life amidst changing elements. The ranks of both the mud show and the railroad show have been decimated, and only a few remain. Likewise, the programmer western movie has long since bitten the dust, and there are no currently active western stars.

The smell of sawdust, the sight of the big top, the swoop of the acrobats, the antics of the clowns, the herds of elephants parading down the hippodrome track, the circus band, the flying trapeze performers, wild animal acts: all of these are fast disappearing, just as is the demise of the wild west concert featuring a Hollywood cowboy. There is nothing like a circus to send one back to childhood for a few carefree hours. Nothing else offers quite the same feeling of nostalgic escape — at least for those older people who grew up in earlier days when circuses roamed the land in all directions. But the day of the circus is over. Only one show of importance is left to carry on the tradition of the big top circus. The Carson and Barnes 5-Ring Circus is the last big traditional circus in America. It has a seemingly perpetual road schedule, visiting a new city or town every 24 hours in a herculean attempt to attract sufficient fun seekers to pay its astronomical daily expense. The truck circus is making its last, magnificent stand in a battle that surely must be lost.

Trail's end has been reached insofar as the movie or television cowboy's chances of reaping fortune or glory as headliners of wild west shows or circus concerts. But the trail could meander a little farther through the thickets of technology, sophistication, inflation, lethargy, and recession. There might yet be time for a few down-on-their luck TV cowboys — if they were of such a mind — to travel the mud show routes of America with the last few remaining small outdoor shows. But at most it would be nothing but a personal appearance, and there would be little of either glory or money. Few people today would be drawn to the sawdust arena on the basis of their names. No longer can a circus afford the wild west concert that once enthralled the multitudes, nor can the public ever again know the same thrill of attending a circus or wild west show as was experienced by earlier generations.

Progress again has taken its toll. But for those of us old enough to remember those summers so far away, there remains a beautiful memory of having seen in person a type of performance distinctly American and head-lined by America's own unique hero—the motion picture cowboy. Oh, the overwhelming ecstasy of it all! To our fading ranks the thoughts of yester-year's sawdust trail and those who rode it are like the refreshing fragrance of honeysuckle and gardenia drifting across a field of cowpats on the first gen-tle breezes of a summer's evening—a welcome relief at the end of reality's tir-ing day.

Notes

Chapter 1

1. Ron Goulart, *Cheap Thrills* (New Rochelle 1972), p. 23.

2. *Ibid.*, p. 135.

3. *Ibid.*, p. 134.

4. Ramon F. Adams, *The Old-Time Cowhand* (New York 1961), pp. 3–4.

5. Buck Rainey, "Guest Editor's Prologue," *Red River Valley Historical Review*, 2, no. 1 (Spring 1975).

6. Joe B. Franz and Ernest Choate, Jr., *The American Cowboy: The Myth and the Reality* (Westport, CT 1981), pp. 95–96.

7. Jack Nachbar, "Horses, Harmony, Hope and Hormones: Western Movies, 1930–1946," *Journal of the West* 22, no. 4 (October 1983): 25.

8. Arthur F. McClure and Ken D. Jones, *Heroes, Heavies, and Sagebrush* (Cranbury, NJ 1972), p. 11.

9. *Ibid.*

10. Michael Parkinson and Clyde Jeavons, *A Pictorial History of Westerns* (London 1972), p. 94.

11. Clifford P. Westermeier, "Cowboy Sexuality," in *The Cowboys: Six Shooters, Songs, and Sex* (Norman, OK 1976), p. 90.

12. Joe Franklin, *Classics of the Silent Screen* (New York 1959), p. 120.

13. George N. Fenin and William K. Everson, *The Western: From Silents to Cinerama*, revised edition (New York: Grossman, 1973), p. 54.

14. Ray Stuart, *Immortals of the Screen* (New York: Bonanza Books, 1965), p. 146.

15. William K. Everson, *A Pictorial History of the Western Film* (New York 1969), p. 40.

16. Kalton C. Lahue, *Winners of the West: The Sagebrush Heroes of the Silent Screen* (New York: A.S. Barnes, 1970), p. 148.

17. Fenin and Everson, *The Western*, p. 10.

18. Buck Rainey, "Reminiscences of Harry Carey," *Remember When* 14 (1974), pages unnumbered.

19. Fenin and Everson, *The Western*, p. 150.

20. Jon Tuska, "From the 100 Finest Westerns: Straight Shooting," *Views and Reviews* 4, no. 3 (Spring 1973): 55.

21. Glenn Shirley, "Harry Carey, Western Natural," *True West* 21, no. 5 (May–June 1974): 7.

22. *Ibid.*, p.9.

23. Ernest N. Corneau, *The Hall of Fame of Western Film Stars* (North Quincy, MA 1969), p. 71.

24. Buck Rainey, *The Saga of Buck Jones* (Nashville: Western Film Collectors, 1975).

25. Jon Tuska, "From the 100 Finest Westerns: Men Without Law," *Views and Reviews* 3, no. 1 (Summer 1971): 34.

26. *Ibid.*

27. Bill Rainey, "The Holts," *Views and Reviews* 5, no. 4 (Summer 1974): 15.

28. Lahue, *Winners of the West*, pp. 288–89.

29. Everson, *A Pictorial History of the Western Film*, p. 212.

30. Paul E. Mix, *The Life and Legend of Tom Mix* (New York: A.S. Barnes, 1972), pp. 76–78.

31. *Ibid.*, pp. 87–88.

32. David Carroll, *The Matinee Idols* (New York 1972), p. 113.

33. Mix, *The Life and Legend of Tom Mix*, p. 94.

34. Everson, *A Pictorial History of the Western Film*, p. 66.

35. Carroll, *The Matinee Idols*, p. 110.

36. Franklin, *Classics of the Silent Screen*, p. 704.

37. Stewart Roberts, "Tom Mix, the Tinsel Cowboy." *Westerner* 4, no. 4 (July–August 1972): 12.

38. Mix, *The Life and Legend of Tom Mix*, pp. 92, 98.

39. Parkinson and Jeavons, *A Pictorial History of Westerns*, p. 97.

40. Fenin and Everson, *The Western*, p. 155.

41. *Ibid.*

42. Jon Tuska, "In Retrospect: Ken Maynard," *Views and Reviews* 1, no. 1 (Summer 1969): p. 17.

43. Jon Tuska, "In Retrospect: Ken Maynard, Part 3," *Views and Reviews* 1, no. 3 (Winter 1970): p. 39.

44. Joel McCrea, "Hoot Gibson: Even the Heroine Blackened His Eye," *Western Stars* 1, no. 5 (Spring 1950): 75.

45. Buck Rainey, "Fred Thomson, Great but Forgotten Hero," in *Saddle Aces of the Cinema* (San Diego, CA 1980), p. 260.

46. Franklin, *Classics of the Silent Screen*, p. 232.

47. Everson, *A Pictorial History of the Western Film*, p. 81.

48. Powell Craig, "We Ride the Range with Daredevil Bob Steele,"*Wild West Stars* 2, no. 6: 2.

49. McClure and Jones, *Heroes, Heavies, and Sagebrush*, p. 69.

50. Buck Rainey, "Tim McCoy, Dignity in the Saddle," in *Heroes of the Range* (Metuchen, NJ: 1987), p. 103.

51. Buck Rainey, "Reminiscences of Tim McCoy," *Remember When* 15 (1974), pages unnumbered.

52. Kalton C. Lahue, *Riders of the Range* (New York: 1973), p. 67.

53. John Stoginski, "Charles Starrett, the Gallant Defender," *Western Film Collector* 1, no. 1 (May 1973): 23.

54. "John Wayne as the Last Hero," *Time*, August 8, 1969.

55. Buck Rainey, "Reb Russell, His Interlude as Western Star," *Filmograph* 3, no. 3 (1973): 36.

56. Nick Williams, "Kermit Maynard as Western Star and Stunt Man," *Filmograph* 2, no. 1 (1972): 25–26.

57. Buck Rainey, "The Film Career of Buster Crabbe," *Western Film Collector* 2, no. 3 (July 1974): passim.

58. Everson, *A Pictorial History of the Western Film*, p. 83.
59. Bill Rainey, "The Holts," p. 18.
60. Alan G. Barbour, *A Thousand and One Delights* (New York 1971), p. 121.
61. Lahue, *Riders of the Range*, p. 51.
62. *Ibid.*
63. Alan G. Barbour, *The Thrill of It All* (New York 1971), p. 47.
64. Raymond Stedman, *The Serials* (Norman, OK 1971), p. 115.
65. Lahue, *Riders of the Range*, p. 9.
66. Gene Fernett, *Next Time Drive Off the Cliff*, Cocoa Beach, FL 1968), pp. 80–82.
67. Everson, *A Pictorial History of the Western Film*, p. 147.
68. David Zinman, *Saturday Afternoon at the Bijou* (New York 1973), p. 108.
69. Lahue, *Riders of the Range*, p. 31.
70. Zinman, *Saturday Afternoon at the Bijou*, p. 111.
71. Jon Tuska, "The Vanishing Legion, Continued," *Views and Reviews* 4, no. 2 (Winter 1972): 43.
72. Richard A. Maynard, *The American West on Film, Myth and Reality* (Rochelle Park NY 1974), p. 61.
73. Les Adams and Buck Rainey, *Shoot-Em-Ups* (Metuchen, NJ 1985).
74. Frederick Woods, "Hot Guns and Cold Women," *Films and Filming* (March 1959), p. 11.
75. Buck Rainey, *The Shoot-Em-Ups Ride Again* (Metuchen, NJ 1990), p. 1.

Chapter 2

1. Carlton Jackson, *Zane Grey* (New York: Twayne, 1973), p. 1.
2. T. V. Olsen, "Zane Grey—How He Grew," *Zane Grey Collector* 7, no. 1: 2.
3. Jackson, *Zane Grey*, p. 1.
4. Gary Topping, "Zane Grey's West," *The Popular Western* (Bowling Green, OH: Bowling Green University Popular Press, 1974), pp. 683/45.
5. T. K. Whipple, "American Sagas," *Study Out the Land* (Berkeley: University of California Press, 1943), p. 24.
6. Topping, "Zane Grey's West," p. 683/41.
7. Buck Rainey, *The Fabulous Holts* (Nashville: Western Film Collectors, 1976), p. 52.
8. George Fenin and William K. Everson, *The Western: From Silents to Cinerama* (New York: Grossman, 1973), p. 165.
9. Buck Rainey, *The Fabulous Holts*, p. 54.
10. Packy Smith, "Zane Grey on the Screen," *Western Film Collector* 1, nos. 4, 5 (November 1973): 24.
11. G. M. Farley, "Zane Grey on the Silver Screen," *Zane Grey Collector* 4, nos. 16, 17 (1972): 5–6.
12. Buck Rainey, "Down Nostalgia Trails with George O'Brien," *Western Film Collector* 2, nos. 1–2 (March–May 1974): 30.
13. Jon Tuska, *The Filming of the West* (New York: Doubleday, 1976), p. 328.
14. Buck Rainey, "The Film Career of Buster Crabbe," *Western Film Collector* 2, no. 3 (July 1974): 4.
15. *Ibid.*
16. Buck Rainey, *The Fabulous Holts*, p. 76.

17. Fenin and Everson, *The Western*, pp. 241–42.
18. Wayne Irish, "Who Wrote Western Union?" *Zane Grey Collector* 4, no. 4 (1972): 15.
19. *Ibid.*
20. Chris Collier, "Rangle River," *Zane Grey Collector* 4, no. 4 (1972): 19.
21. Farley, "Zane Grey on the Silver Screen," p. 6.
22. *Ibid.*

Chapter 3

1. *Contemporary Authors*, new revised series, 30:2.
2. Stanley R. Davidson, "The Author Was a Lady," *Montana: The Magazine of Western History* 23, no. 2 (1973).
3. *New York Times*, January 17, 1926.
4. Jim Hitt, *The American West from Fiction (1823–1976) into Film (1909–1986)* (Jefferson, NC: McFarland, 1990).
5. Gene M. Gressley, "Mr. Raine, Mammon, and the Western," *Arizona and the West* 25, no. 4 (   ): 313–14.
6. Hitt, *The American West from Fiction.*
7. Philip Dunham, Introduction, in Owen Wister, *The Virginian* (Boston: Houghton Mifflin, 1968), p. xi.
8. Andy Adams, "Western Interpreter," *Southwest Review* 10 (October 1924): 124.

Chapter 7

1. Francis Beverly Keller, "The Land of Sawdust and Spangles — A World in Miniature," *National Geographic* 60, no. 4 (October 1931): 478.
2. Fred Gipson, *Fabulous Empire* (Boston: Houghton Mifflin, 1946), p. 232.
3. Reggy Robbins, "Will Rogers: The Immortal Cherokee Kid," *American History Illustrated* 9, no. 4 (July 1974): 9.
4. Kenneth G. Richards, "Will Rogers," *People of Destiny* (Chicago: Childrens Press, 1968), p. 27.
5. Robbins, "Will Rogers," p. 9.
6. Richard M. Ketchum, *Will Rogers, His Life and Times* (New York: American Heritage, 1973), p. 83.
7. *Ibid.*, p. 85.
8. Donald Day, ed., *The Autobiography of Will Rogers* (Boston: Houghton Mifflin, 1926), pp. 27–28.
9. Robbins, "Will Rogers," p. 9.
10. Day, *The Autobiography of Will Rogers*, p. 33.
11. Robbins, "Will Rogers," pp. 9–10.
12. Ray Stuart, *Immortals of the Screen* (New York: Bonanza Books, 1965), p. 194.
13. Paul E. Mix, *The Life and Legend of Tom Mix* (New York: A. S. Barnes, 1972), p. 46.
14. Fred Gipson, *Fabulous Empire*, p. 225.
15. Mix, *The Life and Legend of Tom Mix*, p. 47.
16. *Ibid.*, pp. 81–83.

17. Stuart Thayer, "Tom Mix Circus and Wild West: Part One — Season of 1934 and 1935," *Bandwagon* 15 (March–April 1971): 19.

18. Mix, *The Life and Legend of Tom Mix*, pp. 53, 59.

19. George N. Fenin and William K. Everson, *The Western: From Silents to Cinerama* (New York: Grossman, 1973), p. 110.

20. Mix, *The Life and Legend of Tom Mix*, p. 74.

21. *Ibid.*, pp. 83–85.

22. George E. Virgines, "Adios Amigo," *Frontier Times* 39, no. 5 (September 1965): 21.

23. Glenn Shirley, "Oklahoma's Jack Hoxie," *Westerner* 3, no. 6 (July–August 1971): 48–49.

24. Kalton C. Lahue, *Winners of the West: The Sagebrush Heroes of the Silent Screen* (New York: A. S. Barnes, 1970), p. 175.

25. Shirley, "Oklahoma's Jack Hoxie," p. 49.

26. Lahue, *Winners of the West*, p. 175.

27. Shirley, "Oklahoma's Jack Hoxie, p. 50.

28. Buck Rainey, "Art Acord: An Enigma," *Western Revue* 2, no. 2 (Summer 1975): 4, 11.

29. Tex Jordan, "Art Acord, Destiny of a Drover Silenced by Sound," Western movie memento from W. E. Julison's Ride-M-Ranch, undated, single page.

30. Ernest Carneau, *The Hall of Fame of Western Film Stars* (North Quincy, MA: Christopher Publishing, 1969), p. 54.

31. Buck Rainey, *The Saga of Buck Jones* (Nashville: Western Film Collectors, 1975).

32. Ellsworth Collings and Alma Miller England, *The 101 Ranch* (Norman: University of Oklahoma Press, 1971), pp. 166–67.

33. Buck Rainey, *The Saga of Buck Jones*, p. 12.

34. Jon Tuska, "In Retrospect: Ken Maynard," *View and Reviews* 1, no. 1 (Summer 1969): 6.

35. Hal Jacques, "Palaverin' with Ken Maynard," *Westerner* 4, no. 4 (July–August 1972): 17.

36. Mix, *The Life and Legend of Tom Mix*, pp. 135, 138.

37. Thayer, "Tom Mix Circus and Wild West," p. 19.

38. C. O. Robinson, "Tom Mix Was My Boss," *Frontier Times* 43, no. 4 (July 1969): 18.

39. Thayer, "Tom Mix Circus and Wild West," p. 21.

40. Mix, *The Life and Legend of Tom Mix*, p. 142.

41. Lewis Smith, "Wilder Than the West," *Horse and Rider* (1973 Yearbook), p. 83.

42. Thayer, "Tom Mix Circus and Wild West," p. 23.

43. Stuart Thayer, "Tom Mix Circus and Wild West: Part Two— Seasons of 1936, 1937, and 1938," *Bandwagon* 15, (May–June 1971): 8.

44. *Ibid.*, p. 11.

45. *Ibid.*

46. Fred D. Pfening, Jr., "Buck Jones Wild West and Round Up Days," *Bandwagon* 9 (November–December 1965): 25–26.

47. Joseph T. Bradbury, "Buck Jones Wild West Show and Round Up Days," *Bandwagon* 16 (March–April 1972).

48. Fred D. Pfening, Jr., "Ken Maynard's Diamond 'K' Ranch Wild West, Circus, and Indian Congress," *White Tops* (November–December 1959): 9–10.

49. Virgines, "Adios Amigo," p. 60.

50. Buck Rainey, "Brothers Al and Jack Hoxie, Cinema Trailblazers," *Western Revue* 3, no. 1 (March 1977): 20.

51. Buck Rainey, "Reminiscences of Tim McCoy," *Remember When*, no. 16, 1974, 9 pages unnumbered.

52. Smith, "Wilder than the West," p. 84.

53. Fred D. Pfening, Jr., *Colonel Tim McCoy's Real Wild West and Rough Riders of the World* (Columbus, OH: Pfening and Snyder, 1955), p. 9.

54. *Ibid.*, pp. 29–35.

55. *Ibid.*, p. 49.

56. *Ibid.*, p. 58–59; and Don Russell, *The Wild West* p. 114.

57. Gladys Brewer, "Cowboy Star, Circus to Get Big Sendoff Today," *Hugo Daily News*, (April 28, 1957), p. 6A.

58. Donald R. Carson, "High Grass and Miller Magic," *Bandwagon* 13 (January–February, 1969): 32.

59. *Ibid.*, p. 33.

60. Buck Rainey, "Reb Russell, His Interlude as Western Star," *Filmograph* III, no. 3 (first quarter 1973): 37.

61. *Ibid.*

62. Interview with Reb Russell, May 15, 1976.

63. *Ibid.*

64. Buck Rainey, "Reb Russell, His Interlude as Western Star," p. 43.

65. Fred D. Pfening, Jr., "Circus Train Lithograph," *Bandwagon*, vol. 15 (November–December, 1971): 18.

66. Joseph T. Bradbury, "The Ray W. Rogers Circuses," *Bandwagon*, vol. 19 (March–April 1975): 18–19.

67. Buck Rainey, "Reminiscences of Smith Ballew and Lee Powell," *Remember When* 12 (May 1973), pages unnumbered.

68. Bradbury, "The Ray W. Rogers Circuses," pp. 24–27.

69. Buck Rainey, "Reminiscences of Smith Ballew and Lee Powell."

70. Glenn Shirley, "Cowboy Strongman—Tom Tyler," *Old West*, vol. 11, No. 2 (Winter 1974): 14.

71. Gerald F. Vaughn, "Movie Cowboys' Love Affair with Rodeo," *Rodeo News* (May 1976): 17.

Index